I0137941

Judah in the Neo-Babylonian Period

SBL

Society of Biblical Literature

Archaeology and Biblical Studies

Tammi Schneider, Editor

Number 18

Judah in the Neo-Babylonian Period:
The Archaeology of Desolation

Judah in the Neo-Babylonian Period:
The Archaeology of Desolation

by

Avraham Faust

Society of Biblical Literature
Atlanta, Georgia

Judah in the Neo-Babylonian Period: The Archaeology of Desolation

Copyright © 2012 by the Society of Biblical Literature

All rights reserved. No part of this work may be reproduced or transmitted in any form or by any means, electronic or mechanical, including photocopying and recording, or by means of any information storage or retrieval system, except as may be expressly permitted by the 1976 Copyright Act or in writing from the publisher. Requests for permission should be addressed in writing to the Rights and Permissions Office, Society of Biblical Literature, 825 Houston Mill Road, Atlanta, GA 30329 USA.

Library of Congress Cataloging-in-Publication Data

Faust, Avi.
  Judah in the neo-Babylonian period : the archaeology of desolation / by Avraham Faust.
      p. cm. — (Society of Biblical Literature Archaeology and biblical studies ; no. 18)
  Includes bibliographical references and index.
  ISBN 978-1-58983-640-2 (paper binding : alk. paper) — ISBN 978-1-58983-725-6 (hardcover binding) — ISBN 978-1-58983-641-9 (electronic format)
  1. Jews—History—Babylonian captivity, 598-515 B.C. 2. Palestine—History—To 70 A.D. 3. Palestine—Antiquities. 4. Excavations (Archaeology)—Palestine. 5. Jews—Palestine—Material culture. 6. Material culture—Palestine. 7. Judaism—History—Post-exilic period, 586 B.C.-210 A.D. 8. Iron age—Palestine. I. Title.
  DS121.65.F38 2012a
  933'.4903—dc23

2012017969

Printed on acid-free, recycled paper conforming to ANSI/NISO Z39.48-1992 (R1997) and ISO 9706:1994 standards for paper permanence.

∞

To Iris

Contents

List of Figures, Tables, and Graphs

TABLES

GRAPHS

PREFACE

*M*y first introduction to the debate over the reality in Judah in the sixth century B.C.E. was in 1998, when I heard Joseph Blenkinsopp presenting a paper on the Myth of the Empty Land in The Old Testament Seminar, at the Faculty of Theology, University of Oxford. Later in 1998 I attended a conference in Tel Aviv University on the pottery of the sixth century (organized by Oded Lipschits). Generally speaking, the claims that the Land was not empty were seen as very convincing, although during the discussion I added a reservation that there were also changes, for example the disappearance of the four room house after the end of the Iron Age. In 2001 Oded Lipschits organized another, much larger, conference on the Judah in the Neo Babylonian period, at Tel Aviv University, and he invited me to participate. Specifically, he asked to present a paper on the rural settlements of the Iron Age (which was the topic of my master's thesis). I gave the invitation much thought, and after some time came with the idea that we can examine continuity between the Iron Age and the Persian period in the rural sector. I presented this paper at the conference, and later published it (Faust 2003b).

This is how I was introduced into the study of this fascinating period, and gradually came to hold firm views on the various elements in the ensuing debate. In the course of the coming years I published a few more papers on this troubled era (e.g., Faust 2004b; 2007c), but soon realized that the debate, and the period, deserve a monograph in order to do them at least a partial justice.

I worked on this monograph for the better part of five years, from 2005 to 2010, with some periods of interruption. Some parts of the book were written already in 2005, but I abandoned the manuscript in early 2006, when the preparation for the expedition at Tel 'Eton were gathering speed and I simply couldn't afford the time to deal with the issue. I resumed working on the monograph only in 2007, and most of the research was completed during the early part of 2008, when I was on a Sabbatical leave from Bar-Ilan University, and was a Kennedy Leigh Fellow at the Oxford Centre for Hebrew and Jewish Studies (this book is the first part of a larger study on the Persian period that I initiated at the time). The manuscript was completed later, in the course of 2009, it was accepted to publication at the SBL in 2010, and was edited and updated in early 2011. Only partial updating was possible during the production process.

In the course of the research, I benefited greatly from comments of various colleagues, who read chapters or segments of this book or even the whole of it.

I would like to thank Professors Shlomo Bunimovitz, Aren Maeir, Gabriel Barkay, Garry Knoppers and the late Hanan Eshel for reading earlier versions of some parts of this monograph (either as chapters or as drafts of articles) and commenting on it. Alon De Groot, David Amit, Shlomit Weksler-Bdolah, Hagit Turge and David Vanderhooft allowed me to quote unpublished data. I am also grateful to Hugh Williamson, Barry Cunliffe, Susan Sherratt, Joshua Schwartz, Zeev Safrai, and Avi Shveka who discussed many of the ideas expressed in the various chapters. Special thanks are due to Liz Fried, who read the entire manuscript and commented on it. Needless to say, the responsibility for the ideas expressed in this book and for any mistake or error is mine alone.

The maps were prepared by Yair Sapir, and the text was edited by Rebecca Goldberg. I am grateful to them both.

I should also thank a few bodies and institutions that supported the research financially: The Dr. Simon Krauthammer chair in Archaeology, the Moskovitz foundation, the Kuschitsky foundation, and especially the Ingeborg Rennert Center for Jerusalem Studies—all in the Martin (Szusz) Department of Land of Israel Studies and Archaeology, Bar-Ilan University.

Most of the manuscript was completed at the Oxford Centre for Hebrew and Jewish Studies, and I am grateful to the center for granting me the Kennedy Leigh Fellowship and for supplying me with the suitable environment for completing most of the research.

Finally, for giving me the time and peace of mind to work on this book, I would like to thank my family—my children, Kama, Marvah, and Yannai, and especially my wife Iris. This book is dedicated to her.

Abbreviations

AA	*Archaologischer Anzeiger*
AAR	*African Archaeological Review*
AASOR	Annual of the American Schools of Oriental Research
AB	Anchor Bible
ABD	Anchor Bible Dictionary
AJA	*American Journal of Archaeology*
ANES	Ancient Near Eastern Studies
AWE	Ancient West and East
BA	*Biblical Archaeologist*
BAIAS	*Bulletin of the Anglo-Israel Archaeological Society*
BAR	*Biblical Archaeology Review*
BASOR	*Bulletin of the American Schools of Oriental Research*
BABESCH	*BABESCH, Annual Papers on Mediterranean Archaeology*
CAH	Cambridge Ancient History
CAJ	*Cambridge Archaeological Journal*
CEA	Companion Encyclopedia of Archaeology
DDD	*Dictionary of Deities and Demons in the Bible*
EAEHL	Encyclopedia of Archaeological Excavations in the Holy Land
ErIsr	Eretz-Israel
ESI	Excavations and Surveys in Israel
Hen	Henoch
HS	Hebrew Studies
HUCA	*Hebrew Union College Annual*
IEJ	*Israel Exploration Journal*
JAOS	*Journal for the American Oriental Society*
JAR	*Journal of Archaeological Research*
JBL	*Journal of Biblical Literature*
JCS	*Journal of Cuneiform Studies*
JEA	*Journal of Egyptian Archaeology*

JUDAH IN THE NEO-BABYLONIAN PERIOD

JESHO	*Journal of the Economic and Social History of the Orient*
JHebS	*Journal of Hebrew Scriptures*
JHS	*Journal of Hellenic Studies*
JMA	*Journal of Mediterranean Archaeology*
JNES	*Journal of Near Eastern Studies*
JQR	*Jewish Quarterly Review*
JSOT	*Journal for the Study of the Old Testament*
JSOTSup	Journal for the Study of the Old Testament: Supplement Series
JSRS	*Judea and Samaria Research Studies*
JSS	*Journal of Semitic Studies*
Levant	*Levant*
NEA	*Near Eastern Archaeologist*
NEAEHL	The New Encyclopedia of Archaeological Excavations in the Holy Land
NSJ	New Studies on Jerusalem
OEANE	Oxford Encyclopedia of Archaeology in the Near East
OJA	*Oxford Journal of Archaeology*
Or	*Orientalia*
PEQ	*Palestine Exploration Quarterly*
Qad	*Qadmoniot*
RB	*Revue biblique*
RBL	*Review of Biblical Literature*
TA	*Tel Aviv*
UF	*Ugarit-Forschungen*
WO	*Die Welt des Orients*
ZAW	*Zeitschrift für die alttestamentliche Wissenschaft*
ZDPV	*Zeitschrift des deutschen Palästina-Vereins*

INTRODUCTION

*I*n the summer of 586 B.C.E., the Babylonian army defeated Judah and con-
quered Jerusalem.[1] The Temple was destroyed, and Judah lost its independence.
The Babylonian conquest left clear archaeological marks and destruction layers
in many sites including Jerusalem, Lachish, Ein Gedi, Kh. Rabud, Arad, Tel Ira,
Ramat Rahel, and many others (fig. 1).[2] The destruction of Judah and mainly
Jerusalem that is also recorded in the books of 2 Kings, 2 Chronicles, Jeremiah,
Lamentations and others, was a traumatic event for the population of Judah.
Thus, the opening verses of Lamentations (1:1–3) begin:

> How lonely sits the city, that once was full of people. How like a widow she
> has become, she that was great among the nations. She that was a princess
> among the provinces has become a vassal. She weeps bitterly in the night,
> with tears on her cheeks; among all her lovers she has no one to comfort
> her; all her friends have dealt treacherously with her, they have become her
> enemies. Judah had gone into exile with suffering and hard servitude; she
> lives now among the nations, and finds no resting place; her pursuers have all
> overtaken her in the midst of her distress.

The Babylonian conquest of Jerusalem is, no doubt, an important historical event.
For scholars, this date usually marks the end of the period of the Monarchy or
even the end of the Iron Age and the beginning of the exilic period. For many,

---

1. The exact date of the destruction has received a considerable amount of discussion (e.g.,
Malamat 1983, 243–47, and many references; see also Cazelles 1983; Coogan and Tadmor 1988).
This book will follow the generally accepted 586 B.C.E. date. This is done simply for reasons of
convenience. The exact dating carries no weight for the arguments discussed in this book and is
irrelevant for the conclusions.

2. Jerusalem: e.g., Shiloh 1984; Lachish: e.g., Ussishkin 2004; Ein Gedi: B. Mazar 1993; Stern
2007; Kh. Rabud: Kochavi 1974; 1993b; Arad: M. Aharoni 1993; Tel Ira: Beit Arieh 1993a; 1997;
Ramat Rahel: Aharoni 1993; but see now Lipschits, et al. 2009, 70.

Fig. 1. A Babylonian destruction layer in the City of David, Jerusalem (Shiloh 1984, plate 32:2; courtesy of the Institute of Archaeology, the Hebrew University of Jerusalem).

this date has been regarded as a "watershed."[3] But what was the reality in Judah after the 586 B.C.E. events, in the period known alternatively as the exilic period, the Neo-Babylonian period, or simply the sixth century B.C.E.? The Bible informs us that people remained in the land but gives the impression that they were relatively few and unimportant. Indeed, until recently, the period was viewed as a time of great demographic and cultural decline.[4] This view, however, has been severely criticized over the last decade and a half. Some scholars, mainly following Barstad's *The Myth of the Empty Land*, have accepted the notion that there was not much change in Judah after the fall of Jerusalem.[5] They believe that only a small minority of Judeans were exiled, and for most of the population, life continued after 586 B.C.E. just as before.[6] According to these scholars, most of the population lived in the rural sector and was unharmed by the war and the subsequent

---

3. E.g., Bright 1972, 343; Redford 1992, 471–72; Schniedewind 2004, 139; Liverani 2005; Middlemas 2005, 1.

4. Noth 1960, 296; Kenyon 1965, 298–302; Bright 1972, 343–44; Aharoni 1979; Mazar 1990; Stern 2001; see also Na'aman 1995, 114–15; 2000, 42–44.

5. Barstad 1996; also Carroll 1992; and see already Lemche 1988, 175–79.

6. E.g., Lipschits 1997b; 1998b; 2003a; 2003b; 2005; Blenkinsopp 2002a; 2002b; 2002c; see also Middlemas 2005.

exile. This new understanding of the reality in sixth-century B.C.E. Judah has been criticized, with respect to its understanding of the biblical texts as well as its interpretation of the Babylonian policies, and especially over the way these scholars treated the archaeological evidence from Judah.[7]

Indeed, the evolving debate over the settlement and demographic reality in the sixth century has brought the archaeological evidence to the fore. Unfortunately, as is widely known, no material culture specific to the Babylonian period has yet been identified, and so the debate seems unresolved.

STUDY OF THE NEO-BABYLONIAN PERIOD:
SUMMARY OF PREVIOUS RESEARCH

The period succeeding the Babylonian conquest of Judah, namely, the exilic period, is extremely important for biblical scholars, and various assumptions have been made on the exilic period's contribution to the biblical corpus.[8] The demographic and political reality in sixth-century Judah became a crucial issue for scholars trying to understand when parts of the Bible were written (mainly in the exilic and postexilic eras) and where they were written (i.e., in Judah or in exile).[9] The question of whether Judah was relatively "empty" or had a large and complex society is of significance for scholars who find it essential to understand which parts of the biblical corpus were written in Judah.

Most scholars in the past, although not viewing the land as "empty," accepted the exile as a historical fact and viewed the destruction as significant. Hence, Bright spoke about the "calamity of 587 B.C.E." (1972, 343), and Albertz devoted a large section to the "Babylonian Golah" (2003, 99–111). Only few followed C. C. Torrey (1910 [1970], 285–300; 1930, 24–44; 1954, xxv), who believed that the exile was insignificant. Torrey wrote that "(S)o far as the Jews of the Babylonian deportation are concerned, it is not likely that they ever exercised any considerable influence on the Jews in Judea" (1910 [1970], 288). Elsewhere he added that "the fact is, of course, that Nebuchadnezzar and his officers carried away only those on whom they could lay their hands," (290) noting that those were relatively few. According to him the exile affected only a small part of the population, and

---

7. Stern 2000b; 2004; Oded 2003; Vanderhooft 2003a; Faust 2003b; 2004b; Oded and Faust 2006.

8. Jansen 1956; Thomas 1961; Ackroyd 1968; Seitz 1989; Barstad 1996; Albertz 2003; Lipschits 2005; Middlemas 2005; see also Bright 1972, 347–60; Smith 1989; 1997; Sanders 1997.

9. When: e.g., Ackroyd 1968; Seitz 1989; Albertz 2003; Middlemas 2005; see more in the summary); where: e.g., Middlemas 2005; 2009, and references.

most inhabitants returned to their homes and continued to live in the same way as before the Babylonian conquest (also Torrey 1910 [1970], 300). Torrey (1954, xxvii–xxvii) also believed that there was no significant return. Notable among those influenced to some degree by Torrey in the recent generation (although more moderately) is Hans Barstad (e.g., 1996: 21–22),[10] and following him Lipschits (e.g., 2003a: 365; 2003b: 186–94, 300; 2005: 267), and others (e.g., Carroll 1998). I will return to this issue below.

In the meantime I would like to stress that, although biblical scholars concentrated on discussing the composition and/or editorial process of the biblical text and did not usually address the "reality on the ground" in ancient Judah, all the above discussions were, naturally, based on assumptions regarding the situation in Judah in the exilic and postexilic period. Thus, for example, recent attempts to locate the place of the authorship of the texts that are attributed to this period (e.g., Barstad 1996; Albertz 2003; Middlemas 2005) rely heavily on the "reality on the ground" in Judah. Hence interest among biblical scholars is growing concerning the physical (archaeological) reality in Judah.

While the disinterest until recently of biblical scholars in the physical reality in Judah might be expected, it is surprising that archaeologists did not pay much attention to this period. The literature reflects this gap. Many archaeological and historical books covering the period only briefly mention the Neo-Babylonian period—sometimes devoting to it no more than a paragraph or two—after discussing the destruction of Judah and before mentioning the Persian period. For example, after devoting a long discussion to the destruction, Kenyon (1965, 298) only wrote a paragraph on the Neo-Babylonian period. The same is true for Albright's (1960b) important work, and even in the monumental ten-volume series, *The History of Eretz Israel*, the period seems to fall between the cracks. In the volume on *Israel and Judah in the Biblical Period*, the chapter on the Iron Age ends with 586 B.C.E., and the chapter on the Persian period starts in 538 B.C.E. Oded (1984), who wrote a detailed chapter on the period of the Monarchy, devoted a mere page and a half to "the land of Judah after the destruction" (although it was beyond the "official" timeframe of the chapter). Most of his discussion deals with the short episode of Gedaliah, the governor of the remaining population in Judah after the destruction of Jerusalem (2 Kgs 25:22–26; Jer 40–43). Only the last paragraph addresses 582–539 B.C.E., merely to state that not much is known about the period. Most recent works tend to be smaller in the chronological scope. Hence, works on the "biblical period" end in 586 B.C.E. (e.g.,

---

10. It should be stressed that Barstad is careful to state that one should not follow Torrey in denying any return at all (e.g., Barstad 1996, 43–44, 79) and it is clear that he is not endorsing Torrey's view in full. See more below.

Mazar 1990), while those on the Second Temple period usually begin with the
Persian period (e.g., Avi Yonah 1966).

The most notable exception is Weinberg's (1969) study of the archaeology
of the postexilic period, which concentrated on the sixth century. This study,
which reflects the state of academic knowledge in the late 1960s, however, did
not initiate further archaeological discussion. Barkay (1992), who included the
sixth century in the Iron Age, might also be viewed as an exception. However, he
devoted only a brief discussion (less than two pages) to this period, probably due
to the lack of data (see more below). Interest in the Neo-Babylonian period was
initiated only following the current debate[11] and even this, as far as the archaeological community is concerned, only to a limited extent.

The reason for this archaeological neglect is the dearth of available information on the nature of this period. Hardly any excavated site or stratum was dated
to this period, and this era was subsequently regarded as a period of great decline.
Most of the limited data available is derived from a few tombs. Only in the land
of Benjamin to the north of Jerusalem, which was saved from the Babylonian
destruction, were settlement layers dated to the sixth century B.C.E.[12] Only minimal remains were identified as belonging to the sixth century B.C.E. throughout
the rest of Judah. This came as no surprise to most archaeologists. The Babylonian campaigns were regarded as responsible for this relative emptiness, and
this is indeed echoed in most brief historical and archaeological treatments of the
period. The following are just a few examples.

Albright referred to the destruction of cities and added that "there is not
a single known case where a town of Judah proper was continuously occupied
through the exilic period" (1960b, 141–42). Bright wrote that "as archaeological evidence eloquently testifies, all, or virtually all, of the fortified towns in the
heartland of Judah were razed to the ground, in most cases not to be rebuilt for
many years to come" (1972, 344). More recently, Stern also referred to the lack
of archaeological data from this period (2001), and Mazar's monumental work
stated that the Babylonian period was not "sufficiently known archaeologically"
(and devoted fewer than two pages to it; 1990, 549). He added that only north
of Jerusalem, in the land of Benjamin, "there was no severe destruction, and life
continued under Babylonian rule" (460). The dearth of finds is reflected in the
work of Barkay, who is one of the few that devoted specific efforts to this period
(he even included it within the Iron Age). Barkay referred to the lack of finds by

---

11. Stern (2001) devoted 48 pages to the topic.
12. E.g., Malamat 1950; see also Mazar 1990, 548; Barkay 1992, 372; Stern 1983; 2001; and
now also Lipschits 1999; 2003a; 2003b; the issue will be discussed at length in ch. 9.

stating that the period's material culture was known mainly through surveys and from burials (1992, 372–73; more below).

This short survey demonstrates that from an archaeological perspective, the land of Judah was regarded as devastated during the sixth century. The population was concentrated in limited regions; therefore, the archaeological record provided little to write about. This scarcity of finds matched scholars' expectations. The view that the period's material culture was limited was shared by practically all archaeologists, from scholars like Watzinger (1935), Albright (1940; 1960b; 1963), Kenyon (1965), and Aharoni (1979), to more recent archaeologists like Shiloh (1989), Stager (1996; see also King and Stager 2001), Mazar (1990), Barkay (1992), Herzog (1997b, 278), Dever (2005, 291–94), Master (2007), Holladay (2009, 87–88); Finkelstein (2010, 46), and Stern (2001).[13] In particular, Stern's works (e.g., 1982; 1983; 1987; 2001) have greatly increased the importance of the Persian period in comparison with previous publications (ch. 5), but he stressed that the Babylonian period was underpopulated.

Although these scholars did not treat the land as empty (ch. 8), it is clear that there is an archaeological consensus that the region was devastated. This consensus came under heavy criticism recently, mainly from biblical scholars. Already in 1988, for example, Lemche (1988, 175–76) stressed that "the sources all agree that a remnant was left behind," and although this was composed of the poorest segment of Judahite society, it "may have included as much as 90 percent of the population." Carrol (1992) stressed the creation of the "myth of the empty land" as a dominant idea in biblical writings, but he did not compare/contrast his ideas with the finds "on the ground" in Judah. This line of thinking was developed and elaborated by Barstad (1996; 2003) and later by Lipschits (2003a; 2003b; 2005). While not accepting Torrey's theory in full, those scholars were greatly influenced by him. For example, Barstad (1996, 21–23) referred to Torrey's works as "extreme," but wrote that

> even if he was certainly not correct in every respect, for instance in his dating of Isa 40–55 and in his claim that there was hardly any exile to speak of, or any return whatsoever, he did make several important points which cannot easily be dismissed. Among these are the stress on the importance of those who were left behind in Judah, and an awareness of the exaggerated importance generally attached to such ideological strategies as "exile" and "return" (22).

---

13. Notably, while archaeologists like Barkay (e.g., 1993) attempted to archaeologically identify the period under discussion, they did not claim that the region prospered, or that most of the population continued to live in the region "without any change," and accept the common view regarding the scarcity of settlement. Barkay's views will be mentioned in more detail below.

Barstad also lamented the neglect of Torrey's contribution, and claimed that recent scholarship proved him right with regard to the stress on continuity rather than break in Judah following the events in 586 B.C.E. (22). Barstad's 1996 publication was the most significant contribution to the stress on continuity rather than break. Barstad attacked the notion that the land was empty, and tried to deconstruct the consensus that was based on what he called "the myth of the empty land" (following others, e.g., Carrol 1992). He attempted to examine the biblical texts, the archaeological finds, and additional data on the Neo-Babylonian Empire in order to shed light on the reality in Judah after the destruction of the temple.

As far as the biblical texts were concerned, Barstad attempted to show how the myth of the empty land developed and influenced modern scholarship (1996, 25–27). He believed previous scholarship was based on texts, which were "much more to be regarded as religious and political propaganda than historical documents" (44, regarding the books of Ezra and Nehemiah). When discussing the archaeological evidence, Barstad examined surveys for evidence of the settlement that must have existed in Judah in the sixth century (47–55), since "if the arguments concerning a continuing settlement in Judah during the 'exilic' period presented above [i.e., his chapter on the biblical evidence] are correct, we should expect to find some evidence of material continuation" (47). He also discussed Transjordan where there was evidence of continuity (57–60), and then went on to discuss the Neo-Babylonian Empire and Judah (61–76). Barstad argued that it was against the interests of the Babylonian Empire to destroy Judah, and that the latter had an important role in the Empire's economy. Barstad summarized, "Jerusalem after the fall of Jerusalem constituted yet another wheel in the much bigger economic machinery of the Neo-Babylonian empire" (79).

The bottom line of Barstad's study was his claim that Judah was not empty in the sixth century. The vast majority of the population continued to live just as they had before the fall of Jerusalem, with practically no changes following the Babylonian conquest. The emptiness of the land was a myth created in the Persian period (14–45).

In light of overwhelming evidence from excavations, Barstad acknowledged that the urban centers of the Iron Age were destroyed by the Babylonians (1996, 47). However, he claimed that the large majority of Judah's population lived in villages and hamlets that were not affected by the Babylonian conquest. For this "great majority of the population" (Barstad 1996, 42),[14] life went on after 586 B.C.E. just as before (1996, 41, 79, 81). He felt Judah was simply part of a prosperous Neo-Babylonian Empire (1996, 79).

---

14. Some 90 percent of the population according to Lemche (1988, 176) and some 75 percent according to Kelle (2007, 83).

It should be stressed that as a biblical scholar Barstad was interested in this period because of theological–biblical considerations. As he acknowledged, "my present interest in the exilic period was caused primarily by the claim, originating in the nineteenth century, that no economic, cultural or religious activity could have taken place in Judah during this period because the country simply ceased to exist" (1996, 45). As Middlemas observed (2005, 20; not in a negative manner), Barstad's interest was "part of this wider desire to locate Deutero-Isaiah in Judah rather than Babylon." Therefore, he "sought to redeem Judah from the wasteland to which it had been relegated by historians."

Barstad's work was very influential among biblical scholars, who were interested in the period because it was considered to have been the time in which much of the biblical corpus was written.[15] Many biblical scholars and historians simply followed the lead and did not devote an independent study to the realty "on the ground" in sixth-century Judah (e.g., Albertz 2003; see also Middlemas 2005). Few of those who followed Barstad attempted to study the archaeological reality as revealed by surveys and excavations. Most notable of those who developed this line of research is Oded Lipschits, whose studies incorporate a great deal of detailed archaeological data.

Following Barstad, Lipschits accepted that after the Babylonian conquest there was a break in the urban sector, but not in the rural one (2003b, 222–23; 2005, 190, 368). Lipschits's studies were more detailed than Barstad's. While Lipschits, unlike Barstad, acknowledged that there was a significant demographic decline in the sixth century, he claimed that it was gradual (see ch. 5), that there was significant rural settlement, and continuity in many important traits during the transition from the Iron Age to the Persian period. Thus, Lipschits claimed that the majority of the population in the northern Judean mountains and the area of Benjamin remained in their homes after the Babylonian conquest, and they continued to use the same material culture just as before 586 b.c.e. According to Lipschits (1998b, 21), "in the Judean mountains and Benjamin, the vast majority of the population remained, and most villages continued to exist, with changes and adjustments that the new military, political, and economical struc-

---

15. Some of these scholars do not go beyond the interpretation of the texts and do not refer to the presumed situation in Judah during the sixth century including: who remained in Judah, where they lived, and how they lived (e.g., Carroll 1992). Others try to present a view on how life continued at the time, but they do not support their claim by material evidence (e.g., Berquist 1995, 15–18). Barstad was the first notable exception. He tried to locate these peoples and activities in the "real world." For this reason, it is difficult to relate archaeologically to works such as Carroll's, as there is no real archaeological data or scenario that can be checked.

ture required."[16] Lipschits also believed that the area was of great economic importance for the Babylonians (2005, 69).

Finkelstein and Silberman, following Lipschits, believed that at least seventy percent of the population of Iron Age Judah remained and lived in the region during the Neo-Babylonian period (2001, 306–8). According to their figures, this amounted to over 56,000 people (see, however, Finkelstein 2010 for a contrasting assessment and figures). Many biblical scholars, such as Albertz (2003), Berquist (1995), and Middlemas (2005), presented similar views.

Although those scholars had different interests, and despite some disparity in opinion (e.g., regarding the percentage of the population that continued to live in Judah after the events of 586 B.C.E.), they all stressed continuity between the Iron Age and Neo-Babylonian period and rejected the older consensus that Judah was devastated at the time. Therefore, they will be referred to in this book as the continuity school. It must be stressed that the differences among them are minor when compared with the differences between them as a group, and with the group of scholars who upheld the traditional view (or a modified version of it) of Judah after 586 B.C.E. It is therefore logical to treat them as a school.

The continuity school has come under heavy criticism.[17] This criticism related to Barstad's (and his followers') treatment of the biblical texts, his understanding of the reality in the Neo-Babylonian Empire, and his treatment of the archaeological data.[18] Many aspects of this criticism will be discussed in later chapters. Suffice it to say, the common view among archaeologists is that the Babylonian conquest was a significant event that led to a collapse and left the area in desolation.[19] King and Stager wrote about the Babylonian "scorched-earth policy" (2001, 251–58), and added, "clearly the population of Judah was severely diminished. West of the Jordan it is difficult not only to find a settlement site that continues to be occupied during the period (586–525 B.C.E.), but also to point to individual artifacts that fill the gap" (257). Aharoni wrote that "the destruction of

---

16. Note that in most of his writings, Lipschits attributed settlement continuity and prosperity mainly to the northern part of the Judean highlands and the region of Benjamin; e.g., Lipschits 2003b, 222; 2005, 190–91, 196, 258, 374.

17. See, e.g., Vanderhooft 2001; 2003a; Oded 2003; Oded and Faust 2006; Faust 2003b; 2004b; 2007c; Stern 2001; 2002; 2004; Schniedewind 2004, 141–47.

18. Treatment of the biblical texts: e.g., Oded 2003; Oded and Faust 2006; understanding of the reality in the Neo-Babylonian Empire: e.g., Vanderhooft 2001; 2003a; treatment of the archaeological data: e.g., Stern 2002; 2004; Faust 2003b; 2004b; 2007c; Oded and Faust 2006; see also Master 2007; Schniedewind 2004, 141–47.

19. E.g., Shiloh 1989; Mazar 1990; Stager 1996; Herzog 1997b, 278; King and Stager 2001; Stern 2001; Faust 2003b; 2004b; 2007c; Dever 2005, 291–294; Master 2007; Holladay 2009, 87–88; Finkelstein 2010, 46.

the 587/6 B.C.E. was total. No place that has been examined in the Shephelah or in the hill country escaped its fate except Mizpah, to which the seat of government was transferred with the destruction of Jerusalem..." (1978, 279). Finkelstein recently assessed the population of the Persian period and concluded that the population was so limited that the demographic estimates "work against scholars who tend to belittle the scope of the catastrophe which befell Judah in 586 BC" (2010, 46). Mazar claimed that the prosperity of the seventh century "came to an end with the Babylonian conquest of 586 B.C.E., when most Judean cities were destroyed and abandoned" (1990, 438). After reviewing the evidence for destruction (458–60), he concluded that "only in the land of Benjamin ... was the Babylonian conquest not obliterative." Holladay expressed a similar view, writing "there is virtually no clearly defined period that may be called Babylonian" (2009, 88), and then he quoted Stern (2001, 350) saying that "it was a time from which almost no material finds remain." Holladay then added the words (alluding to the present debate), "an empty land!" (2009, 88). A similar view was expressed by the historian M. Liverani, who referred to "a real overall collapse" (2005, 231–34, esp. 232), and that "it is thus easy to understand how, seen from Babylon, Palestine seemed to be an 'empty' land, a country of miserable squatters camped in the ruins of ancient cities, infested by nomadic incursions, a country abandoned by God and humans" (234).[20] The debate, however, continues.

This Book

This debate triggered the present monograph. The book's central aim is to reexamine the archaeological reality in the Neo-Babylonian period, mainly in the territories of the former (Iron Age) kingdom of Judah, in order to shed new light on this troubled period. The chapters will aim to resolve the impasse, by expanding research into new avenues and examining new data, as well as by offering new methods to examine older data. On this basis, the book will arrive at new insights about life in the region. Notably, while scrutinizing the evidence regarding Judah in the sixth century B.C.E., this monograph will concentrate mainly on the archaeological aspect of the debate. Before presenting the structure of this book, however, a few preliminary notes regarding chronology and the difficulties we face are in order.

---

20. Needless to say, many historians share this view. See, e.g., Na'aman 1995, 114–15; 2000, 42–44.

Most archaeologists use 586 B.C.E. as the traditional date that ends the Iron Age II.[21] A few archaeologists, most notably Gabriel Barkay, have challenged this view. According to Barkay (1992, 372–73; 1993), the date 586 B.C.E. is historical and marks the Babylonian destruction of Jerusalem, which means it is unlikely that changes in material culture would be so abrupt as to take place in the same year. Moreover, it is only Judah that experienced destruction and abrupt changes in 586 B.C.E.; most of the country was unaffected by the 586 events. Barkay, therefore, claimed that biblical descriptions of the destruction and its impact strongly influenced archaeological thinking and, hence, historic periodization. He believed that the processes by which the Iron Age material culture changed were much slower, and hence the point in time when the traditional Iron Age assemblages ended should be later, probably around 530–520 B.C.E. (Barkay 1992, 373; 1993). While not accepted by many archaeologists, this point, as we will see below, influenced the debate over the reality in Judah during the sixth century, since it allows (although it does not necessitate; Barkay accepts the traditional view) for many sites to have existed at the time—sites that were traditionally identified as late Iron Age, that is, ceramic assemblages generally attributed to the seventh century (for a late Iron Age assemblage, see fig. 2).

ATTEMPTS TO IDENTIFY THE POTTERY OF THE NEO-BABYLONIAN PERIOD

As we have seen, no clear-cut archaeological assemblages dated to the sixth century have been identified in Judah, and this makes the attempts to date sites to this period very problematic. Several explicit attempts, however, have been made in this direction, mainly since the heated debate on the nature of Neo-Babylonian Judah commenced.

Barkay postulated that a tomb he excavated in Keteph Hinnom was in use during this period (1998b). He tried to reconstruct the period's pottery forms based on this conclusion. Zorn also attempted to identify a stratum dated to this period at Tell en-Nasbeh (biblical Mizpah) and to define the period's assemblage (1993a; 1993b; 1997a; 1997b; 1997c; 2003). Finally, Lipschits tried to delineate the period's pottery in detail (1997b; 2005, 192–206). Much of the discussion was based on several layers dated to the sixth century at sites in Benjamin (see, e.g., Lapp 1978c; the finds in Benjamin will be discussed in ch. 9). These attempts, however, were all problematic.

Barkay's most important attempts at reconstructing sixth-century ceramic assemblages refers mainly to a sixth-century ceramic assemblage observed by

---

21. E.g., Amiran 1970; Aharoni 1978; Mazar 1990; Dever 1995; see also Stern 1993.

Fig. 2. A seventh- century B.C.E. assemblage from the Ashlar House, the city of David, Jerusalem (Shiloh 1984, plate 24:1; courtesy of the Institute of Archaeology, the Hebrew University of Jerusalem).

Barkay in his excavations at Keteph Hinom and in a few additional tombs (e.g., Barkay 1998b). This, however, is a putative assemblage. The tomb contained Iron Age and Persian period pottery. Barkay chose some forms, and on the basis of their assumed stage of development attributed them to the sixth century. While not impossible, this is not the appropriate method to identify the pottery of the sixth century, nor any century for that matter. To identify such pottery accurately, we need either a "sealed" assemblage at a stratified site, or one homogeneous assemblage from a unique context, such as a "single period" tomb. Only then could pottery be placed in its appropriate place within a relative chronology or sequence of pottery assemblages. In the absence of either, any selective attempt to identify the pottery of the sixth century is hazardous and cannot be proven.

As of yet, no form has been identified as unique to the sixth century. Given the lack of any pottery from a secure sixth century context, the failure to identify *fossiles directeurs*[22] is expected. With the absence of such forms, attempts to identify the pottery of the period would require constructing hypothesized "battleship

---

22. A *fossil directeur*, or *type fossil*, is a geological term referring to a particular type of pottery form or artifact which is unique to one period or culture and is not found in other eras. Such a form is, therefore, diagnostic of one period only, and when it is found, even without context, one may conclude that this period is represented in the site.

curves"[23] for various vessels and then extrapolating a possible "typical" assemblage for the sixth century. Given the nature of the available data, such an exercise would be speculative. However, the exercise was never attempted by Barkay (who devoted insightful, but brief, discussion to the issue), or other scholars.

Zorn conducted the most detailed attempt to identify the pottery of the sixth century, and his was the only study that produced pottery plates (1993b; and esp. 2003). He used historical reasoning and architectural analysis to reconstruct a "new" stratum at Tell en-Nasbeh, which he dated to the sixth (and the fifth) century B.C.E. Zorn then attempted to trace the pottery of this period. However, this pottery was never found in homogeneous assemblages; it was always mixed. In some cases, the sixth-century putative assemblages included "earlier Iron Age material" (e.g., regarding cisterns 304 and 361; Zorn 2003, 429), and in other cases Persian period pottery. Some elements Zorn hypothesized dated to the Neo-Babylonian period without any stratigraphical basis (e.g., Zorn 2003, 433–42), and "virtually none of these pieces comes from a clean stratigraphical context" (433). Zorn's attempts are exemplary (ch. 9), but even if his stratigraphical analysis is correct (and many doubt it; Herzog 1997b, 237; Faust 2005a, 81–83, n. 148; see also De Groot 2001, 79, and more below), all we have is an artificial assemblage. Even Zorn (2003, 445; 416–17) asserted, "we are left with a collage of objects mixed together that covers the entire life of the stratum" (i.e., sixth–fifth centuries B.C.E.). This reconstruction is insufficient to salvage the pottery of the sixth century, and the picture of sixth century pottery remains unclear.

Lipschits's attempts were more detailed than Barkay and Zorn but were less grounded in specific data. His discussion was lengthy and detailed but did not include any pottery plates (2005, 192–206). Lipschits described many forms which showed continuity or development, mainly from the late Iron Age, to the Persian period, through the sixth century (198–203). However, he acknowledged that going beyond a description of each form and identifying the "real" pottery of the sixth century was a tricky issue (203): "nevertheless, familiarity with the assemblages of the late Iron Age and the Persian period is not sufficient to identify all the characteristics of the pottery assemblages that existed in the sixth century." Therefore, Lipschits turned to the finds from "stratified" sites in Benja-

---

23. A battleship curve, or a battleship-shaped curve, refers to a curve that represents the popularity of vessels through time (the term is used in seriation). In most cases, a vessel is less frequent when it first appears, gradually becomes more popular, and then declines in popularity until it disappears (Deetz 1967, 26–33; Sinopoli 1991, 74–75; Orton, Tyres and Vince 1993, 190). The level of popularity (even at peak) and the speed with which each vessel gains and loses popularity changes from one vessel to another. The graphs that represent this popularity look like a World War II battleship, hence the name.

min (which are dated to the period under discussion by the majority of scholars), mainly at Tell el-Ful (Lipschits 2005, 204), and compared them to the pottery from Tell en-Nasbeh, Bethel, Gibeon, and so on (204–6).[24]

However, he compared forms but not assemblages.[25] This is a problematic procedure, since the forms have a long life (a fact of which Lipschits is aware, given his discussion on pages 198–203). Using the existence of ceramic forms to raise claims about the "importance and significance of the sixth-century occupation at Gibeon" (205) is invalid (see also ch. 9). Unless some *fossiles directeurs* of the sixth century are discovered in sealed or clear contexts, no form can be dated exclusively to this century on the basis of such argumentation. Moreover, forms that, on the basis of their "development," are "likely" to be common in the sixth century (a dangerous suggestion by itself) were in most cases already in use in the seventh century B.C.E.[26] Hence, those very forms can be found in sites that did not exist in the sixth century.[27] With a lack of *fossiles directeurs*, we must study assemblages, and not forms. Good assemblages, and not hypothesized ones, remain to be discovered.

Clearly, the attempts have failed to identify any *fossils directeurs* from the sixth century, and even the suggested assemblages are problematic since no clear and "clean" pottery assemblage from this era was excavated anywhere (see also De Groot 2001, and more below). This is not to say that there was no pottery at the time, but instead our archaeological resolution is not good enough, and we are currently unable to identify it (ch. 9).

Moreover, even the relative chronology of the assemblages is not straightforward. For example, the site at Bethel, located just north of Judah, is regarded by many as having clear evidence for sixth-century occupation (e.g., Kelso 1968, 37; 1993; see also Albright 1948; Lipschits 2005, 204–5; more below). Another site that is regarded as almost a site-type for this period is Tell en-Nasbeh (Zorn 1993a; 2003; Lipschits 2005, 204–5). Some scholars equated the pottery at

---

24. It should be noted that none of these sites provides a good assemblage from a domestic context that can be dated to the sixth century (e.g., Lipschits 2005, 204–6 for references; see ch. 9). The issue will be discussed further in ch. 9.

25. As we will see in ch. 9, in most of these sites no assemblages can be dated to the sixth century.

26. The same is true regarding his other comparisons, even if (supposed) "assemblages" are mentioned, e.g., at Keteph Hinom. To reiterate, only sealed or stratified contexts can be used to define assemblages. Any other attempt is artificial and involves an arbitrary collection of forms.

27. For some well-known forms, see the discussion of the Gibeon Jar: Kelm and Mazar (1985, 114–16); Mazar and Panitz-Cohen (2001, 79) (and already Amiran 1975); for the Iron Age date of the "carrot shaped" bottles, see Kelm and Mazar (1985, 114–15); Mazar and Panitz-Cohen (2001, 131). The issue will receive more detailed discussion in ch. 9.

both sites, and dated it to the sixth century (e.g., Lipschits 2005, 204–5). But as Albright (1948, 205) commented many years ago, "thanks to the fact that there was an important sixth-century occupation at Bethel after the final destruction of Jerusalem by the Chaldeans, we can say confidently that Tell en-Nasbeh was abandoned during most of this century, since the Bethel pottery in question is conspicuous by its absence" (see also ch. 9). Notably, Albright's comment referred to the relative chronology, and should, therefore, be seriously considered. This shows that the issue of "identifying" the pottery of the sixth century is more difficult than it might appear at first glance,[28] and this is without even mentioning the criticism on the sixth century date for the pottery of Bethel itself.[29]

This means that we cannot at the present state of knowledge, identify the pottery of the sixth century B.C.E. This has a devastating impact on our ability to use surveys in the study of this period. Many of the sites referred to in the debate over the reality of the sixth century are known from surveys. A major aim of identifying the pottery of the sixth century is therefore not only to date the few sites that were excavated, but to produce *fossiles directeurs* of the sixth century B.C.E. Discovering such "type finds" would help date sites that were only surveyed. This is especially important because the debate centers around the rural sector, and rural sites are usually only known from surveys (but see ch. 2).[30] In the absence of such "type finds" the surveys simply cannot identify the sixth century (through its pottery).

In sum, no pottery forms can currently be attributed with any degree of certainty to the sixth century B.C.E., and even all the suggested assemblages are putative (ch. 9). De Groot discussed the state of knowledge of Persian and Neo-Babylonian pottery:

---

28. The detailed discussions that attempt to organize a sequence of the assemblages (e.g., Lapp 1978a; 1978b; Lipschits 2005: 204–6, and references; see also Wright 1963) are nearly impossible. It is not viable to work in such a resolution, and the differences observed in the finds of different strata need not have anything to do with chronology. They can be attributed to regional factors or can even result from the different nature of the activity in the limited areas that were exposed. The issue will be discussed at more length in ch. 9.

29. The sixth-century date for the assemblage at Bethel (Kelso 1968, 37) was doubted by Dever (1971; 1997a), who claimed that the pottery did not come from a secure context, and it was more likely that the site ceased to exist in the time of the Babylonian conquest (see now also the criticism of Finkelstein and Singer-Avitz 2009; for a detailed discussion see ch. 9).

30. It must be noted that even if sealed or stratified sixth-century assemblages would be found in the future, it is possible that there will be no fossiles directeurs found, and all we will have are the assemblages. That would mean that even the identification of a Neo-Babylonian settlement through excavations might not solve the problem of identifying the period through surveys.

At the present state of research we have no (data from) stratified excavations that enable us to distinguish between early and late in the Persian
period ceramic assemblages in the highlands ... Recently, several scholars
have claimed that it is possible to define, archaeologically, the short period
of time between the Babylonian destruction and the Persian conquest—i.e.,
the Neo-Babylonian period. A reexamination ... cast doubts on this claim
(2001, 79; my translation).

After discussing the sites and loci involved, De Groot summarized that "the lack
of ceramic assemblages that can be attributed to the Neo-Babylonian period in
Judah" makes the attempts to identify this period in the surveys in Benjamin
untenable (2001, 80; see also the cautionary note of Master 2007, 29–30). In light
of the above it is clear that we cannot date sites to the sixth century B.C.E., and
this leads us to the fundamental "problem" of the archaeology of the sixth century
B.C.E.: the dearth of finds attributed to this century.

FOCUSING THE PROBLEM: EXPLAINING THE DEARTH OF FINDS

The lack of sixth-century archaeological evidence is explained in two contrasting
ways.

1.   The region was only sparsely settled; therefore, the population left only
      scant remains. This approach was adopted in the past by almost all
      scholars (e.g., Albright 1960b; Kenyon 1965), and is still followed today
      by most of them.[31] The dearth of evidence, therefore, was a result of the
      low demography and scarcity of settlements which were typical of this
      era.

2.   The period did not have a distinct material culture that differed from
      the previous period (Barkay 1992; 1993). The material culture of the
      period should be viewed as a continuation of the late-seventh and early-
      sixth centuries B.C.E., and also as a predecessor of the Persian period,
      without any specific major characteristics for this era, which lasted
      about fifty years. This approach views the Babylonian period's mate-
      rial culture as a continuation of the Iron Age (see now Lipschits 1997b;
      1998b; 2003b; 2005; Barstad 1996; 2003). This view allows for many
      sites to exist during the sixth century. Many supporters of this outlook

---

31. E.g., Stern 1997a; 1998; 2000b; 2001; Mazar 1990; Stager 1996; King and Stager 2001,
251–58; see also Vanderhooft 2003a; Oded 2001; Liverani 2005, 194–96, 231–34; Finkelstein
2010, 46.

(the continuity theory) regard the sixth century as more populated than
supporters of the first school, since in their view sites that were usually
dated to the Iron Age should be reassigned to the sixth century. Since
many of the major sites were already excavated, and sixth century B.C.E.
destruction layers were unearthed, supporters of the continuity theory
suggest that the rural sector was not affected by the war and that many
of the small Iron Age sites discovered in the surveys were representative
of the sixth century B.C.E.

Both explanations could account for the lack of detailed and specific knowledge
of sixth-century B.C.E. material culture. For this reason, the debate continues concerning the demographic reality in Judah during this period: "empty" or not (a
way to circumvent this problem will be discussed in chapter 2, and another solution will be offered in ch. 3).

THE STRUCTURE OF THE BOOK

In chapter 1, "The End of the Iron Age in Judah: Primary Archaeological Data,"
I discuss the data from the central sites in Judah and its vicinity. The data mainly
include tells, which were usually destroyed in the early-sixth or late-seventh century B.C.E. The widespread destruction of these sites gave rise to the traditional
view that Judah was desolate in the sixth century B.C.E. Due to the persuasive-
ness of the evidence, followers of both schools of thought accept that the urban
sector was destroyed, and supporters of the continuity school attribute continuity
to the rural sector only. The aim of the chapter 1 is, therefore, to present the basic
settlement data regarding the end of the Iron Age of Judah in order to establish
common grounds for discussion.

Due to the continuity school's view that life in the rural sector continued as
usual, chapter 2 "Judah in the Sixth Century B.C.E.: A Rural Perspective," examines the reality of settlement in the rural sector. Since no sites can be identified as
belonging to this period on the basis of ceramic *fossiles directeurs*, in this chapter
I suggest a method to enable us to identify sites that were settled at the time. The
method involves examining patterns of continuity and discontinuity in excavated
small sites from the Iron Age to the Persian period, since continuities in such
sites (unlike in central mound) might indicate settlement also in the intervening
sixth century B.C.E. The method has already been published (Faust 2003b; Faust
and Safrai 2005), but the chapter is updated, includes many more sites, and refers
to additional issues (see Lipschits 2004; Faust and Safrai 2005).

In chapter 3, "Greek Imports and the Neo-Babylonian Period," I discuss
the sixth century from a different perspective. While the local pottery cannot

be securely dated to the period under discussion, Greek pottery can be dated to the sixth century with great precision. A close examination of the find spots of this pottery, both in the region and abroad, can shed new light both on the reality on the ground and on dating local pottery. While the dating of Greek pottery can also be debated, both schools of thought regarding sixth century B.C.E. Judah follow the traditional chronology of Greek pottery. When compared with the situation in other parts of the Mediterranean, and especially in the Phoenician colonies in the west, the findings in Judah and the surrounding regions are indicative not only of the prosperity or devastation of the region, but also of the Babylonian policy and economic interests in the region.

Chapter 4, "Social and Cultural Changes in Judah: The Iron Age to the Persian Period," examines the social and cultural processes in Judah during the transition from the Iron Age to the Persian period. Identifying socio-cultural changes allows us to understand the nature of this transition. Some of the data (from burial practices and domestic architecture) have already been published (Faust 2004b). However, the discussion here is updated, expanded, and includes aspects of religion, language, and kinship.

Chapter 5, "Settlement and Demography in Judah: Seventh to Second Centuries B.C.E.," takes a broader perspective in examining settlement fluctuations and demographic trends during the settlement peak of the late Iron Age in Judah (seventh century B.C.E.), the Persian period, the Neo-Babylonian period, and the Hellenistic period.[32] Understanding the nature of these long-term processes (and their causes) affords a deeper understanding of the settlement reality and demographic situation in Judea during the Neo-Babylonian period. The chapter also presents a new perspective on the demographic reality in Persian-period Judah, and also in the Neo-Assyrian provinces in the late Iron Age.

Chapter 6, "The Babylonian Destruction in Context: Nebuchadnezzar and Sennacherib Compared," in which I discuss the results of the Babylonian campaigns of the late-seventh and early-sixth centuries from a comparative perspective. The chapter will compare the archaeological results of Nebuchadnezzar's and Sennacherib's campaigns (study of the latter is based on Faust 2008b), which will provide a way to assess the degree of the Babylonian destruction within what can be viewed as its ancient Near Eastern context.

In chapter 7, "Sixth-Century Judah as a Post-Collapse Society," I analyze the implications of the previous chapters to create a deeper understanding of sixth-century Judah. This analysis will be studied in light of data from other societies

---

32. Much of this chapter is based on Faust (2007c).

that went through processes of collapse and post-collapse (esp. in light of the seminal works of Tainter 1988; 1999; see also Faust 2004b; 2007c).

Chapter 8, "Consequences of Destruction: The Continuity Theory Revisited," examines additional aspects of the reality in the sixth century B.C.E. and evaluates the main arguments of the continuity school: was Judah part of a Babylonian imperial economy; was a drastic demographic decline possible, and under what circumstances can such changes occur? I also explain how the entire debate, as far as the archaeological interpretation is concerned, was erroneously conceived.

Chapter 9, "The Land of Benjamin Revisited," looks at settlement in the region of Benjamin. The area has received a great deal of scholarly attention because of the consensus among scholars that settlements existed in the Neo-Babylonian period. Can the old excavations and/or new interpretations stand scrutiny, or are the conclusions and interpretations based on the biblical texts?

Chapter 10, "Life in Judah in the Sixth Century B.C.E.," will attempt to reconstruct life in Judea during the sixth century. The chapter will try to assess where people lived, the economy, and the type of life that existed in the region at the time.

Chapter 11, "Judah in the Sixth Century B.C.E.: Summary and Conclusions," concludes the volume. Here I also comment on aspects of the debate not dealt with in previous chapters.

CHAPTER 1

THE END OF THE IRON AGE IN JUDAH: PRIMARY ARCHAEOLOGICAL DATA

The common view until the 1990s was that the sixth century B.C.E. was a period of desolation. This view was based on the data from dozens of excavations, mostly in urban sites.[1] Herzog summarized the consensus: "the destruction of Jerusalem by Nebuchadnezzar in 586 B.C.E. is the event which terminated the rather short third urban phase [i.e., the Iron Age urban phase] in the history of ancient Israel" (1997b, 278).

Those who challenged the traditional view of sixth-century Judah as desolate claimed that it is the archaeologically less-known rural sector that prospered during this period. Generally speaking, they agreed that the urban sector was destroyed by the Babylonians (e.g., Barstad 1996, 47; 2003, 6; Lipschits 2003b, 222–23; 2005, 190, 368). For example, Lipschits referred to the "sharp decline in urban life" (2005, 190); elsewhere he wrote, "large, important cities were laid waste, and urban life effectively came to an end" (368). A few, however, have suggested that the common view of the urban sector was exaggerated (e.g., Blenkinsopp 2002b, 184–87). In this chapter, I present and reexamine the data from the major excavations on which past discussions have relied.

JUDAHITE CITIES AND CENTERS AT THE END OF THE IRON AGE

First, I will review the fate of Judah's cities and central sites (e.g., major forts) at the end of the Iron Age in geographical order according to regions (for their location, see figs. 3, 4).[2]

---

1. E.g., Bright 1972, 344; Kenyon 1965; Albright 1960b, 141–42; Aharoni 1978, 279; Stern 2001, 324–25; Mazar 1990, 438, 458–60.

2. For more data on the Iron Age finds in those sites, see ch. 6.

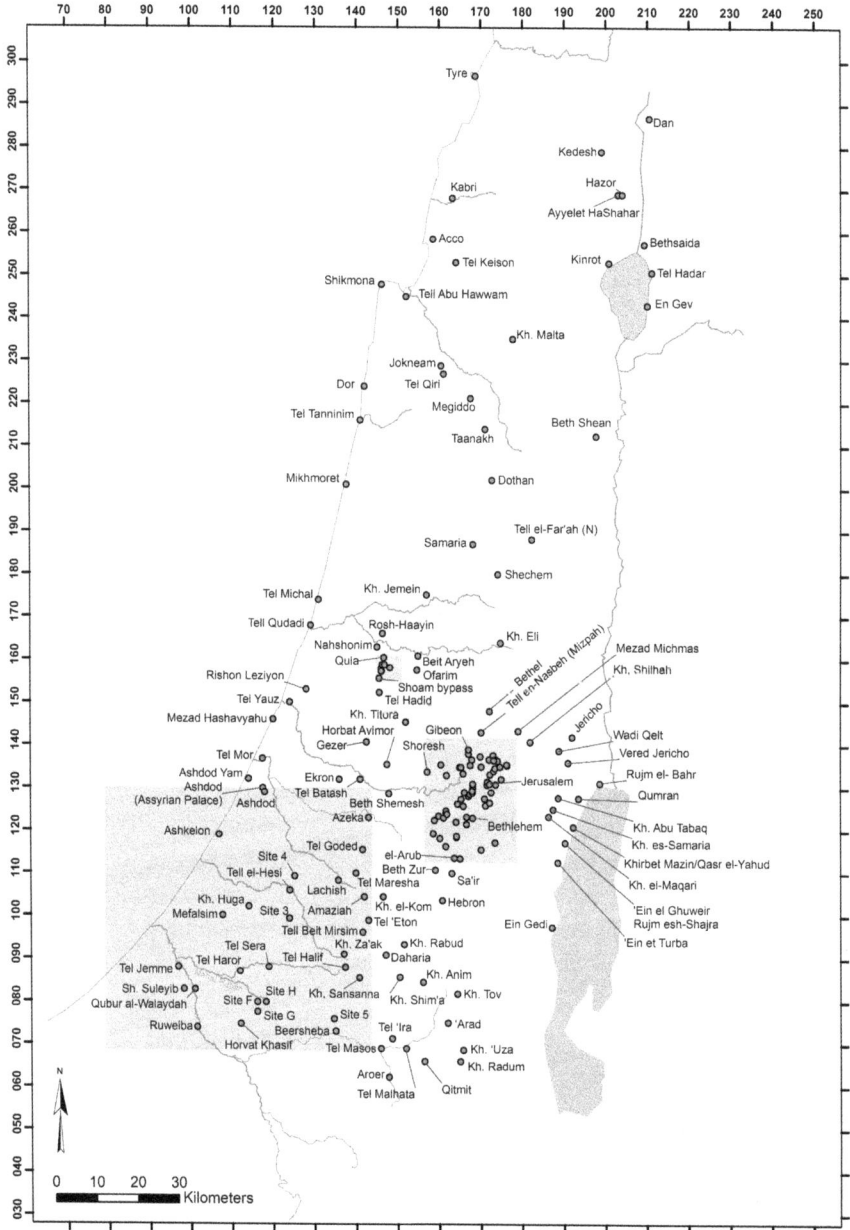

Fig. 3. Map showing the sites mentioned in the text.

CITIES IN THE LAND OF BENJAMIN

A number of cities were excavated in this region, and there is a consensus that Benjamin differed from other regions in that the region prospered in the sixth century.[3] While the region will be discussed in more detail in ch. 9, it is worth mentioning that from the available data it appears that some of the sites were at least partially destroyed or abandoned at the time discussed, for example, Gibeon,[4] and probably also Gibeah/Tell el-Ful (Stratum IIIa).[5] The reality at Mizpah/Tell en-Nasbeh is more complex, but even there destruction in the late Iron Age cannot be ruled out (see discussion in ch. 9; see also Albright 1940, 205). Even according to Zorn (e.g., 1993a; 1993b), Stratum 2 was not a continuation of Stratum 3 at the site, but was superimposed on it. Another large site that prospered in the seventh century, but not later, was Deir el-Sid (Biran 1985, 211–13).[6] In any event, the situation in Benjamin was very complex and will be discussed in detail in ch. 9. For the time being, we can conclude here that the consensus agrees that the region was unique and was not devastated by the Babylonians.

THE HIGHLANDS FROM JERUSALEM SOUTHWARD

Jerusalem
    The site reached its zenith in the seventh century B.C.E., when the city and the extramural neighborhoods covered 900–1,000 dunams, and was surrounded by a dense network of rural settlements.[7] The site was destroyed in the Babylonian campaign of 586 B.C.E., as is evident in the findings in various areas. For example, in area G of the City of David (fig. 1), a destruction layer showed that

---

3. E.g., Stern 1982, 31–34; 1983, 120; 2001, 321–23, 350; Mazar 1990, 548; Barstad 1996, 48–50; Lipschits 1999; 2003a, 347–51; 2003b, 272–83; 2005, 237–49.
    4. Pritchard 1962, 163; see also Finkelstein 2010, 42.
    5. See, e.g., Lapp 1993, 447, even though it is commonly agreed that the site was still settled in later parts of the sixth century.
    6. The site at Kh. el-Kharruba was probably occupied in the Iron Age, although on a very small scale. During the Persian period it was a large site, hence indicating change. In any event, the site was of a rural nature in the Iron Age and will not be discussed here (chs. 2 and 9).
    7. The scholarly consensus is that Jerusalem reached a demographic peak in the seventh century B.C.E. (e.g., Barkay 1989; Mazar 1990, 438; Faust 2005b, and many others). Na'aman (2007) challenged this consensus; and while admitting that Jerusalem's environment was more densely settled than before, he claimed that Jerusalem itself was less dense than during the eighth century B.C.E. I believe Na'aman's reconstruction is wrong on this point. However, the issue will not be addressed in this monograph, and whether the peak in Jerusalem's demography was during the eighth or seventh centuries is immaterial for the present discussion.

the residential houses that existed in the late Iron Age were burned (e.g., Shiloh 1984, 18–19; Steiner 2001, 108–9, 114–15). A similar picture was observed in other excavation areas. Regarding area E1, Shiloh (1984, 14) wrote, "the clear-cut destruction level—the total destruction of the series of building in area E1—was accompanied by traces of fire and destruction." A layer of ash, in which arrow-heads were discovered, was also observed near the "Israelite tower" in the Jewish Quarter, near the "broad wall," and was attributed to the Babylonian conquest (Avigad 1983, 53–54; Geva and Avigad 2000, 155). The same picture was reported in the Ophel excavations, where the large Iron Age complex "was destroyed in conflagration when Jerusalem was razed by the Babylonians in 586 B.C.E." (Mazar and Mazar 1989, 59).

Most scholars believe that the city was thoroughly destroyed (e.g., Auld and Steiner 1996, 44–45; see even Lipschits 1998a; 2005, 210–18), and Lipschits has even suggested that Jerusalem was totally empty after the destruction (2005, 211, 218). However, a few scholars believe that the evidence shows that some of the population continued to live amid the ruins (e.g., Barkay 1993; 2003).

Moza

In the late Iron Age, Moza probably served as an administrative center for storage purposes (e.g., Greenhut 2006, 195–282; De Groot and Greenhut 2002; Greenhut and De Groot 2009). The site ceased to exist at the end of the Iron Age, and was not settled in the Persian period (Greenhut 2006, 195; Greenhut and De Groot 2009, 226–27).[8]

Ramat Rahel

The site's original excavator attributed the destruction of Stratum 5A to the Babylonians. The later Persian occupation exhibited a different plan (Aharoni 1993, 1265; Barkay 2006, 44; for a sixth-century gap, see also Naʾaman 2001, 274). The excavations at the site, though mainly outside the palace, which was excavated almost in its entirely by Aharoni, had been renewed by Lipschits et al. (2006, 227), and initially they reported only "small remains dating from the Iron Age II," and only "sherds and seal impressions dating from the Persian and Hellenistic periods." Recently, Lipschits et al. suggested that "it seems to us that the palace … was not destroyed by the end of the Iron Age," adding that "the question of its continued use during the sixth century B.C.E. is, archaeologically, an open question" (2009, 70; my translation; also 2011, 34). Interestingly, salvage

---

8. The existence of *mwsh* inscriptions (usually dated to the Persian or Babylonian period; see more below) led Greenhut (2006, 194–95) to suggest that perhaps the name Moza was preserved, and served as the name of another site in the region, where Persian period remains were found.

excavations carried out recently on the edge of the site reported Iron Age remains but no Persian period remains (Solimany and Barzel 2008b). Overall, the evidence seems to support the view that there was a clear difference between the Iron Age palace and the later one. However, in light of Lipschits's excavations, this is not certain (Lipschits et al. did not deny a gap, but rather left it as an open archaeological question).

Beth Zur

It appears that the Iron Age II site was already established in the eighth century (as is evidenced by the *lmlk* impressions[9] unearthed at the site), and prospered during the seventh and early-sixth centuries B.C.E. The excavators believed that the site ceased to exist in 586 B.C.E., but it is not clear if the site was destroyed or not, as evidence for a destruction layer is partial (Funk 1968, 8; 1993; see also Alpert Nakhai 1997). It is quite clear that the site did not "continue" to exist in the Persian period (see also Finkelstein 2010, 41–42).[10]

Hebron

It appears as if the Iron Age city continued to exist until the early-sixth century (Chadwick 2005, 70). The excavations on the slopes revealed remains from the seventh century B.C.E., which indicated that the city was large at the time.[11] This was followed by a settlement gap in the Persian period (Eisenberg and Nagorski 2002, 92; see also Lipschits 2005, 250).

---

9. Recently, Lipschtis et-al. (2010; see also Lipschits et-al., 2011) attempted to challenge the late-eighth century dating of some of the impressions. This is a very problematic suggestion, which was already rejected by a number of scholars (see Ussishkin 2011 for a detailed refutation; see also Barkay 2011: 170), and is not accepted by me either (more below, ch. 6).

10. Lipschits (2005, 250–51) tried to question the destruction of the site, based mainly on his interpretation of the surveys in the region. This is very problematic (for the surveys, see ch. 5). It must be stressed that in contrast to the abundant Iron Age material at the site, the Persian period finds are limited, although they are not absent (Dever 1971; Stern 1982: 36), hence indicating a break or at least a great decline at the end of the Iron Age (see recently Finkelstein 2007, 53; 2010, 41–42). Lipschits's (2005, 251) attempts to oppose this view on the basis of forms found in mixed loci is misguided, since pottery forms exist for long periods. Many "Persian" forms began to appear during the Iron Age and were still found until the fourth century and later; their presence in surveys or mixed loci is meaningless and does not indicate anything about the Persian period, as they were used, even if in small quantities, already in the Iron Age (for the process of appearance and disappearance of ceramic forms, see Deetz 1967, 26–33; Wesler 1999; Sinopoli 1991, 74–75; Orton, Tyres and Vince 1993, 190–91).

11. Emanuel Eisenberg and Alon De Groot, personal communication; see also Eisenberg and Nagorski 2002, 92*, who referred to finds from the eighth–seventh centuries B.C.E.

Khirbet Rabud (Debir)

The town of the seventh century was relatively large, and in addition to the fortified city, included an unwalled settlement. Both "were completely razed with the destruction of the First Temple." The later Persian period settlement was very limited (Kochavi 1974; 1993b, 1252; also Lipschits 2005, 250).[12]

Eastern Judah

The seventh century was the peak of settlement in the region of Jericho and the Judean Desert (see also the detailed discussion in ch. 6).

Jericho

The late Iron Age settlement, that of the seventh century, was relatively extensive, and existed until the Babylonian campaigns (Kenyon 1993, 680–681; see also Stern 2001, 134, 324; Lipschits 2005, 232–33). The Persian period settlement was much smaller (e.g., Lipschits 2005, 233).

Ein Gedi

The first settlement was erected during the late Iron Age (Stratum 5). The excavators suggested that it was destroyed in 582 B.C.E., but the exact date is far from secure and is based on non-archaeological considerations. It is clear however, that it was destroyed in conflagration in the sixth century, and probably even early-sixth century (e.g., Stern 2007, 362; Mazar 1993, 402; see also Lipschits 2005, 233). As Stern (2007, 362) noted, "layers of destruction and ashes (were) noted on the floor of the building from this time. ... Moreover, in one of the walls surrounding building 207 on the north was found a barrage of arrows of the Scythian-Iranian (Babylonian) type which had been fired at the building."

Many other sites, e.g., Rugm el-Bahr, Qumran, Khirbet Mazin/Qasr el-Yahud, Ein el-Guweir, Ein et-Turaba, Rujm esh-Shajra, and others (most of which were forts and served royal purposes, though a few were probably rural in nature) prospered in the seventh century B.C.E. along the shores of the Dead Sea. Several additional sites were excavated in the Boqe'ah valley, and they also prospered in the seventh century B.C.E. (since they were probably rural in nature, they will

---

12. Lipschits (2005, 250) wrote that "there is no obvious proof that the site was destroyed, and the reasons for its abandonment are not clear." Even if he is correct in his first statement, and this is doubted, there is no reason to doubt the connection of the abandonment with the Babylonian campaign. Moreover, for our purposes it is sufficient to show that the site was abandoned at the time, and this is agreed upon by Lipschits (for a more detailed discussion of the entire region, see ch. 5).

be discussed in ch. 2). Settlement in all of these sites ceased in the sixth century and was not resumed for at least several hundreds of years (e.g., Bar-Adon 1989; Cross and Milik 1956; Stager 1976; De Vaux 1973, 1–3, 58–60, 91–93; 1993).

THE NEGEV (BEERSHEBA AND ARAD VALLEYS)[13]

The late Iron Age seems to have been the peak of settlement in the Negev region.[14]

Tel Ira

The last Judahite city at this location (Stratum 6) was built in the mid-seventh century B.C.E., and existed until it was violently destroyed by fire around 600 B.C.E. or early in the sixth century. Beit Arieh (1997, 176–77) mentioned that "traces of the disaster are visible everywhere in this stratum" (see also Beit Arieh 1993a, 644; Lipschits 2005, 227). After a gap, a new settlement was established in the Persian period, but it was much smaller in scope (Beit Arieh 1997, 173, 177).

Aroer

Stratum 2 is dated to the late-seventh and early-sixth centuries B.C.E., and came to an end "with the Babylonian conquest." This was followed by a 500-year settlement gap (Biran 1993, 91).[15]

Arad

This important Judahite fort was destroyed in the early-sixth century B.C.E., and the site was abandoned until the mid-fifth century (e.g., M. Aharoni 1993, 85; Herzog 1997a, 242, 244, 245).

Tel Malhata

The Iron Age city was destroyed by fire in the early-sixth century B.C.E. (Kochavi 1993a, 935–36). This was followed by a long settlement gap until the

---

13. Note that no significant seventh-century material was found at Tel Beersheba (Tell es-Saba) or under the Roman-Byzantine town of Beersheba (Bir es-Saba) (see the updated studies of Panitz-Cohen 2005; Fabian and Gilead 2007).

14. While almost all scholars agree that the seventh century represented the peak of Iron Age settlement (e.g., Herzog 1997a; Finkelstein 1995a), Tahareani Sussely (2007) suggested that settlement in the eighth century was about the same size. While it appeared that seventh-century settlement was still larger than in the eighth century, this is of no significance for our purposes.

15. Note that Lipschits (2005, 228) claimed there was no evidence of destruction. He does not deny that there was destruction, only that the Iron Age remains were "badly damaged" later by Herodian activity. This, however, is irrelevant as it is agreed that the site was abandoned.

Hellenistic period (Kochavi 1998, 35–38; see also Kochavi 1993a, 936; Lipschits 2005, 228).

Tel Masos

Scant seventh century B.C.E. remains were found in area G. These remains probably represented a fort, which was "destroyed in a violent conflagration" (Kempinski 1993, 989; see also Lipschits 2005, 227).

Khirbet Uza

According to the excavator, the Iron Age Israelite fort and the nearby village appear to have fallen to the Edomites and were then deserted for four hundred years (e.g., Beit Arieh 1993c, 1496). Similar was the fate of the nearby small fort at Kh. Radum: the site was abandoned in the early-sixth century and was not resettled (Beit Arieh 1993b; see also Lipschits 2005, 224–25).

Khirbet Tov

A large fort dated to the late Iron Age was excavated by Cohen. He reported that it was a single period site, that is, it did not exist after the Iron Age (Cohen 1985, 115–16; see also Lipschits 2005, 225–26).

It is debated whether some of the sites in this region were destroyed by the Babylonian army or by the Edomites, who took advantage of Judah's weakness. For our purposes, the answer to this question is irrelevant. The discussed sites were all destroyed or abandoned at the end of the Iron Age. After describing the prosperity of the Negev in the seventh century B.C.E., Herzog (1997a) summarized:

> this settlement prosperity came to an abrupt end by the early sixth century, as a result of the Babylonian conquest … All the Beersheba valley sites were destroyed and deserted for some 150 years, until a partial resettlement of a few forts in the Persian period (242; see also Lipschits 2005, 225).

THE SHEPHELAH

Lachish

Probably second in importance in Judah during the late Iron Age, the city was destroyed in the Assyrian campaign of 701 B.C.E. (Ussishkin 2004, 88–90). Lachish was later rebuilt on a more modest scale (91). The new city was destroyed again in 586 B.C.E. (91). A massive destruction layer was observed throughout the site (91–92).

Beth-Shemesh

The last Iron Age city was destroyed in 701 B.C.E. (Bunimovitz and Leder-man 2003). However, there was some short-lived resettlement in the seventh century. This phase came to an abrupt and violent end. Excavators attributed the destruction to the Philistines (Bunimovitz and Lederman 2003), but Fantalkin (2004) suggested that it was destroyed by the Babylonians. While I find the interpretation from the excavators more convincing, we should remember that this occupation, as ephemeral as it was, was destroyed during the end of the Iron Age. The site was not resettled in the following periods.

Azeka

The excavations carried out in the early-twentieth century are difficult to interpret with certainty. In light of the scant remains from the Persian period, and on the basis of the historical evidence (Jer 34:7; and perhaps also ostracon 4 from Lachish), it is likely that the site was destroyed in the early-sixth century, and was not settled during most of the century (Albright 1960b, 30–31; Stern 1993a; Lipschits 2005, 219–20). However, this conclusion should be treated cautiously.

Tel Goded

Dagan (2000, 91–93), and following him Lipschits (2005, 220), suggested that the late Iron Age settlement existed until the early-sixth century, and this was followed by an occupational gap until the Hellenistic period. This view is not universally accepted, and it is possible (and even likely) that the city ceased to exist in 701 B.C.E. (Gibson 1994). The data from this site should therefore be treated with caution (see also Broshi 1993; Manor 1997), but in any case it does not show continuity from the Iron Age onward.

Tel Maresha

The site was apparently destroyed in the late Iron Age (Avi Yonah 1993), and this was followed by a certain settlement gap until the site was resettled in the Persian period (Avigad 1993, 951; Lipschits 2005, 220). Although Vaughn (1999, 27) and Dagan (1992, 47) doubted the existence of a seventh century city, the existence of such settlement is now supported by the findings of various remains, including walls, pottery, and an ostracon (Kloner and Eshel 1999, esp. 150; additional references).

Tell Beit Mirsim

It was previously accepted that the Iron Age settlement at the site was destroyed by the Babylonians (e.g., Albright 1943; Stern 1975). This view is not accepted today, with most scholars believing that the site did not exist at the time (e.g., Blakely and Hardin 2002, 22–24; Finkelstein and Naaman 2004, 63–64). While some disagreement can be related to the old debate over the dating of Lachish III (and consequently other sites, see, e.g., Aharoni and Aharoni 1976, 73–74; Ussishkin 1977),[16] this is only a partial explanation, and many scholars who accept the dating of Lachish III to 701 B.C.E. still identify a seventh century occupation (Stratum A3), though on a smaller scale, at Tell Beit Mirsim (e.g., Barkay 1992, 356, 373; see also the tables in Aharoni and Aharoni 1976; Shiloh 1989, 103; Stern 2001, 149–50). It is clear that Tell Beit Mirsim, like Beth-Shem-esh, was not of real significance during the seventh century B.C.E., let alone at the early-sixth century, and is therefore of little importance for the present discussion.

Tel Batash (Timnah)

The site was "violently destroyed" by a "severe fire" during the Babylonian campaign of 604 B.C.E. Mazar and Panitz-Cohen (2001, 282) wrote: "In each of the excavation areas of Stratum II at Timnah, clear evidence of Babylonian destruction was found. In areas D, E, and F, massive conflagration resulted in destruction debris over one meter deep." The site was not resettled in the sixth century (nor really in the Persian period), and only an agricultural installation was dated to this period (Mazar and Panitz Cohen 2001, 282). It is not certain whether the site was part of Judah at the time, and it might have been a Philistine city (Mazar and Panitz Cohen 2001, 282).

---

16. Until the renewed excavations at Lachish, there was debate over the dating of Lachish level III. While it was agreed that Lachish II was destroyed by the Babylonians in 586 B.C.E., some scholars attributed the destruction of Lachish III to Sennacherib's campaign in 701, while others suggested that the city was destroyed in an earlier Babylonian campaign in 597 B.C.E. (for reasons that are beyond the scope of this note). As a consequence, many scholars dated the assemblage of Lachish III to 600 B.C.E., while others dated it to the late-eighth century. It is now clear that level III was destroyed in 701, but the implications of the old, mistaken date still cause confusion. The uncertainties around the dating of Kh. el Qom can serve as a good example. The site was excavated about forty years ago, when the debate was not yet solved, and the excavators appear to have followed the "low" chronology of Lachish III. The preliminary publications suggested that the Iron Age city reached its zenith in the seventh century (Holladay 1971, 176; see also Dever 1969–1970, 188) and this was repeated in various encyclopedic entries (Dever 1993; 1997b, 392; see also Dagan 2000, 101). Since no reports were published, and no pottery plates were presented, the data were simply followed by others (e.g., Stern 2001, 165, 324). However, an unpublished Ph.D. dissertation from the University of Toronto (Defonzo 2005) examined the Iron Age pottery uncovered in the excavations, and concluded that the site was destroyed by the Assyrians, and probably did not exist (or was of little significance) in the seventh century. The old debate over the dating of Lachish III is also significant for the study of the Land of Benjamin (ch. 9).

The evidence from Philistia shows that the Babylonian policy was similar throughout the south.

Ekron (Tel Miqne)
The large Philistine city was destroyed in the late Iron Age, probably during the Babylonian campaign of 604 B.C.E. (Gitin 1995, 74–75; 1998, 276; Gitin and Dothan 1993; for the dating, see also ch. 3). The site was not settled during the sixth century.

Ashkelon
The huge Philistine port was devastated at the end of the Iron Age, probably by the Babylonian army during the campaign of 604 B.C.E. Evidence of destruction was massive and abundant. The site was resettled in the Persian period following a gap (Stager 1996).

Ashdod
It is likely that Tel Ashdod should be added to this list. The excavators write that "(A) sole chronological anchor in areas H and K is the destruction of stratum VI, dated to the Babylonian conquest of Nebuchadnezzer" (Ben-Shlomo 2005, 8). Since, however, Finkelstein and Singer-Avitz (2001; 2004) claim that the site was not settled (or hardly settled) in the seventh century B.C.E., and in order to err on the side of caution, we can leave this site outside the discussion (but see Ben Shlomo 2003; 2005). Notably, Ashdod Yam had existed during the seventh century (Kaplan 1993; Finkelstein and Singer-Avitz 2001), and can probably be added to the sites which ceased to exist at the end of this century—whether this is Ashdod of the time, as Finkelstein and Singer-Avitz suggested or not. Clearly, Ashdod of the seventh century (either Tel Ashdod or Ashdod Yam) ceased to exist by the end of this century according to all views.

SUMMARY AND DISCUSSION

The data presented in this chapter clearly show that almost every seventh century city and central fort excavated was destroyed or abandoned during the time of the Babylonian campaigns—both in Judah and in Philistia. Many were razed, and others were abandoned and ceased to exist. In almost all the sites, this destruction (or abandonment) was accompanied by a settlement gap during at least part of the Persian period. This clearly shows a major collapse and settlement decline in the urban sector, even if one challenges the exact circumstances of the destruction at different sites.

Such a clear-cut picture naturally gave rise to the common view that the region was devastated in the sixth century. This is not to deny, of course, that people remained and continued to live amid the ruins (ch. 10). Supporters of the continuity school agree that the urban sector was destroyed by the Babylonians (e.g., Barstad 1996, 47; 2003, 6; Lipschits 2003b, 222–23; 2005, 190, 222–23, 368; only a few seem to challenge this consensus, e.g., Blenkinsopp 2002b, 184–87);[17] therefore, the survey of this chapter is accepted by both schools of thought. The debate revolves around whether the rural settlement continued to exist uninterruptedly in the sixth century. It is the latter sector which stands at the heart of the ensuing debate, and its fate is therefore the subject of the next chapter.

---

17. Although, generally speaking, accepting this truism, some supporters of the continuity theory "hinted" that the reality was more complex. Blenkinsopp stressed that not all the sites that were supposed to have been destroyed in the early-sixth century (listed, for example, by Stern or Albright) were indeed destroyed at the time (2002b, 184–87). He referred to places like Beth-Shemesh and Tell Beit Mirsim. While Blenkinsopp might be technically correct in some cases (as there is a debate regarding the situation at Tell Beit Mirsim, and it is likely that Beth-Shemesh did not exist at the time of the Babylonian destruction), this is less important than Blenkisopp makes it. None of the sites continued to exist in the sixth century, and hence the new data does not support the view that there was continuity after the Iron Age. If those sites were not destroyed in the early-sixth century, it was because they were destroyed earlier—not because they continued to exist in the sixth century. Furthermore, in his attempt to minimize the number of sites destroyed by the Babylonians, Blenkisopp eliminates any site, even if violently destroyed in the early-sixth century, with no direct evidence that the Babylonians destroyed it (see, e.g., his claim regarding Kh. el Qom on page 55; I am commenting, of course, on Blenkinsopp's methodology. As we have seen above, the site itself was destroyed earlier, and did not exist at the time of the Babylonian conquest). Lipschits also hinted that the "list" of destroyed sites was inaccurate, since we do not really know who the agent of destruction was (e.g., 2005, 250–51, see also ch. 5). This was a problematic claim. The destruction and abandonment of so many sites precisely at the time of the Babylonian campaigns was not likely to be mere chance. If Lipschits believed that it was not connected with the Babylonian campaigns which he agrees are historical, he carries the burden of proof. Moreover, while all the above might be important in regard to the Babylonian policy, it does not have an impact on the main debate, i.e., over the settlement and demography of the sixth century. Regardless of who destroyed the cities (or what was the cause of the destruction)—all scholars agree that they were destroyed (or at least not settled after the early-sixth century).

CHAPTER 2
JUDAH IN THE SIXTH CENTURY B.C.E.:
A RURAL PERSPECTIVE

A s we have seen, there is an agreement that the urban centers in Judah and Philistia were destroyed during the Babylonian campaign, and the debate over the reality in the sixth century concentrates on the situation in the rural sector. It is in this settlement sector that the various scholars claim settlement continued to exist and even flourished in the sixth century B.C.E. Thus, Lipschits, for example, after referring to the "termination of one of the characteristic features of Judean settlement: large, important cities were laid waste, and urban life effectively came to an end," added that "in contrast, the majority of rural settlement had been in the Judean highlands …; this continued almost unchanged" (2005, 368).

This claim drags the debate into unknown territory. Rural settlements in general, and those of the Iron Age in particular, received little scholarly attention from the archaeological community. Near Eastern archaeology is notorious for being "tell minded" (Ahlstrom 1982, 25), and suffers from a strong "urban bias" (London 1989). Scholars who believe that the rural sector flourished in the sixth century, therefore, could not point toward sixth-century excavated sites, and as a result relied mainly on the large body of data available from surveys.

As mentioned, however, no assemblages that can be dated to the sixth century have been recognized so far, let alone *fossiles directeurs* that can be used to date surveyed sites to the Neo-Babylonian period. We have seen that the dearth of finds attributed to this century was explained as either representing huge settlement decline or as resulting from our lack of archaeological knowledge. Regardless of the interpretation, the result is the same: we are currently unable to identify any material markers of this brief period, and it is impossible to date sites to this era. How can we judge these contrasting views and decide the fate of the Iron Age rural settlements? Were they destroyed and/or abandoned in the early-sixth century, or did they continue to exist uninterruptedly during much of this century?

As the debate over settlement reality in the Neo-Babylonian period cannot be resolved on the basis of the data from securely dated sixth-century sites, in this chapter I will attempt to identify the fate of the rural settlements from a different perspective. First, I will suggest a new method to solve the problem. Second, I will examine the data on settlements in Judah in light of this method. Finally, I will discuss the implications of this examination on our understanding of the settlement reality in Judah during the sixth century B.C.E.

METHOD

The debate centers around the reality in the rural sector. Since the rural sector has not received much scholarly attention, there have been minimal excavations in rural sites. Fortunately, there have been many salvage excavations in recent years, which have accrued a large body of data on the rural sector.[1] The key to solving the problem of identifying the sixth century lies in an examination of patterns of continuity and discontinuity in rural settlement, which we call the instability index (Faust and Safrai 2005; in press a; see more below).

THE INSTABILITY INDEX

The instability index relates to considerations that influence the location of new settlements. Sometimes a new settlement is established on the ruins of a settlement that has been abandoned for many years. The builders of the new settlement might have been interested in the same topographical location, or wanted to use the building stones and the cisterns. Such resettlement is certainly true regarding major settlements, which are located at advantageous sites. The sitting of urban centers in ancient times was a result of complex considerations, whose "freedom" was quite limited; the need to concentrate a large population in one site is somewhat deterministic, resulting in a pattern in which urban settlements were repeatedly located in the same place. This is one of the reasons for the formation of tells in various regions.

Understanding this characteristic of urban settlements, an examination of urban settlements' continuity upon which there is a wealth of information, will

---

1. E.g., Riklin 1993; 1995; 1997; Dar 1986; Seligman 1994; Covello-Paran 1998; Maitlis 1989; Baruch 2007; for a summary, see Faust 1995a; 2000b; 2003c; 2012.

Notably, Zeev Safrai and I are currently working toward the publication a project that will examine the published data from these salvage excavations, and the preliminary results enable us to improve and elaborate on past conclusions (see, e.g., Faust and Safrai 2005; in press a).

prove fruitless since it is likely that a Persian period center would be located on top of an Iron Age one, even if there was no continuity (i.e., no sixth-century occupation) between the two. Consider a site in which a Persian period settlement is uncovered on top of an Iron Age city. Can it be claimed that since these two periods are represented, it is reasonable to assume that the site existed continuously? The answer is of course "no," or "not necessarily." It is likely that a new settlement, erected in the Persian period, would have been located in the same location as its Iron Age predecessor, owing to the site's qualities, without any necessary continuity or connection between the two. The mere fact that the two settlements were located on top of each other cannot serve as evidence of continuity. It is possible that after a gap of one hundred years or more the same site was chosen for the location of a new settlement.

However, the situation in the rural sector was different. The sites were smaller and were inhabited by smaller populations. The factors which influenced the siting of a village, hamlet, or farmstead were local in nature (relating mainly to local land divisions and ownership), enabling many possible positions in any given region, or even within the micro-region (as can be seen in the Iron Age, when hardly any excavated Iron Age II villages or farms were built on the same sites as their Iron Age I predecessors; see Faust 1999b; 2003a; 2007b).[2] Therefore, if one identifies a rural site with both seventh-century B.C.E. and Persian period occupations, it is reasonable to assume continuity. A Persian period rural site would usually not be situated on the same spot as its Iron Age predecessor—unless it existed without interruption. The likelihood exists that a few rural sites were incidentally (or in order to use building stones, etc.) located on ancient ones, but the overall pattern should count. If all or most Persian period rural settlements were located on top of Iron Age rural settlements, one could speak of continuity.[3] If the pattern is to the contrary, and Iron Age rural sites are not

---

2. The size of rural settlements and their locations (in many cases) on slopes and valleys made them susceptible to security problems, and hence in periods of crisis, rural settlements tended to be abandoned. Some sites can be abandoned, of course, due to local reasons, but the pattern is important. This increases the importance of the rural sector as an indicator of changes (see also Faust and Safrai in press a; Faust and Erlich 2008; 2011).

3. In areas where Persian period settlement was dense, one should allow for more cases of "incidental" resettlement. Theoretically, we could have developed a method to calculate this, but this is not necessary, since even in such regions (e.g., the northern Judean highlands, below), continuity was, as we will see below, very limited. Notably, differences in the scale of settlement between the observed periods should be considered too. A full theoretical discussion is beyond the scope of this chapter.

succeeded by Persian period sites, then there seems to have been a gap, at least in the rural sector.[4]

To conclude, when the majority of rural sites from period X are located on rural sites from period Y, this apparently shows the continued existence of the sites from period Y in period X. However, when the pattern is different, and most of the period X rural sites are not located on top of the preceding Y period sites, we must conclude that something happened at or around the transitional period—"something" that accounted for the abandonment of the settlements. When a typical site is built at some distance from the previous settlement, this is evidence of a temporary abandonment of the settlement. Had that not been the case, the inhabitants would not have built a new settlement, and would have continued to use the previous site. The moving of sites and the building of new settlements testifies to settlement movement.

The "instability index" hints at settlement movement, even if there are not necessarily any obvious changes in the size of the population during the periods compared (i.e., even if the number of sites and/or the settled area are similar in the two periods; see more below). This method of analysis was used in studies of the traditional Arab village in modern times (Grossman 1994b), and a large number of digs in a given region enable us to use this index for ancient periods as well (Faust and Safrai 2005).

Since most scholars who support the continuity theory believe that it was manifested mainly in the rural sector (Barstad 1996, 54–55, 81; Lipschits 1997b; 2003a; 2003b; 2005; see also Weinberg 1969, 84, 88, 96), it seems as if the model suggested here is especially suited for this period and for the question under discussion. Reactions to the proposed method first suggested in 2003 (Faust 2003b) were positive and it was accepted even by supporters of the continuity theory, e.g., Lipschits (2004; for his reservations about the conclusion, see below). This strengthens the importance of the instability index.

BIASES IN THE METHOD

1. If the method errs, it errs on the side of continuity. We do not know how many sites are expected to be situated on top of earlier sites even with-

---

4. As we will see in ch. 5, almost all Persian period sites were rural. The question is whether those sites were situated on top of Iron Age rural sites. If the answer is yes, we can hypothesize continuity. The fact that Persian period sites, even if rural, are situated on top of Iron Age cities does not prove anything since we have seen that it is likely that people would be attracted to those central places because of the sites" qualities.

out continuity (incidentally). Hence, we might identify continuity even where it did not exist.

2.   Even if continuity is found, this does not rule out the possibility that there was still a decline. For example, consider a situation in which ninety percent of the inhabitants of a settlement died, fled, or were exiled. The remaining ten percent continued to live at the site, and a Persian period village developed from these individuals. Our scenario would count this as "continuity," although there was a major break and decline. Therefore, instances of continuity can be suspected; however, a break in the archaeological record produces sound conclusions (providing the data is sound).

In both cases, the method might err on the side of the continuity theory, which reinforces our conclusions.

Methodological Notes
1.   This stage of the analysis will use mainly data from excavated sites, as surveys are more ambiguous and inaccurate, especially for identifying transitional periods (in relation to another transitional period, see the discussion in Faust 1999b; 2003a; 2007b; Faust and Safrai 2005; for several examples see also Kh. el-Burj 1973, 26; Bienkowski 1998, 164; Dessel 1999, 12–14; Cresson 1999, 97; see also Wolff 1998, 449). Surveys are an important tool in reconstructing settlement history.[5] However, when there is enough data from excavations, the latter should serve as the backbone of any reconstruction, and surveys should be used for supplementary purposes (Faust 2003a).[6]
2.   The present study will therefore use mainly data from excavations, and surveys will be used only to supplement a picture that is initially supported by, or built from, data from excavations.
3.   Most of the data on rural sites is taken from salvage excavations (Faust and Safrai 2005). This is a result of a lack of planned excavations in rural sites, but it does insure that the data are random and does not result from a biased research agenda or collection methods. The sampling that results from modern construction activities, although not spread evenly

---

5. For the advantages and disadvantages of each set of data, see Faust and Safrai (2005; in press a).

6. When examined carefully, surveys are in accordance with our conclusions (below). A full discussion on surveys' reliability and their relation to salvage and planned excavations exceeds the scope of the present paper; see Faust and Safrai (2005; in press a), Faust (2007b).

across the landscape, provides a clear and non-biased picture which is not influenced by any a priori assumptions or specific research questions. The limitation and uneven distribution of modern activity should be considered, but it is at least "objective" in terms of sampling and data collection (Faust and Safrai 2005).[7]

4. Two or three regions have gone through exceptional rates of development over the last two decades, and have produced many salvage excavations. The first is the environs of Jerusalem, and the second is Samaria's foothills (where the new towns and cities of El'ad, Shoam, and Modiin were built, Rosh Ha-ayin expanded, etc.). The area near Gush-Etzion, southwest of Bethlehem, also went through intensive development. The main debate over settlement in the sixth century concerns the region of the (former) kingdom of Judah, and the area around Jerusalem falls within the area of interest, as does the area near Gush-Etzion. The data from these regions will be supplemented by information from other parts of Judah, where the data are less detailed but the accumulated picture is nevertheless significant, and even impressive. The data from Samaria's foothills, which was outside the territory of the Iron Age kingdom of Judah, will serve as a control group, as will be shown below.

RURAL SETTLEMENT IN JUDAH DURING THE IRON AGE–PERSIAN PERIOD TRANSITION

Some fifty late Iron Age rural sites were excavated in Judah, scattered from the region of Benjamin in the north to the Beersheba-Arad valley in the south, and from the shores of the Dead Sea in the east to the western slopes of the Hebron hill country in the west (figs. 3–4). These sites will be discussed region by region.

---

7. It should be noted that tells are less influenced from construction activities (owing to the high cost of excavations, constructors prefer to avoid them). This might cause bias since it is possible that the inclusion of such sites would alter the picture. However, tells comprise only a minor percentage of settlement sites in general, and of rural sites in particular (in most cases tells inhabited cities). Therefore, the inclusion of more tells would not have altered the discussion significantly, especially since tells were excavated in planned excavations and the data are well known.

Many Iron Age rural sites were revealed in and around the modern city of Jerusalem.

Khirbet er-Ras 1

A farmstead (16700/12820) near Manahat. The farmhouse is of the four-room type. It was probably established during the eighth century and was destroyed at the end of the Iron Age (Edelstein 2000; Maitlis 1989, 82; see also fig. 5).

Khirbet er-Ras 2

A farmstead was excavated some forty m from Kh. er-Ras 1. During the eighth century, a four-room house was erected, and during the seventh century, major changes took place. The building existed until the end of the Iron Age (Feig and Abd Rabu 1995, 65; Feig 1996).[8]

Malhah

A rural site (RP 1673/1286), adjacent to Kh. er-Ras 1 and 2. The excavator reported architectural remains—a storehouse—dating to the "Late Iron Age-Persian period," that "was uncovered on the south part of the spur" (Zehavi 1993, 66–67). The time period indicates possible continuity between the Iron Age and the Persian period.

---

8. Feig suggested that the two farms were part of a village. The data derived from the two excavations seems to negate Feig's suggestion, and given the distance between the two structures (40 m.; Feig and Abd Rabu 1995, 5; Feig 1996, 3, 4, fig. 1), I interpreted the structures to be two separate farmsteads, part of a dense concentration of farms surrounding the capital city of Jerusalem (cf., Faust 1997; 2003d). The site is being reexcavated now, however, and the first season was carried out in the summer of 2011 by Yuval Gadot. According to Gadot (2011: 46) the distance between the two above mentioned structures is only some 10 m., and he actually unearthed parts of additional walls in the area adjacent to the buildings and between them (see especially his figures 1 and 2, on pp. 45, 46). Although it is not clear what was actually the distance between Kh. er-Ras 1 and Kh. er-Ras 2, if Gadot is correct, this seems to support Feig's suggestion that the site was a village, and it is likely that the two structures should be combined with the finds at Malhah. Still, we need to wait for more data in order to assess the nature of the finds. Notably, the finds at Malhah (below) include Persian period pottery, and if indeed part of the same village this means that the settlement significantly shrank in size after the Iron Age (as no *in situ* Persian period pottery was unearthed at Kh. er Ras 1 and Kh. er Ras 2; Gadot reported a few Persian period finds, but those were out of context and simply indicate that the area was used for agricultural purposes at the time (for the significance of the finds in agricultural areas, see below, especially pp. 52–53).

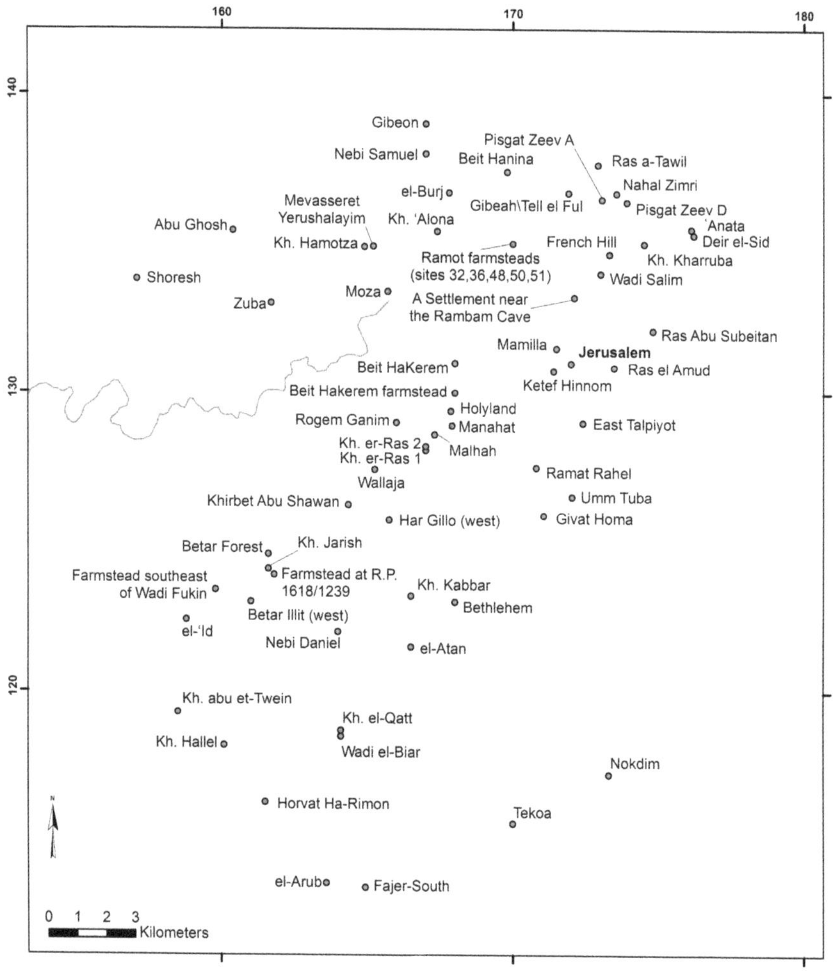

Fig. 4. Enlarged map showing the sites in Jerusalem's vicinity.

Nahal Zimri

A farmstead (RP 17354/13669) about 1 km east of Tell el-Ful. The farmstead is composed of a typical four-room house and adjacent features. It is dated to the late Iron Age (Maitlis 1989, 51; Yogev 1985, 29).

The French Hill

An Iron Age farmstead (17330/13465) that was excavated in the French Hill neighborhood of Jerusalem. This farmhouse was probably established in the eighth century and went out of use by the end of the Iron Age (early-sixth century B.C.E.). It was later reused in the late Second Temple period (Mazor 2006).

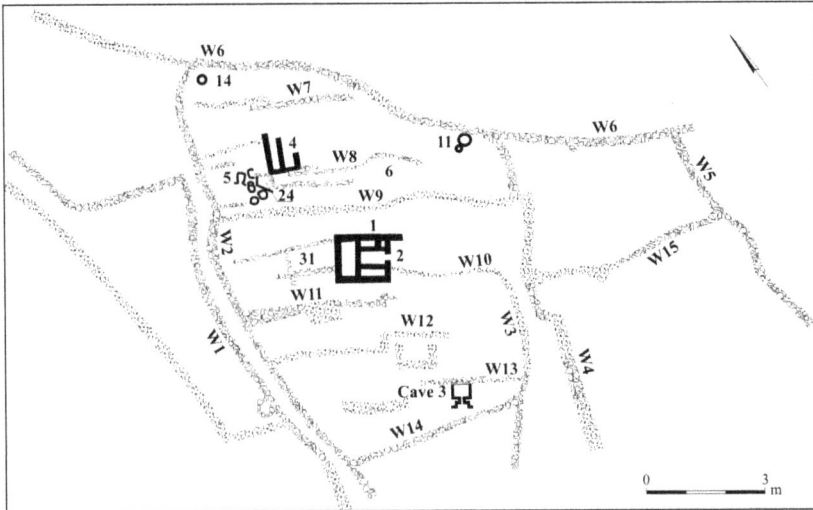

Fig. 5. Plan of the Iron Age farm at Khirbet er-Ras 1 (Edelstein, 2000, 40;
courtesy of the Israel Antiquities Authority).

Ketef Hinnom

Poorly preserved remains of an Iron Age site (RP 1714013075) were excavated near the famous tombs at this site (Barkay 1995, 12-13). The finds consist
mainly of pottery of domestic character, unlike that of the nearby tombs. Much of
the pottery predates the tombs, and it seems as if the site was founded during the
eighth century B.C.E., and existed until the Babylonian conquest. The excavator
suggested that the site was an agricultural farmstead or a village (Barkay 1995,
13). No Persian period remains were reported.[9]

Pisgat Zeev A

A farmstead (1728–1733/1362–1368) was excavated near the modern neighborhood of Pisgat Ze'ev A (Seligman 1994). It is possible that this farm was
originally of the four-room type (Faust 2003c), but this is not certain. The pottery is chronologically homogeneous and clearly dates to the end of the Iron Age
(Seligman 1994, 67, 73).

---

9. I am grateful to G. Barkay for supplying me with this information.

Pisgat Zeev D

A small, probably rural, Iron Age site (1739/1364) was uncovered (Nadelman 1993, 54–55). During the Persian period, a fortress was built on top of the Iron Age site. In the brief report, the excavators reported that pottery dating to the Babylonian period was also found, although its nature was not clear.[10]

Givat Homa

A farmstead near Ramat-Rahel (17105/12590). Two structures were excavated, including one three-room house. The house was used during the late Iron Age (Mai 1997, 93).

Khirbet Alona

A three-room house was excavated at the site (1677/1349). It was poorly preserved and no pottery was found on the floors. In publication, the house was described as an Iron Age structure (Weksler-Bdolah 1997, 98), but the excavator informed me that later analysis revealed that the structure should probably be dated to the Persian period. Iron Age pottery was found under the floor, but it is not clear whether this indicates an earlier occupation of the same structure (Shlomit Weksler-Bdolah, personal communication), or not (Alon De Groot, personal communication). Since there are other Iron Age remains nearby, it is clear that following the above mentioned method, continuity is possible at this site, though, perhaps not in the same building.

Umm Tuba

Iron Age structural remains and agricultural installations were unearthed (171/126). No Persian period finds were reported (Seligman 2009, 10).

Mevasseret Yerushalayim

Parts of an Iron Age village (16530/13346) were uncovered near Jerusalem (Edelstein and Kislev 1981). It appears that the site was not inhabited during the Persian period.

Khirbet Hamotza

The site is located west of Jerusalem. The main periods of occupation were during the classical periods, but the site was first settled during the Iron Age (R.P. 1648/1349). No Persian period remains were reported (Billig 1995).

---

10. The site does not meet the requirement for continuity, as the Persian period site is of "royal" character, and not a rural one, making any assumption regarding continuity between the two sites problematic.

Fig. 6. Plan of the Beit Hakerem farmstead (Davidovich et al., 2006, 64; courtesy of Uri Davidovich and the Ingeborg Rennert Center for Jerusalem Studies).

Ramot Farmsteads (sites 32, 36, 48, 50, 51)

Five isolated dwelling structures (CRP 220/635), located in the agricultural area, were discovered and excavated by a team from Hebrew University (Davidovitz et al., 2006). Sites 32 (Davidovitz et al., 2006, 68-69), 36 (70–72), 48 (72–75), 50 (75–76) and 51 (77–79), were all small structures which probably served as dwellings in the late Iron Age. The excavators (91–93) have raised several explanations for the function of the structures, including the possibility that they were all part of a larger unit, which was inhabited by an extended family. Whether the dwellings were all parts of the same unit or five separate farmsteads carries great importance for the study of Iron Age Israelite society (see also Faust 2012), but for our purposes it is important that the structures were not in use in the Persian period, and that even the agricultural area was probably not in use at the time (Davidovitz et al., 2006, 66–67; 86–88; see also 93–94).

A Settlement near the Rambam Cave

In a quarry, a large collection of late Iron Age pottery sherds was unearthed (RP 1721/1332). The large size of the sherds along with their quantity suggest that they came from a settlement. The excavator suggested that the stones were taken for rebuilding, and pottery was all that remained from this small agricultural settlement (Zissu 2006).

Beit Hakerem Farmstead

In this farmstead (RP 168/130), poor remains from the late Iron Age (seventh century), Persian period, and early Hellenistic period were discovered (Davidovitz et al., 2006, 80–82, 86–87, 93–94). The scant remains do not provide enough evidence (fig. 6), and in a previous publication (Kol Ya'akov and Har-Peled 2000), no Persian period pottery was even mentioned. Still, according to our method, this a possible site of "continuity."

East Talpiyot

Remains of a building (RP 1724/1290) with two construction phases were reported (Solimany and Barzel 2008a). The earliest occupation was from the end of the Iron Age II, and the second from the Early Roman Period.

Beit HaKerem

A rural settlement (RP 168/131) with remains from five periods was reported recently (Billig 2007). The earliest period of occupation was the Iron Age II, and the following settlement was from the Roman period.

Mamilla

Remains of a large building, which the excavator interpreted as a farmhouse (RP 1715/1315), was reported recently (Amit 2009, 102–4). The building was erected in the eighth century and functioned until the end of the Iron Age. Resettlement at the site did not take place before the second century B.C.E. (104). The excavator raised the possibility that the building was more than a farmhouse, and that it might have been connected to a nearby pool. Still, a rural nature for the site is the most plausible interpretation.

In addition, there are many other excavations in Jerusalem's vicinity where late Iron Age pottery was reported, but no Persian period remains were found (e.g., the Third Wall excavations, the Municipality Square Givat Shaul). These are not quantified (below) but should be noted because they supplement the picture from other sites.[11]

Discussion of Jerusalem's Environs

Only three out of twenty-two excavated farmsteads and villages (counting all structures at Ramaot) in Jerusalem's vicinity could indicate continuity. It is interesting to note that although the available database of sites in Jerusalem's environments has almost doubled since the original analysis (Faust 2003b), the statistics have not changed significantly. They even suggest a stronger discontinuity. This strengthens the importance of the available information. Such a small degree of continuity could either indicate an extremely low level of continuity or even be coincidental.

Notably, Malhah and Beit HaKerem farmsteads, two of the excavated sites which indicate possible continuity, are located only 1.5 km apart (Davidovitz et al., 2006, 93–94).[12] This might indicate a small "island" of stability amidst a "sea"

---

11. The above discussion addressed the relevant small sites in the vicinity of Jerusalem. There are additional small sites that were excavated, but were not discussed here since they are irrelevant for the present discussion. For example, at Shuafat Ridge a structure was recently reported, but it probably was not a dwelling (Rapuiano 2006; although the function of the building is open to different interpretations) and is therefore irrelevant for the present discussion. Moreover, the site did not exist in the Persian period, and appears to have ceased to exist in the middle of the seventh century. This also pertains to a number of similar structures that were used for agricultural purposes (see more below). Other sites, like Binyanei HaUma (e.g., Arubas and Goldfus 2007, 14) were relatively large and served as central sites, and should not be discussed here. The rudimentary nature of the finds—mainly pottery with some patches of walls—precludes discussing them in the previous chapter, as not much can be said about their nature.

12. Davidovitz et al. (2006, 94) also added the site at Rogem Ganim, which is only 1 to 1.5 km away. Rogem Ganim, however, was not a settlement (Greenberg and Cinamon 2000; 2006), and the pottery found there indicates only periods of agricultural activity. Such usage in both the

of destruction. If this is indeed the case, this is similar to what happened in other parts of the country, where such "islands" were observed (below). It is also possible that the area was simply more densely settled in the Persian period, and this is the reason for a certain degree of incidental resettlement on Iron Age settlements. However, since the surveys do not seem to suggest dense Persian period settlement in the region (Kloner 2003, 24–26), it is more likely that we are indeed discussing a small area of relative settlement stability.

The scarcity of even Persian period settlements (let alone Neo-Babylonian ones) was already observed by Greenhut (1994, 140). In a paper discussing settlement in Jerusalem's hinterland throughout the ages, only two paragraphs were devoted to the Persian period, and part of this discussion referred to the lack of data. Greenhut wrote, "actually, of all the expeditions working in Jerusalem's region in recent years, remains from this period were found only by one expedition—in Pisgat Zeev east" (my translation). The excavations at this site revealed remains of a poorly preserved rectangular fortress (Greenhut 1994, 140; Greenhut notes that one should also consider the Persian period finds at Tell el-Ful). Greenhut's summary is dated, but although the more updated list presented above includes three sites which might indicate continuity (Greenhut did not find any such site, as a fortress is not a rural site), Greenhut's summary gives a correct impression regarding the scarcity of Persian period remains in comparison to those of the Iron Age. I will deal with the reality in the Persian period in ch. 5, but it should be stressed that despite the limited settlement at the time, some of this period's sites were located on new sites.

Notably, some of the rural sites are located to the north of Jerusalem, bordering the region of Benjamin (and they will be addressed below).

Iron Age and the Persian period does not necessitate continuation in settlement throughout the Iron Age to Persian Period time-span, since settlers in the Persian period were likely to use the same agricultural lands, even if their settlement was not situated at the same spot as the Iron II settlement (see also below). Interestingly, in a publication of the finds from Rogem Ganim, the excavators (Greenberg and Cinamon 2006, 241, n. 5) claimed that there was "no severe disruption in rural settlement around Jerusalem after 586 B.C.E." In addition to Rogem Ganim, they point to the tombs at Ketef Hinnom, the handles at Ramat Rahel, and pottery from Manahat and the Holyland sites (the former is indeed a site, but the latter is a cave!). It appears that of all the places they discuss, including Rogem Ganim, only one is a rural settlement. Given the nature of Rogem Ganim as an agricultural area, it is impossible to use in a discussion of settlement patterns.

The Data from Surveys

In addition to the above mentioned excavated Iron Age rural sites, the region around Jerusalem was surveyed extensively. Although data from surveys are somewhat problematic, these sites can supplement the above mentioned data.

According to Kloner (2003, 24*) there were hundreds of late Iron Age sites (grouped together into 140 "sites") in the area around Jerusalem, including over three hundred farmsteads. The Neo-Babylonian period shows a drastic decline—almost to nothing[13]—and "to a certain extent, this situation continued into the Persian period," when only some fifteen sites were discovered in the entire area (Kloner 2003, 28*).

Nurit Feig (2000) also analyzed the data concerning Jerusalem's hinterland during the Iron Age (based mainly on Kloner's Jerusalem survey, before its final publication). As Feig's paper was not intended to supply all the information relevant for the present discussion, there is some difficulty in quantifying the data with absolute precision. When examining what Feig defined as "single structures," "agricultural areas," "towers," "stone mounds" (though some of these are the famous "rojums"), and "sherd concentrations," Persian period material seems to have been found only in two[14] out of nearly fifty possible Iron Age rural sites (Feig 2000).[15]

These data correspond with the excavations summarized above and indicate that in the rural sector there was a drastic decline and no real continuity between

---

13. Kloner (2003, 28*) spoke of "the absence of settlement in Jerusalem and its surroundings in this period."

14. The two sites are Wadi Salim (Feig 2000, 406) and Ras Abu Subeitan (406). It is possible that the Shuafat ridge should be added to this list. Feig does not mention any Persian period pottery at the site (2000, 407; the ridge was partially excavated; Onn and Rapuanu 1993), but the surveyors mentioned such pottery being found at the ridge. This pottery might not be connected with the activity at the Iron Age site, but these data are noteworthy, even though they do not seem to change the overall picture. It is possible that forts exhibit much stronger continuity, but this might result from sitting considerations, similar to those mentioned above in regard to urban sites. Notably, caves or agricultural remains with Iron Age and Persian period pottery were found at the Holyland hotel (a cave; Ben Arie 2000), east Talpiyot (Amit and Seligman 2010, 16) and south of Har Homa (Seligman 2008, 11). All those (and Reogem Ganim, above note 12) were not "sites," but rather agricultural areas and are irrelevant for the study of settlement continuity (for "agricultural areas," see below, pp. 52–53). In other agricultural areas, however, like Ras el Amud (Seligman 2007, 10) only Iron Age pottery was unearthed, indicating that even in such areas the great decline is evident (cf., pp. 52–53).

15. Excavated sites are not included in this figure, and neither are large sites or khirbets. Feig's paper (in addition to those mentioned above) also names the category of "rural settlements." The latter, however, comprises only sites that were excavated and already discussed above.

the Iron Age and the Persian period. It is likely that the sites were abandoned at some point, and when the rural settlement was renewed, much later, most of the new sites were naturally located elsewhere.

RURAL SITES IN OTHER PARTS OF JUDAH[16]

Although the data from Jerusalem's environs are the most detailed, they can be supplemented by information from other parts of Judah (including the Gush Etzion-Bethlehem region in northern Judah, in which Lipschits and others suggested that settlement continued uninterrupted; e.g., Lipschits 2003a, 351–55; 2003b, 283–90; 2005, 250–58). The data in the next section are taken from excavated sites, or in some cases from intensively surveyed sites (where the surveyors were even able to draw the plan of the site).[17] It should be noted that the rural nature of a few of the sites can be doubted, and it is possible that one or two will eventually prove not to be such. This would not change the overall picture as most of the sites discussed below are undoubtedly rural.

---

16. The present section will discuss all the late Iron Age rural sites excavated so far in the kingdom of Judah. Since we are discussing settlement and demographic changes in this region following the destruction of the kingdom, the entire kingdom should be examined. An examination of only part of this region, i.e., the territory of the later province of Yehud, is problematic since the fate of the rest of the region's population would be concealed and will remain unnoticed. When the entire area is examined the fate of the entire population of Judah is studied. However, if one wishes, for whatever purposes, to study what happened to a certain part only of Judah's population (e.g., Lipschits 2004), one can always refer to the relevant region and to the sites within it. As a matter of clarity it should be stressed that while the present study discusses some fifty rural sites within what used to be the kingdom of Judah (as well as more then twenty outside this region), only three of them lie in regions which were probably south of the borders of Yehud. (One should also remember that the date of the emergence of the political unit of Yehud with its much more limited boundaries is not clear, and considering its borders might be not only methodologically problematic, but also completely irrelevant for the present discussion, which focuses on the sixth century B.C.E.). In any event, the patterns are the same throughout the region.

17. The inclusion of these sites might raise objections, as they are not excavated, and might insert bias (one-period sites are more likely to be surveyed intensively, as they are more likely to be well preserved). It, therefore, should be noted that they are very few in number, and have no real impact on the overall picture. Moreover, they generally correspond with the situation revealed in excavated sites, and perhaps even slightly increase the impact of "continuity" (see, e.g., Horvat Ha-Rimon, below). Even if this is methodologically wrong, our data will err on the side of continuity. The inclusion of these sites is important, since they were part of the Iron Age rural settlement system, and we have good information on their nature and date.

While the following discussion is divided into regions, the settlement reality in all regions is similar. The division does not change the overall picture. The rural settlements throughout Judah went through similar processes during the Iron Age-Persian period transition.

Benjamin Area

Mezad Michmas

This is a seventh century B.C.E. site in the eastern part of the land of Benjamin (1789/14335). Though the exact nature of the site is unclear, it was most likely a farm. No Persian period pottery was found at the site (Riklin 1995).

Khirbet Shilhah

This Iron Age farmstead or estate in the Benjamin desert's fringe (RP 1818/1408) did not exist during the Persian period (Mazar, Amit, and Ilan 1996).

Khirbet Kharruba

Small-scale excavations were carried out at the site by Biran (1985), and revealed a large Persian period settlement, as well as some late Iron Age remains. The two settlements were very different, and this is not what one expects of "typical" continuity. The change reflects sharp shifts in settlement patterns. Still, since the site could have been a rural site in the Iron Age and seems to have existed also in the Persian period, in order to err on the side of caution this settlement is referred to here as a site with possible continuity.

Anata

A late Iron Age farm complex that was uncovered east of Anata (RP 2261063550). The main farm building identified in the excavations was a large three room house, and it was accompanied by agricultural installations and a cave. The site existed in the late Iron Age, i.e., seventh to early sixth centuries BCE (Reuben and Peleg 2009).

Discussion of the Benjamin Area

Of the four sites mentioned, at least three did not exist in the Persian period, and the fourth probably reflected a break, although continuity cannot be ruled out. The number of excavated rural sites in Benjamin is small because we have included only sites in the northern part of Benjamin. The border between Jerusalem's environment and Benjamin was not clear, and many of the sites which were discussed in the former can also be considered part of the latter. This is the case with Nahal Zimri, the French Hill, Pisgat Zeev A, Pisgat Zeev D, Kh. 'Alona,

Mevasseret Yerushalayim, the five Ramot farmsteads, and the settlement near the Rambam Cave. The reality in those sites is similar to the pattern observed above, and if we include them within Benjamin, only two (including Kh. Kharruba) out of sixteen sites north of Jerusalem show possible continuity from the Iron Age to the Persian period. Like the other regions in Judah, the rural sector of Benjamin was devastated in the sixth century B.C.E. The reality in this region will be further discussed in ch. 9.

Eastern Judah and the Judean Desert

Vered Yericho
The site is situated 6 km south of Jericho (191/136). The site could have been royal or rural in nature. The site existed only during the late Iron Age (Eitan 1983). Due to its unclear nature (Eitan 1986, 30–32), it should be treated cautiously.

The Boqeʿah Sites
Several isolated structures were uncovered in this part of the Judean Desert (Kh. Abu Tabaq, Kh. es-Samaria, and Kh. el-Maqari). The structures probably existed during the seventh century B.C.E. (but not in the Persian period) and were used in organized agriculture (Stager 1976; see also Faust and Weiss 2005).

The same is true for several nearby Iron Age sites located on the shores of the Dead Sea, such as Ein el Ghuweir, Ein et Turba, and perhaps also Rujm el-Bahr, Qumran, and Rujm esh-Shajra (e.g., Bar Adon 1989; De Vaux 1993; since it is possible that some of these sites were of semi-military nature, in order to err on the side of caution, none of them will be "counted" among the Iron Age rural sites).

Discussion of Eastern Judah and the Judean Desert
Notably, all sites in this region ceased to exist in the late Iron Age, similar to the picture that emerged in other parts of Judah.

Northern Judah

Khirbet Abu Shawan
This is a farmstead (16435/12625) near Beit Jala that was composed of two buildings, a cave, and a wine press, and is dated to the late Iron Age (Baruch 2001a; 2007).

Har Gillo (west)

Remains of what was probably a farmstead complex were unearthed near the modern settlement of Har Gillo (16575/12575). The structures (including a wine press) were dated to the late Iron Age (Iron Age III according to the excavators' terminology, i.e., seventh century). No Persian period remains were unearthed (the only remains that were later than the Iron Age were a few sherds dated to the Early Islamic period; Peleg and Feller 2004b).

Khirbet el-Qatt

A large farmstead (1641/1187) near Gush-Etzion. The site existed during the late Iron Age, that is, the seventh to sixth centuries B.C.E. It should be noted that several other structures, probably also farmsteads, were identified, but not excavated, nearby (Amit 1989–1990a). Notably, a few Persian period pottery sherds were collected on the surface, indicating possible continuity (Amit and Cohen-Amin, in press; the very limited amount of Persian period sherds hints against real continuity, see more below).

Farmstead Southeast of Wadi Fukin

A large farmhouse (1598/1234) was surveyed southeast of the village of Wadi Fukin near Gush-Etzion. The farm existed during the eighth to sixth centuries B.C.E. No Persian period pottery was reported (Amit 1991, 77; Amit and Cohen-Amin in press).

Farmstead at R.P. 1618/1239

A farmstead in the Gush Ezion area was surveyed and most of the finds were dated to the Iron Age. No Persian period pottery was reported. It should be noted that another Iron Age structure was reported nearby, but its rural nature was not obvious (Amit 1991; Amit and Cohen-Amin in press).

Khirbet Jarish

A village in the Hebron hills country near Gush-Etzion (1616/1241) was surveyed during the 1968 emergency survey (Kochavi 1972, 38; followed by Carter 1999, 168–69, 377; Lipschits 1997b, 267). The site was dated to the Persian period (and even Babylonian period, Kochavi 1972, 23). Later, the site was excavated, and the pottery from the excavation was assigned to the late Iron Age (Amit 1989–1990b; Ofer 1993b, 2, 88–89). In the final publication, a few Persian period pottery sherds are reported to have been found, but only on the surface (Amit and Cohen-Amin in press). In order to err on the side of caution, we will treat the data as if it might hint at a possible continuity, though the limited amount of sherds and the fact that they were unearthed only on the surface makes this very unlikely (see more below).

Khirbet abu et-Twein (village)

This site is a fort and a village in the Hebron hills country (1585/1193), near Gush-Etzion (Mazar 1982). The village, which is our concern here, was probably established during the late Iron Age, and did not continue to exist in the Persian period. There was some continuity in the use of the fort or parts of it, but since this continuity was observed only in the fort, and not in the village, this is irrelevant for the present discussion (see more in ch. 10).

Khirbet el-Id

A similar situation (no Persian pottery) probably existed in the nearby village (1588/1224) below the fort of el-Id (Baruch 1997).

Khirbet Hallel

Most of the finds at the site (RP 1601/1182) were dated to the late Second Temple and the Byzantine periods, but the site was probably first settled during the Iron Age (Amit 1991).

Horvat Ha-Rimon

This small site (1615/1163) was surveyed, and pottery from both the late Iron Age and the Persian period was discovered (Amit and Cohen-Amin, in press), indicating possible continuity.

Nokdim

A number of structures (17330/11725), probably all part of a farmstead, were excavated at the desert fringe of northern Judah (Peleg 2004). The houses were built in the Iron Age II, and functioned in the eighth to seventh centuries B.C.E. The site was reoccupied in the first century B.C.E. As summarized by the excavator in the abstract (Peleg 2004, IX) "the site was abandoned toward the end of the Iron Age, perhaps during the Babylonian conquest. It was populated again during the first century BCE." The excavator, however, suggested that perhaps three sherds should be dated to the Persian period (41). Clearly, three sherds cannot indicate continuity, let alone three sherds that were not identified as belonging to the Persian period with any certainty. Still, since the excavator raised the possibility that there was some activity during the Persian period, we will not count this site as indicating discontinuity either.

Agricultural Areas

Notably, excavations at agricultural areas are relevant for our discussion, since they are expected to show continuity in the usage of fields, even when no continuity in settlement existed. After all, since we are discussing agricultural fields, even if Iron Age and Persian period pottery had been found together, it would still be insufficient to prove continuity. This is because even if there was a gap, Persian period settlers, who established new settlements and did not dwell in the same places as their Iron Age predecessors, could still use (some of) the same fields. It is therefore interesting to note that excavations in agricultural areas, although expected to show continuity in the usage of the area for agriculture (and given the large number of Iron Age and Persian period sites in the region, the area was expected to be used extensively in both eras), reveal a more complex picture, and indicate almost a break. This can be seen, for example, at the excavations at Fajer-South (a wine-press). Here, a large wine press (16495/11345) was excavated near the village of Beit Fajer, and sherds from an "enormous amount of storage jars" were uncovered, dating to the eighth to seventh centuries B.C.E. (Ofer 1993b, 2, 87–88).

This should be supplemented by the excavation of a large number of Iron Age field towers in the nearby Betar Forest and at Betar Illit (west), where no Persian period pottery was found. Notably, "Betar Forest" relates to an agricultural area and not to a settlement site. In the survey which was conducted in the forest (1616/1246), sherds from the Iron Age II, and Persian and Hellenistic pottery were collected (Baruch 2000). Following the survey, several field towers were excavated. The towers were probably built during the Iron Age, and Hellenistic period pottery was found in one tower. The excavator concluded that the area was cultivated from the Iron Age II until the Hellenistic period. It should be stressed that, in contrast to the survey, no Persian period pottery was reported from the excavations. The same is true regarding the excavations of a number of field towers at Betar Illit (west), located nearby (161/123). Here, thirteen Iron Age towers were excavated and no Persian period pottery was unearthed (Peleg and Feller 2004a). This indicates not only discontinuity between the Iron Age and the Persian period, but also that Persian period settlement in this region was more limited than is commonly assumed on the basis of the surveys.

Discussion of Northern Judah

Clearly, rural settlement in northern Judah was practically devastated during the transition from the Iron Age to the Persian period. It is also important to stress two interrelated issues. First, due to the high development rate of this region, we have a wealth of information on rural settlement—approximately ten excavated sites—so the situation is quite clear. Second, this is precisely the region (northern Judah) in which supporters of the continuity school suggest continuity. The archaeological data refute this notion. Persian period pottery was observed in only three Iron Age sites,[18] and even at those sites the amount of pottery seems to have been very limited, and was found mainly on the surface (this could have resulted from various post-settlement activities.). Hence, the finds seem to indicate a decline or cessation (if the finds were a result of agricultural activity) in settlement even within those sites. Moreover, because this area was densely settled in the Persian period (ch. 5), it is probable that at least some Persian period sites (more than in other regions) would incidently be located on top of Iron Age ones, or that Persian period pottery would end up on the surface of Iron Age sites as a result of various (e.g., agricultural) activities.

The archaeological evidence shows that the level of possible continuity in the rural sector was small, even if all the sites in which Persian period pottery was found were considered as indicating continuity. The argument is strengthened by the scarcity of evidence for continuity in the agricultural areas, where it is expected to be found. In order to err on the side of continuity, we can summarize that three out of 10 sites show possible and at best limited continuity from the Iron Age to the Persian period.

SOUTHERN JUDAH/NEGEV

Khirbet Sansanna

A small Iron Age building was uncovered in salvage excavations (RP 14075/08565). The finds comprised a number of Iron Age III (late Iron Age) sherds (Peleg and Feller 2004c, 65*). No Persian period pottery was reported.

Khirbet Be Shim'a (Industrial Zones)

A cave that served as a dwelling during the Iron Age was unearthed in salvage excavations (RP 1505/0856). The finds were dated to the Iron Age III (late Iron Age), and to the Mamluk period. The excavators believe that "the cave was used as a dwelling and later, as a shelter for local shepherds" (Peleg and Feller 2004d, 64*). No Persian period pottery was reported.

Khirbet Anim

The Iron Age fort ceased to exist in the eighth century, and the seventh century remains discovered below the later synagogue were of a rural nature (David

---

18. Also at the fort/estate at Kh. Abu et-Twein, but this was a fort, and not a settlement in the Iron Age. See more in ch. 10.

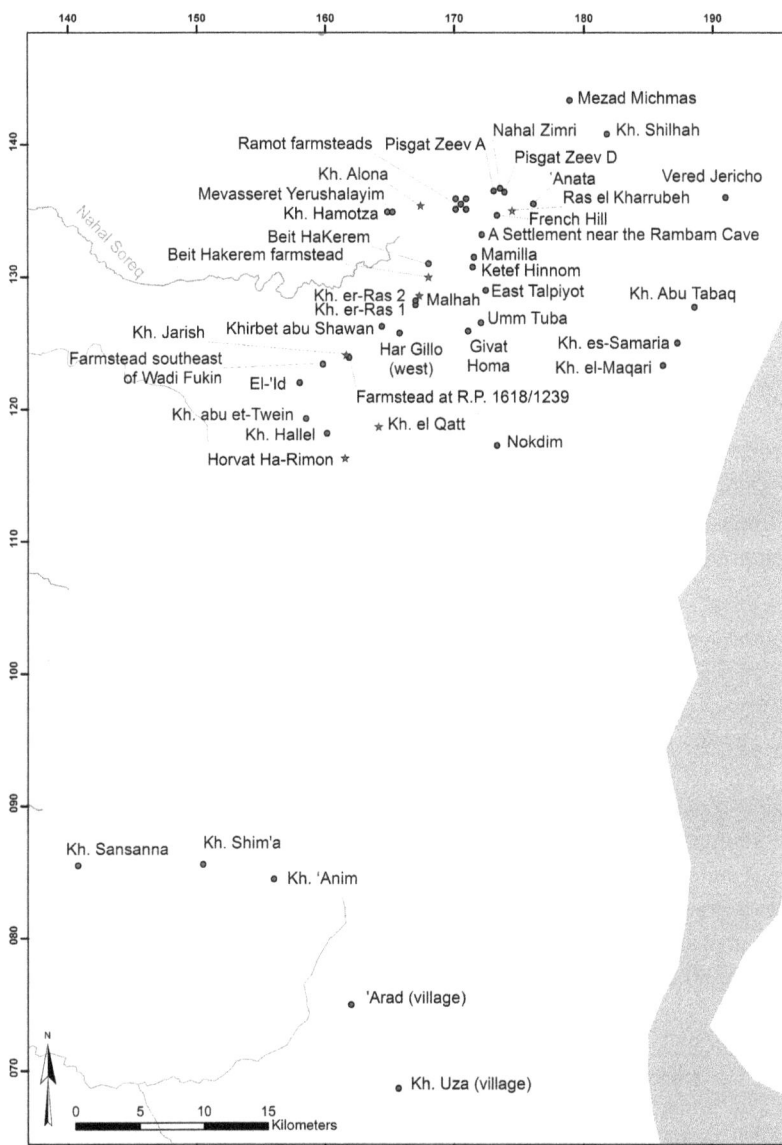

Fig. 7. Map of excavated Iron Age II rural sites in Judah, marking sites with possible settlement continuity from the Iron Age to the Persian period. (Possible continuity is marked by a star.) The map includes sites whose rural nature during the Iron Age is not certain; it represents maximum possible continuity.

Amit, personal communication; RP 1560/0847). No Persian period pottery was uncovered (see also Lipschits 2005, 226; note that the he connects it with the settlements of the Negev, but this is immaterial for the present discussion).[19]

Arad (village)
    An Iron Age fort and a village beneath (162/075). No continuity with the Persian period was observed in the limited excavations in the village (Goethert and Amiran 1996).

Khirbet Uza (village)
    The small village which existed below the fort (1657/0687) ceased to exist by the end of the Iron Age (Beit-Arieh and Cresson 1991; 2007: 49–52).

Discussion of the Southern Judah/Negev
    Data on excavated rural Iron Age settlement in southern Judah is scarce, but the limited data hint at the same conclusion as in other parts of Judah. There was a major break in rural settlement.

INTERMEDIATE SUMMARY

The overall picture is unambiguous: there is a low level of continuity between the Iron Age and the Persian period in the rural sector in the regions that were part of the kingdom of Judah (fig. 7). Out of forty-five late Iron Age rural sites discussed (this figure excludes the sites not discussed in order to err on the side of caution), only seven sites present us with possible continuity—usually with limited Persian period material. Since very few sites exhibit the possibility of continuity between the two periods, it is difficult to judge whether this is an indication of small-scale continuity at these sites or that some or even most of these sites were incidentally located on top of earlier ones. Furthermore, because some Persian period

---

19. Batz published, in a preliminary fashion, a number of late Iron Age farmsteads in the southern Hebron hill country (2006). Because Batz dated the farmsteads to the eighth century only, they are not discussed here (in his view they did not exist during the final years of the Iron Age). However, it is likely that the farmsteads existed in the seventh century, as can be seen by a few of the sherds that were published (59–60, 64; see also Faust 2008b). Since no Persian period pottery was found, it appears as if the farmsteads should be added to the list of discontinuity. These sites were not included here, since this possibility runs counter to the interpretation of the excavator, and in order on err at the side of caution. A similar problem exists with Beitar Ilit (west). Har-Even (2009) suggested that the site ceased to exist in the late-eighth century, but an examination of the data makes an eighth–seventh century date for the site more plausible. In order to err on the side of caution, I will not discuss the site here (more below, ch. 6).

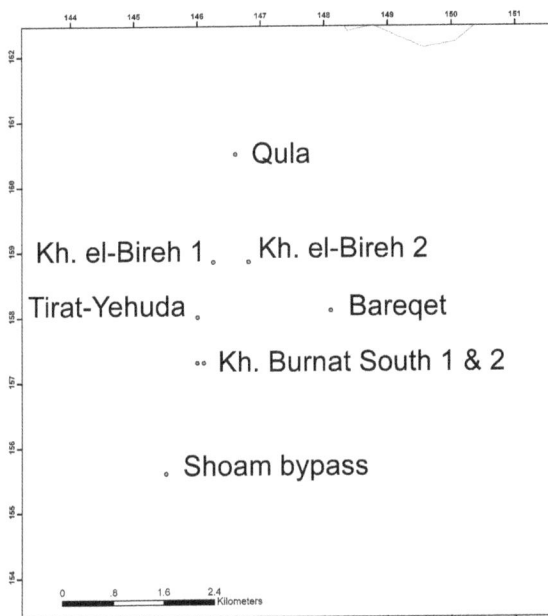

Fig. 8. Map of Samaria's foothills, with rural sites mentioned in the text.

sites were identified in new locations—such as Kh. Kabbar north, Kh. Kabbar south (Baruch 2001b; 2006), Wadi el-Biar and Daharia (Yuval Baruch, personal communication)—and showed no continuity from the Iron Age, these sites support the fact that there was a break in settlement between the two periods (for the settlement reality in the Persian period, see chs. 5 and 6). At best, there was extremely low continuity and at worst, (almost?) no continuity at all. This conclusion seems to be solid enough, and it should be noted that it is unlikely that when additional sites are discovered in the future, they would significantly alter the above picture.[20]

20. The reality in some additional surveys will be discussed briefly below, but one should note that they are, just like the Jerusalem survey, in general agreement with the conclusions presented here on the basis of the data from rural (mainly salvage) excavations.

Rural Settlements in Other Regions

But how do we know that the method suggested here works? After all, rural sites are "expected" to have a shorter lifespan than their urban counterparts. Since such sites are abandoned frequently, can a "break" be discerned at any given time? Broadening our survey might answer this question. Looking at the situation in Samaria's foothills can be used as an example.

The Samaria Foothills

A large number of farmsteads was identified in this region in surveys conducted by Israel Finkelstein (1978; 1981), Shimon Dar (1982), Moshe Kochavi and Izhak Beit-Arieh (1994), and Ram Gophna and Beit-Arieh (1997). The foothills of Samaria is one of the regions in which major construction takes place, and this development was followed by several intensive and detailed surveys that were carried out in micro-regions of this area.[21] All the surveys conducted in this region indicated definitive continuity from the eighth century B.C.E. to the Hellenistic period. More importantly, excavations of such farmsteads (as well as other rural sites) confirm this continuity (see fig. 8; for a detailed discussion of the phenomenon see Faust 2006a; ch. 5).

Tirat-Yehuda
A large farm complex, 87 × 45 m (146/158), was excavated (Yeivin and Edelstein 1970). The site was established during the Iron Age and existed during the Persian and Hellenistic periods.

Bareqet
An enclosure (22 × 23 m), probably the remains of a farmstead (1481/1581), was investigated. The scant finds include sherds from the Iron Age, Persian period, and Early Roman period, therefore indicating continuity between the Iron Age and the Persian period (Ayalon 1982).

Khirbet el-Bireh 1 and 2
Two farmsteads, 1 km apart, were excavated. The first (1476/1589) was established during the late Iron Age and continued to exist during the Persian period (see Scheftelowitz and Oren 1996, 3–5; 1999, 42*). The second farmstead

---

21. Haiman 2000; Amit and Zilberbod 1998; following the construction activities, and in tandem with the excavations that will be discussed below.

(1565/1590) was also built during the Iron Age and continued to exist during the Persian period (Oren and Scheftelowitz 2000, 50*). In both sites, sherds from later periods were also found, but this is irrelevant for the present discussion.

Khirbet Burnat South 1 and 2

Two similar farms were excavated at Nahal Bareqet. Both were established during the Iron Age, existed during the Persian period, and ceased to exist during the Hellenistic period (Hagit Torge, personal communication).

The picture that emerges from the analysis of the six excavated farmsteads is strengthened by the excavations of other rural sites, hamlets, and villages that reveal a similar pattern.

Rosh-Haayin

Remains of a village were excavated near the modern town of Rosh-Haayin (1461–6/1660-3). The village existed throughout the Iron Age II, the Persian and Hellenistic periods, until the second century B.C.E. (Avner-Levy and Torge 1999; Hagit Turge, personal communication).

The Shoam Bypass

Remains of a rural site were excavated near Shoam (1455/1556). Stratum 8 was dated to the end of the Iron Age and the Persian period (Dahari and 'Ad 2000, 56*).

Qula

Though the main occupation at the site (1466/1605) is of later date (a crusader settlement), earlier remains were found in area E2. Most of the finds were dated to the Hellenistic period, but some pottery was dated to the Persian period and the end of the Iron Age (Avissar and Shabo 2000, 51*). It is likely that the earlier site was established during the late Iron Age, and it continued to exist during the Persian period, and well into the Hellenistic period (final conclusions should await more data).

Tel Hadid

The exact nature of the site (1526/1454) is unclear, but it was probably urban. This site also exhibits continuation from the Iron Age to the Persian period (Brand 1998).

Other Sites

An additional site, which was recently excavated and might be part of a similar phenomenon although it is located more to the south, is Horbat Avimor (RP

1974/6355). Late Iron Age and Persian period pottery was also uncovered here, and practically on the same floor (Golani 2005). Continuity was also observed in Kh. Titora, although the nature of the site is less clear (Gudovitz and Feld-stein 1998; note that continuity was not observed in every area, e.g., Birman and Goldin 1999, 54*–55*).

In all, about eleven excavated rural sites exhibit clear continuity from the Iron Age to the Persian period in these other regions.[22] It should be noted that a few excavations in this region do not show (full) continuity, e.g., at Ofarim (Riklin 1993, 53–54), but exceptions are expected. The majority of Iron Age rural sites in this region continued to exist into the Persian period, and in many cases also into the Hellenistic period (see extended discussion in Faust 2006a). This book will not discuss the possible reasons for the different settlement history of Samaria's foothills. Suffice it here to stress that the rural settlements were part of a different political unit, and were the hinterland of the nearby coastal plain, or of the international highway from Syria to Egypt that passed in the trough valley (e.g., Faust 1995b; 2006a).

Discussion of Samaria's Foothills

The data from Samaria's foothills can serve as a control group indicating that when there is continuity, archaeological examination of excavated rural settle-ments reveals that continuity.[23] Therefore, the archaeological evidence from this region strengthens the significance of the lack of continuity in Judah.

VALIDITY OF THE DATA

Interestingly, Lipschits (2004, 102; 2007, 46) rejected the validity of the foothills farmsteads as a control group. He said,

---

22. Some continuity can be observed in Nahshonim, where burials found near Kibbutz Nachshonim (RP 1457/1633) also indicate continuity from the Iron Age to the Persian period (Nahshonim 1961, 7–8). However, burials are less indicative than settlements. In addition, Iron Age and Persian period pottery were excavated in the agricultural area near Mazor (Zilberbod and Amit 1999, 63*). Finds in an agricultural area, however, cannot serve as proof of continuity, since new settlers will use the same fields, even if they came later and settled on a different site (above).

23. Other factors, such as the accessibility of building materials, should also be considered, as they might influence the pattern of reuse of older sites. However, it is not clear if such con-siderations are relevant for the present case. In any event, they cannot explain the clear cut dichotomy between Judah and Samaria's foothills.

this is a very limited and defined area, part of the Samaria province since the end of the 8th century B.C.E., and one of the most stable regions in de- mographic and political terms from the 7th to the 4th centuries B.C.E., with clear continuity between the end of the Iron Age and the Persian period. The Samaria data, thus, provide no control for assessing processes in Judah (2007, 46).

Those arguments, however, are extremely problematic. As mentioned above, the data from Samaria's foothills show that when there is continuity, it can be identified archaeology. Nothing in Lipschits's claims challenge that. The data can therefore be compared and contrasted with the data from Judah (notably, due to the high level of construction in the foothills, this is one of the only regions out- side of Judah that can be used for such purposes; see above).

More revealing, however, is the fact that Lipschits claimed, as we have just seen, that the situation there was exceptional and was "one of the most stable regions in demographic and political terms from the seventh to the fourth centu- ries BCE." This continuity is indeed rare.[24] But Lipschits's quote also means that even according to him there was not much continuity in other regions, including northern Judah. Lipschits cannot hold the stick from both ends.

Finally, it appears that Lipschits misunderstood the purpose of having a control group. If the control group produces different results from the examined group, according to him, it is invalid. The purpose of having a control group is to be able to compare and contrast the results of one set of data in relation to another set of data. If the results are different, one should ask what are the causes for the differences. And at minimum, the data from the foothills sites show that continuity in the settlement of rural sites can be observed archaeologically, and that frequent breaks in occupation (though common) are not an integral and inevitable part of the history of such sites. When there is a break or continuity, it needs an explanation.[25]

In conclusion, the data from Samaria's foothills, and the contrast between it and the data from Judah (including northern Judah), clearly indicate that the latter reflects a break and a real crisis in the transition from the Iron Age to the Persian period (including in the rural sector).

---

24. A certain degree of instability is expected in rural settlements. But the low degree of con- tinuity in Judah is just as rare, and perhaps even more so, as the level of continuity in Samaria's foothills (for more data on the expected levels of continuity, see Faust and Safrai, in press a).

25. That the foothills group is an exception, and the sites in Judah fit into the general pattern of this period, does not disqualify the comparison. The reasons will be discussed in chs. 6 and 7. Ironically, as we will see in ch. 8, the mere fact that Judah fits into a larger scheme and was not unique seems to disprove some of the basic arguments of the continuity school.

ADDITIONAL DATA

The data on rural settlements in other regions are much less detailed (for reasons given in ch. 7), and prevents a similar analysis. I would like to mention, however, two additional regions.

Northern Samaria and the Galilee

The survey of the land of Manasseh also indicated a high level of continuity between the discussed periods (Zertal 1992; 2001), although the different periodization on one hand, and the fact that the data are derived only from surveys on the other, make any comparison problematic.

Similar to other regions, most Iron Age rural sites excavated thus far in Samaria (mainly western, central, and southern Samaria) did not continue to exist into the Persian period, although the date of their destruction/abandonment seems to be earlier than in Judah (e.g., Kh. Eli, Kh. Jemein, and Beit Aryeh; see Hizmi 1997; Dar 1986; Yezersky 2011: 230; and Riklin 1997). In the Galilee, the situation was more problematic. At Kh. Malta (Covello-Paran 1997), for example, there was an Iron Age II village and Persian period material has been found. But, it is possible that there was a gap between the two settlements, and owing to a different historical reality (and therefore different archaeological division into sub-periods), one should examine the continuity from the Iron II, through the (so called) Iron III, to the Persian period (see also Gal 1992, 108–9). Northern Israel deserves further discussion, which is beyond the scope of the present monograph, and any discussion should await further information (see a brief and general discussion at the end of chapter 7).

Southern Coastal Plain

Quite a few rural sites were reported by Gophna in this region (1963; 1964; 1966; 1970). Although several of the sites were excavated on a very small scale, the data should be treated with caution. These sites represent (methodologically) a different case from the other sites mentioned above. On the one hand, the survey was intensive, and in many cases included an examination of trenches dug into the site during construction or agricultural activities (usually, surveys only collect material found above the ground). On the other hand, the excavations were in most cases on an extremely small scale ("trial excavations"). It is possible that in this particular case, the data from the surveys are not less reliable than the data from the excavations.

Gophna reported nineteen Iron Age sites dating to various parts of the Iron Age, and an additional site was excavated recently by Lehmann, et al. (2010). Out

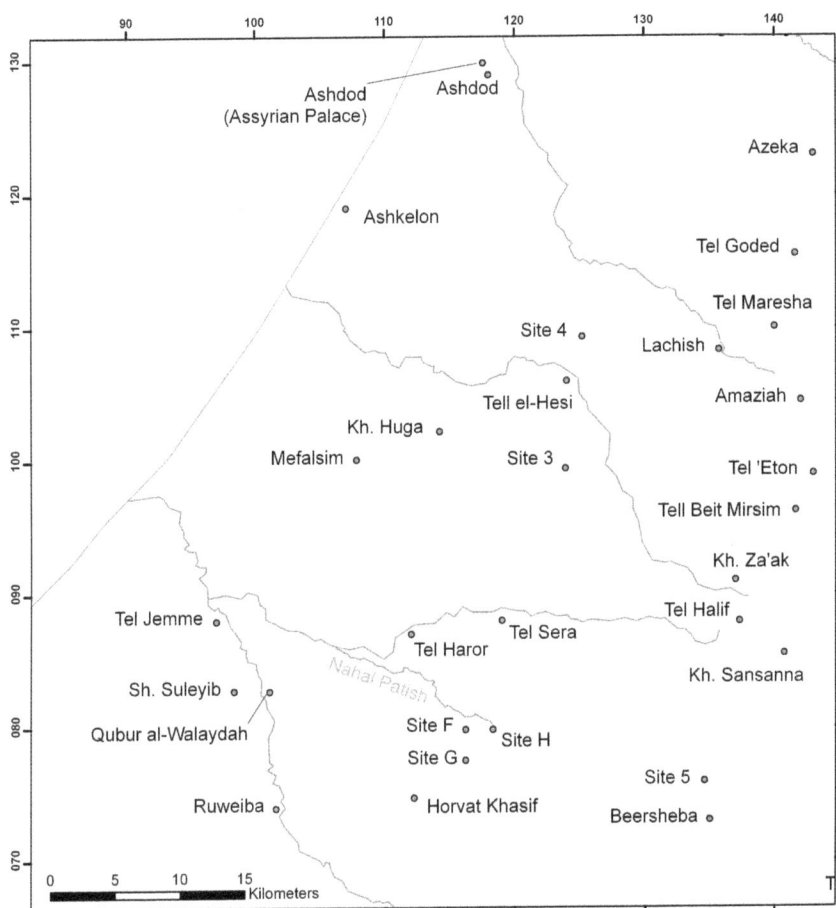

Fig. 9. Map of the southern coastal plain, with sites mentioned in the text.

of twelve sites that existed during the late Iron Age,[26] four sites had possible Late Iron Age to Persian period continuity (Gophna 1963, site 5; Gophna 1964, sites F–H). When referring to the entire data set (the twelve sites; see also fig. 9), an interesting picture arises. A first examination indicates a great decline in the rural

---

26. Those are sites 3, 4, 5 (Gophna 1963), F, G, H (Gophna 1964), Mefalsim (Gophna 1966), Kh. Ruweiba, Horvat Khasif, Kh. Suleyib, Kh. Huga (Gophna 1970), and Qubur al Walaydah (Lehmann, et al. 2010, 156–57).

sector, though not as extensive as in Judah.[27] However, it is possible that there is more that can be learned. An examination of the sites' locations indicates that all four sites that exhibited continuity were located in one zone: three of them near Nahal Patish, and the fourth was 15 kilometers to the east. The remaining sites were located to the south, west, and north of this group, but not between these sites. It is possible that while the rural settlements in most parts of the southern coastal plain were almost eliminated at the end of the Iron Age, other micro-regions, like the one mentioned above, flourished or at least survived. If this is correct, then a closer examination of rural sites can provide insight into the events that accompanied the Babylonian campaigns, and perhaps even into the Babylonian policy toward different regions. Final conclusions, however, should await more data (esp. more large-scale excavations).

In summary, the data from rural sites in other parts of ancient Israel seem to indicate that the suggested model works. Moreover, these data show that a close examination of the rural sector might identify the different histories of the various regions, and perhaps can even help us in understanding the Babylonian "policy" on a micro-level.

Notably, not all regions were discussed. A broader examination might reveal more about the Babylonian policy and activities, but will not add much to the main issue discussed in this chapter—the situation in Judah.

RURAL SETTLEMENTS IN JUDAH: A DISCUSSION

WHY WAS THE COUNTRYSIDE DEVASTATED?

Why were the villages and farmsteads destroyed or abandoned? Wasn't this in contrast to Babylonian interests (see Barstad 1996; 2003; Blenkinsopp 2002b; Lipschits 2005)? The Babylonians' interest in the region will receive a more detailed discussion in chapter 8, but it is important to stress that devastation of the countryside happened frequently during wars, especially siege warfare. The destruction of the countryside can be attributed to several reasons.

1. Initially, it is expected that rural inhabitants would leave their unde-
    fended houses and would find refuge in a nearby city upon the approach
    of an attacking army (see Faust and Erlich 2008; 2011). If they did not

---

27. Again, it is possible that some the sites were incidentally located on top of earlier ones, but it is not likely that all of them were.

return to their houses, gradual deterioration, and finally collapse, would be expected even without deliberate destruction by the attacking army.

2. In most cases, the attacking army would actively destroy the country-side for a number of reasons. First and foremost, the army needed food, which it would take by ravaging the countryside, fields, orchards, and houses.[28] Secondly, destroying the countryside demoralizes a popula-tion. Destroying the countryside causes long-term agricultural damage to the country, further frustrating the defenders (Eph'al 1997, 54; also Wright 2008). The attacking army would generally gradually destroy the city's environments. Eph'al stresses that this is done gradually so the besieged population can be kept under constant pressure, with the attackers using the available "cards" one by one (54–55). This can also be seen as part of the attackers' psychological warfare (e.g., Saggs 1984, 248, ch. 5).

3. Furthermore, besieging a city can be a long and frustrating process. In addition to destroying the land in order to subsist on it and as an intended policy to demoralize or punish the enemy, the frustration of the army can lead to further destruction (Kern 1999, 71). Notably, the coun-tryside is not devastated due to this reason immediately upon the arrival the attacking army. Frustration, too, is built up over time, and it is likely that the destruction of the countryside was indeed a gradual process.

All the above led to the devastation of the countryside. As Erdkamp (1998, 13) wrote: "The result of plundering or 'foraging' in this manner was that it depleted the resources of the countryside." He added, "the loss of seed corn and the loss of animal labor power could cause more damage than simply the loss of the plun-dered or foraged goods, since it depleted the means of future production. As a result of rural flight and population loss, part of the land would lie bare." He added that if the army intended to come back to the region, the depletion would be a disadvantage. This is irrelevant for the present discussion, as the Babylonian army was not expected to come back to Judah (and the number of soldiers who were stationed there was quite minimal in comparison to the number of soldiers who participated in the campaign). Moreover, for some commanders "the deple-tion of local resources was not an unfortunate side effect, but was part of their strategy." Van Creveld (2004, 37) also mentioned examples of regions that were devastated to such a degree that armies who returned there could not have relied

---

28. Van Creveld 2004, 17, 36–39; Wiseman 1989, 51; see also Keegan 1993, 302; Bellamy 1990, 11; Erdkamp 1998, 11–26, 122–40; Roth 1999; Wright 2008.

on the local resources simply because there were none (the issue will be further discussed in ch. 8).[29]

Our examination of the rural sites in Judah shows hardly any continuity between the Iron Age and the Persian period, indicating a clear break in the sixth century B.C.E. It should be noted that rural settlements are more responsive to changes in security conditions, and at times a new regime might choose to transfer the rural population into cities (e.g., Demand 1990; Marcus and Flannery 1996; Bunimovitz 1998; Faust 1999b, 2003a, and there additional bibliography). In addition, as mentioned above, we do not know much about sixth century B.C.E. material culture. Theoretically, one might suggest that the break occurred later than the early-sixth century B.C.E., perhaps as a result of the Persian Empire's policy. However, if these farmsteads/villages were abandoned during the "real" Persian period (fifth to forth centuries B.C.E.), one would expect to find "real" Persian material. In the absence of such material one must conclude, archaeologically, that they were abandoned at some time during the sixth century, but not later (probably before 530/520 B.C.E., as this is the time, even according to Barkay, in which the Iron Age tradition finally gave way to Persian period pottery). It is true that, archaeologically, we cannot distinguish the year 600 B.C.E. from the year 550 B.C.E. However, anyone who wishes to claim that these sites were not abandoned during the 586 B.C.E. war and as a consequence of the events which followed (below), but rather, for example, in 540 B.C.E., carries the burden of proof. Since all scholars involved in the debate agree that there were Babylonian campaigns and that they caused considerable damage, those campaigns are the logical candidates for being responsible for the observed pattern. Therefore, it would be difficult to attribute the destruction to another, unknown event.

A Later Date for the Abandonment?

This challenge was met recently by Middlemas (2005, 47). She followed Hoglund (1992), who believed that the Persian Empire initiated major changes in the province of Judah as a consequence of the Egyptian revolt. These changes included the establishment of many forts in Judea and a resettlement of the local population as part of "an intentional imperial policy of ruralization." These were

---

29. The lack of administration and the "disappearance" of the elite made the effects even more disastrous, as we will see in ch. 8, and prevented real recovery (see also Jamieson Drake 1991, 145–47; Tainter 2000, 12).

the reasons for the abandonment of the villages. According to Middlemas, it was not the Babylonian destructions which caused the break in the rural sector, but rather the Persian Empire policy of ruralization. Hence, Middlemas concludes that the date of the abandonment of the Iron Age rural sector should be set in the late-sixth century, rather than in the beginning of the sixth century.

Middlemas's attempt tried to "save" the Neo-Babylonian rural settlement that was otherwise proven to be non-existent. However, Middlemas's argument suffers from a number of serious shortcomings.

1. According to Hoglund (1992), the process by which the Persian Empire consolidated its control over the region was a response to the revolt in Egypt. Therefore, Hoglund dated the sites to the mid-fifth century B.C.E. (Moreover, he connected the changes with the mission of Ezra and Nehemiah.) He believed the changes were not the late-sixth century, let alone before 520 B.C.E. (the last date to which the Iron Age assemblages were down-dated), but instead were some seventy years later. Should the villages have existed until then, we would have easily found plenty of Persian period pottery. This fact is sufficient to disqualify the alternative scenario.

2. Moreover, to which sites were all the settlers transferred? As we will see below, the number of Persian period settlements is much smaller than their Iron Age predecessors. If the population of those sites simply "moved," we should have found many more Persian period sites (although it is not clear how to identify the pottery of the new sites; did they change the pottery as a consequence of the transfer?). A demographic decline explains the discrepancy, but not a simple "one to one" population transfer.

3. The abandonment of the rural sector was almost complete. Did the Persian regime transfer all the population? This is almost impossible. Moreover, why was that necessary? Wasn't there any value to leaving some of the population in its place? And to which area were they transferred?

4. In addition, there were serious social and cultural changes between the Iron Age and the Persian period. We interpret these changes as social and cultural collapse (chs. 4 and 7). Was this also caused by Persian Empire policy? When compared to what we know about the destruction and the crisis during the early-sixth century, it is clear that the Babylonians were much better candidates to cause such disruption.

5. The reasons behind the presumed "ruralization" are not clear, but the population in the discussed settlements was already rural, so there was

no need to "ruralize" it. The biblical data, if of any value at all, teaches of attempts at "urbanization" at the time (Neh 11: 1, 13: 4–14; see also Eshel 2000, 341; Weinberg 2000, 315–16).

6. Finally, whether historically possible or not, Hoglund's (1992) entire discussion on which Middlemas is relying is (archaeologically) seriously flawed. Most of the sites Hoglund discussed, used to build his typology, and to reconstruct the Persian Empire policy in Judah were really forts that were located outside of Judah. Meanwhile, the examples from Judah are speculation and at times, not a single Persian period sherd was found at a site. Khirbet Abu et-Twein, which Hoglund treated as a Persian period fort, was excavated by Mazar (1982) and is really an Iron Age fort that was reused (probably in a different manner) in the Persian period. Furthermore, dating by architecture in the way Hoglund suggested is untenable, even if he would have treated the archaeological data appropriately (i.e., even if there were Persian period remains in all sites, and they would have corresponded with the architecture in the way he reconstructed it). Clearly, Hoglund's dating and interpretation cannot be accepted, let alone developed, uncritically. The issue will receive more attention in chapter 10.

Any of the above should suffice to show that the alternative scenario is not feasible. Using Hoglund's postulated scenario regarding the mid-fifth century in order to explain the abandonment of the villages in the sixth century is untenable.

Quite clearly, the rural data indicate that there were major changes and drastic demographic decline during the sixth century B.C.E. in Judah. The 586 B.C.E. campaign and the events which followed are the most likely candidates to be responsible for it.

THE IMPORTANCE OF THE RURAL SECTOR

One can raise the claim that the rural sector was not important, and that owing to the wars and insecure conditions that probably followed the Babylonian conquest it is likely that the rural sites would be especially affected. The claim could further be made that the abandonment of such settlements would be expected. This is, of course, correct, but it goes along with, as has already been established by many, the almost total destruction of urban sites (ch. 1).

Furthermore, such a claim would run against the explicit claims for continuity in the rural sector raised by the supporters of the continuity theory.[30]
Moreover, it is precisely this relative lack of continuity in the urban sector that
drove them to this argument. This is not to deny the possibility that some of the
few sites in Judah that do have Iron Age and Persian period material did continue to function during the sixth century. There were, no doubt, such sites, both
among those already excavated (and discussed above), and among the sites that
were not. But the number would have been so small, so it would support the
above conclusion regarding discontinuity in the rural sector. Moreover, even if all
these sites with late Iron Age and Persian period material existed during the sixth
century—not a very plausible suggestion as such a small figure might, at least
partially, be accidental—a major break remains.

ARE THE DATA REPRESENTATIVE?

But are the discussed data from the rural sector representative of the processes
that the rural sector in Judah went through? I believe that our discussion shows
that it was. Since, however, Lipschits (2004; 2007, 45–46) attempted to question
this (on the basis of my earlier paper), I would like briefly to address his rejoinder.
    While accepting the method I employed to identify continuity in the rural
sector, Lipschits claimed that there were some methodological problems in the
research. His main concern was that I did not differentiate between Judah's sub-
regions. According to Lipschits (2007, 46), "the main methodological problem
with Faust's study is the discussion of all the territory of the former kingdom of
Judah without any attention to the different fates of the different regions."
    This, however, is not the case. The fate of the rural sector in all parts of Judah
was the same, and almost all rural settlements were destroyed or abandoned. One
can follow the above division of the rural settlements of Judah—the Benjamin
area, the Jerusalem environs, the Judean Desert, the northern Judean highlands,
southern Judah and the Negev, and the Shephelah—or can suggest a different
subdivision, but the results would be the same (above). It does not matter how
one wishes to manipulate the data or to make subdivisions within the territory of
Judah. The rural settlements of Judah were devastated in the sixth century B.C.E.
    Moreover, Lipschits failed to notice that a large group of abandoned or
destroyed settlements was excavated precisely where he believed there was con-

---

30. Barstad 1996, 54–55, 81; see also Lipschits 1997b, 153–98; 1998b; 2005; Berquist 1995,
15, 17; McNutt 1999, 187–88; see also Weinberg 1969, 84, 88, 96.

tinuity (see Lipschits 2007, 46)—northern Judah—therefore undermining his arguments for continuity in this region altogether.

Lipschits also raised the point that salvage excavations were a problematic source of information. The problematic nature of each set of data should be acknowledged, but salvage excavations, if numerous enough, are the best source of information for our purposes. Salvage excavations represent mainly the rural sector, just like the surveys, but are far more reliable than the latter (see above; for an extended discussion see Faust and Safrai 2005; in press a).

Finally, even if Lipschits's methodological notes were correct—and this is not the case—the overall settlement picture of Judah would not be affected, and one would still have to conclude that the rural sector was devastated. It is particularly revealing that Lipschits does not mention even one excavated rural site out of those he believes existed in the sixth century B.C.E. Notably, the conclusions presented in 2003 are now supported by a larger dataset, which was discussed in this chapter (see also Faust and Safrai 2005; in press a).

A NOTE ON THE DATA FROM SURVEYS

As mentioned above, when examined carefully most surveys are in general agreement with the conclusions presented in this paper. Since the issue will be discussed in ch. 5, it will be addressed only briefly below.

The results of the Jerusalem survey, as summarized by Kloner and Feig, are in accordance with the excavations (see discussion above). The surveys also revealed a great decline in the region north of Jerusalem (Milevski 1996–7, 20; Finkelstein 1993b, 27; Feldstein et al. 1993, 138; Goldfus and Golani 1993, 279; Dinnur and Feig 1993, 346; Magen 1995, 78, 84; see also Magen 2004, 2; Gibson 1996, 17*; for another interpretation, see Lipschits 1999, and extended discussion in ch. 9).[31] Decline was also observed in the Shephelah (Dagan 1998, 8) and in the Judean highlands (Ofer 1998, 47–48; see also Ofer 1993b, 2, 131–32). In this region, Ofer identified large Persian period settlement in some regions, but the pattern of settlement changed during the transition from the Iron Age to the Persian period (Ibid., and especially Ofer 1993b, 2, 131–32) indicating that this should not be viewed as continuity. Continuity (according to the surveys) might have occurred in a sub-region south of Jerusalem (Ofer 1993b, 2, 131–32; but see Kloner 2003, 29*). However, we have seen that the relatively large number of excavations in this region indicates otherwise, and it is more likely that there was

---

31. Note that Hizmi (1993, 100) reflects the reality in the nearby Coastal Plain and Samaria's foothills.

decline in settlement in the beginning of the sixth century B.C.E., and renewal of settlement (not at the same sites) in the Persian period. A more detailed discussion of the situation in Judah, and the discrepancy between the data from surveys and from excavations in the Bethlehem-Gush-Etzion region, will be conducted in chapter 5.

SUMMARY AND CONCLUSIONS

The idea that Judah was not seriously harmed during the Babylonian conquest has been gaining support over the last decade, mainly among biblical scholars. Archaeologically speaking, we have seen that the excavated tells show the area suffered a major blow. Therefore, we should not look in this sector for the prospering population of Judah in the sixth century. Barstad, Lemche, Lipschits, and other scholars who claimed that most of Judah's population was unharmed by the destructions therefore turn to the little-known rural sector as the potential location of the prosperous population of sixth-century Judah.

A growing number of rural sites were excavated over the years, however, mainly in salvage excavations. Today we know of some fifty excavated rural sites from the late Iron Age in Judah, from the region of Benjamin in the north to the Beersheba-Arad valley in the south, and from the Judean Desert to the slopes of the Hebron hill country in the west. The vast majority of the rural sites of the late Iron Age simply ceased to exist, and did not continue into the Persian period; only some seven sites exhibit possible continuity into the Persian period, usually with limited Persian period material. This extremely limited continuity from the Iron Age indicates that during the sixth century B.C.E., very few rural settlements continued to exist in Judah. This stands in contrast to the view that most of the population of Iron Age Judah continued to live in such sites during the Babylonian period. There were survivors in some villages, but this settlement sector suffered a major blow, just like the urban sector.

Furthermore, the view that the rural sector can be completely separated from the urban one is erroneous. Once the centers and the administration collapsed, so did the countryside (Jamieson-Drake 1991, 75, 145–47; see also Liverani 2005, 196). As Tainter (2000, 12) wrote regarding Ur, "(W)hen the administration apparatus collapsed it took the countryside with it." The processes that brought about such a reality will be discussed in detail in other chapters, especially ch. 7. To reiterate, Judah was not "empty." But such was never a common view. Balanced views regarding the situation in Judah during the sixth century B.C.E. have been prevalent among scholars in the past (e.g., Aharoni 1979; Bright 1972), and many scholars have stressed that the land was not literally empty (see also Noth 1960, 296). For example, while stressing that "the catastrophe was nevertheless appalling and one which signaled the disruption of Jewish life in Palestine," Bright (1972, 343–44) wrote that "… the popular notion of a total deportation which left the land empty and void is erroneous and to be discarded." Such balanced views also match the archaeological evidence (the issue will receive extended discussion in ch. 8).

The settlement picture discussed matches the fundamental cultural changes that took place in tandem with the processes of abandonment and destruction described above. Those and other aspects will be discussed in ch. 4. However, the next chapter will examine one type of pottery, which, in light of the problems with dating the sixth century pottery (above), might prove fruitful for our discussion: Greek pottery.

Chapter 3
Greek Imports and the Neo-Babylonian Period

*T*he previous chapters have shown that with the present state of knowledge, we cannot identify pottery specific to the sixth century B.C.E. Our lack of knowledge was explained as resulting either from the fact that there was little settlement at the time or because the pottery did not have any unique characteristics and was similar to the late Iron Age and the Persian period. The two arguments are not mutually exclusive. It is possible that the settlement in this period was sparse and that the pottery was of transitional character. The former is responsible for the fact that even the transitional "assemblages" are hardly known.

As a result of the confusion, a group of scholars have suggested that there were many settlements in the sixth century that cannot be identified because the pottery was similar to that of the Iron Age, so the sites were labeled as Iron Age sites. This claim is disputed, but methodologically it is possible. This is the reason that in the previous chapter we developed other methods to understand the reality at the time without turning to pottery. The archaeological evidence shows that there was very limited settlement in accordance with the traditional view.

This chapter will discuss the possibility that pottery can be used to learn about the sixth century and to date this settlement decline with more precision. Trying to use local pottery to date sites to this period leads to a dead end. However, Greek pottery can be dated with precision, and imported Greek pottery can help date local pottery.

Painted Greek pottery had been studied thoroughly. Proto-Geometric, Geometric, Archaic, and Classical pottery are all well known (e.g., Cook 1997). Greek decorated pottery is easily identified and, therefore, used to date assemblages elsewhere. While not without chronological problems, the sequence of Greek pottery is sound (e.g., Cook 1997; Cook and Dupont 1998; Sparks 1996; see also Coldstream 2003, 247). Painted Greek pottery from the seventh century onward is dated with precision even within centuries, and in many cases even to specific subphases of several dozens of years. Such precision exceeds the dating of local pottery in ancient Israel, where pottery is estimated to a period of a century or more. Finding Greek imported pottery can greatly refine the dating of a locus or stratum.

Greek painted pottery has been found in a fairly large number of seventh-century Iron Age sites in the Land of Israel, and was more numerous in the Persian period. Examining the frequency of this pottery in the late Iron Age to Persian period will prove significant for understanding the reality in sixth-century Judah.

GREEK POTTERY IN THE LAND OF ISRAEL DURING THE LATE IRON AGE AND THE PERSIAN PERIOD

Greek imports were found quite often in the late Iron Age, especially along the coast, and were common in the Persian period. However, there are hardly any such vessels that are dated to the sixth century.

GREEK IMPORTS IN THE LATE IRON AGE

As the late Iron Age came to a close, the number of Greek imports grew significantly. Fantalkin referred to the "sudden and massive appearance of East Greek pottery on the coastal plain of Israel toward the end of the seventh century" (2006, 202). Greek pottery of the late Iron Age is indeed found in a number of sites in the region, especially along the coast.[1] Those sites include Ashkelon, Tel Miqne-Ekron, Tel Batash-Timnah, Mezad Hashavyahu, Dor, along with Kabri, Tell Keison, and others, as well as the more inland sites such as Tel Malhata and Dan.[2]

The exact nature of the connection between these sites and the Greek world has been a topic of debate.[3] How did Greek pottery arrive in the region? Were there Greek settlers, merchants, or soldiers at those sites? Or was the pottery only an indication of trade? Was it some combination of the two? Regardless of how

---

1. The list below is taken from Waldbaum 1994, and is slightly updated; see also Niemeier 2001.

2. Ashkelon: Stager 1996; 2006; Master 2001; 2003; Niemeier 2001, 16; Ekron: Gitin 1989, 40, 48; 1995, 70, 71; see also Waldbaum 2007; Tel Batash: Magness 1991; also Niemeier 2001, 16; Waldbaum 2007, 64; Mezad Hashavyahu: Naveh 1962; Fantalkin 2001b; Niemeier 2001; Dor: Cook 1995; Kabri: Niemeier 1990: XXXV, fig. 22: 2; 2001; 2002; Tell Keison: Briend and Humbert 1980: 125, fig. 35; Tel Malhata: Kochavi 1993a; 1998, 35; Dan: Niemeier 2001, 16.

3. E.g., Waldbaum 1994; 1997; 2007, Boardman 1999; see also Stern 2001, 217–27, and esp. 217–21; Sorensen 1997; Stager 1996; Fantalkin 2006.

this pottery arrived in the region, its appearance helps in dating. Since the dating of Greek pottery is much more refined than the dating of local pottery, the identification of seventh-century Greek imports is sufficient to date a level or site to this period with relative precision (for every scholar that accepts the basic chronological scheme of the seventh century).

While the causes for the appearance of Greek pottery are doubted, the bottom line is that Greek pottery is found in a relatively large number of seventh-century sites. Waldbaum concluded her paper on the "Early Greek Contacts with the Southern Levant" with:

> In any event, the growing number of sites at which it is found (Greek pottery; AF), and the generally wider distribution throughout the country, suggest that by the end of the seventh century B.C., Greek pottery was growing in popularity and the mechanisms for acquiring it were becoming more established. (1994, 61)

While not infrequent in coastal sites in the seventh century, the number of imports was much larger in the Persian period.

GREEK IMPORTS IN THE PERSIAN PERIOD

Greek imports reached a peak during the Persian period.[4] As Waldbaum observed, "Greek pottery of the Persian period, now primarily Attic but with some 'East Greek,' is found throughout the southern Levant, in greater abundance at coastal sites, but also in more limited quantities inland" (2003, 302).

Indeed, Greek pottery was found at almost every site in the region, even those with limited settlement.[5] A partial list of sites includes the coastal sites of Acco, Tell Abu Hawwam, Shikmona, Dor, Mikhmoret, Tel Tanninim, Tel Michal, Tel Yauz, and Ashkelon.[6] Imported Greek pottery is also found in more inland sites such as Tel Batash, Tel 'Eton, Tell el-Hesi, and highland sites such as Tell en-

---

4. Stern 1982, 138; Fantalkin 2006, 204; see also Stern 2001, 518–22.

5. E.g., Waldbaum 2003; Weinberg 1969, 78; Stern 2001, 518–22; Armon 2002; Ambar-Armon 2005.

6. Acco: Dothan 1985, 13; Tell Abu Hawwam: Balensi, Herrera and Artzi 1993, 9; Ambar-Armon 2005, 17; Shikmona: Elgavish 1968, 42, 59, plate LII; Ambar-Armon 2005, 17; Dor: Marchese 1995 [most revealing is the graph on page 172]; Mook and Coulson, 1995; Mikhmoret: Porath, Paley and Stieglitz 1993, 1045; Ambar-Armon 2005, 17; Tel Tanninim: Yankelevitch 2006, 112–15; Tel Michal: Herzog 1993, 1038; Ambar-Armon 2005, 17; Tel Yauz: Segal, Kletter and Ziffer 2004, 15*–18*; and Ashkelon: Stager 1993, 108–9; Ambar-Armon 2005, 17.

Nasbeh, Shechem, and even in small highland sites such as Kh. Kabbar.[7] Imports in the Persian period surpass the number of imports in previous periods, perhaps even in the Late Bronze Age, and certainly the Iron Age. The increase in imports is consistent with the numbers from other areas along the Mediterranean, where an increase in the amount of Greek pottery from the seventh century to the Persian period is noticeable.[8]

GREEK IMPORTS IN THE SIXTH CENTURY

Although the Greek pottery of the sixth century is no less distinctive and widespread than that of the other periods (e.g., Cook 1997, passim), during this intervening period there were hardly any Greek imports in the region, if any at all. Some have suggested that a few scattered sherds appeared in Dor,[9] but others dismiss even those.[10] It is irrelevant to list the sites at which no sixth century Greek pottery was found.[11] This "absence" is significant, and scholars such as Weinberg, Waldbaum, Boardman, and Fantalkin have taken note of this phenomenon. Already in 1969, Weinberg stated,

> To the classical archaeologists coming to work in Israel, and wishing to remain within his field of competence, the problem of relations between the Greek world and the eastern shores of the Mediterranean Sea is of paramount importance. Even the most cursory examination of the question, with respect to Palestine in particular, reveals a tremendous unevenness of knowledge. Going back only to the Mycenaean times, one finds a highly illuminated picture of interrelations, but the light begins to fade rather rapidly at the beginning of the first millennium B.C.E., becomes *almost totally extinguished at the time of the Babylonian conquests ending in 586 B.C.E., and remains so for the rest of the sixth century.* Only very slowly does that light begin to increase during the fifth century, but the increase becomes much more rapid in the fourth century and reaches another crescendo with the

---

7. Tel Batash: Johnson 2001; Tel 'Eton: Faust 2011a; Tell el-Hesi: Fargo 1993, 633–34; Tell en-Nasbeh: Zorn 1993a, 1102; Shechem: Campbell 2002, 306–7; Kh. Kabbar: Baruch 2006, 69*.

8. For Spain, see Dominguez and Sanchez 2001, 459–63.

9. Mook and Coulson 1995, 94, 99; see also Marchese 1995, 171.

10. E.g., Stern 2001, 316; for Dor, see now also Shalev 2009, esp. 364–65; Gilboa and Sharon 2008, 167. Note that a sherd unearthed in Tel Tanninim is also dated to the sixth century, on the basis of the date of similar sherds at Dor (Yankelevitch 2006, 115; cf. Mook and Coulson 1995, 94, type C).

11. Notably, there were other types of imports (e.g., Etruscan pottery) that were found in various locations around the Mediterranean during the sixth century (e.g., Naso 2006). Those are also absent from the land of Israel.

arrival of Alexander and the beginning of the Hellenistic period (1969, 78; my emphasis).

He later concluded,

> there is still very little Greek pottery found in Palestine that can be dated to the last quarter of the sixth century, and only a few pieces that date from the previous quarter. One can as yet see little difference between coastal sites and inland sites; if there is material from the last quarter of the sixth century at 'Atlit, there is also some at Shekhem. *There seems, then, to have been no considerable exchange between Palestine and Greece between the destruction of 586 and the last quarter of the sixth century* (1969, 89; my emphasis).

Finally, after defining the upper and lower limits of Greek importation, he wrote, "With the upper limits thus defined, we are left with a gap of almost a century for which we have so little imported pottery that it is of no help just when it is most needed" (1969, 90).

One can question Weinberg's historical reconstruction, but the lack of imports cannot be denied. While our data in 2010 are more detailed and updated, and we know of many more imports in the seventh century, there is still a noticeable gap in Greek pottery during the sixth century b.c.e.

In a similar vein, John Boardman wrote that "there are very few other finds of Greek pottery in the Near East from some sixty years after the beginning of the sixth century—the Babylonian 'interregnum' between the Assyrians and the Persians" (1999, 52). He added that "the gap in the Greek record at Al Mina seems matched in Palestine."

Ephraim Stern also wrote, "surprisingly, a similar gap exists for Greek imports of the sixth century BCE" (2001, 344). After quoting Weinberg, Stern stated, "this gap occurred ... as the result of the complete devastation of the Palestinian coastal harbor towns by the Babylonians in 604–603 BCE." Again, the causes for the phenomenon can be debated, but not the data on which they rest.

On the basis of the accumulating data, Jane Waldbaum wrote about the contacts between the Levant and the Aegean,

> The nature of the finds changes over time as well, with different areas of the Aegean playing more or less dominant roles as exporters in different periods. Archaic East Greek pottery, manufactured in the Greek cities of western Turkey and the Aegean islands, had been imported to the Near East in considerable quantities at the end of the seventh century b.c.e. *This is all but disappeared from the southern Levant with the Babylonian conquests of 604–587 b.c.e.* (Waldbaum 2002, Waldbaum and Magness 1997). *There is almost no sign of revived contact with the Aegean before the beginning of the*

Persian period in the late-sixth century. The usual Greek trade wares of this pe-
riod—early Attic Black Figure, Middle or Late Corinthian, and East Greek pot-
tery of the early to mid sixth century—are almost or completely lacking. Since
many of the sites where early Greek pottery had been found were abandoned
or seriously reduced in wealth and population after the Babylonian destructions, this is no surprise. Trade with the West revived in the Persian period
(from 539 to 326 B.C.E.) and flourished from that time on (2003; 301–2; my
emphasis).

Fantalkin (2006), too, discussed the significance of Greek pottery found in the
eastern Mediterranean from the Iron Age until the early Persian period. He
divided the Greek pottery unearthed in the region (and the connections between
the Levant and Greek that it represented), into five different periods and types of
interconnections. The Neo-Babylonian period was the "fourth period" in Fantalkin's terminology, and he wrote, "The Neo-Babylonian period is characterized
by a total lack of Greek material in the southern part of the Eastern Mediterranean. During the major part of the sixth century BC … this part of the Levant,
except for a few inland areas, is in ruins …" (2006, 204).

The fact that practically no Greek imports were found in the region during
the sixth century indicates that international trade came almost to a halt. Since
at least some of the imported pottery came to the area through trade (below),
the lack of Greek pottery suggests that the area was of no importance for the
maritime trade of the sixth century. Maritime trade was the largest form of long-
distance trade, and the absence of trade from most of the Levant is significant.
Notably, sixth century Greek pottery is found in other regions, sometimes in
large quantities.[12] From a Mediterranean perspective, trade peaked in the sixth
century B.C.E. (Sherratt and Sherratt 2003, 371). The (almost?) complete lack of
Greek pottery on the coasts of Israel begs explanation. Before elaborating on this,
however, first we will discuss a few possible reservations concerning the dating of
Greek pottery.

---

12. E.g., Weinberg 1969, 91–92, 94; Cook 1997, 77, 84, 95, 110; Dominguez and Sanchez
2001, 459–60; Foxhall 2005, 240–41, 245; see more below.

Validity of the Data and the Problem
of Circular Dating

Chronology of Greek Pottery

The chronology of Greek pottery is debated. Before advancing the discussion, I should stress that since all scholars involved in the present debate, including Stern, Stager, Vanderhooft, Barstad, and Lipschits, accept the traditional chronology of the seventh century in Israel, the discussion below does not have any direct implication on the debate over the reality in the sixth century. Recourse to an alternative Greek chronology would force those scholars to change their entire historical reconstruction and would make their current historical scenario irrelevant. Since the chronology itself is debated, however, the issue has to be addressed, even if briefly.

The relative chronology of Greek pottery is firmly based. Coldstream equated it with a "strong 'suit of cards,'" in a firmly based relative sequence: firmly based on many hundreds of closed groups of whole pots with painted decoration, found in single graves" (2003, 247). The available data "help us to build up a comprehensive network for the relative chronology" (248).

However, while the relative chronology of Greek pottery is well established, its absolute chronology is problematic. Without any historical synchronisms in the Greek world prior to the eighth century, when some parallels exist with Greek colonies in the west, the dating relies heavily on parallels with the Levant. Prior to and during the late Iron Age, the chronology and dating of the Greek sequence is based mainly on synchronism with the east.

The Land of Israel, with a large number of excavations, was one of the main sources for dating Greek pottery. Greek pottery found in various levels in the region was used to give exact dating to this pottery in Greece. The problem is that many of the strata in the southern Levant were dated on the basis of historical assumptions, which are not always accepted. Moreover, many of the sherds came from disturbed contexts (and in one case, several fragments of the same pot came from four different strata at the site; e.g., Fantalkin 2001a, 120, and references). In addition, archaeologists working in Greece were not always aware of changes in views regarding Iron Age chronology in Israel in general, let alone about subtle changes in the dating of one level or another in particular. Hence, they sometimes used outdated data from Israel to date Greek pottery. The issue came to the fore due to the extensive discussion of Iron Age chronology that resulted from Finkelstein's low chronology (for Greek pottery, see Fantalkin 2001a; Coldstream 2003; Mazar and Coldstream 2003).

Leaving the chronology of the Iron I and IIA aside, we should note that there is a large body of data from Israel which helps to date late-seventh century Greek pottery. I am not referring to the "problematic" site of Mezad Hashavyahu, whose dating was circular to some extent (Fantalkin 2001b), but to the more secure destruction levels of Ashkelon (Stager 1996) and Ekron (Miqne; Gitin 1989; 1995, 74–75), and perhaps also Tel Batash (biblical Timnah; Mazar and Panitz-Cohen 2001). Those sites, whose dating is not questioned by anyone working in the region (see, e.g., Barstad 2003, 12; Lipschits 2005, 41–42, n. 54, p. 64, n. 98; but see James 2006, and more below), serve as an excellent anchor for Greek pottery of the period (e.g., Waldbaum and Magness 1997).

"Circular Dating"?

Attempts to use Greek pottery to date Iron Age strata in Israel is to some extent futile, and even circular. This was noted by scholars (e.g., Fantalkin 2001b, 128, n. 57;[13] Waldbaum and Magness 1997, 25–26; see also Lemos 2002, 24–25). Using seventh-century Greek pottery to date a site in Israel is not based only on Greek dating, but also on the initial dating of this pottery in Israel (notably, however, in this period there are also synchronisms from the west). This does not make Greek pottery useless for dating. We should be aware of the limitations, and know that when we find seventh century Greek pottery, we can use it to date our level to the seventh century, only that this is not "external" evidence, but just another type of pottery, whose dating is based on the local scheme. In other words, Greek pottery cannot be used as "external" evidence to solve chronological debates, but when chronology is not disputed, it can be used for dating, just like other pottery. And if its resolution is for some reason (e.g., good internal phasing) better (as is the case with the painted Greek pottery), then we even gain something from using it.

And here lies the main importance of Greek pottery for the current discussion. Greek pottery from the seventh century onward is well known in the Greek world, and the strong relative sequence is revealing when examining the presence of this pottery in the Land of Israel in general, and when confronting its absence in the sixth century in particular.

---

13. Though he notes the existence of independent dates from the second half of the eighth century.

ALTERNATIVE CHRONOLOGIES FOR GREEK POTTERY

Although irrelevant for the present discussion, since all participants accept
the current chronology, it should be admitted that the accepted chronological
scheme for Greek pottery had been challenged by several scholars over the years
(e.g., Francis and Vickers 1983; 1988; James 1991). The critics can be divided into
two groups:

1. James and his colleagues, the most extreme revisionists of the traditional
    chronology, require down-dating of some Iron Age strata by several
    centuries (James et al. 1991)! Notably, the big differences between the
    alternative chronologies end earlier within the Iron Age, and at the time
    discussed here, the differences are "relatively minor," and cover only
    a few decades (e.g., James 2004; 2006).[14] However, this critique was
    rejected by almost every scholar working in the Greek world and the
    Levant, and even in other parts of the Mediterranean.[15] While some of
    the problems to which James et al. 1991 points exist, James et al. 1991
    failed to address all the relevant data, and their solution is not accepted.
    This is not the place for a lengthy discussion, but among the problems in
    their method, there is a partial treatment of most of the data. For exam-
    ple, according to Whitley, "their attempt to abolish the Early Iron Age is
    partially based on a misconception—namely, that this is a period where
    the archaeological evidence is sparse in the extreme" (2001, 71; see also
    Ward 1994). Moreover, the recent detailed examination of the Iron Age
    chronology in Israel, resulting from the debate over the historicity of
    the United Monarchy,[16] while not solving this debate, seem to have
    proved that strata usually attributed to the tenth to ninth centuries, are
    at least approximately accurate (the differences between the high and
    low chronology are about fifty to seventy years). This disproves James's

---

14. James et al.'s (1991) chronological disparity from the conventional chronology of the period discussed here appears to have been smaller than that of Vickers and Gill, discussed below
(although the disparity was much larger regarding earlier phases of the Iron Age).

15. E.g., Kitchen 1991; Kemp 1991; Postgate 1991; Snodgrass 1991; Sherratt and Sherratt
1991; Ward 1994; Waldbaum and Magness 1997, 25; Ridgeway 1999, 147–48, n. 21; Whitley
2001, 71; Lemos 2002, 25, n. 153; Gilboa and Sharon 2003, 72, n. 31; for the western Mediterranean see Nijboer 2005, 264–65.

16. E.g., Finkelstein 1996; 1998; Mazar 1997; Bruins, van der Plicht and Mazar 2003; Sharon,
Gilboa, Jull and Boaretto 2007; and various papers in Levy and Higham 2005.

chronology (which would place those strata in the eighth century; e.g., James et al., 1993, 195).

7. The second critique was forwarded by Francis and Vickers (Francis and Vickers 1983; 1988; Vickers 1987). This is a much more nuanced criticism of the accepted chronology (Whitley 2001, 72). First, it changed the chronology only by dozens of years, and not by hundreds. Second, it was based on serious, mainstream scholarship. Francis and Vickers base their chronology on the assumption that the archaeological finds should "closely coincide with historical events" (Biers 1992, 83). They see contradictions between the way they interpret the historical record and the archaeological evidence. To reconcile the two contradicting sources of information, they adapt a lower date for the finds. While there is almost a consensus that Francis and Vickers have identified real problems with the traditional chronology, their chronology is not accepted, as it creates larger problems than it is supposed to solve.[17] There is much evidence from within the Greek world that does not suit their chronology, and which they have not addressed (e.g., Whitley 2001, 73–74). Another problem lies in the fact that if their chronology would be accepted, three generations of known potters (with numerous signatures on vessels), would have existed over a span of only thirty-five years (Boardman 1988). In the traditional chronology, these potters lived over a century. Moreover, some recent works dealing specifically with the Levant have also questioned their chronology and retained the traditional ones (e.g., Waldbaum and Magness 1997).

It is accepted that most of the problems Francis and Vickers have raised can be solved within the parameters of the traditional chronology, and that the latter better tackles the large array of available data (e.g., Cook 1989; Whitley 2001).

THE LEGITIMACY OF USING GREEK POTTERY IN THE SIXTH CENTURY DEBATE

Although the traditional chronology of Greek pottery seems to prevail, the debate might pave the way for severe criticism of its use as a chronological tool in the debate over the reality in the sixth century. Would this be circular reasoning?

For several reasons, the answer is no.

---

17. E.g., Boardman 1988; Cook 1989; see also Biers 1992, 82–85; Waldbaum and Magness 1997; Ridgeway 1999, 147–48; Lemos 2002, 24–26; Whitley 2001, 71–74.

1. If one accepts the late-seventh century dating of the destruction layers at Miqneh and Ashkelon, then this scholar also accepts the chronological scheme discussed here, which is responsible for Greek chronology. In such an instance, the sixth century dating of Greek pottery must also be accepted. Hence, the absence of this pottery would require an explanation.

    To reiterate: Greek pottery is not used to create the basic chronological scheme—that would indeed be circular argument. It is used to refine the dating of sites whose general dating is based on others grounds (e.g., local pottery). As already stressed, all scholars involved in the present debate explicitly accept the dating of the destruction of Miqneh and Ashkelon to the late-seventh century.[18] Therefore, they all have to accept the dating of Greek pottery and have to face the question, "Why is Greek pottery of the sixth century missing?"

    Only scholars who question the traditional dating of the destruction of Ekron and Ashkelon can doubt the sixth century dating of Greek pottery, and its relevance to the debate (see James 1993, 170–82; 2004, 48, 54; 2006).[19]

2. We should remember that as far as Greek pottery is concerned, there is clear sequence and strong internal relative chronology. Even if one wishes to change the exact dating of a certain type of pottery, or even of the entire sequence, there would still be a certain period of time in this sequence for which there would be no evidence of contact between the southern Levant and the Greek world. This break would require an explanation. In a sense, the mere existence of the gap supports the traditional chronology. After all, the traditional chronology creates a logical

---

18. See, e.g., Stern 2001, 307, 317–18; Stager 1996; Barstad 2003, 12; Lipschits 2005, 41–42, nn. 19, 52, n. 55, 64, n. 98.

Lipschits accepts the dating of the destruction of Ashkelon to 604, but questions the dating of the destruction of Ekron to this year. He suggests a later date of 601/600 B.C.E. (2005, 41–42), 599/598 (42), or 598/597 (52) for the destruction of Ekron. Whether he is correct or not, for all practical matters he follows the traditional chronology.

19. James (2004, 54), for example, suggested that the destruction layer identified by the excavators at Ashkelon and attributed to the Babylonians was later in date. He also suggested that there might have been an earlier destruction layer, and that this (as yet undiscovered destruction level) should be attributed to the Babylonians (after all, the Babylonian destruction is known historically and cannot be ignored). Notably, the lack of publications of the excavations at Ashkelon enabled this suggestion Recently, however, Stager (2006, 2008a, 2008b) reported the finds from Ashkelon, although in a preliminary fashion, and he did not mention any Iron II destruction layer prior to 604.

and firm historical reconstruction that can account for the lack of Greek imports. The fact that the "gap" in Greek connections with the eastern Mediterranean coincided with what according to the traditional Greek chronology is the sixth century, strengthens this same chronology. Later we will see that the gap in importation of Greek pottery is contemporaneous with additional changes in the western Mediterranean, and this also supports the traditional chronology and overall reconstruction.

3.   Finally, we should remember that the traditional chronology of Greek pottery is still accepted today! This is the scheme on which anyone should begin to work.

IMPLICATIONS OF THE DATA

Since the data are important for all parties involved, they must be addressed. Why do we not find Greek imports of the sixth century in the Land of Israel, in contrast to the situation in preceding and succeeding periods?

Theoretically, one could suggest that perhaps the cessation in contacts between the southern Levant and Greece (or the Mediterranean world at large) had to do with events in the Greek world. But there is nothing to support such a claim. Ships continued to cross the Mediterranean Sea during the sixth century B.C.E., and Greek pottery dated to this century was found in many other places.[20] As Weinberg wrote more than forty years ago, "with the exception of Al Mina, which shows a gap very close in date to that present everywhere in Palestine, Greek pottery is especially plentiful at some sites not far to the north or south during the sixth century" (1969, 94). One must look at the Levant for an explanation of this absence.

The reason for the lack of imports seems straightforward. The country was devastated. The region had very little surpluses, and not much to offer international trade at the time.[21] This does not mean that there was no trade at all. It is likely that there was some imported pottery in the region, but since what we find is only a fraction of past activity, the very limited trade that took place in the region had not yet found its archaeological mark. I am positive that there were

---

20. E.g., Weinberg 1969, 91–92, 94; see also Venit 1988, 1, 60, 67, 71, 113; Osborne 1996; Cook 1997, 77, 84, 95, 110; Dominguez and Sanchez 2001, 459–60; Foxhall 2005, 240–41, 245; D'Angelo 2006, 181.

21. Another indication of economic collapse was the complete cessation in the use of the "Judahite" weights system after the Iron Age (Kletter 1998, 42–43; Dever 2001, 227). See more in ch. 8.

some Greek imports in the sixth century[22] and that Greek pottery will be found in the future. However, Greek imports will always remain just bits and pieces when compared to the Persian period and even the seventh century—representing the extremely low level of economic activity and international trade at the time. Thus, the lack of Greek pottery is an indication of the desolation of the sixth century.

We have noted that scholars often claim that (local) pottery of the sixth century is indistinguishable from that of the seventh century, and that it is only our inability to identify it correctly that creates an artificial "gap" in the archaeological record. This cannot be argued when Greek pottery is involved. Greek pottery is both easily identified and dated! The fact that sixth-century Greek pottery is practically missing from the region could imply either (1) that there was no significant settlement at the time, or (2) that the settlement was completely blocked from Mediterranean trade.

Since there was nothing in the Greek world that prevented contact, even if we chose option (2) we must admit that "something bad" was going on in the region. That is, life did not continue as usual even in the economically important coastal region. As there was also no biblical myth or even bias for this area, the data are quite straightforward.[23] The two options (no/minimal settlement and no/minimal contact) are not contradictory and are probably complementary. That is, there was very little settlement, and hence very little contact. The only reason for the minimal contact was the desolation of the region—both in Judah and Philistia. Furthermore, since the coastal plain was the most important region from an economic perspective (Faust and Weiss 2005; 2011, and references), the lack of international trade reflected the country's economic "unimportance" in the Neo-Babylonian economy (ch. 8).

The first to mention the absence of Greek pottery in the context of the current debate was (to the best of my knowledge) Vanderhooft (1999, 83–84), and the issue was not usually addressed by supporters of the continuity theory. Lipschits is the exception. Lipschits very briefly (in a footnote; 2005, 41, n. 18) addressed the lack of imported Greek pottery and suggested that the presence of Greek pottery in the seventh century resulted from the presence of Greek mercenaries. These mercenaries left the region in the sixth century, and therefore no

---

22. E.g., Mook and Coulson 1995, 94, 99; see also Yankelevitch 2006, 115; for little Attic pottery, see Merchese 1995, 171; we have seen above, however, that even this dating is contested.

23. Notably, the lack of imports in Judah can theoretically be explained along cultural lines, as was done for the Iron Age (Faust 2006b; 2006c); not only does such a claim require some support, but the fact that imports are missing in the coastal plain makes it clear that there was not any real contact between the land of Israel and the Mediterranean world system at the time.

Greek pottery was found. In attributing Greek pottery found in late-seventh century contexts to Greek mercenaries in the service of the Egyptian army, Lipschits
is relying on the work of Fantalkin (2006, 202; but see below for Fantalkin's own
view of the sixth century B.C.E.). Even if Fantalkin is correct, and much of the
Greek pottery was brought and used by Greek mercenaries, it is factually and
methodologically untenable to connect every sherd to such activity in the way
Lipschits does. Archaeological evidence does not connect "sherds" to people in
such an extreme way.

Before continuing the discussion, it is important to stress that the common
view connected Greek imports to trade, and not only to the movement of
people.[24] For example, when discussing various imports throughout the Mediterranean, Aubet (2007, 448) wrote, "these imported Ionian wares cannot be related
to the arrival of Greek Mercenaries." Aubet (2007, 450–53) showed that East
Greek and Etruscan pottery were often found in Phoenician colonial contexts,
and arrived through trade, which she labeled the "international trade network
of huge scope" (453–58). The view that imported pottery did not signify only
the presence of foreign population is also shared by those (e.g., Boardman) who
stress the movement of people in the Mediterranean. When discussing "minor
vases" unearthed outside the Greek world, Boardman (1999, 16) concluded that
"in quantity they should imply some kind of settlement, but the presence of just a
few such vases may be an indication of regular trade in other commodities which
they accompanied casually, or perhaps of temporary quarters for Greek traders or
their agents" (see also Boardman 1999, 272).

Waldbaum recently examined the contexts in which the various Greek
imports were found in the coastal plain during the seventh century (2007, 64–65).
She showed that the contexts varied greatly, from bazaar quarters (Ashkelon), to
domestic contexts (Timnah and Ekron), to Greek mercenary garrisons (Mesad
Hashavyahu). Waldbaum, therefore, reexamined the view that the pottery was
used by Greek mercenaries only and summarized:

> The commercial contexts at Timnah and now Ekron speak against this blan-
> ket interpretation. Furthermore, the appearance of these imports together
> with far larger quantities of locally-made wares that serve the same functions
> as the imports does not present a picture of an enclave of foreigners keeping
> to themselves and using only the familiar wares they brought with them.
> What seems more plausible for Timnah and Ekron is the acquisition of some
> exotic fine ware by a few high-status individuals, accompanied perhaps by a

---

24. E.g., Luke 2003, 60; Lemos 2002, 228; Dominguez and Sanchez 2001; Waldbaum 1997;
2007, see also Osborne 1996; Aubet 2007, 447, 448, 450–58.

container of imported Samian wine and a cooking pot or two purchased by a couple of adventurous Timnahites, possibly picked up on occasional shopping trips to Ashkelon, the nearest large emporium for imported goods from around the eastern Mediterranean (2007, 64–65).

The view that all Greek pottery was brought by Greek mercenaries is not well-founded and is not supported by the vast majority of scholars. This issue is beyond the scope of this chapter, but I would like to stress that even if one accepts Fantalkin's interpretation of the presence of Greek pottery and connects the major sites in which such pottery was unearthed with mercenaries, one cannot attribute all the sherds to Greek mercenaries (as suggested by Lipschits). Greek pottery is found in many late-seventh century sites in various contexts, and even if the main and intended clientele were Greek mercenaries, it appears to have spread also by other mechanisms, that is, exchange or trade.[25]

This is similar to the situation in other parts of the Mediterranean in the seventh century, when Greek pottery was widely circulated. It is accepted that the major mechanism for the transportation and movement of this pottery was exchange or trade.[26] The situation in the Levant was similar; even if Greek mercenaries were the main consumers of Greek pottery, they were not the only ones, and some pottery arrived through "regular" trade. Notably, the total lack of Greek imports in the sixth century, which contrasts not only the presence of such imports in the seventh century but also their abundance in the Persian period (and also their presence in most parts of the Mediterranean in the sixth century), requires a more thorough explanation—the lack of Greek mercenaries is insufficient.

Consider for example the situation at Tell en-Nasbeh. According to Zorn (1993a, 1102; following von Bothmer 1947), "twenty-nine fragments of Greek pottery, dated mainly to the late sixth to fifth centuries BCE" were unearthed at the site (see also Zorn 2003, 443–44). Tell en-Nasbeh is a remote highland site, but even there "contact" was resumed in the late-sixth century B.C.E. Did Greek mercenaries settle there at that time, as would be implied by Lipschits's scenario? Clearly not. This means that the "gap" in importation of Greek pottery cannot be attributed to the "lack" of Greek mercenaries.

---

25. Consider, for example, the few sherds (rare, probably due to cultural reasons—Faust 2006b; 2006c—but nevertheless present) uncovered at seventh-century Jerusalem (Auld and Steiner 1996, 70) and Tel Malhatah (Kochavi 1993a; 1998, 35). Were they brought there by Greek mercenaries and used by them?

26. E.g., Domingues and Sanchez 2001; Luke 2003; Osborne 1996; Lemos 2002, 228; Waldbaum 1997; Boardman 1999, 16.

Moreover, one should remember that there were Greek mercenaries in the service of the Babylonians (Boardman 1999, 52; Niemeier 2002, 328; see also Trundle 2005, 2). If Greek pottery was brought by mercenaries, where is the pottery from those mercenaries? While Lipschits appears to rely on Fantalkin, it must be emphasized that the latter (Fantalkin 2006, 204), after noting the lack of imports in the sixth century, wrote, "this part of the Levant, except for a few inland areas, is in ruins." The temporal correspondence between the lack of imported Greek pottery and Babylonian rule is too precise, and this also supports the connection between the decrease in trade and the Babylonian destructions.

Moreover, it appears as if the decline in the eastern Mediterranean not only made it less appealing to trade with, but it also had an impact on the situation in the central and western Mediterranean. I am referring to the relatively sudden decline in Tyrian influence in the west, the abandonment of many of its colonies, and the subsequent rise to power of Carthage as the leading colonial power.

The Western Mediterranean in the Sixth Century

It appears that the Phoenicians started their explorations in the western Mediterranean no later than the ninth century B.C.E.[27] This was followed by colonization and the erection of settlements that resulted in major socio-economic changes among the local population.[28] While by no means static, Phoenician hegemony in the region lasted some 200 years, from the eighth to the sixth centuries (Aubet 2001; Aubet Semmler 2002). In the first half of the sixth century, major and abrupt changes took place. Many settlements were abandoned and others changed in character.[29] Throughout the western half of the Mediterranean, Phoenician hegemony waned and Carthage became the new colonizing empire that controlled the area[30]—control that lasted until the Roman period (Aubet 2001; 341–46; Cunliffe 2001, 275). But what were the changes that occurred in the sixth century, and what were their causes?

---

27. E.g., Aubet 2001, 372–81; Docter et al. 2004; Nijboer 2005; Nijboer and van der Plicht 2006.

28. E.g., Aubet 2001; see also Cuntliffe and Fernandez Castro 1999, and various papers in Bierling and Gitin 2002.

29. Aubet 2001, 307, 321, 325, 341–46; Cunliffe and Fernandez Castro 1999, 431; Cunliffe 2001, 275, Mata 2002, 192–96; Markoe 2000, 186; Sagona 2004, 259; Gonzales-Ruibal 2006, 127.

30. Carthage replaced Tyre as the Hegemonic power in many parts of the region, but other forces seem to have gained more influence at this time.

First and foremost, the changes involved settlement patterns.[31] Thus, many settlements in the coastal stretch of the provinces of Malaga, Granada, and Almeria, settled by Phoenicians from the mid-eighth century, were abandoned between the years 580–550 B.C.E. (Aubet 2001, 307). At Toscanos (Toscanos V), the great central warehouse ceased to be used at the beginning of the sixth century, shortly after the settlement's commercial and urban "high point." The "grand residences of the town centre were abandoned and the settlement was reorganized, to be finally abandoned around 550 BC. Something similar seems to have occurred in other nearby settlements" (Aubet 2001, 321). At Cerro del Villar, the types of imported pottery "fix the end of the Phoenician occupation of the island at around 580/560 BC. All the signs indicate that the abandonment occurred very suddenly" (Aubet 2001, 325; note that at the same time another site in the vicinity was settled, hence indicating that the abandonment was not a regional phenomenon, but part of the overall decline of the Phoenician colonies in the west). Similar changes took place throughout the central and western Mediterranean, including on the islands of Ibiza and Sardinia (Aubet 2001, 341–46; Cunliffe and Fernandez Castro 1999, 431).

Some of the changes can be attributed to the rise of Carthage (Aubet 2001, 343), but what was the cause of the disruption of the previous system, centered to a large extent on Tyre?[32] Several reasons have been given for those drastic changes. One reason was the overuse of accessible silver ores in the west (near Tartessos), along with the usage of other sources of silver, for example in Attica.[33] The increased influence and activity of the Greeks was also regarded as an unsettling factor (e.g., Cunliffe 2001, 275; Mata 2002, 192).

Another factor mentioned by practically everyone dealing with this period in the western Mediterranean as the possible cause for the changes was the siege of Tyre and its fall to the Babylonians. Cunliffe wrote, "the siege of Tyre by the Babylonians from 586 to 573 BC was a major disruptive event" (2001, 275). Aubet added, "the fall of Tyre into the hands of Nebuchadnezzar after a siege lasting thirteen years (586–573 BC) … could not but have repercussions in the west" (346). And Mata mentions "the economic disequilibrium provoked in the West

---

31. For other changes, see Mata 2002, 194–96; those are connected, but are beyond the scope of the present discussion.

32. For the economic system, see also Faust and Weiss 2005, 85–86; 2011.

33. E.g., Cunliffe 2001, 275; Cunliffe and Fernandez Castro 1999, 431; Aubet 2001, 343; Mata 2002, 192.

by the fall of Tyre around 573 B.C., toward which a large part of the Phoenician market was directed."[34]

This is significant. Tyre was a major economic force behind the prosperity of the Mediterranean basin in the seventh century. Its decline in the first half of the sixth century (whether it was destroyed or not) had an immense impact on the entire economic system, severely damaging the colonies that were connected with it.[35] The decline of Tyre led to the rise of Carthage in the western part of the Mediterranean (as a substitute of Tyre in this region),[36] and probably to the strengthening of the Greek traders.

Why did Tyre decline? The Babylonian campaigns to the west (i.e., the eastern shores of the Mediterranean) caused havoc and destruction. The siege of Tyre and the destruction of many sites led to Tyre's decline, and its influence in the western Mediterranean waned. In this sense, the abandonment of Toscanos and Iberia was a result of the Babylonian destructions in the southern Levant.

The fate of the Phoenician colonies in the western Mediterranean, as well as that of sites and areas that were on the maritime routes between Tyre and its colonies, is just a mirror image of the processes that caused the lack of Greek pottery in parts of the eastern Mediterranean. Both were a result of the Babylonian

---

34. 2002, 192; see also Cunliffe and Fernandez Castro 1999, 431; Mata 2002, 192; Hodos 2006, 91–92; for the history of Tyre at the time, see also Katzenshtein 1973, 295–347; Elat 1991, 30; Ward 1997; Sommer 2010, 21.

It appears that archaeology does not yet contribute much to our understanding of the history of Tyre at this time (see, e.g., Bikai 1978, 67–68, 75).

35. Interestingly, a severe decline in the sixth century is also evident in other parts of the eastern Mediterranean, e.g., at Crete. Here, a collapse in the sixth century is well known (e.g., Hutchinson 1962, 349–50; Pendlebury 1963, 339; Whitely 2001, 243–52; Prent 1996–1997). Thus, Hutchinson (1962, 350) refers to population decline at the time. Whitely (2001, 244–45) wrote that "central Crete around 550 B.C.E. is an archaeological desert." Although the decline appears to have started earlier than in the western Mediterranean, it can be suggested that it was also connected with the decline in Phoenicia (Tyre suffered greatly also during the seventh century, see e.g., Markoe 2000, 46; Aubet 2001, 59). Notably, Crete is on a maritime commercial route which led from Phoenicia to the Phoenician colonies in the west (e.g., Boardman 1999, 269, 274; Markoe 2000, 172). It is therefore possible that the decline on the eastern shores of the Mediterranean was the cause for the significant settlement collapse in Crete (I am grateful to Sue Sherratt for this suggestion). That the decline started early, if not mistaken, can be attributed perhaps to the disruption caused by the early Babylonian campaigns in the Levant, which started in the late-seventh century B.C.E., or perhaps to Assyrian pressure in the seventh century B.C.E. (e.g., Markoe 2000, 46; Aubet 2001, 59).

36. In the Levant, the decline of Tyre most likely led to the rise of Sidon (Eilat 1991, 30; Aubet 2001, 60), only that the latter did not fill Tyre's place as a Mediterranean power, and was only of local importance.

activity and its damaging impact on the economic system at the time. The importance of the southern Levant was decreased to such an extent that the region was
simply wiped off the economic map of the period.[37]

Summary

The evidence regarding Greek pottery in the Levant shows that there was a cessation of international contacts between the Mediterranean world and most parts
of the land of Israel during the sixth century. This could have only resulted from
the changes that took place throughout the country at the time. Since the basic
logic behind the chronology of Greek pottery of this period is accepted by all
scholars who participate in the sixth century debate, the absence of Greek pottery requires an explanation. Greek activity in other regions of the Mediterranean
continued, and even peaked at the time, and it is therefore clear that the explanation lies in the internal situation within the Levant. The population was greatly
reduced, agricultural production diminished drastically, and due to the lack of
surpluses in the region it was not a real part of international trade. The decline in
the Levant affected not only the role of the region in the world economy, but also
caused changes in the western Mediterranean—where Tyre lost its hegemony and
was replaced by Carthage (and also by the Greeks).

There are several important conclusions to be drawn:

1. While the decline in trade is clear, the reasons for it cannot be sought
   in the Greek world, but in the Levant. This means that settlement was
   drastically reduced, and there were not enough clients for Greek pottery
   on the one hand, and the region did not have much to offer international trade on the other. Hence, the phenomenon clearly supports the
   traditional view of the sixth century b.c.e.
2. The decline occurred already in the early years of Babylonian rule. This
   is important because in previous chapters we identified decline, and
   while we showed that the only candidate to cause it was the Babylonian
   destruction, the date of the decline within the sixth century could not be
   demonstrated archaeologically. As far as Greek pottery was concerned,
   however, the early date of the disruptions within the sixth century was
   demonstrated, implicating the Babylonians as the cause for the great
   decline.

---

37. As we will see below, this is another indication that the Babylonians were not interested
in economy, and did not invest in the peripheral area of Judah for economic purposes.

3. The decline occurred not only in Judah, but throughout most of the country (and in this case mainly in the coastal plain). Hence, it is not a result of a "biblical myth." This seems to invalidate much of the logic behind the "myth of the empty land" claim, since if the "myth" is responsible for the scholarly invention of "emptiness" and decline, it should have been invented in Judah alone, and not in the coastal plain, for example (detailed discussion in ch. 8). Not surprisingly, the situation in the entire region accords well with information regarding a decline throughout large parts of the Near East (e.g., Liverany 2005, 230–31).

4. The decline in the east did not only make it less appealing for trade, but also had an impact on the political and economic constellation in the western Mediterranean. After more than 200 years of colonial enter-prises in the west, the hegemony of Tyre disappeared during the first half of the sixth century, many of the colonies were abandoned, and Carthage took Tyre's position as the leading colonial power in the region (and the Greeks also strengthened their position). There is practically a consensus that at least part of the reason for the decline in the status of Tyre and its disappearance from the western arena was the Babylonian siege and the consequent conquest of Tyre (even if it was not conquered, let alone destroyed, the siege was sufficient to reduce Tyre's status). Hence, the weakness of the east was not seen only by its disappearance from international trade, but also by the decline and even disappearance of the Tyrian colonies in the west.

5. The economic "desolation" of the region, and especially the fate of Tyre and its colonies, indicate that long-term economic planning did not influence Babylonian activities in the west.

The bottom line is that the lack of imported Greek pottery is not only an indi-cation of the desolation of the region, but is also important for dating this desolation, which can be safely attributed to the time of Babylonian rule.

CHAPTER 4
SOCIAL AND CULTURAL CHANGES IN JUDAH:
THE IRON AGE TO THE PERSIAN PERIOD

*I*n the previous chapters we have attempted to overcome the problem of our inability to identify ceramic assemblages of the sixth century B.C.E. First, we developed a method to recognize the rural settlement that could have existed during the transition from the Iron Age to the Persian period through reference to settlement continuity (instead of dating sites through pottery). Second, we discussed the presence and absence of Greek pottery in the region. We have seen that almost all settlements, both urban and rural, suffered a major blow during the transitional period from the late Iron Age to the Persian period. Additionally, the lack of Greek imports corroborates the great economic decline that occurred throughout the country (and help us to date it). Settlement in Judah and its environs was limited and poor. The present chapter will examine cultural and social practices in Judah before and after the sixth century B.C.E. as another means to examine continuity and change.

SOCIAL AND CULTURAL CHANGES IN THE
SIXTH CENTURY B.C.E.

Several material traits were of great importance in late Iron Age Judahite society, and an examination of their fate in the sixth century B.C.E. can inform us about the social and cultural situation at the time. The main traits to be discussed are the Judahite tomb, which was extremely prevalent outside the settlements' walls in late Iron Age Judah, and the four-room house, which dominated Judah's urban and rural landscape. After that, we will also address a few other elements (terminology and linguistic changes as well as some material ones), some of which will be shown to be connected to those two. The discussion in this section will deal mainly with socio-cultural changes. While the implications for the study of demography will be mentioned throughout this chapter, demography will be addressed in ch. 5.

The Judahite Tomb

Judahite tombs received a great deal of discussion (e.g., Barkay 1992; 1994; 1999; Yazersky 1995; 1999; Bloch-Smith 1992; 2002; Mazar 1990, 520–526; Faust and Bunimovitz 2008). The term referred to a new type of burial that appeared in Judah in the Iron Age II, and mainly in its crystallized form during the eighth to seventh centuries b.c.e. (Faust and Bunimovitz 2008, and references). The typical Judahite tomb (fig. 10) was composed of a hewn burial cave with a *dromos* (a passageway or a corridor leading to a subterranean tomb). From the *dromos*, one entered the cave by stepping down on a rock step(s). The cave itself was usually composed of a single space of approximately 2.5 × 3 m. The chambers were cut in straight lines, although the quality and the finish varied greatly.

After entering the cave, one reached a central passage. Surrounding the passageway on three sides were benches, which were organized like a Hebrew ח; one faced the doorway, and the other two were on each side of the central passageway. The deceased were laid on the benches, until their flesh decomposed. On one of the inner corners, or below one of the benches, there was a repository, into which the bones of the deceased were collected for the secondary burial. The bench was thus freed to accommodate a new body. The caves were used for multiple burials, usually dozens, and were used by extended families for many generations (in one instance almost 100 people were buried in a single tomb; Barkay 1999, 97; 2000, 268). Many funerary gifts accompanied the burials, and these were also found in the repository.

While hundreds of caves followed these general guidelines, there were also many differences. Some of the caves were hewed in a high quality: the benches were uniform, and the walls and roof were smooth. Others were very rough. In addition, while most caves included a single chamber, others were composed of a cluster of adjoining chambers or caves.

Today, we know of hundreds of such burials throughout Judah. About fifteen years ago, Yezerski (1995, 109) counted 395 burial chambers in 278 tombs (in thirty-nine sites), the vast majority of which belonged to the discussed type. Such caves were unearthed all over Judah, from Tel 'Ira in the Beersheba basin in the south (Beit Arieh et al. 1999), through Kh. Anim, Tel Halif, Kh. Za'ak, Ein Gedi, Tell Beit Mirsim, Tel 'Eton, Kh. el-Kom, Ras a-Tawil, Sair, Tel Goded, el-Arub, Tekoa, Nebi Daniel, el-Atan, Bethlehem, Manahat, Zuba, Moza, Shoresh, Abu Ghosh, Jerusalem, to Nebi Samuel, Tell el-Ful and Gibeon in land of Benjamin in the north (a partial list from Yezerski 1995, plate 1; 1999, 265; see also fig. 11).

Admittedly, the caves do not represent the burials of the entire population of Judah. Only the middle and upper classes, that is, the rich, the nobility, and the landowning peasants, buried their dead in this way (Barkay 1992; 1994;

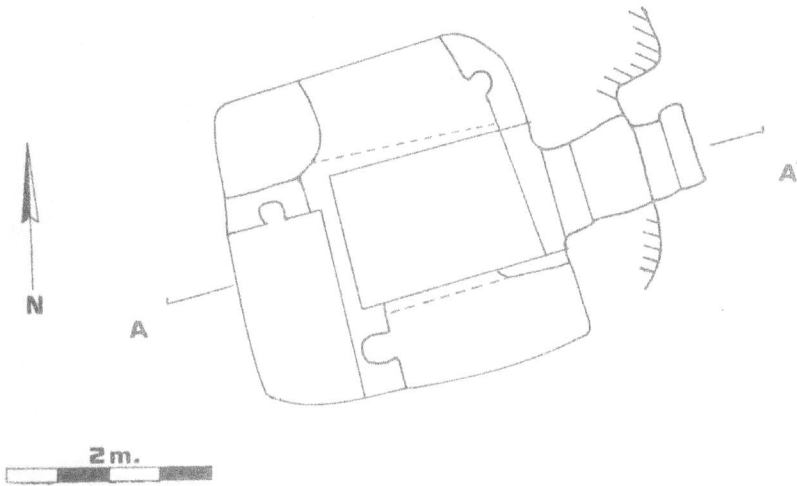

Fig. 10. A Judahite tomb from Gibeon (Eshel 1987, fig. 9;
courtesy of the Israel Exploration Society).

1999; Faust 2005a; 2012; see also Bloch-Smith 1992, 49). The majority of the
urban poor probably disposed of their dead in simple inhumations in the ground
(Barkay 1992; 1994; 1999; Faust 2005a; in press a).

The Judahite tombs were used by extended families (the biblical *bet av*) for
many generations. The tombs stressed the element of generational continuity and
the permanent nature of the family, which were important in Iron Age society.
When located in the countryside, the tombs might have signified the possession
of land (Faust and Bunimovitz 2008). They also might have shown beliefs about
death and the relationship between the living and the dead (e.g., Barkay 1994;
1999; Bloch-Smith 1992). The tombs appear to have gradually become a family
emblem, and there was no doubt as to their social importance (Faust and Bunimovitz 2008). Moreover, several scholars had also noted the similarity between
the tomb and the typical house of this period (the four-room house, see below),
and have suggested that the former was viewed as the house of the dead, where
all family members went after their death (Mazar 1976, 4, n. 9; Barkay 1994;
1999). This clearly connects these two important features in a "non-functional"
way. It is clear, therefore, that the Judahite tomb had became an important social
phenomenon, both reflecting Judahite values and structuring them (Faust and
Bunimovitz 2008; cf. Bourdieu 1977; Giddens 1979).

It is striking that no such caves are known from the Persian period (e.g., Stern 2001, 470–79; Yezerski 1995, 113–14; Wolff 2002, 132, 133, 136; see also Kloner and Zelinger 2007, 219[38]). The absence of the typical Judahite burial custom in the Persian period indicates that an important social institution had disappeared rather suddenly. This could have only resulted from a cultural break in the sixth century B.C.E.[39]

Admittedly, there is some evidence for the continuous use of a few of these Iron Age tombs during the sixth century, but not into the Persian period. Continuity was perhaps observed at some sites in the land of Benjamin, and also in Keteph Hinnom, tomb 5 at Mamilla (both at Jerusalem), Beth-Shemesh (tomb

---

38. Kloner and Zelinger (2007, 219) wrote that no such tombs were hewn in the Persian period. However, after describing the Iron Age tombs, they added that "(S)ome of these may have continued in use during the Babylonian, Persian, and Early Hellenistic periods, *since* there is no archaeological evidence of newly hewn tombs of this type from these periods" (emphasis added). While they are right in observing that no tombs were hewn in the Persian period, the conclusion that the existing tombs continued to be used in subsequent periods is problematic on the ground of both method and data, and does not follow the facts (see also Kloner and Zissu 2003, 15, 67). As far as method is concerned, tombs are not necessarily found from all periods, and finding them depends on the way in which the period's population buried the dead. In some periods, simple inhumations were used that do not leave easily identifiable traces. Because archaeologists concentrate on excavating settlements, simple inhumations in the field are not usually found. Moreover, such burials are difficult to identify and date, and as a result there are periods from which we know of very few tombs (e.g., Kletter 2002; Faust 2004a; and see especially Faust and Safrai 2008, and many references). This does not mean that tombs from previous periods were in use! As far as the data is concerned, we simply do not have archaeological evidence for a continual use of tombs from the Iron Age through the Persian period to the Hellenistic period. Not even one example exists (see also the data in Batz 2007)! If reuse was typical, we would expect a few such tombs to be excavated. Still, none of the tombs discussed by Kloner and Zelinger (2007) and Kloner and Zissu (2003) exhibit such continuity. In most cases there is a gap of a few hundred years between the Iron Age material and the Hellenistic period. (See also Kloner and Zissu 2003, 42; and the information supplied for the various caves; for a similar phenomenon in additional sites, see also Batz 2007). The limited formal resemblance between the Iron Age tombs and those of the later Second Temple period do not require continuity in usage. It is possible, and even likely, that during the latter period (mainly the late Hellenistic and Early Roman periods, when the usage of hewn caves for burial in the vicinity of Jerusalem reached a peak; Faust and Safrai 2005, 149–50; 2008; in press a) the population simply reused older tombs, which were already hewn, either because of the need for many tombs or because they were seen as "authentic" and, therefore, suitable to the needs of the period's population. It is therefore likely that some of the Second Temple period's tombs, which were similar to the Iron Age tombs, might have been reused Iron Age burials. The issue will be further developed below.

39. For the suggestion that a few tombs were hewn in the Persian period, see below.

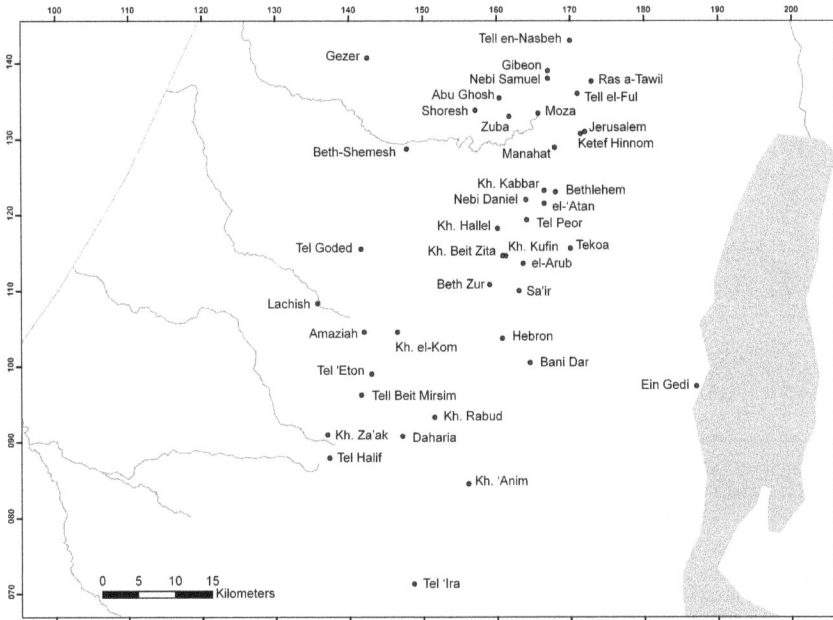

Fig. 11. Distribution map of Judahite tombs (not all sites are shown on the map).

14), and in one tomb at Tel Ira.[40] The fact that there is some ephemeral use of these tombs in the sixth century reinforces our position that their significance indicated a major social break at the time, for a number of reasons.[41]

1.   With the exception of the region of Benjamin,[42] only a few tombs exhibit this continuity: one in Tel ʿIra, two in Jerusalem and probably one in

---

40. Land of Benjamin: e.g., Barkay 1992, 372; 1994, 164; Carter 2003, 307; Kloner 2004, 108; Keteph Hinnom, tomb 5 at Mamilla: Carter 2003, 307; Barkay 1992, 372; but see Stern 2001, 324; Beth-Shemesh: Barkay 1992, 372; Tel Ira: Beit Arieh et al. 1999, 162–66.

41. Interestingly, these tombs comprise almost all the archaeological evidence for the sixth century (Barkay 1992, 372). I will discuss this phenomenon in ch. 7.

42. As noted, continuity was observed in the land of Benjamin (e.g., Barkay 1994, 164; Carter 2003, 307; but see Yazerski 1995, 114), but this is of less importance for the debate. There is an agreement among scholars from all schools that Benjamin was either the only or one of the only regions where significant settlements existed in the sixth century (Malamat 1950; Stern 2001, 321–23; Lipschits 1999; Barstad 1996, 48). It is possible that continuity was less than believed, but there is currently agreement that settlement continued there (for a reanalysis, see ch. 9).

Beth-Shemesh. The continuity that was observed in these tombs in the sixth century was extremely limited. The vast majority of the Iron Age tombs were not used at the time. It is clear that the sixth century population that remained in Judah did not immediately change its habits and the limited use of these tombs reflected the diminished population. These few tombs indicate that the limited population of sixth-century Judah continued to practice the traditional Judahite burials at least in the first generation after the collapse (see also Oded 2003, 67, n. 10).

2.   These burials represent the last phase of usage in Iron Age cemeteries (of which they were part; e.g., Stern 2001, 340). The tombs were used for a short period of time—hardly any of them exhibited a continuous and prolonged usage in the Persian period (at best, they existed into the beginning of this period, e.g., Reich 1993, 106–7 for Mamilla and Barkay 1998b for Keteph Hinnom). This means that, after a few generations, the old Judahite practice simply died away (see more below).

"Continuity" in the use of the tombs is an ephemeral episode and statistically insignificant. It is important for someone who wants to prove that the land was not literally empty in the sixth century, but it does not prove the existence of more than a very small number of people, and does not indicate any real and significant settlement. The later burials were probably practiced by those who remained in Judah after its fall, and still conducted traditional burials. This ephemeral use of the tombs is an indication that these remaining inhabitants were few. Otherwise, we would expect to find many more caves in use during the sixth century. The usage of the tombs was not only limited, but also of short duration; ch. 7 will discuss why the custom gradually faded away and was not practiced in the Persian period.

The fact that no Judahite tombs were hewn during the Persian period clearly poses a problem for these who assume almost full continuity between the Iron Age and the Persian period.[43] A major social institution ceased to exist at

---

43. Baruch (2006, 67*–70*) reported three tombs near Kh. Kabbar, which he classified as the discussed type, and which he dated to the Persian period. In two of the tombs, no sherds were found, while in the third, a few Persian pottery sherds were discovered out of context. It is likely that this was an Iron Age tomb which was used, for whatever purposes (probably not for burial) in the Persian period (perhaps by the inhabitants of the nearby fort, who probably had no "respect" for those buried in the tomb, and hence they cleaned the place and reused it). Nothing can be said regarding the other two tombs except that they probably were hewn in the Iron Age. Baruch (2006, 70*) gave parallels to this "Persian period tomb," but they do not withstand scrutiny. The tomb at Beth-Shemesh (tomb 14) is an Iron Age tomb, part of an Iron Age necropolis that was perhaps used in the sixth century. The tomb at Amaziah was dated by the

some point between the end of the Iron Age and the Persian period. Since these tombs were not hewed (or even used[44]) in the Persian period, it is clear we are witnessing a break between the late Iron Age and the Persian period. While archaeologically we cannot date the time when this change took place within the sixth century, anyone who doubts that it is a result of the 586 B.C.E. events and the processes that followed will have to produce another reason. Whatever the exact date, only major population shifts or societal collapse (or both) could have caused such an abrupt change.[45]

The cessation of hewing and using the Iron Age Judahite tombs is there-fore indicative of both a major socio-cultural change, and also of a demographic decline. The Judahite tombs were used mainly by the middle and upper classes of Judahite society—those who maintained the traditional (extended) family struc-ture of the biblical *bet av*. Those, however, were the majority of the population. One could claim that the lower classes (mainly the urban poor), who were buried in simple inhumations in the ground, were less affected by the 586 B.C.E. events. This claim cannot be examined archaeologically as such burials are rarely found (and their absence in the sixth century cannot be used as an evidence for the lack of population; for the rationale behind using burials to infer on population

---

excavator to the Iron Age (Naveh 1963) and the limited Persian period pottery found outside the cave was deemed later (75). Baruch's reference to Stern is also problematic. The latter mentions mainly coastal tombs that he considers to be of Phoenician influence. The same can be said of Batz's (2007) survey. Batz's list included many Iron Age tombs, which contained Hellenistic or Roman period remains (showing that there was no continued use in the tombs; see also above). Baltz also listed three places in which only Persian period pottery was found in or in the vicinity of rock-cut tombs. It must be stressed that in none of the cases is it clear that the caves were used for burial in this period, and in all three instances there was a large Persian period site in the im-mediate vicinity of the caves, hence suggesting that the caves were simply cleaned and reused at the time. The fact that most of the tombs were different from the typical Iron Age Judahite tombs might suggest that they were modified in the Persian period (if indeed used then, which is not certain) to fit other needs (e.g., storage). I should also note that Batz explicitly referred to chang-es in burial customs between the Iron Age and the Persian period (2007, 54, 55). It is important to stress that no "Judahite" tombs can definitely be dated to the Persian period, and that all the burials that can positively be dated to this period are not of the discussed type (e.g., Wolff 2002).

44. Even if the limited amount of Persian period pottery found in the "sixth century" tombs should be interpreted as representing some continuous use into the Persian period, the overall picture remains the same. This use was extremely limited both in terms of the number of tombs and length of their use in the Persian period (on the basis of the usually limited amount of Per-sian period pottery).

45. Interestingly, Niehr (2003) identified (on the basis of texts) changes in the status of the dead at the same time. These changes indicate that profound social changes occurred during the time discussed here.

and the problems involved, see Faust and Safrai 2008; in press a; in press b), but should be rejected on several grounds. First, scholars looking for continuity are searching in the rural sector and not among the urban poor—after all, there is an agreement (ch. 1) that the cities were devastated. Second, the disappearance of the middle and upper classes signified the collapse of the entire society (ch. 7). If someone would postulate a reality in which the Iron Age urban poor were unaffected by the Babylonian campaigns and prospered at the time, this person would have to suggest a reasonable scenario. As of yet, no one has come up with such a suggestion. Finally, there are other socio-cultural phenomena that, just like the Judahite tomb, disappeared in the sixth century. The most important is the four-room house, which was used by the entire population. Therefore, the theoretical claim that the Iron-Age urban poor prospered during the sixth century seems baseless.

THE FOUR-ROOM HOUSE

Another dominant feature of Israelite and Judahite society during the Iron Age II was the four-room house (fig. 12), which has received much scholarly attention over the last couple of decades.[46] The term "four-room house" is used here, as elsewhere, as a generic term.[47] A house of this type has a few long spaces (three, in the ideal type) and a broad space in the back (many rooms are sometimes subdivided). The number of rooms thus varies, even greatly, but most houses have either four or three "spaces." Typically, the entrance is in the center of the short wall, and in many cases pillars are used to divide the long spaces, although this is not a necessity. The four-room house, along with its subtypes, was the most dominant house during the Iron Age. The house appeared during the early Iron Age, slowly crystallizing into its more familiar form, and becoming dominant in the Iron Age II. Not only were most dwellings in Israel and Judah built following this form (or its subtypes), but even some public structures were built in this fashion (e.g., the fort in Hazor). Moreover, we have seen that this plan probably influenced the Judahite tombs, which were built following a similar perception of space.

In the early stages of research, many scholars viewed the house's temporal and spatial distribution (fig. 13) as matching those of the Israelites. Therefore,

---

46. Shiloh 1970; 1973; 1978; Stager 1985; Holladay 1992; 1997; Netzer 1992; Braemer 1982; Faust 1999d, 190–206; 2005a, 237–55; 2012; Faust and Bunimovitz 2003; in press; Bunimovitz and Faust 2002; 2003.

47. Most houses actually have three-rooms (or spaces).

the house was labeled the "Israelite House" (e.g., Shiloh 1973). Later scholarship attributed the house's dominant position in the Iron Age to its superb functionality, whether accepting the ethnic label or not (e.g., Stager 1985; Holladay 1992; see also Ahlstrom 1993, 340). The functionality referred to the house's assumed suitability for the Israelite's (and possibly others) way of life and practical needs. According to scholars who believed the functional explanation for the structure's popularity, the uniform plan was adapted because it suited the daily life of the population—certain rooms were used for storing animals, others for food preparation, sleeping, and so forth.

However, the functional explanation falls short of accounting for the phenomenon of the four-room house.[48] The functional explanation was disqualified because the plan was used in both urban and rural settings whose functional needs were different, for rich and poor dwellings, and even for public buildings. The four-room house was even used as a template for the period's tombs. Moreover, the finds in the rooms do not reflect any uniformity in the use of these spaces (Faust 2005a, 241; see also Cassutto 2004, 133–34; Aizner 2011). An additional fact that disproves the functional explanation is that the construction of these houses ceased in the sixth century B.C.E. (e.g., Shiloh 1973, 281; Holladay 1997, 337; Fritz 2007, 114). No technological changes took place in the sixth century; if the house was adopted because of its suitability for peasant life in the Iron Age, why was it not suitable for peasants in the Persian period?

In a series of papers, Bunimovitz and I attempted to show that the "Israelite" label was justified. We claimed that whether or not all houses were inhabited by Israelites, they did use this house extensively, much more than any other group. We showed that the house suited the Israelites' world views, kinship and perceptions of space, and suited their daily practices. This was the reason for its dominant position. Part of the structure's architectural characteristics (some revealed by access analysis) reflect Israelite values and ethnic behavior, for example, egalitarian ethos, privacy, and cosmology. Moreover, the Israelites were preoccupied with order (e.g., Douglas 1966; see also Bunimovitz and Faust 2003; Faust and Bunimovitz 2003; in press), and therefore once this kind of house became typical, it eventually became the appropriate and "right" one. It is thus the dialectic between function, process, and mind that created the "Israelite House."

Whether we are correct in our explanations, the house's ubiquity clearly indicates its importance in the social landscape of Judahite society. In light of the importance of the four-room house for Iron Age society, its demise in the sixth

---

48. For more details, see Faust 1999d; 2000a; Faust and Bunimovitz 2003; Bunimovitz and Faust 2002; 2003, and references.

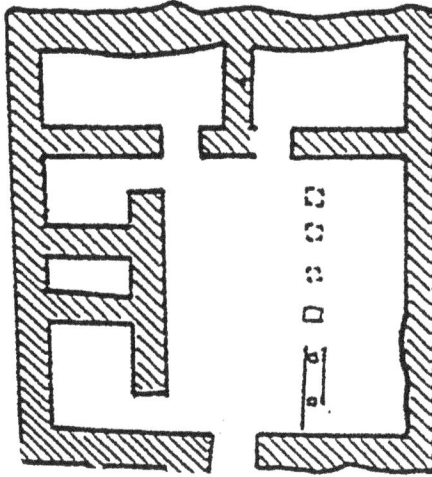

Fig. 12. A typical four-room house. Redrawn after house 2A at Hazor.

century is interesting. While this fact indicates that the functional explanation is faulty, as no major changes that could influence the functionality of the house took place at this time, it is also important for our discussion. The house, which practically embodied the Israelite world, simply ceased to exist in the sixth century, and this clearly indicates that major socio-cultural changes took place. This can only be explained by a cultural break.

To reiterate: one need not accept all of our interpretations of the four-room house in order to see the importance of the house's disappearance in the sixth century. The disappearance of something which must be seen as an important cultural feature of the Iron Age society begs an explanation. If life went on as usual after the Babylonian destruction, as suggested by a number of scholars, why did the people not continue to use and build the same houses?

It is possible that there was an ephemeral use of these structures in the sixth century. The four-room house uncovered at Alona (not far from Jerusalem), could be dated to the sixth century. In the publication, the house was described as an Iron Age structure (Weksler-Bdolah 1997, 98). However, the excavator informed me that later analysis revealed that the structure should probably be dated to the Persian period. Iron Age pottery was found under the floor, but it is not clear whether this indicates an earlier occupation of the same structure (Shlomit Weksler-Bdolah, personal communication), or not (Alon De Groot,

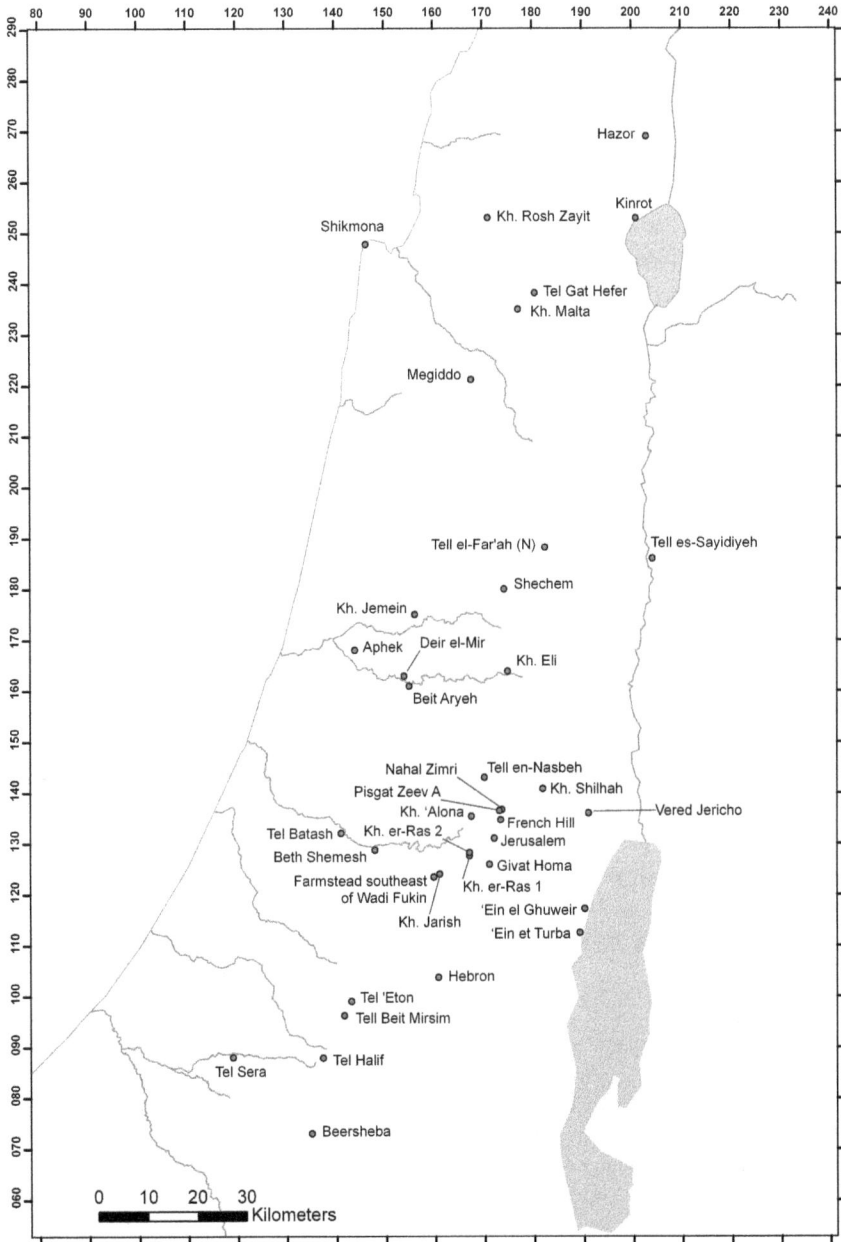

Fig. 13. Map of Iron Age II sites with four-room houses
(not all sites are shown on the map).

personal communication). The house should probably be dated to the sixth century.[49]

Moreover, Zorn attempted to date several large four-room houses from Tell en-Nasbeh to the sixth century (e.g., Zorn 1997a; 1997b; 1997c). According to Zorn's reconstruction, startum 2 at Tell en-Nasbeh was the city that became the new capital of Judah in the early-sixth century after the destruction of the Kingdom of Judah and Jerusalem, and this is the stratum to which, according to Zorn's reconstruction, the large four-room houses that were unearthed at the site should be dated (contra the common view, e.g., Branigan 1962, see more below). If Zorn was correct, then the fact that the inhabitants built four-room houses would strengthen the notion that the people of Iron Age Judah built such houses whenever they lived (see also Lipschits 2003b, 275; 2005, 239). The destruction of Jerusalem did not prevent the survivors from building the type of houses of which they were familiar. The absence of these houses elsewhere begs an explanation, and might suggest that the survivors were few. It should be admitted that Zorn's redating of the structures is doubted,[50] and the most we can conclude is that perhaps these structures were reused in the sixth century. In any event, the number of houses up for discussion is extremely limited.

Notably, Lipschits accepted the Judahite nature of the four-room house. He wrote (regarding Tell en-Nasbeh) that "most of the dwelling units in Stratum 2 were built according to the classic 'four-room house' plan, which is evidence that at least some of the people who lived there were Judeans" (2003b, 275; 2005, 239). But if one accepts the connection between the four-room house and the Judahite population, then one must admit that the fact that there were so few four-room houses in the sixth century, and that even these few ceased to function after a short while, means that there was at most very little continuity, even in Benjamin. And even there for a very short period of time![51]

In summary, just like the Judahite tomb, the quantity of sixth-century four-room houses is exceptionally restricted, exhibiting that there was a great

---

49. Note that De Groot (e.g., 2001; see also above) rejected all attempts to date finds to the sixth century, rightfully pointing to methodological problems with some of the datings, and to the difficulties such dating would create for our understanding of the Persian period (and he is probably right in his discussion of the finds on the western hill, for example). However, if indeed the pottery of the sixth century does not have any special characteristics of its own, then there is no reason for an outright rejection of every sixth century date, if based on other (circumstantial) evidence.

50. E.g., Herzog 1997b, 237; Faust 2005a, 81–83, n. 148; see also De Groot 2001, 79; the issue will be discussed in ch. 9.

51. If the structures at Tell en-Nasbeh are not from the sixth century, then the continuity was even more limited (ch. 9).

demographic decline when compared to the Iron Age. After all, the entire sixth century population would have been expected to use these houses, at least in the first generation or two after the destruction. If a large segment of the population survived, we would have expected to find many such houses. Moreover, we are not familiar with any four-room house that was built in the Persian period in the Yehud province, or even in the larger territory of what used to be Judah (Alona could be the only exception). This means that even the ephemeral use of these houses ceased during the sixth century, probably a generation or two after the destruction.

Just like the demise of the Judahite tombs, the four-room house was still used by the limited population that lived in Judah in the sixth century B.C.E., but even this ephemeral use by the limited population that remained declined and eventually died out.

The Judahite Tomb and the Four-Room House

The traits discussed are of importance for the study of daily life, as they accompanied the individual from cradle to grave. The house structured the individual's *habitus* (Bourdieu 1977) on a daily basis, and the tomb was the eternal resting place. Both markers of life and death, which were prevalent in Iron Age Judah, exhibited an abrupt change with the transition into the Persian period. This transition must indicate an extreme social and cultural break. The changes reflect fundamental changes in lifestyle, ethos, and beliefs, and only a significant event could have caused them.

Archaeologically, the changes cannot be dated with precision within the sixth century. However, it is clear that they occurred during this century. The traditional view of the Babylonian conquest—that many died in the war and the catastrophes that followed, many survivors fled and others were exiled, leaving Judah with little population—easily works with these data. The new school of thought, which viewed Judah in the Neo-Babylonian and Persian periods as a continuation of the Iron Age where life went on almost "as usual," cannot accommodate the changes that took place. If the 586 B.C.E. events and the processes that followed did not cause a break, then what could have caused these drastic changes? In the absence of another explanation, one must turn to the traditional and widely accepted explanation that attributes the changes to the Babylonian campaign. The dating of the changes to the early part of the sixth century is also supported by the lack of Greek pottery during most of this century, as we have seen in chapter 3.

It should be noted that the lack of Judahite tombs and four-room houses could partially be explained differently. Persian period Yehud was sparsely settled. Most scholars consider the Persian period population to be a third or even less of its late Iron Age predecessor (e.g., Carter 1999, 247; Lipschits 2003a, 363–66; Meyers and Meyers 1994, 280–82; see more in ch. 5).[52] As a result, the small population of Persian period Yehud left very little remains. Theoretically, it is possible that such minimal cultural continuity results from the fact that there was a small population, and as a consequence, few remains. If this is true, then we can expect more four-room houses and Judahite tombs to be discovered in Persian period Yehud in the future (see also Wolff 2002, 137 n. 1, who suggests that perhaps some of the few sixth century tombs represent Persian period usage of the tombs).

I should therefore note that if the lack of Judahite tombs and four-room houses in the Persian period is a result of a diminished population, then it is still of great importance for the current debate. Such a large population decrease[53] supports the notion that Judah was devastated in the sixth century. Moreover, such a decline inevitably resulted in a social and cultural disintegration. This issue will be discussed at length in chapter 7.

Finally, there are additional traits, whose identification cannot be explained as resulting only from the great demographic decline of the Persian period, and should be attributed to subsequent social processes.

ADDITIONAL CHANGES

The Biblical Bēt ʾaw and Mišpāhâ in the Persian Period

It is well known, on the basis of a textual analysis, that the meaning of various kinship terms had dramatically changed in the Persian period (in comparison to the Iron Age). This is discussed by many scholars (e.g., Smith 1989, 99–120; Williamson 2003; Vanderhooft 2009).

The change from the Iron Age *bet av* to the *bet avôt* of the Persian period, which differ not only in name but also in size and composition, was observed by various scholars. The Iron Age (preexilic) *bet av* was a relatively small unit that was usually identified as an extended family (e.g., De Vaux 1965, 28–29; Reviv 1993, 47; Wright 1990, 1, 53–55; Faust 2000b; 2005a). In the Persian period, the term used was *bet avôt*, which referred to much larger demographic groups (e.g., Smith 1989; Williamson 2003). The process by which the change came about is

---

52. Note that even these (generous) estimations are enough to characterize Judah as a devastated society (compare, for example, Tainter 1999, 1016). The issue will be discussed at length in chs. 5 and 6.

53. Note that the number of postulated Persian period remains actually represents the peak of their usage in the Persian period, and the nadir was much lower, see ch. 5.

not completely agreed upon, but as Smith wrote, "the familial terms and 'close-knit' nature of the pre-exilic *bet av* were used to impose a familial fiction on a sociologically necessary unit of survival—the bands of 'remnants' in exile who settled together" (1989, 115). Williamson attributed the change from the *bet av* to the *bet avôt* to the fact that the exiled population to whom the term *bayětî 'awôt* is usually referred (when they resettled in Judah), did not have inheritances in Babylonia and the kinship groups did not have to divide (2003, 477–78). Therefore, they simply became larger and larger. This was in contrast to the "original" *bet av* in Judah, whose inheritance was limited, and could not have supported large groups, leading to the fragmentation of the *bet av* and imposing demographic limits on its size. Hence, when the exiled population resettled in Judah, the groups were much larger than these of the Iron Age.

Regardless of the exact scenario through which the terminology changed, it is clear that there was a change not only in social reality but also a linguistic one, since the new terminology was accepted. The change from the small *bet av* to the large *bet avôt* is indicative of the social changes that took place between the Iron Age and the Persian period.

Other changes in terminology were observed. Vanderhooft (2009) also discussed changes in kinship terminology, such as the transformation of the term *mišpāhâ*. Vanderhooft examined the position of the Priestly source (P) in this regard, and he concluded that P was akin to other preexilic (i.e., Iron Age) sources. While his arguments are convincing, discussing P will drag me into a discussion of issues that are irrelevant for the main argument of this section, and I will therefore pursue Vanderhooft's exercise in a slightly more limited way.

To learn about P's position vis-à-vis other sources, Vanderhooft examined the meaning of the term *mišpāhâ* in other non-Priestly sources. He divided those less "problematic" texts as far as dating is concerned into preexilic and postexilic, and he found major differences between them. In order to circumvent a debate regarding P, I will use only Vanderhooft's basic division and will avoid discussing P.

During the period of the monarchy, the *mišpāhâ* was frequently mentioned in the texts. Vanderhooft (2009, 490) concluded that "during the monarchic era the *mišpāhâ* was defined by the territory it occupied and the economic activity and familial rites associated with that territory." In later, postexilic sources, however, the *mišpāhâ* only scarcely appears in the sources. According to Vanderhoof,

> both the scarcity of the term in Chronicles and the writer's reinterpretation of earlier sources suggest that Israel's kinship organization, and hence the semantic range of the term, had changed by the time of the Chronicler. Proof of this appears in several cases where the Chronicler uses *mišpāhâ* as no pre-exilic source did. Twice Chronicles refers to guild-like institutions … (2009, 490–91).

He added, "the Chronicler, thus, feels no constraint to use the term as his pre-exilic sources do, and on occasion alters his sources' conception of the term" (491). The differences in usage reveal the changes the society experienced in the transition from the Iron Age to the Persian period. As Vanderhooft concluded,

> The reduction and alteration of the use of the term *mišpāḥâ* in Chronicles and Ezra–Nehemiah suggest that in the post-exilic period it lost its concrete associations with the spatial dimension of Israel's earlier kinship organization. It is likely that the political disruptions of the sixth century, which upset the territorial distribution of the kinship groups that had prevailed through the end of the Judahite monarchy, helped to undermine the older geographical associations of the *mišpāḥâ*, and that this process accelerated with the territorial and demographic diminution of the Persian province of Yehud. (491)

The social changes that were expressed in language (the meaning of *mišpāḥâ* and the *bet av*) are parallel to the changes observed archaeologically and architecturally. The four-room house[54] and the Judahite tomb, which were both connected to the traditional extended family, ceased to exist because the entire social world and kinship structure to which they belonged collapsed (ch. 7). The changes observed by biblical scholars simply mirror the same processes, and they were reflected in the text and in the language. Those who remained in Judah lost their extended families in the war and subsequent destructions. And they could not transmit the reality of living within an extended family, and the ideological "package" that accompanied it, to their children (for the process, see below, ch. 10). Those who returned from Babylonia, no matter their number, probably could not have come as "real" extended families (as oppose to fictive kinship group—the latter resemblance to the real ones, however, was probably limited), even if they maintained it in exile (migration is notorious for breaking such formations, which means that it is unlikely that the exiled really kept this structure, let alone that the returnees would still have it).

The social changes observed by biblical scholars on the basis of textual evidence are therefore complemented by the archaeological changes. When the *bet av* and the *mišpāḥâ* dissolved, so did their archaeological correlates. This further illustrates that major social changes took place in the sixth century.

---

54. We are referring to the large four-room houses that housed large extended families (Faust 1999a; 2005a; 2012), and not to the smaller houses (mainly of the three-room type, although those also fall under the generic name four-room house; see Faust 1999a; 1999c; 2000b; 2005a; 2012).

Fig. 14. Iron Age pillar figurine (Zemer 2009, 13;
courtesy of the National Maritime Museum, Haifa).

Religion: Figurines in Persian Yehud

The Persian period also exhibited clear differences from the Iron Age traditions in what is usually regarded as religious or semi-religious practices. Stern (e.g., 2006) convincingly demonstrated that figurines were absent from Jewish sites of the Persian period.[55] The figurines of the Persian period were generally divided into those of the so-called Phoenician style with eastern influences, and western, Greek figurines. While absent from Persian period Jewish sites, figurines were frequent in non-Jewish sites in the coastal plain, Idumea, and the Galilee (e.g., Stern 1982, 158–86; 2006; Erlich; 2006; Armon 2005, 20). The situation in Jewish sites was unique and requires an explanation (notably, Samaria presents a similar pattern; Stern 2006).

For our purpose, it is important to stress that the situation in Persian period Yehud differed not only from its contemporary neighbors, but also from the reality in Iron Age Judah. Figurines were a frequent find in Judah of the eighth, seventh, and early-sixth centuries B.C.E. (fig. 14); hundreds of figurines dating to those centuries have been unearthed over the years (Kletter 1996, and many references; see also Byrne 2004; Meyers 2007). Therefore, the lack of figurines in

---

55. Here, we refer only to his observation regarding the absence of figurines in Jewish sites and will not treat his other arguments.

Persian period Yehud not only demarcate clear boundaries with the population of the coastal plain and Idumea, but also from the Iron Age practices in Judah itself.

While the reasons behind this change and the processes that brought it about—whether it were the "reformists" who were exiled and returned, "reformists" who stayed behind (for some speculations on the "reformists" and "nationalists" at the time, see, e.g., Albertz 2003, 95), or any other mechanism— are of paramount importance for understanding the social reality in the Persian period, for our limited purposes in the present section the exact scenario is of less import. Such an abrupt change in Judahite practices—which probably reflected a religious change or a different understanding of the objects themselves—was most likely a result of a major societal collapse, and also of a great demographic decline that allowed new traditions to develop. We should remember that Josiah's reform apparently did not manage to get rid of the figurines.[56] It is the great demographic decline of the sixth century that enabled this major cultural change. A crushed society is a fertile ground for the development of new traditions.

The great settlement decline of the Persian period is insufficient to be responsible for the fact that no figurines were found in Jewish sites of the period; such objects, if they existed, would be found in excavations. Figurines were not found because they were much less popular (and probably not used) in Jewish sites.

Linguistic Changes

The differences between the Classical Hebrew (Standard Biblical Hebrew; SBH) that dominate parts of the biblical corpus and the Late Biblical Hebrew (LBH) that is more prevalent in other works, and where Aramaic influences are more clearly evident, are well-known, mainly due to the works of Avi Hurvitz (e.g., 1974; 1982; 2003; 2006) and others. Those works have become very influential (see also, e.g., Rendsburg 2003; Polak 2003; 2006; Eshult 2003; Wright 2003; 2005). According to this view, SBH was prevalent during the Iron Age, while LBH was dominant in the Persian period. The transition between the two, which is the subject of the present section, is usually attributed to the sixth century (but see below). This view also tends to date some of the texts that are traditionally regarded as late—e.g., the Priestly source—to the late Iron Age. While not accepted by all, the logic behind the early date is quite clear (e.g., Levin 2006).

---

56. Subtle chronological distinctions are not always possible, but the figurines were found until the Babylonian destruction. Should this not be the case, other explanations might be possible for the observed pattern, e.g., that Josiah's reforms were responsible for the change (e.g., Ackerman 1992). At the present state of our knowledge, however, this seems unlikely (e.g., Byrne 2004, 140–41).

Notably, a number of scholars "challenged" (following the terminology in Zevit 2004) this basic scheme. Some have rejected it altogether (e.g., Davies 2003; Rezetko 2003), while others questioned the dating of the transition (e.g., Talshir 2003; Levin 2006; see also Ehrensvard 2006). The latter view, however, has not rejected the basic logic behind Hurvitz's scheme.

Since the vast majority of scholars accept, if not Hurvitz's entire scheme, than at least its logic and the idea of a "relative" chronology of "Hebrews," I intend to discuss this majority (and will refrain from discussing those who completely challenge Hurvitz's scheme; a view that is rejected by the majority of scholars, including many of the "challengers" themselves). The brief discussion below is, therefore, based on the basic scheme. Those who do not accept it, will find the entire discussion irrelevant.

Levin (2006) for example, commented that while the differences between the two "Hebrews" are clear, the date of the transition between them is less so, "The real question is when the transition from SBH to LBH can be *dated*. The assertion that the borderline was the exile is unproven and also unprovable" (2). According to this view, Classical Hebrew was indeed dated to the Iron II (the period of the Monarchy), but while the Late Biblical Hebrew was generally dated to the Persian period, it should actually be dated to the fourth century B.C.E. If this is the case, claims Levin, "a gap of two centuries yawns between the beginning of the exile and the observable beginning of LBH" (2006, 2). Ehrensvard's critique of Hurvitz's scheme is similar (2006). While there are texts that are clearly early and others that are clearly late, there are a few that while later than the destruction of Judah, are still more akin to the earlier texts than to the later ones. He therefore concluded "that the ability to write proper Early Biblical Hebrew did not end with the exile," adding that the end date is not clear (188).

Talshir placed the transition from one Hebrew to the other only in the fifth century. He attributed the change to the more significant wave of return from Babylonia (Ezra and Nehemia). According to Talshir, "it seems as if the Babylonian exile played a considerable role in the development of LBH; without their energetic influence, Hebrew would have developed differently" (2003, 255). Young raised similar claims, suggesting that the two forms of Hebrew coexisted for some time (such coexistence is inevitable), and that the question is for how long did the two coexist (2003: 309–10).

The implications of the reservations for biblical scholarship are clear. One can accept Hurvitz's compelling linguistic observations, while still dating the Priestly source to the Persian period (where it is traditionally dated) since it is possible that Classical Hebrew was used throughout the sixth and fifth centuries. Levin wrote:

As long as it is merely asserted and not proved that the transition from SBH
to LBH was contemporary with the exilic period—and not, perhaps, with
the transition from the Persian to the Hellenistic period—the dates proposed by F. W. Winnett and J. Van Seters [i.e., the Persian period; AF] lose
none of their probability. (2006, 4–5)

Clearly, there are scholars who reject Hurvitz's sixth-century watershed between
the two "Hebrews," and claim that the transition could have been at a later stage.

I am not a linguistic expert, so caution should be practiced; but first and
foremost, I note that Hurvitz was aware that the transition from SBH to the LBH
was a long process that did not happen overnight (e.g., Hurvitz 1982, 152–53;
2006, 206–7). He attributed to the sixth century (the exilic period) a "post-classi-
cal phase of BH" (Hurvitz 1982, 153, n. 36), that is, the writing of Ezekiel. Thus,
Hurvitz presented a more gradual shift from SBH to LBH. Levin, for example,
would have had to place Ezekiel in the fifth or early-fourth century in order to
allow both the positioning of the Priestly source in the Persian period and a
development between the various stages—and even this might be too condensed.

My main point is that, with caution, I would like to suggest that the reasonable setting for such a linguistic change would be the great demographic decline
of the sixth century, which allowed a new form of Hebrew to become dominant.
Anyone who accepts the relative dating of the various Hebrew "stages"—the
vast majority of scholars including many of the "challengers" (e.g., Talshir 2003;
Ehrensveard 2006)—will need a setting for that change. The sixth-century
destruction and the decline that followed are in my view the best setting to enable
the reception of the "new" language.

In his overview "Language Death and Dying," Wolfram (2002, 767) wrote,[57]
"the factors leading to language death are non-linguistic rather than linguistic"!
Those factors "include economic, political, ideological, ecological and cultural
factors" (Wolfram 2002, 767). In an influential study, Milroy and Milroy (1985)
claimed that the most important factor is social network. When society is characterized by strong ties, linguistic changes will be slow; whereas, a society with weak
social ties will experience rapid linguistic changes. Milroy (2002, 563) wrote, "a
type of social organization based on overlapping close-knit unit networks will

---

57. Notably, the following discussion of language change and even language "death" is based
on studies of such processes elsewhere that usually relate to changes between languages; whereas
in the current case we are discussing the internal development within a language. I argue, nevertheless, that the logic behind the change is the same, and it was the processes discussed that
allowed it.

inhibit change, while one characterized by mobility (for whatever reason), with concomitant weakening of close ties, will facilitate it."

Weak ties can result from various reasons, but as Trudgill argued, "weak ties have to do with lack of social stability" (2002, 709). Trudgill added that (emphasis added) "societal *breakdown*, such as that caused by the Anglo-Saxon invasion of Britain ... accelerates change." Although not a necessity, conquest and colonization are in many cases among the causes for weak social ties within a society (Milroy and Milroy 1985, 379–80). As Campbell mentioned, among the factors responsible for the "death" of languages (1994, 1963) are "repression, rapid population collapse, lack of economic opportunities, resettlement, dispersion, migration ... cultural destruction, war ... famine, epidemics ... resource depletion ... lack of social cohesion ... particular historical events."[58] These factors, which can be summarized as a social breakdown or collapse, existed in sixth-century Judah and led to the weakening of kinship ties (see ch. 10)—something which enabled the reception of the changes.

We have seen that some scholars suggested that the "new language," LBH, was brought by the returnees (Talshir 2003, 255; whether in the late-sixth century or the first half or middle of the fifth century). Their status as elite enabled "their" language to disseminate to the population at large. This is a likely proposition. But it seems to me that it was the great decline that enabled the new form of Hebrew to become dominant, regardless of the exact date of the transition (which was clearly gradual) during the sixth to fifth centuries. This fits Hurvitz's (1982, 153, n. 36; 2006) chronological scheme, and probably that of Talshir (2003) and other challengers. In light of the above it would be more difficult to attribute the changes to the fouth century B.C.E.[59]

If indeed brought by the returnees,[60] and given the existence of at least some degree of hostility between the returnees and the population that remained in the country, we might view the process as a weak form (as we are still discussing the same language) of language replacement. One can speculate that this was carried

---

58. The situation in sixth century C.E. Britain was similar, and historical events (wars) led to social changes and subsequently to drastic language replacement (Jackson 1953, quoted by Trudgill 2002, 708–9). Trudgill (2002, 709) wrote that "sixth-century Britain was a socially very unstable place indeed." Given the drastic and catastrophic changes that took place in Judah in the sixth century B.C.E., one can suggest that society was far less stable there than in sixth century C.E. Britain.

59. The general process described cannot aid in determining the date of the disputed biblical texts.

60. I do not wish to dwell on the issue of the period of the restoration, the number of returnees, etc. Suffice it to state that the majority of scholars believe that there was at least some "return."

out by "elite dominance" (Renfrew and Bahn 2004, 482–83), that is, when "a small number of incomers secure power and impose their language on the majority." One can, therefore, suggest that the elite (the returnees) spoke LBH, while those who remained spoke a form of language closer to SBH. The social weakness of the latter (resulting mainly from the collapse of the sixth century b.c.e.) made them susceptible to changes and enabled LBH to become dominant.

It should be stressed that the linguistic issue is beyond the scope of this book, and my main aim in the present section was to tentatively show that the destruction in the sixth century might have provided an appropriate social context for the linguistic changes that occurred. Firm conclusions, however, will require a much more thorough and detailed discussion.

Interestingly, in his discussion of the development of scribal culture, Sanders (2009, 166) noted "the total disappearance of Hebrew from the epigraphic record between the Babylonian exile and the Hellenistic period." It is not that writing disappears—"writing continues as before, but in Aramaic." Sanders's explanation is straightforward: "This shift finds its cause in the destruction of the Judean political infrastructure in the early-sixth century by the Babylonians, combined with the economic devastation and mass deportation of craftspeople and artisans." Clearly, this fits well with the other language related changes that took place at the time.

Cosmology

The archaeological evidence indicates that during the Iron Age the Israelites tended to orient their houses and settlements toward the east and avoided the west (see extended discussion, including statistics, in Faust 2001, and many references). This pattern is manifested in the dwellings of the period, both in urban and rural settings, as well as in the orientation of other structures, and even city gates. No functional explanations seem to account for the phenomenon, and it seems as if the solution should be sought in another realm.

It seems that the east was of special importance in Iron Age Israel, as in other Near Eastern societies in antiquity. A tendency for eastward orientation was observed by ethnographers in many societies, and can be, generally speaking, attributed to a "natural" preference toward sunrise rather than sunset—both with the accompanied "package" of meaning (life versus death, etc.; e.g., Lubetski 1978; Waterson 1997; North 1996, 7, 9). Though comparisons with other societies cannot give definite explanations for the behavior of past societies, archaeologists have used the above mentioned pattern to explain a similar archaeological pattern (e.g., in Britain; see, e.g., Fitzpatrick 1997; Oswald 1997). We cannot know whether they are right, but this explanation is possible and the Israelites could have preferred the east for similar reasons. For Iron Age Israel, however, we have additional information, derived from the ancient Israelites' language and text. Those can be used as a partial substitute for human informants in order to understand a people's world views, beliefs, and so forth. The meaning of the Biblical Hebrew word for east is *qēdmâ*, that is, "forward," and that serves as an indication for the preference given to this direction; also one of the words for west is *'āḥôrâ*, that is, "backward" (e.g., Malamat 1989, 67; Drinkard 1992a; 1992b). These words indicate that the Israelites oriented themselves toward the east, a fact that might have affected their cognition. Moreover, there are other words for east and west, and they indicate that the east had a positive connotation while the west—usually called *yam* (sea)—had a negative one (e.g., Lewis 1993, 335; Ahlstrom 1986, 49; Stolz 1995, 1397–98; Keel 1978, 23, 35, 49, 50, 55, 73–75) thus strengthening the above presented conclusion (Faust 2001, with literature). Several passages in the Bible demonstrate this tendency quite clearly and exhibit the preference given to eastern orientation and the avoidance of a westerly one. This is most clearly evident in Ezekiel's (40–48) description of the temple and its courts. The temple itself was oriented to the east. The courts had gates in the north and south, and those entering in one left through the opposite gate. There was also an eastern gate, but no western one. So how do those that entered through the eastern gate leave? This is not really a problem, as nobody actually entered through the east— this was God's gate (Ezekiel 43:1–4; 44:2). The description in Ezekiel is probably not historical, but this is immaterial for our purposes. Ezekiel's vision fits with the picture that emerges from the archaeological record: a preference for the east and avoidance of the west (for detailed discussion, see Faust 2001).

Unfortunately, we do not have enough archaeological data to statistically examine the orientation of houses in the Persian period. Given this widespread "orientational tendency," it is possible that such an eastern orientation was prevalent even at this time, but probably not to the same extent and not with the same importance as that of the Iron Age. The later texts, however, imply that this element of cosmology/belief did not exist anymore, or at least, lost its significance. First Chronicles 9:23–24 (see also 1 Chr 26:12–19) was clearly written after the Iron Age. Here, in the description of the Temple and its courts that in many respects is similar to that of Ezekiel, there is also a western gate. The existence of a western gate in the Chronicler's vision of the Temple Mount, as opposed to Ezekiel's, hints that the Iron Age cosmological beliefs that were still evident in Ezekiel's perception of the world died out and did not influence the writing of 1 Chronicles.

Discussion and Conclusions

It should be noted that in some aspects, there seems to be continuity between the Iron Age and the Persian period (e.g., the persistence of the negative view toward imported pottery, Faust 2006b: 49–64; 2006c). Continuity, however, seems to have been overstressed recently. Socially, culturally, and to a large extent religiously, there were drastic changes during the transition from the Iron Age to the Persian period. The Judahite tomb and the four-room house were important social institutions, which dominated the Iron Age social landscape and accompanied the individual from cradle to grave. Both, however, disappeared during the sixth century, and were practically unknown in the Persian period. These social and cultural changes are connected with transformations, or disintegration, in the position of the traditional family. Similar changes in the meaning of the terms *bet av* (*bet avôt*) and *mišpāhâ*, between the preexilic and postexilic sources seems to match the archaeological ones. Significant changes can also be seen in other practices, for example, the disappearance of figurines from the archaeological record of Judea. While those changes should be treated more cautiously, it appears as if dramatic changes were also observed also in cosmological beliefs and in language.

To reiterate, the land was not empty. This was clearly demonstrated above (see also ch. 5). After all, the houses and tombs were both still used in the first generation(s?) after the destruction. However, this usage was very limited, and lasted only a short period of time. The disappearance of the Judahite tomb, the four-room house, and the figurines, along with changes in linguistic terms and other changes, represent the break in the sixth century. Within a generation or two after the destruction, the limited number who remained continued to use the houses and tombs to which they were accustomed. Due to their limited numbers and the collapse of their social institutions (ch. 7), they gradually ceased to use the Iron Age type tombs and houses. It is precisely this collapse that enabled, perhaps somewhat later, additional changes, that is, in language and also in religious and cosmological beliefs. Some of these changes might have occurred in the fifth century, but they were all consequences of events of the early-sixth century. As Schniedewind (2004, 143) wrote, "every cultural institution of Judean life changed." Clearly, nothing continued as before. Understanding the cultural and social decline that accompanied the sixth century events is even more important than studying the "exact" figures of those who remained in Judah, or "playing" with population estimations (see also Dever 2005, 293–94; Liverani 2005, 196).

In chapter 7 I would like to put the social changes that took place in Judah during the sixth century within a broader anthropological context in order to understand them better, but before that we would like to examine the settlement and demography of the sixth century B.C.E. within a broader perspective.

Chapter 5
Settlement and Demography in Judah:
The Seventh to Second Centuries b.c.e.

The five hundred years that spanned the late Iron Age, the Neo-Babylonian, the Persian, and the Hellenistic periods were troubled ones in Judah. This period started during the seventh century b.c.e. with Assyrian domination. After an interlude of Egyptian hegemony, Babylonians ruled during the late-seventh century and most of the sixth century. Persian rule followed, and lasted two hundred years. The conquests of Alexander the Great ended Persian domination, and this was followed by contesting Hellenistic dynasties, which fought over the region. Finally, the second century saw the Hasmonean revolt and expansion.

This chapter looks at the long-term settlement and demographic processes as observed in the archaeological record of this period. Archaeological evidence from excavations, salvage excavations, and surveys will be at the forefront, and historical information will be used only as complementary data. Interestingly, such an endeavor has hardly been attempted. Most studies of the biblical period conclude with the end of the Iron Age, and while several have discussed the Persian period, they do not include a detailed analysis of the data from the Hellenistic period.[1] The same is true regarding studies of the Second Temple period. These studies have usually begun with the Hellenistic period, and even if the Persian period was examined, it was not compared to the late Iron Age. The Persian period's exclusion from studies of long-term processes seriously hampers the study of this period. Only when such a study is embedded within a larger frame-

---

1. Carter's 1999 study is a notable exception. While not giving the same amount of discussion to all three periods, settlement in all was examined (e.g., 233–48). Note that even Lipschits's detailed studies (2003a; 2003b; 2005), while stressing the importance of discussing the timespan from the late Iron Age until the Hellenistic period, do not really examine the settlement and demography of the latter.

work of archaeological data can we truly assess the demographic and settlement reality of the time.

Most of the chapter will not address the sixth century specifically. Only through first examining the Iron Age, the Persian period, and the Hellenistic period will the implications of the reality in the Neo-Babylonian period become apparent. Finally, while more subtle regional distinctions will be made, the basic diachronic comparison will refer to the territory of the Iron Age kingdom of Judah, and I will examine the settlement and demographic history of this region. Notably, the region probably encompassed both Judea and Idumea in the Hellenistic (and Persian?) period, but this is the only way to examine changes in demography and settlement (see also ch. 2).

Settlement Dynamics

Our knowledge of settlement dynamics derives from several related sources of archaeological information. We will begin by analyzing the vast database of surveys. While surveys are problematic (ch. 2; see also Faust and Safrai 2005; in press a), the overall patterns observed from the data are relatively reliable. If their findings are in accordance with the information from excavations, then we can work with this data.

Surveys

The aforementioned regions have been extensively surveyed. While this data is far from conclusive (e.g., Faust and Safrai 2005; ch. 2), the patterns are straightforward and confirmed by the data from excavations (below). The surveys conducted in Judah were mostly published (either in print or as part of an unpublished but available Ph.D. dissertation).

Table 1 represents the results of surveys[2] from the land of Benjamin survey in the northern part of the discussed region, through the surveys of Jerusalem,

---

2. Note that I used the rough data presented by the surveyors, and did not reanalyze it. This means that in some rare cases the figures also included tombs. Admittedly, using all the reported "sites" is a problematic procedure, but it resulted from the available data. In most cases the trends should not be affected, therefore permitting the usage of the data. The relative accuracy of the trends can be seen in the reality in Benjamin, in which the "rough data" were analyzed by Carter, but the trends were not altered (see note 9 below). Notably, in many cases, the surveyors made the distinction and offered listing of settlements only.

the Nes Harim map and the Hebron Hill Country, to the surveys of Tel Malhata and Nahal Yatir maps in the south, and from the Herodium and Deir Mar Saba survey maps in the east to the Shephelah survey in the west. While some statistical differences can be observed within the various subregions, the pattern of settlement dynamics is clear. The late Iron Age II, a settlement peak by all standards, is followed by a decline in the Persian period,[3] and a significant recovery in the Hellenistic period.[4]

Notably, data from the regions that were closer to the coast (but were parts of Judea during part of the time discussed) show a different pattern. A comparison with the area of Rosh Ha'ayin-Shoham-Modiin,[5] is most revealing. Here, the surveys gave the results illustrated in table 2. The trends within this region are not identical, but none of these surveys resemble the picture from Judah, in which there was always a decline followed by recovery. The Rosh Ha'ayin-Shoham-Modiin region behaved differently, and settlement was shaped by different processes (interestingly, the more reliable data from the salvage excavations is more similar to that from the Beit Sira map, mentioned below).[6] The Modiin-Shoham region was an "island of stability" in the aftermath of the Babylonian campaigns. The data from this region present us with a settlement reality against which to compare the information from Judah proper.[7]

---

3. Most studies do not report finds from the Neo-Babylonian period; the few that do identified very little activity at the time. The issue will be discussed in detail below.

4. Our information on the marginal areas of the Negev and the Judean Desert are more partial than those of other regions. Since scholars from all schools seem to agree that these areas suffered devastation in the early-sixth century (e.g., Lipschits 2003a, 338–41; 2003b, 260–72; 2005, 224–37), if the data from this region were more complete, the overall picture of the decline in the Persian period would have been greater (though the demographic importance of settlements in these regions was somewhat limited).

5. The results of the excavations conducted have already been discussed in ch. 2.

6. This area is outside Iron Age Judah and is therefore a convenient "control group" against which to compare the data from Judah (see ch. 2—the region addressed here encompasses not only the area in which the farmstead phenomenon was observed, but is much larger, and includes additional subregions).

7. Notably, the results of the survey are in general accordance with the excavations (see ch. 2).

Table 1. Settlement (number of sites) in Judah during the Late Iron Age, Persian and Hellenistic periods according to the data from surveys.[8]

	1	2	3	4	5	6	7	8	9	10	Summary
Iron Age	16	64	21	68	24	143	113	87	27	23	586
Persian period	7	27	0	13	12	15	87	47	7	1	216
Hellenistic period	35	70	10	27	33	110	98	110	7	10	510

1) Ramallah and el-Bireh (North) (Finkelstein 1993b)[9]; 2) Ramallah and el-Bireh, (South), Ein Karem (north) (Feldstein et al. 1993); 3) Wadi el-Makukh (Goldfus and Golani 1993); 4) Eastern Jerusalem (Dinur and Feig 1993); 5) Nes Harim (Weiss, Zissu, and Sulimany 2004); 6) Jerusalem (Kloner 2000, 2001b, 2003); 7) Hebron Hill country (Ofer 1993b)[10]; 8) Shephelah[11] (Dagan 2000); 9) Tel Malhata and Nahal Yatir (Beit Arie 2003; Govrin 1992; 10) Herodiom (Hirschfeld 1985) and Deir Mar Saba (Patrich 1994).

---

8. I did not include the results of the emergency survey (Kochavi 1972), which despite its great importance, is dated. Also, the table does not include the results of the Beit Sira map (published as part of the Benjamin survey), as it relates to another area (below).

Nes Harim: There were sixteen sites identified only as "Iron Age." Since most identified Iron Age sites were dated to the Iron Age III, it is likely that most of these sixteen should be added to the Iron III, hence increasing the number of settlements in this period.

Jerusalem: Note that the Iron Age figure relates also to groups of sites, and the real figure was much larger (Kloner 2001, 92). The figure 110 refers to the late Hellenistic/Hasmonean period, which seems to have been the peak in this (Kloner 2003, 26), as well as in other regions (e.g., Finkelstein 1993b, 27). From the early Hellenistic period only thirty-seven sites were reported. There were many additional remains that were reported as "Second Temple" period only (49), and it is likely that some of these belonged to the Hellenistic\Hasmonean period.

Tel Malhata: While in the summary it appears that at the Map of Tel Malhata there was only one site with Hellenistic finds, the text indicated the existence of another (Beit Arieh 2003, 12*–13*).

9. Carter (1999, 235) examined the number of actual settlements in the entire region of Benjamin and came up with the following results: Iron Age: 157; Persian period: 39; Hellenistic period: 163. The trends clearly follow the more general data supplied by the surveyors.

10. Note that according to Finkelstein (1994, 174–75), Ofer underestimated the number of seventh-century settlement, due to methodological problems (below).

11. The figures relate only to settlements (or buildings) of various sorts. In his summaries, Dagan differentiated between sites and other find spots (cemeteries, agricultural activities, and find spots), and I followed suit. The Iron Age figure relates to the seventh century. Note that according to some, Dagan also underestimated (due to methodological problems) the number of sites from this period (Ofer 1993b, 2, 153, see more below). Should this criticism be true, the

Table 2. Settlement in the Rosh Ha'ayin-Shoham-Modiin Region during the Iron Age, Persian, and Hellenistic periods according to the surveys.[12]

	Beit Sira	Lod	Rosh Ha'ayin	Summary
Iron Age	5	46	34	85
Persian period	13	28	37	78
Hellenistic	28	19	26	73
Summary of trend	Gradual increase	Gradual decline	Relatively Stable	Very modest gradual decline

A Note on Chronology

The Iron Age data presented are representative mainly of the seventh century. While many surveys do not differentiate between the various sub-periods within the Iron Age II, and the data could have represented the eighth century that is usually regarded as the settlement peak in the land of Israel (e.g., Broshi and Finkelstein 1992; regarding Judah, see Na'aman 1993; 2006; but see Finkelstein 1993a; 1994; Faust 2008b), this is not the case here. Dagan (2000) and Ofer (1993b), who surveyed the larger part of the region, made the distinction between the two centuries (perhaps even underestimating the seventh century B.C.E.).[13] The same is true for the Nes Harim map (Weiss, Zissu, and Solimany 2004). As far as the Jerusalem area is concerned, the seventh century, and not the eighth, seems to have been the peak of settlement in the region around the city (Faust 2005b; Faust and Weiss 2005; see also Na'aman 2007). The same is true for the Negev and the Judean Desert (Finkelstein 1994). Regarding the Benjamin area, in some cases the surveyors explicitly claimed that the date represented the last phase of the Iron Age (Finkelstein 1993b, 27). Therefore, it is clear that the data represent the last century of the Iron Age.

Iron Age figure should be even higher. The inclusion of find spots might have changed the data from this region significantly.

12. Beit Sira: Hizmi 1993; Finkelstein 1993b; Lod: Kochavi and Beit-Arieh 1997; Rosh Ha'ayin: Gophna and Beit-Arieh 1994.

13. Several scholars have claimed that seventh-century settlement was underestimated because it was identified on the basis of a few types of pottery that were easily missed. In the absence of these finds, the eighth- to seventh-century assemblages were regarded as reflecting only the eighth century. Finkelstein (1994, 174–75) raised this claim regarding the survey of the Judean hill country, and Ofer (1993b, part 3, 153) raised a similar claim regarding the survey in the Shephelah (see also Faust 2008b).

A similar problem exists regarding the Persian period and the Hellenistic period, since the finds are usually not divided into sub-periods. The two-hundred-year long Persian period will be discussed below. Regarding the Hellenistic period, some surveyors commented that the peak was at its later stage (Finkelstein 1993b, 27). Others conducted a subdivision of this era and also found the peak at the later stage (Kloner 2003, 26). The data support that the peak of the Hellenistic was indeed toward its end.

Before analyzing the trends observed above, we will first study the data on settlement in the Iron Age–Hellenistic period, as revealed in the excavations. Data from excavations should be analyzed according to the type of excavation: planned excavations and salvage excavations.

Planned Excavations

Planned excavations are usually carried out in central, larger sites. There are no exact statistics available for these excavations, but the overall phenomenon is clear and well known in the research literature.

Iron Age

Remains from the later Iron Age are well attested throughout the region, including its fringes, e.g., at Jerusalem, Lachish, Ramat Rahel, Moza, Tell en-Nasbeh, Jericho, Ein Gedi, Tel Batash, Hebron, Kh. Rabud, Arad, Aroer, Tel Ira, Tel Masos, and many other towns and villages (chs. 1 and 2; see also, e.g., Finkelstein 1994; Stern 1994; Faust 2008b; Faust and Weiss 2005, and others).

Persian Period

The dearth of Persian period remains in Judah (Stern 1983, 120, e.g., excludes the area of Benjamin, but see more below) is a well-known phenomenon, which has been addressed by many scholars (Carter 1999; Stern 1983, 119–20; 1997a, 25; 2001, 461–62; Lipschits 2001). The lack of substantial finds prevented scholars from discussing archaeological details, such as town planning (e.g., Stern 1997a, 25; 2001, 461–62). The dearth of finds also attracted several explanations (e.g., Stern 1983; 2001, 461–62; Lipschits 2001), including suggestions that the houses in this period were built outside existing settlements, that the Persian period strata were destroyed by later activities, and that the tells housed only palaces.

These suggestions, even if they account for part of the problem, are insufficient to explain the phenomenon (as observed already by Stern 1983, 120), as the dramatic decrease in remains was much more significant in the highlands (Lipschits 2001, 46–47; Stern 2001, 462, 466). The finds from the same period were relatively numerous in the coastal plain, and this seems to disprove these suggestions, according to which the decrease in both the highlands and lowlands should have been to the same degree. Clearly, the finds attest to a much higher degree of human activity in the coastal plain.

In addition, much of our knowledge is based on data from salvage excavations, and these were conducted outside the main tells (below; see also Faust and Safrai 2005; in press a). Lipschits suggested that the dearth of architectural finds should be attributed to the Persian imperial policy in the highlands, which only allowed settlement in villages (2001). Such a policy is not attested anywhere, and only the scant remains in the highlands led Lipschits to suggest it. Furthermore, even if the Persian Empire had a policy that prevented the establishment of cities in Judea, houses leave the same kind of remains whether built in an urban or rural settlement. The relative lack of building remains (even in salvage excavations) cannot be fully attributed to any of the above.

The simplest explanation for the rarity of finds in Judah is that there was relatively little settlement in the Persian period. Settlement was simply sparse at the time, and the decline in settlement during the Persian period is therefore clearly well attested in planned excavations. While some of the above suggested explanations might increase the statistical significance of the settlements that have been found from the Persian period, we are still witnessing a phenomenon that resulted from the fact that settlements—especially large settlements that are best reflected in the planned excavations—were sparse at the time discussed here.

Hellenistic Period

Settlement gradually resumed in the Hellenistic period, mainly in its second half. According to Berlin (1997, 8), "throughout the third century B.C.E., the central hill country continued for the most part to be thinly populated ... Jerusalem continued to be the only city in Judea and the archaeological evidence shows it to have been small and materially rather poor throughout the third century." Settlement, however, grew significantly during the second century B.C.E. (Berlin 1997, 15, 16, 28; see also Smith 1990; Kloner 2003, 26). New settlements were established throughout the century, and "Jerusalem's population was now large enough to have expanded beyond the confines of the City of David to the southwestern hill" (Berlin 1997, 16).

Notably, if one wishes to attempt to quantify the data, we can use the New Encyclopedia of Archaeological Excavations in the Holy Land (Stern 1993b) as a general index for trends in this settlement sector to quantify the data.[14] Of

---

14. The issue will be discussed at length in Faust and Safrai in press a.

the sites, thirty to thirty-five yielded "architectural remains" from the late Iron II Judah, while only some thirteen sites yielded such remains from the Persian period.[15] There is not only a decrease in the number of sites, but most of the sites in which Persian period remains were revealed were much smaller in scale than their predecessors. The figure climbs again to approximately thirty-five when examining Hellenistic sites. The "quantified" data exhibit the decline observed above in the Persian period.

SALVAGE EXCAVATIONS

As of 2005, well over three thousand salvage excavations had been carried out in the modern state of Israel. However, until recently no systematic attempt had been conducted to use this large database. In the last couple of years Zeev Safrai and I carried out a systematic study of all published data from these excavations (e.g., Faust and Safrai 2005; 2008; in press a; in press b). The data from salvage excavations is detailed enough for us to observe settlement patterns and dynamics. With the exception of the Rosh Haʿayin-Shoham-Modiin region, thirty salvage excavations[16] from greater Judea reported findings[17] from the Iron Age II.[18] Only seventeen excavations reported finds from the Persian period,[19] and thirty had relevant finds from the Hellenistic period. The data from the salvage excavations database is similar to that of the planned excavations and surveys; they both show a significant decline after the Iron Age and recovery in the Hellenistic period.[20]

---

15. This has nothing to do with the question of settlement continuity, which should be examined on a site by site basis (see ch. 2; Faust 2003b; Faust and Safrai 2005; in press a).

16. In reality, there were probably more Iron Age II sites that were excavated; several sites were reported as Iron Age IIC, and others were reported as Iron Age, with no subdivision. I did not count these when using the database because I preferred to err on the side of caution.

17. Including what was defined as architectural remains and pottery finds.

18. I refer only to the database that includes information from *Hadashot Arkheologiyot*, as information from other sources is biased for statistical purposes (Faust and Safrai 2005; in press a).

19. This has nothing to do with the question of settlement continuity, which should be examined on a site by site basis (see ch. 2; Faust 2003b; Faust and Safrai 2005; in press a).

20. The data from the Rosh Ha'ayin-Shoahm-Modiin region (*Hadashot Arkheologiyot* database only) are completely different. Here, the number of excavations increases from the Iron Age (8), through the Persian period (14) to the Hellenistic period (29),showing a different pattern. The farmsteads phenomenon mentioned in ch. 2 occurred in part of this area. It is likely that the data regarding the Hellenistic period are comprised of two separate settlement phenomena, before and after the Hasmonean expansion, hence artificially increasing the figure. This is true

Similar results can be obtained by examining the relative importance of the region during the various periods. This can be done by examining the importance of the region of Judea in relation to the rest of the country during each period. We have calculated the percentage of the sites[21] that existed in Judea, out of the total number of sites that existed in each relevant period. Hence, during the Iron Age, the relative importance of the region was almost 27 percent (i.e., almost twenty-seven percent of the salvage excavations from the entire country were conducted in the area defined as greater Judea). During the Persian period,[22] the relative importance of the region was sixteen percent, and during the Hellenistic period it was twenty-five percent.

The data from salvage excavations clearly show a decline in the Persian period and recovery in the Hellenistic period, both in terms of number of sites and of the relative importance of the region.

A Note on Regional Variation

Almost every region in Judea proper[23] reported a decline in the Persian period, followed by a recovery in the Hellenistic period. Still, differences between the regions were observed. Ofer (1993b, 2, 132), for example, reported that according to his survey in northern Judah (north of Beth-Zur) there were only minor changes at the transition to the Persian period (and even an increase in settlement during this period). I will return to the significance of the data (from surveys) later, but this should not obliterate the importance of the general pattern—even if not in all of Judah, settlement in the Persian period was much smaller than that of both the Iron Age and the Hellenistic period.

As far as the region of Benjamin is concerned, there is a discrepancy between the results of the surveys and the results of the excavations. The surveys reported a great decline (see also Magen 1994, 5; 2004, 2; Gibson 1996, 17*), while the planned excavations reported continuity for some time after the fall of Jerusa-

---

regarding the data from surveys as well, but I do not wish to go into detailed discussion of settlement processes in the late Hellenistic period, which are well beyond the scope of this volume.

21. Including all types of finds, from the whole territory of Judea as defined in the database (Faust and Safrai in press a).

22. Since all of Judea is included in these statistics, there is a bias toward the Persian period because the statistics include the region of Rosh Ha-ayin-Shoham-Modiin. This strengthens the significance of the trends, and the decline in the Persian period in comparison to both periods is highlighted.

23. Not including the Rosh Ha'ayin-Shoham-Modiin region, which was not part of Judah during the Iron Age.

lem (e.g., Malamat 1950; Stern 1983, 120; 2001, 321–23). Lipschits attempted to correct the surveys to match the data from the excavations (e.g., 1999, 180–84; 2003b, 280; 2005, 245–48). However, it is possible that the major centers (i.e., the sites that were excavated in planned excavations) "behaved" differently than the rural sites which were reported in the surveys. The data from salvage excavations (ch. 2) was in accordance with the data from surveys, further supporting this suggestion. The issue will be discussed in length in ch. 9.

Settlement Dynamics: An Intermediate Summary

The late Iron Age was a period of relative prosperity as far as settlement was concerned. The surveys reported 586 sites from this period. The number of Persian period sites decreased dramatically. At the peak of the Persian period, the number of sites was 216, that is, about 35 percent of the late Iron Age.[24] These settlements were relatively small and rural in nature. Jerusalem was the only "real" center, and even it was quite small (see more below). Later, settlement grew again, reaching 510 sites during the height of the Hellenistic period, and the settlement was comparable to that of the Iron Age.

Similar trends were observed in other data. As far as settlement dynamics are concerned, the Persian period was in the shadow of the Iron Age and the Hellenistic periods. Notably, the figures regarding the Persian period represent the peak of settlement within two hundred years, and during most of this era the number of settlements was significantly lower. Before examining the significance of these trends, the next section will discuss demographic changes.

Demographic Trends

Many studies have attempted to count the population of ancient Israel in various periods (e.g., Broshi 1979; Broshi and Finkelstein 1992; Broshi and Gophna 1984; 1986). However, counting ancient populations is a dangerous endeavor. Even calculating the number of inhabitants of a single site is unreliable and results in a margin of error of some 400 percent (Postgate 1994; see also Faust 2005b). Therefore, it is almost impossible to study an entire region where there are numerous unknown variables. The specific figures are quite meaningless. What can be studied, and even this very cautiously, is demographic trends.

---

24. It is doubted whether all the Persian period sites coexisted even during the height of the Persian period.

The periods under examination here did have their share of demographic studies. The demography of the Iron Age (throughout the country) was studied in detail by Broshi and Finkelstein (1992; see also Finkelstein 1993a; see additional studies below), as was the demography of Persian period Judah.

Carter (1999, 201–2), in his detailed study of Persian Yehud, concluded that the population of Persian Yehud was 13,350 people in the early Persian period (his Persian period I), and it grew to some 20,650 in the later Persian period (his Persian II period). Meyers and Meyers (1994, 282) reached similar conclusions. They calculated a population of 10,850 people in the Persian I period, and estimated that this was about one-third of the population of the late Iron Age. It should be noted that their estimation of the Iron Age was based to a large extent on their interpretation of literary sources, not on firm archaeological data. Carter (1999, 246–47) estimated the Iron Age population in the areas that later encompassed Persian Yehud as 60,000–68,500 people (based on previous studies), also concluding that the population of the Persian period was about one-third of these figures (during the peak of the Persian II period; settlement in the Persian I period was one-fifth of the population of the Iron Age). Carter only examined the reality in the area that was part of the Persian Yehud province, excluding the Shephelah, the Judean Desert, and so on, from his calculations. If these regions were included, the demographic decrease would be even larger because these regions were devastated at the end of the Iron Age. While comparing only the limited area of Yehud is legitimate—after all, Carter's study focused on the Persian period—to understand the demographic processes that occurred from the Late Iron Age to the Hellenistic period, the entire territory of the Iron Age kingdom of Judah should be examined. This is because when examining demographic changes from the Iron Age onward, the fate of the entire population of Judah is of importance, and all Judah's territories should be investigated. For such an enterprise, Carter's figures underestimate the Persian period decline.

The most detailed attempt to calculate the population of ancient Judah in the Persian period was conducted by Lipschits (2003a; 2003b; 2005). Lipschits concluded that the population of Judah in the seventh century was 108,000, and the population of Yehud in the Persian period was 30,125 (i.e., about 28 percent of the population of Iron Age Judah; 2003a, 364; 2003b, 304; 2005, 270).

Lipschits's demographic study is problematic. For example, he did not compare the same regions in all periods. The Persian period's demographic estimation did not include regions that were outside the Yehud province; however, these regions were included in his Iron Age calculations. Therefore, the comparison is misleading, and the population of the Persian period should be increased (see below for corrections, based on his own data). Lipschits's figures, on the other hand, err in favor of the Persian period for many reasons.

1. A number of Iron Age sites were not included, decreasing the relative importance of the period. For example, Lipschits correctly regarded the city of Jerusalem as a large metropolis (about a 1,000 dunams following Barkay 1989; Lipschits 2003a, 361–63), but failed to take into account the large hinterland, which included large towns and centers such as el-Burj (some 40 dunams; De Groot and Greenhut 1994), Moza (Greenhut and De Groot 2009),[25] and others, as well as hundreds of farmsteads (e.g., Kloner 2001a; Faust 2007a).[26] The demographic reality in the Iron Age was thus underestimated.

2. Lipschits also exaggerated the demography of the Persian period because he used the same coefficient to study the populations of the Iron Age and the Persian period. While rural settlements comprised the majority of settlement during the Iron Age and the Hellenistic period, during these periods there were many large and more crowded settlements. The situation during the Persian period was different, and this should have been taken into account. Lipschits did not take into account the fact that most of the sites were small and rural in nature (see also Carter 1999, 249), and their density was therefore impossible to calculate according to "typical" coefficients (although Lipschits is aware of this shortcoming e.g., Lipschits 2003b, 294; 2005, 261). Rural sites are usually much less crowded.[27] Farmsteads, or isolated buildings, com-

---

25. In the past, the site's size was estimated at 100 dunams (De Groot and Greenhut 1994). Today, however, the excavators have a different interpretation, suggesting that the site was only about 10–15 dunams (Greenhut and De Groot 2009, 222). This figure should still be taken into account and added to Lipschits's calculations.

26. Lipschits (2003a, 361–62) stated that ninety percent of the settled area in Jerusalem was within the city-walls, making it clear that he did not calculate the many settlements in the city's vicinity.

27. E.g., Portugali 1988, 29; Grossman 1994, 1, 2; Efrat 1995, 57; see also Bunimovitz 1990, 152; Finkelstein 1988, 67–68; and Gophna and Portugali 1988, 15, when they compare urban to non-urban sites.

Some studies indicated that in "pre-modern" eras in the land of Israel, rural sites were crowded (e.g., Biger and Grossman 1993). This, however, seems to be the exception rather than the rule, and could result from specific political conditions (at times, large rural sites tended to be less dense than their smaller counterparts, e.g., Gophna and Portugali 1988, 13, 14; it is possible that the sites studied by Biger and Grossman fall into this category). It should be noted that there could be cultural variation regarding density in different types of sites, but when one examines the reality in Iron Age villages, the low density in relation to cities is obvious. For example, compare Bet Arye (Riklin 1997) and Kh. Jamain (Dar 1986) to the well known plans of Tell Beit Mirsim, Beersheba, etc. Kh. Jarish also seems to have been less crowded (e.g., Amit 1989–90b; contra 'Ofer 1993b).

posed an important part of the Persian period's small sites and were inhabited by a limited number of people (probably an extended family; cf. Safrai 1998, 38; Faust 2003c).

3. Lipschits compared the data of the entire Persian period, which was much longer than the seventh century.[28] It is likely that not all the sites existed contemporaneously, which reduces the figure even further.

The contrast between the treatment of the Iron Age, when many settlements were not taken into account, to the Persian period, when the population was exaggerated, exemplify the problems with the figures presented above. The actual demographic decrease in the Persian period in comparison with the Iron Age was therefore much larger then envisaged by Lipschits (more below).

IRON AGE AND PERSIAN PERIOD DEMOGRAPHY

Carter estimated the population during the height of the Persian period as being one-third of the population of the Iron Age (and one-fifth during the beginning of the period). Lipschits's figures put the Persian period at less than twenty-eight percent of that of the Iron Age, but since he compared a small Persian Yehud to the larger Iron Age Judah, his figures are also off and the relative importance of the Persian period should be increased. Based on Lipschits's own figures (2003a, 356–64, tables 1–3; 2005, 258–71, tables 4.1–4.3) we should add 8,375 people, putting the population of the Persian period at 35 percent of the Iron Age. Both Carter and Lipschits identified similar trends in demography. While both estimations favor the Persian period, I will still use their figures, in order to err on the side of caution.

Clearly, when two-thirds of the population disappears, one must acknowledge not only a major demographic collapse (contra Barstad 1996; Lipschits 2003b; 2005), but also a social and cultural one (chs. 4 and 7). Such a large decrease in population is sufficient to disprove the theory that life for most people continued with no changes in the Neo-Babylonian period. But there is more to it than that. An interpretation of these figures as comprising a decrease to one third of the population is simply wrong.

---

28. Even the data from Jerusalem's environments reflect mainly the late Iron Age, and not the entire Iron Age II (contra Lipschits 2003b: 250–51, n. 45). On this, see Kloner 2003: 20; Finkelstein 1994: 174 Faust 2005b; 2007a; 2008b).

The decline was much larger than can be seen by a quick glance at those figures (we refer mainly to the general trends of course). This brings us to the next issue.[29]

METHODOLOGY: ANALYZING THE TRENDS

The one-third estimation of Judah's Persian period population in relation to the Iron Age will be used as the point of departure; however, this section will attempt to show that understanding the data as indicating a decrease to 30 percent is not only wrong, but even impossible. Our aim is to show that such a simple analysis of the data is misleading, and the decrease from the Iron Age to the Persian period was much larger than sixty-five to sixty-seven percent as interpreted by Lipschits.[30] Notably, the same analysis that is conducted below in relation to demography is applicable for the discussion of settlement dynamics and vice versa.[31]

The dates in the following graphs are also basically taken from Lipschits, who referred (in the Iron Age) to the seventh century (our point of departure), and suggested that the peak of the Persian period was during the fifth century (e.g., Lipschits 2003b, 194, 292; 2005, 166; 259; see also 363 and the title of his 2003a paper). The date for the Hellenistic period was randomly chosen, as it was not discussed by Lipschits. The dates are not necessarily accurate (see below) and are given as a general guide only. More detailed chronology will be discussed later. Since the purpose of the present section is methodological, the exact dates are of no importance.

---

29. The demographic reality in the Hellenistic period did not receive much attention by these scholars, and since I find the exercise to be futile, I will not attempt it either. The following discussion on settlement and demographic dynamics will be based on the trends observed in the number and size of settlements, and not on a new reconstruction of this period's demography (it should also be noted that constructing my own estimation might be accused of being biased due to the issue at hand—this is why I prefer to stick to existing figures although I showed them to be biased).

30. Carter identified a decline by 80 percent in the early Persian period. Even if Carter's reasoning can be questioned (for a critique critics on his methods, see Lipschits 2003a) his logic is correct.

31. The following discussion will concentrate on demography, although from time to time I will refer also to settlement changes. The trends in both are similar, and this makes the interchange in terminology legitimate. Theoretically, of course, demography and settlement can behave in a different manner, but this does not seem to be the case here.

We have seen that according to Lipschits (e.g., 2003a, 364; 2003b, 292–305; 2005, 267–71; see above) and Carter (1999, 201–2) the Persian period's population was about 33 to 35 percent of that of the Iron Age. Assuming that the demography of the Hellenistic period was somewhat similar to that of the later Iron Age (based on the data from settlement dynamics, above, this seems to be the case; the demography of the Hellenistic period has not yet been studied), then the demographic trends are apparently represented in Graph 1.

Graph 1 represents a decrease to thirty-five percent in the Persian period,[32] which is a major decline by all standards. This graph, however, is false. Each of the three "points" on the graph, which is based on accumulating all the available data on settlements and occupations, represents the demographic peak of each period—the time in which settlement and demography was at its climax and all (or at least most) settlement existed. While important for all three periods, this has grave consequences for the demography of the Persian period. In the current graph, 35 percent represents the nadir of the Persian period while, in reality, it should represent the peak.[33] The vast majority of the Persian period should actually be below this point.[34]

If the peak of the Persian period was during the fifth century (as postulated by Lipschits), Graph 2 would more accurately represent the demographic trends of the periods discussed.

The exact nadir is of course, a mere guess, but the trends are clear. If the peak of the Persian period was during the fifth century, then the decrease after the Iron Age was more significant than 65 percent. The Persian period peak came only after a nadir, and in this scenario, the peak was followed by another nadir. Only then did demographic growth begin toward the Hellenistic period. If Graph 2 is correct, then according to Lipschits's demographic estimations, the decline after the Iron Age was sharper than he claims.

---

32. That this line of thinking governed some past reconstructions is apparent in Lipschits's work. He (2003a, 349; 2003b, 279–80; 2005, 246–47) explicitly claimed that the find from the Persian period in Benjamin represented the nadir of settlement in the period, rather than the peak. He wrote that "… the finds of the Persian period discovered in the survey reflect this low point, rather than a peak in settlement activity or a stage of rebuilding." This is of course impossible. Whatever one thinks of the date of the peak, the Persian period finds represent it (or, in case not all the sites were contemporaneous, then the peak was even lower than that). See more below.

33. If this graph was correct, then the demographic peak of the Persian period was not some thirty-five percent of that of the Iron Age, but rather more than sixty percent.

34. The degree to which the graph goes below this point is a mere estimation, and the figures used might be far from accurate.

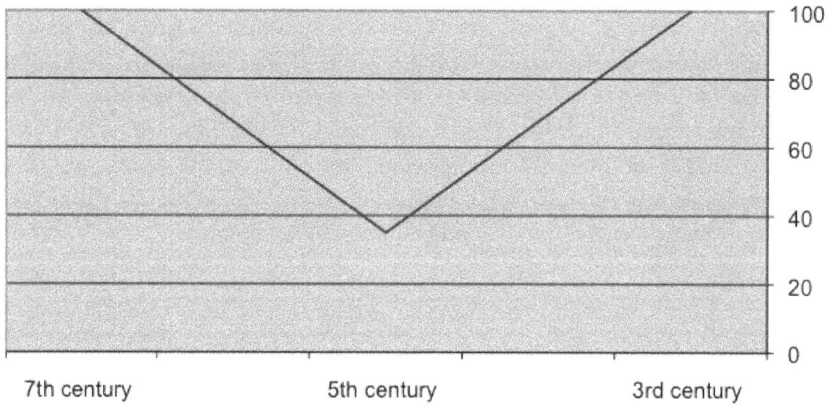

Graph 1. Demographic trends from the seventh to the third centuries B.C.E., with the demographic peak of the Persian period represented as a nadir.

There are, however, several problems with this suggestion. Demographic trends are long-term processes. While various events can have great impact on demographic trends, we cannot "invent" such episodes. Graph 2 has too many unexplained ups and downs, which are are not based on any data on the demographics of the region.[35]

Graphs 3 and 4 present two alternative scenarios. The settlement peak could have been either at the beginning of the Persian period, or toward its end. Graph 3 locates the thirty-five percent peak at the first stage of the period.

Graph 3 is more logical than Graph 2 in terms of long-term processes. There is a sharp decline in the transition from the Iron Age to the Persian period. The decline continues through most of the Persian period, although the rate of decline decreases (assuming the same rate of decline would leave the end of the Persian period almost entirely unpopulated). A quick and significant population increase starts at some point toward the end of the period, until the peak of the Hellenistic period.

Graph 4 shows a demographic peak toward the end of the Persian period.

There is a sharp decline at the end of the Iron Age until the Persian period. This decline is followed by a gradual increase in settlement until the end of the Persian period (where the thirty-five percent peak is represented), and finally settlement/demography intensifies in the Hellenistic period.

---

35. Naturally, there were demographic/settlement fluctuations within the Persian period. However, these were on a small scale in comparison to the relatively long-term processes discussed here. It is likely that the peak of the Persian period was part of such long-term processes, and not part of small-scale fluctuations.

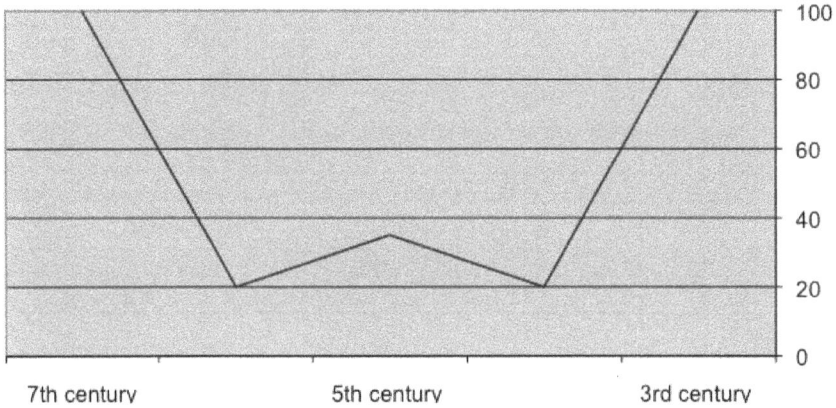

Graph 2. Demographic trends from the seventh to the third centuries B.C.E., with the fifth century as the peak of Persian period settlement.

How do we choose which graph best represents the reality of the time? As mentioned earlier, the last two graphs (Graphs 3 and 4) are more reasonable than the Graph 2 (above), but is there a way to chose between them?

When examined within the historical background of the period, it is obvious that there is a big advantage to the Graph 4. We do not know of any reason for a huge demographic decline in the Persian period, let alone toward the Hellenistic period. On the contrary, we do know of a major crisis at the beginning of the sixth century B.C.E. The Babylonian conquests of the region brought about settlement instability and demographic decline that is acknowledged not only by supporters of the traditional view of this period (e.g., Stern 2001; Mazar 1992; Stager and King 2001, and many others), but also by supporters of the continuity theory (e.g., Barstad 1996; 2003; Lipschits 2003a; 2003b; 2005). Although the latter greatly underestimate the importance of the demographic changes, they still acknowledge them. We therefore have "positive" and "negative" evidence that support a decline at the beginning of the Persian period, and a gradual recovery during this period (and not vice-versa). The Babylonian conquests in the early-sixth century serve as "positive" historical evidence, and the lack of evidence for significant demographic catastrophe in the later Persian period act as "negative" evidence to support Graph 4.

Another advantage of Graph 4 lies in the general nature of population increase and decrease. Graphs 3 and 4 both show gradual and abrupt demographic changes, but those in Graph 4 are more logical. Graph 3 involves gradual decline and a relatively abrupt increase, whereas Graph 4 depicts an abrupt decline and gradual increase. While decline can be either abrupt or gradual, there are some limitations on the possible speed of population increase. Unless some-

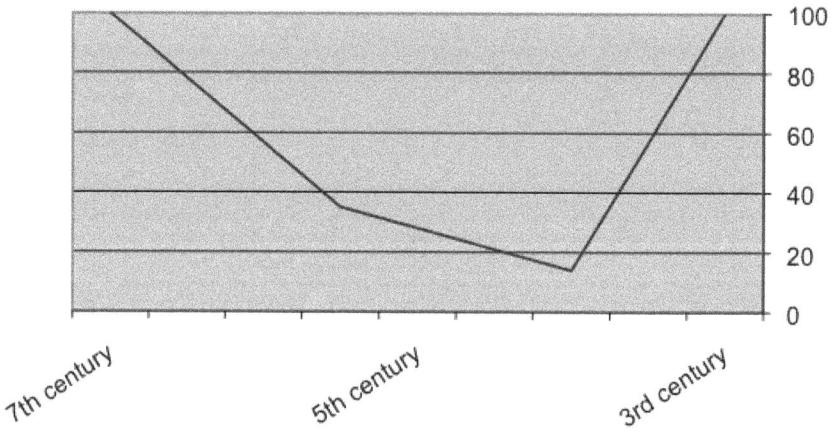

Graph 3. Demographic trends from the seventh to the third centuries B.C.E., with the demographic peak of the Persian period represented in the sixth century B.C.E.

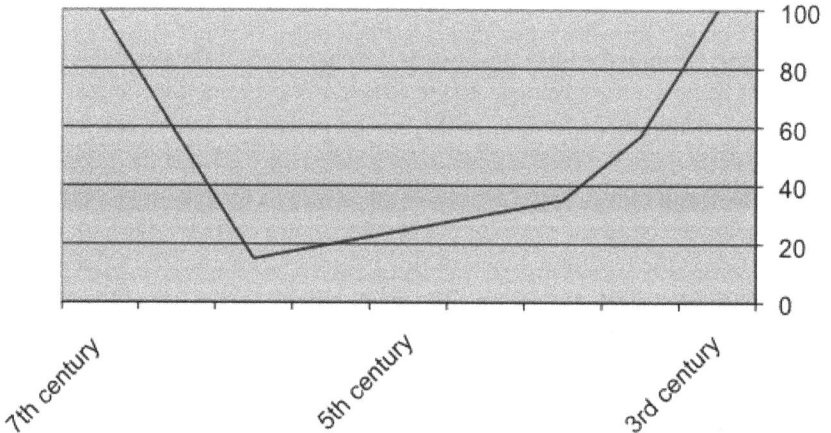

Graph 4. Demographic trends from the seventh to third centuries B.C.E., with the demographic peak of the Persian period represented in the fourth century.

one assumes that there was a large influx of people to the region in the Hellenistic period, population growth must have been gradual. Since there is no reason to suspect large-scale migration, an abrupt increase in population is not feasible. This makes Graph 3 less likely, and points again toward Graph 4 as the only viable possibility.

Clearly, Graph 4 better represents demographic trends at the time discussed here. Similar trends of gradual increase were presented by scholars like Carter

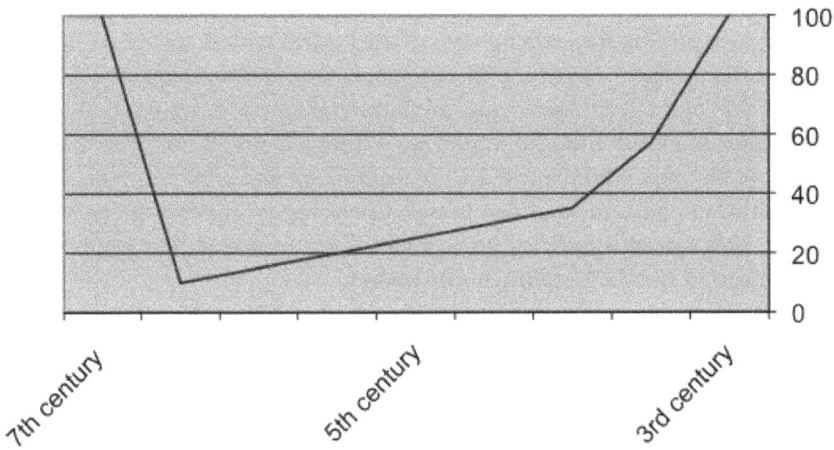

Graph 5. Demographic trends from the seventh to third centuries B.C.E., acknowledging the decline in the sixth century B.C.E. and the Persian period demographic peak is represented in the fourth century B.C.E.

(1999), Stern (2001, 581), Kloner (2003, 25–26), Berlin (1997) and Meyers and Meyers (1994).[36] Still, we need to slightly adjust our picture. Since the Babylonian conquests are the reason for the decline, the decline should not be viewed as so gradual, encompassing the entire century. Graph 5 more accurately reflects the reality.

In light of the fact that previous studies underestimated Iron Age settlement, and overestimated Persian period settlement, it is possible that the decline was even more severe. As mentioned, the figures only serve as an estimation, but Graph 5 best suits the demographic reality of the period.

DEMOGRAPHIC TRENDS: A SUMMARY

The demographic studies by Carter and Lipschits err in favor of the Persian period, but even they indicate that during the peak of this period, which was

---

36. Contra Lipschits (2003a; 2003b; 2005). Lipschits presented contrasting estimations regarding the trends during the Persian period. In some places he suggested that the fifth century was the peak of the Persian period, but in others he wrote that the decrease from the Iron Age to the Persian period was gradual and hence (though he did not realize it) placed the peak at the period's first day (see Oded and Faust 2006; see also ch. 8). Both his (contrasting) estimations are wrong, and the peak was toward the end of the Persian period. Interestingly, it appears that even in the coastal plain the recovery was gradual (Shalev 2009, and references).

probably toward its end, the population was only about one-third of that of the Iron Age. Regarding the earlier phases of the Persian period, it appears that one has to accept Carter's estimation that the population was only about twenty percent of that of the Iron Age. These estimations allow us to appreciate the crisis that occurred by the end of the Iron Age—after all, after a few generations of recovery, the population reached 20 percent or so, and after 250 years it only reached 33–35 percent (and this is even according estimations given by Lipschits). This carries significant implications for our understanding of both the Persian period and the Neo-Babylonian period.

IMPLICATIONS FOR THE STUDY OF THE PERSIAN PERIOD

In the past, scholars like Watzinger (1935; quoted by Stern 1983, 119) claimed that urban life ceased during the Persian period. Kenyon (1965) also wrote,

> the low ebb of civilization in Palestine, which lasts for the next three centuries or so, makes it difficult for archaeology to recover any evidence. Town life suffered a severe setback, and such reduced settlements as there were, with little in the way of substantial buildings, were most likely obliterated by later building operations (296–97).

She added,

> The great cities of the Israelite period therefore play little part in the life of the country under the Babylonians and the succeeding Persian empire. The slight glimpses we get of the culture of Palestine come largely from unimportant sites. It is perhaps significant that most of them come from the coastal belt (302).

Albright also claimed that "to judge from the results of excavations, the resettlement of Judah was a slow process, and it was not until the third century B.C. that the country recovered anything like its old density of population" (1960b, 142; cf. also Fritz 1997, 24). Admittedly, some of these evaluations were exaggerated. Urban life prospered in some regions, mainly in the coastal plain (see also Berlin 1997, 4).[37] While such gloomy estimations might not be an accurate reflection of the reality in the entire region, they are surely accurate regarding some areas. Even Stern, whose seminal studies to a large extent saved the study of the Persian

---

37. As noted above, even in this region recovery was gradual, and started only in the fifth century B.C.E. (Shalev 2009, and additional references).

period from oblivion, admitted that there was a great decline (although not all over the country), and the available explanations (above) were not sufficient to explain the lack of finds in the region (e.g., 1983, 120).[38]

As far as Judea was concerned, the above quotes represent the bleak reality in the region (see now also Finkelstein 2010, 43–46). A real recovery did not take place before the Hellenistic period, and the entire Persian period was only a shadow of the Iron Age. Even in regions in which many settlements existed in the Persian period, such as northern Judah, settlements were smaller and less dense than in the Iron Age (see more below).[39] This has important implications for our understanding of the long-term processes the region experienced (ch. 7).

A Note on Regions Outside Judah

Processes of collapse and recovery took place in other parts of the land of Israel following the Assyrian and Babylonian conquests, but a detailed discussion is beyond the scope of the present chapter (see ch. 7). Both the extent of collapse and the rate of recovery should be examined within the specific context of each region. For example, we have seen that both urban and rural settlements in the coastal plain flourished in the Persian period, as is evident by both planned and salvage excavations (e.g., Stern 1983, 120; 2001, 385–422, 462; Lipschits 2001). This supports Stern's claim that past estimations regarding the extent of the decline in the Persian period were exaggerated and that the decline did not affect the entire country to the same extent (1983, 120). Here, I would only like to point to this direction, and to note that "collapse" and "post-collapse" (ch. 7) should be taken into consideration when discussing the Assyrian, Babylonian, and Persian periods throughout the country (see more in the summary).

Implications for the Debate over the sixth Century b.c.e.

Our analysis shows that the decline in the sixth century b.c.e. must have been drastic—to a greater extent than the supporters of the continuity theory acknowledge. These theorists erred partially because they assumed that the peak of the

---

38. Regarding Judah, Stern (1983, 120) states that the northern Judah and the region of Benjamin fared better than others, but all the examples he brings are of sites in Benjamin (and many of those sites did not exist throughout the Persian period). Both regions will be discussed in more detail (below).

39. The estimation that Yehud province was poor is accepted by many today (e.g., Carter 1999, 285; Berlin 1997; Schniedewind 2004, 168–70).

Persian period was the nadir, that is, they followed Graph 1 (above), and partially because of their basic assumptions on the nature of this period; after all, even the first graph does not really support the continuity theory.

The problematic foundations of the continuity school are attested by the archaeological evidence discussed in the previous chapters, for example, its inability to find real settlement in the sixth century despite the large database, its failure to address evidence for social and cultural break during this century, and the lack of Greek pottery that showed that the entire region was "wiped off" the map of Mediterranean trade. Here we have seen that the mere figures used by supporters of this school prove them wrong and force us to realize that the decline between the Iron Age and the Persian period was great, even if the figures they use were correct (and they are not).

The processes observed above are quite straightforward. It is possible that the nadir of the sixth century was not as low as presented in the graph (approximately ten percent), and was somewhat higher—maybe even reaching twenty percent. This is still a huge decline. Furthermore, when taking into account the above considerations, we must concur with Carter (1999, 201–2), and estimate that the peak of the Persian I period could not have been more than twenty percent of that of the Iron Age. The reality in the sixth century was probably closer to ten percent, as shown in the graph. Still, even the improbably high figure of twenty percent completely disproves the minimalist stance. Similar estimates were recently suggested by Liverani (2005, 195–96), who referred to a decline of 85 to 95 percent.

THE "MECHANISMS" OF DEMOGRAPHIC DECLINE

What caused such a great decline? Surely the Babylonians could not have exiled the population of Judah almost in its entirety. Most scholars who addressed the issue, and especially those who support the continuity theory, paid a great deal of attention to exile[40] as a possible mechanism for population decline following the Babylonian campaigns.[41] They questioned whether it was possible that the entire population of Judah was exiled and concluded that it was impossible. Although such a conclusion requires more systematic study, these scholars are probably right in this observation. As a consequence, they concluded that the population

---

40. Their interest in the exile derived from their interest in the issue of authorship of biblical texts.

41. Barstad 1996, 18, 30, 33–34, 37–38, 40, 42–43, 62–63, 68, 79–80; 2003, 3, 14; Lipschits 2003b, 219; 2005, 187; see already Torrey 1910 [1970]; ch. 8.

decrease was much smaller than originally thought, and from these views came the emergence of the continuity theory.

It should be stressed that the mechanisms which decreased the population in Judah involved not only deportations to Mesopotamia, but also included death from wars, epidemics and famine (during the war, and following it), executions following sieges, and people who fled to other regions (and the Babylonian imperial policy).[42]

Death. The death toll in wars in antiquity was high. With the lack of any real means of evacuation of the wounded, effective medicine, and sterile conditions, many wounds ended in death (for the treatment of wounds in the Greco-Roman world, see Salazar 2000). This was much more so during (and after) siege warfare. The death toll among the defenders (if they lost) was great (cf. Eph'al 1996, 37–39; Kern 1999), and Judah lost the war with Babylon.

Famine and Epidemics. War, especially during siege (and afterward, see below), led to famine among the besieged population, and hence a growing death rate (Ephal 1996, 57–64; cf. also 2 Kgs 6:28–29; Lam 2:20; 4:10). The poor conditions in the besieged cities, where dead were lying around, resulted also in the spread of epidemics that accelerated the rate of death enormously (Ephal 1996, 64–65).

Executions. Following the war, the conquerors executed many survivors, especially members of the royalty, military commanders, and leaders (e.g., Kern 1999, 69–71, 73, 75). This can be seen, for example, in the Lachish reliefs (uncovered at Sennacherib's palace at Ninveh), which depict scenes of the conquest of the city of Lachish in 701 b.c.e. (e.g., Barnett 1958; Ussishkin 1982). While executions may seem unnecessary, and perhaps even be attributed to the sadistic nature of one ruler or the other, this does not seem to be the case. Brutality and executions following the fall of a besieged city was a deliberate and calculated policy. Saggs (1984, 248) explained that in order to maintain stability in the region, the Assyrians had to "persuade" their potential foes or rebels that it would be futile to oppose Assyria. This was done by demonstrating an overwhelming might, as well as through using propaganda. Demonstration of power, including punishment of offenders, was consciously directed not only toward those who suffered, "but also upon those who heard of it at a distance." Saggs wrote, "the Assyrian king, in perpetrating actions—sometimes atrocities— ... put the enemies into panic. ... This represented a conscious use by the Assyrians of terrorism not for sadistic

---

42. See Weinberg 1969, 84; Stern 2001, 323; Jamieson-Drake 1991, 75, 145–47; Schniedewind 2004, 143.

purposes, but for psychological warfare." Executions, therefore, were another mean for demographic decline.

Death Amid the Ruins. All the above made famine and epidemics ever worse, leading to more and more death even after the war (and the subsequent executions) had ended. While the corpses increased epidemics, the sacking by the conquering army of all the available food increased famine (see Wiseman 1989, 51; Van Creveld 2004, 37; Erdkamp 1998, 13; see also Keegan 1993, 302; Bellamy 1990, 11). The collapse of the administration and the lack of organization in production made the famine worse (e.g., Jamieson–Drake 1991, 145–47; cf. Tainter 2000, 12; for the effect on the countryside, see also Kern 1999, 73).

Archaeological Evidence of Death. The archaeological evidence supports a great decline. The overall death toll among the population was great. A hint of this reality can be seen by the thousands of burials unearthed at Lachish and Ashdod. At both sites mass burials, probably dated to the eighth century B.C.E., were unearthed (Eph'al 1997, 37–38).

At Ashdod in locus 1151 alone, remains of 2,434 human beings were unearthed, 22.1 percent of whom (i.e., 538 individuals) were younger than 15 years at the time of death. In another locus (1114) the remains of 376 people were found; the majority of the dead were below the age of 15. In other loci (1115, 1113, 1006), additional skeletons were found (about 61–62 individuals), many of whom had been beheaded (Eph'al 1997, 37; Hass 1971, 212–14). Dothan (1971, 21) attributed the massacre to Sargon's conquest of the city in the late-eighth century. Since the entire area of the city was not excavated, it is possible that more burials are still below ground. However, the figures present us with the horrible outcomes of the siege(s) and the executions that followed. Eph'al noted that those whose heads were cut off were usually buried separately. It is likely that they were executed after the war ended (1997, 37, n. 67).

At Lachish, too, mass burials were discovered in caves during the excavations in the 1930s (Eph'al 1997, 37–38). Remains of more than 1,500 individuals were thrown into the caves (numbered 107, 108, 116, 120), probably as result of a massacre following the conquest of the city by Sennacherib (Ussishkin 1982, 56–58; though other wars cannot be ruled out, e.g., the destruction of the Late Bronze Age city; Eph'al 1997; 38). It is also likely that not all the dead were unearthed, but the above figure is sufficient to present us with the horrible outcomes of the war. While the data relate to the Assyrian conquest of the cities discussed, the fate of the defenders was probably the same in other epochs. Clearly, death in the war (and following it) was a major cause for population decrease.

Notably, death in the wars and immediately afterward was not the only means of demographic decline, and this was followed by other processes.

Insecurity. Following the war and as part of its consequences, security was shattered. The conquering army could do as it pleased, killing, robbing property, and raping women (e.g., Kern 1999, 81; see also throughout this section of Kern's book), and this resulted with a period of lawlessness. Gangs, composed of some of the survivors and outsiders, roamed the area (Tainter 1999, 1023). Thus, insecurity led to more death, famine, and eventually, additional migration.

Refugees Fleeing the Region. The devastation of cities and villages led to a process of mass migration. Many of the survivors fled the region and migrated to safer and more hospitable places (for the period under discussion, see, e.g., Jer 41–44).

Exile. Exile was practiced by many empires, including the Assyrians and Babylonians (Oded 1979; see also Smith 1989, 29–31; Kuhrt 1993, 532–34). The exiled included the elite, craftsmen, and more, hence this contributed to demoralization, instability, and lack of organization (even beyond the exile's mere demographic importance).

In summary, many factors—famine, epidemics, instability, and more—contributed greatly to the population decrease. Deportations to Mesopotamia were only one mechanism—probably not the most important one demographically—that led to the great demographic decline of the sixth century B.C.E.

REGIONAL VARIATION WITHIN JUDAH

Overall, although the area was divided between different political units after the Iron Age, the territories of the former kingdom of Judah behaved (demographically) quite uniformly. Almost all regions show a sharp decline that was followed by recovery. However, every micro-region had its own history, so a few comments are in order.

Benjamin

The region of Benjamin has been mentioned throughout this book and will be discussed at length in chapter 9, but a few words are in order in the present context. The region of Benjamin has received more attention than any other region, due to the suggestion that it was not destroyed in the sixth century by the Babylonians (e.g., Malamat 1950; Stern 1983, 120; 2001, 321–23; Lipschits 1999). Indeed, it appears that the collapse was somewhat less rapid in the area of Benjamin, but after some time the region did follow suit (for the decline of the central settlements, see also Lipschits 2003b, 272–79; 2005, 237–45). In contrast to the "planned" excavations, major decline is evident in the surveys and in the salvage excavations that represent mainly the rural sector. If the interpretation of the "planned" excavations did not result from biblical bias (Vanderhooft 2003a, 254, n. 18; see also the "archaeological" criticism of De Groot 2001, 79–80; ch. 9), then the discrepancy shows that the decline in the rural sector was immediate, while that of the urban sector was more gradual. This should not be a surprise as such a dichotomy is to be expected, and insecurity could easily lead to an immediate settlement decline in the rural sector. The specific history of the area of Benjamin—where the remaining administration under Gedaliah survived[43]— might also explain why some central sites did not immediately collapse but had a lengthier "dying" process (more than sites in other parts of Judah).

Northern Judah

Along with Benjamin, northern Judah is also a region that is discussed extensively by supporters of the continuity theory. Many Persian period sites have been reported in northern Judah, leading some to believe that the region (along with Benjamin) was not harmed by the Babylonians and continued to prosper in the sixth century.

However, an in-depth archeological analysis of settlement trends indicates that the area of northern Judah, like other parts of the kingdom, suffered a major blow by the Babylonians. The excavated central sites were destroyed or abandoned (Stern 2001, 324; see even Lipschits 2003b, 283–85, though the latter claims that the agent of destruction is unknown,[44] see ch. 1). The same is true of the rural sites; the vast majority of which did not exist in the Persian period (ch. 2). The disastrous consequences of the Babylonian campaigns are attested archaeologically throughout the region.

---

43. This is according to the biblical testimony (2 Kgs 25:22–26; Jer 40–43) that is usually accepted by scholars and is of special significance for supporters of the continuity school.

44. This region is of paramount importance for Lipschits's thesis, and the fact that the excavated sites were destroyed or abandoned seems to be at odds with the continuity school. Lipschits (2003b, 283; 2005, 250–51) therefore tries to claim that there was no real evidence of destruction, although he does admit when discussing the sites themselves that they were probably abandoned and not resettled until the late Persian period. Lipschits tried to discuss every site separately, and showed either that there was no evidence of actual destruction, or that it was not clear that the Babylonians were responsible for it (ch. 1). It is essential to stress that Beth-Zur, Hebron, and Kh. Rabud (the sites were discussed in Lipschits 2005, 250–51; see also ch. 1) did not continue to exist uninterruptedly into the Persian period. There was a clear break between the Iron Age and the Persian period (even if one accepts Lipschits's view that there was no destruction layer, and this is doubted). Every site exhibits this break, and the claims that the agent of destruction is unknown or that circumstances in every case are unclear (see also Blenkinsopp 2002b, 185) cannot "cover-up" the clear archaeological pattern. Furthermore, not only are the Babylonians the only logical candidate to cause the destruction, but when discussing the settlement and demography of the sixth century, does it matter who is responsible for the destruction? It is clear that the settlement in the Judean Hills suffered a major blow during the Babylonian conquest, and this is the important fact in the debate over continuity and demography.

Gradually, however, this region became the center of the Yehud province in the Persian period, and its population grew.[45] This was probably not only a result of natural growth, but was accompanied by migration from the devastated areas in the south, east, and even west—areas whose recovery was much slower. It is likely that some of the growth should be attributed to the returnees, but at present we cannot archaeologically estimate their demographic significance.

The relative importance of this region in the province of Yehud and its central location led to a faster recovery that attracted more people, and this escalated the process of demographic growth. This led to its relative prosperity in the Persian period. However, this prosperity was not a continuance of the settlement peak of the Iron Age; it was a result of a process of recovery and resettlement after a crisis.

The demographic reality in the region was discussed by Lipschits (2003a, 351–55; 2003b, 283–290; 2005, 250–258), and a few words on his study are in order, at least as a methodological cautionary tale. Lipschits, following Ofer (1993b, 2, 131–34), realized that settlement in this region during the Persian period was relatively significant, and quite similar to that of the Iron Age (and even larger than that of the Iron Age in terms of the number of sites). Due to this similarity, he assumed that there was no break between the two periods (e.g., 2003a, 353; 2003b, 285–291; 2005, 250–258).[46] Methodologically, however, this is wrong. The demographic peaks of the Early Bronze Age (e.g., Broshi and Gophna 1984) and of the Middle Bronze Age (e.g., Broshi and Gophna 1986) were similar, but we cannot conclude that there was no break in between them. The demographic decline at the end of the Early Bronze Age and during the Intermediate Bronze Age is well attested (Gophna 1992). The same is true here—the similarity between the seventh century and the Persian period (which is not complete, see even Lipschits 2003a, 354) does not say anything about the situation in the sixth century.[47]

---

45. Many of the Persian period settlements were new, and were not located on Iron Age sites. For such excavated sites, see the two sites near Kh. Kabar (Bruch 2006). For the survey, see below.

46. One should note that there were many differences in settlement patterns and distribution, of which Lipschits is aware (e.g., 2003b, 289; 2005, 256; despite speaking about continuity, the data themselves indicate a major change. See also Master 2007, 31).

47. In regard to Lipschits's analysis of Ofer's data, Master (2007, 31) wrote, "in some ways this conclusion reminds me of a photograph of the City of David taken from the Mt. of Olives. From the photograph alone one might be misled into believing that the walk between Silwan and the City of David is a gentle downhill slope. But to anyone who has walked that path, it is clear that between the two ridges is a deep gorge of the Kidron valley."

Furthermore, when the level of continuity between the two periods is examined at the site level, a major break is evident (cf. Faust 2003b; Faust and Safrai 2005; see also Master 2007, 31). We have seen that both planned and salvage excavations that represent all settlement sectors show this break (chs. 1 and 2). Lipschits, however, attempted to base his conclusions on the survey. Not only are surveys less reliable as a source of information for such studies (e.g., Faust and Safrai 2005; in press a), but they tend to "flatten" the graphs and make settlement fluctuations appear less extreme than they really were (Faust 2007b; Faust and Safrai in press a). Moreover, Ofer's survey clearly reveals the same trends of changes. An examination of all the small seventh century sites (sites whose overall size was smaller than 10 dunams)[48] shows that almost half did not continue to exist in the Persian period,[49] while half of the Persian period sites were new.[50] This shows that continuity was limited. If one would argue that fifty percent (even slightly more) is a high degree of continuity, then the figure, derived from Ofer's survey must be put in proper context. When examining the transition from the eighth century to the seventh in the same survey, it appears that twenty out of twenty-two small sites continued to exist after Sennachrib's campaign.[51] Moreover, due to his methodology (dating the typical eighth to seventh century pottery by default only to the eighth century), Ofer underestimated the number of seventh century sites (Finkelstein 1994, 174–75; Faust 2008b), so the decline in the Persian period was even greater. The change during the Iron Age–Persian period transition is therefore extremely significant, and this confirms the major break which is evident in this region by the more reliable analysis of the excavations.

Even if slightly less than other regions, northern Judah was devastated in the sixth century. There were survivors, and the region eventually attracted more population from nearby regions. This, along with natural growth (and probably with some who returned from Babylon), led to its recovery in the Persian period. The Persian period peak in this region, therefore, represents the results of a gradual recovery and not of a continuation of settlement.

---

48. The importance of rural sites for the debate is stressed by all scholars. These sites are especially suitable for an examination of continuity, as I have shown in ch. 2.

49. Fourteen small late Iron Age sites, all located north of Beth Zur, did not continue to exist in the Persian period; seventeen sites did continue to exist.

50. Seventeen Persian period sites were established de novo, and not on top of earlier, seventh-century sites.

51. In reality, there were probably more changes, but as already stated, surveys tend to flatten trends. For Sennacherib's campaign, see ch. 6.

Conclusions

An examination of the various data regarding demographic and settlement trends during the late Iron Age to Hellenistic era shows that the relative prosperity of the seventh century was followed by a major decline, and then a gradual recovery. While there are several theoretical scenarios that can outline the demographic ups and downs, we have seen that the most plausible reconstruction is that of a sharp and abrupt decline immediately after the Iron Age, and then a gradual recovery that lasted during the Persian period and matured only during the (late) Hellenistic period.

The demographic and settlement peak of the Persian period was at most about one-third of the populations of the late Iron Age and the Hellenistic period. The nadir of the Persian period, however, was much lower. The lowest demographic point (sixth century B.C.E.) was probably around ten percent of the late Iron Age. Twenty percent would be a highly exaggerated figure. Clearly, the land was not literally empty; the inhabitants numbered in the thousands, but life did not continue as usual.

The figures presented are lower than recently assumed. We must therefore stress that they are not based on new "reading" of the data (although we hinted that this is needed), but rather on putting the figures advanced by Carter and Lipschits in their proper perspective. To reiterate, I have followed the figures presented by Lipschits and others, but these very figures necessitate a new estimation of the Persian period in Judea, and inevitably lead to an evaluation that the period was of a greater settlement and demographic decline than appeared at first glance.[52] Realizing how low the nadir is on the one hand, and the overall processes described above on the other, are also the first steps in assessing the Persian period. The implications for the study of the sixth century are clear: understanding the situation in the sixth to fourth centuries B.C.E. carries great importance for the analysis of the social situation in Judah in the Neo-Babylonian period and to the processes of collapse and post-collapse, which will be discussed in chapter 7.

The following chapter aims to examine the results of the Babylonian campaigns in the late-seventh century and early-sixth century from a comparative perspective, in order to allow a better understanding of their results.

---

52. The estimates reached above are relatively close to those of Carter, and the greater disparity is with Lipschits's figures (which by themselves indicate a much greater decline then he usually acknowledges).

Chapter 6
The Babylonian Destruction in Context:
Nebuchadnezzar and Sennacherib Compared

The Babylonian destructions of the late-seventh and early-sixth centuries were one wave of destruction experienced by the region's inhabitants in the late Iron Age. Another notorious wave of destructions was carried out by the Assyrians in the late-eighth century (see also the postscript of ch. 7). Both empires inflicted heavy blows upon the kingdom of Judah: the Assyrians in the time of Sennacherib in 701 B.C.E. and the Babylonians during the reign of Nebuchadnezzar. The campaigns were landmarks in the history of Judah—much more than any other campaign or war. The present section will compare the outcomes of both campaigns, in order to put the above discussion of Judah in the sixth century and the "rigorousness" of the campaigns in a proper comparative context.

Sennacherib's Campaign and Its Implications for Settlement and Demography

Judah in the Eighth Century

The Iron Age II is regarded as an unprecedented settlement and demographic peak in ancient Israel, and the eighth century is usually regarded as the zenith of the period (e.g., Broshi and Finkelstein 1992, 47–48; see also Ofer 1993b; 1998; Dagan 2000; Na'aman 1993, 114–15). The Iron Age is considered a period of gradual demographic increase, which ended with the fierce destructions of the Assyrian campaigns in the last third of this century.

Indeed, the outcomes of the Assyrian campaigns, in the form of fierce conflagration and destructions, were evident in many eighth-century settlements (e.g., Mazar 1990, 405, 438; Stern 2001, 7–10). As far as Judah was concerned, the campaign was disastrous. Sennacherib reported the destruction of forty-six fortified cities and many rural settlements, and the exile of 200,150 people (e.g.,

Pritchard 1969, 287–88). While the number of exiled is doubted,[1] the number of settlements destroyed is usually viewed as a more reliable number (Halpern 1996, 319; Rainey and Notley 2006, 243, 245; see also Gallagher 1999, 261). Archaeologically speaking, a destruction layer attributed to this campaign was unearthed in almost every site excavated in Judah (Stern 2001, 10). The most famous site is Lachish, whose destruction is also depicted on the walls of Sennacherib's palace in Ninveh (Ussishkin 1982; see also 2004), but evidence of Assyrian destruction was also found at Beth-Shemesh, Hebron, Tel Halif, Beersheba, Arad, Tel Malhata, Tel 'Eton, Tel Goded, Tell Beit Mirsim, Kh. Rabud, Ramat Rahel, and many others.[2]

The one notable exception was Jerusalem, but it is clear that there was widespread destruction in Judah. Many sites in Judah were destroyed. Many inhabitants were exiled; many died from the war, starvation, epidemics, or executions. In addition, territories were torn from Judah and given to the Philistines (Tadmor 1984, 76). There is a consensus that Judah suffered a major blow at the hand of Sennacherib.

JUDAH AFTER SENNACHERIB: THE CONSENSUS

It is agreed that the outcomes of the 701 campaigns are attested almost everywhere, and there appears to be almost general agreement that Judah never fully regained its demographic strength after the Sennacherib campaigns in 701 B.C.E. Many of the destroyed sites did not recover, or at least did not fully recover. Lachish, for example, was resettled in the seventh century, but never regained its density during the eighth century and was actually relatively empty (Ussishkin 2004, 90–92). Beth-Shemesh, too, did not recover, and with the exception of remains found within the earlier water system, no seventh century remains were unearthed. The meager finds at best indicate an unsuccessful attempt at resettlement, and even this on a very modest scale (Bunimovtiz and Lederman 2003). Tell Beit Mirsim did not recover either. Here, the seventh century occupation is regarded as limited in scope (e.g., Aharoni 1973, 6; see also Finkelstein and Na'aman 2004, 61–64, and references). Beersheba II, the last Iron Age settlement,

---

1. E.g., Halpern 1996, 318; Gallagher 1999, 131–32; De Odorico 1995; Zevit 2006, and references.

2. Beth-Shemesh: Bunimovitz and Lederman 1997; Hebron: Eisenberg and Nagorski 2002; Tel Halif: Seger 1993, 558; Beersheba: Aharoni 1973, 6–7; Arad: Herzog 1997a, 136; Tel Malhata: Kochavi 1998, 35; Tel 'Eton: Faust 2009; 2011a; Katz and Faust 2011; Tel Goded: Gibson 1994; Tell Beit Mirsim: Aharoni and Aharoni 1976; Greenberg 1997; Kh. Rabud: Kochavi 1974; 1993b; 1997; Ramat Rahel: Aharoni 1993; Barkay 2006, but see Lipschits et al. 2009.

was destroyed by the Assyrians, and no seventh century city existed at the site (e.g., Aharoni 1973, 6–7; Herzog 1997b, 247). At Tel 'Eton, too, the recent excavations indicate that after the destruction of the eighth century, no large-scale resettlement took place at the site in the seventh century (Faust 2009; 2011a).

The data from the excavations were corroborated by the data from surveys. Dagan surveyed the Shephelah, which is regarded as the most densely settled part of Judah. He wrote (2000, 208; my translation), "following Sennacherib's campaign the settlement in the Shephelah went through an acute change—the number of sites decreased significantly, many settlements were destroyed and abandoned, and the settlement did not regain its former size." On the basis of Ofer's survey of the Judean highlands, the heartland of Judah, he also expressed the view that the settlement peak was in the eighth century until the widespread destruction of 701 (1998, 47). He added that during the "Iron Age III (701–587/6 B.C.E.)" there was settlement recovery, but "the highland population did not approach the peak of the earlier phase" (see also Ofer 2001, 27).

Indeed, the results of the excavations and surveys gave rise to the common view that the seventh century was a shadow of the eighth century, which is expressed by most scholars (though not by all, see below). Na'aman (1993, 114–15) referred to the "extreme weakness of Judah in the 7th century," and elsewhere he (Na'aman 1994, 248; emphasis mine) wrote that "Even in the late-seventh century, following a hundred years of recovery, the kingdom's settlement, population and economy was considerably less than in the 8th century B.C.E." Similar views were expressed by Halpern (1996, 319; see also 1991), Eshel (1991, 155), McLellan (1978), and others.

JUDAH AFTER SENNACHERIB: A NEW EXAMINATION

However, the reality in the seventh century may have been more complex. It is well-known that the Judean Desert and the Negev prospered in the seventh century B.C.E., and settlement in both areas was more significant than in the eighth century (e.g., Stern 1994; Finkelstein 1994, 175–16; 1996; 144–153; Bar Adon 1989; Na'aman 1987). The prosperity of these regions, however, was always explained as an exception that resulted from unique circumstances (Finkelstein 1994; Na'aman 1987, and others). On closer look, other regions also prospered. Jerusalem was not destroyed in 701 and reached its settlement peak in the seventh century B.C.E. (e.g., Barkay 1988; Faust 2005b; 2008b; contra Na'aman 2007). The same is true regarding Jerusalem's environs (Barkay 1988; Faust 2005b; and even Na'aman 2007), the land of Benjamin, and even the highlands of Judah (below). It is therefore worthwhile to review the data of the settlement situation in the seventh century, after Sennacherib's campaign.

I will examine the situation in seventh century Judah by reviewing the results of the known excavated sites.[4] The discussion will be divided into the following sub-regions: the Shephelah, the Judean Desert, the Negev, Benjamin, Jerusalem and its environs, and the Judean highlands. By reviewing the different regions, we will be able to see if there were areas whose peak was in the seventh century and not the eighth century.

The Shephelah

The Shephelah during the eighth century is thought to have been the most densely settled area of Judah, with a large number of sites, and the majority of Judah's towns and cities (e.g., Broshi and Finkelstein 1992, 52, 54, Table 1). However, the reality of the seventh century was grim. The Iron Age excavated sites in this region were practically all destroyed by the Assyrians.

Lachish
Despite limited recovery, the site was much smaller than its eighth-century predecessor (Ussishkin 2004, 90–92).

Tell Beit Mirsim
The last Iron Age city was apparently destroyed in 701 b.c.e., and the seventh century-occupation was of limited nature only (e.g., Aharoni 1973, 6; Greenberg 1997; see also Finkelstein and Na'aman 2004, 61–64; Blakely and Hardin 2002, 14–24; note that the latter article dates the major destruction slightly earlier, and only a second destruction to the 701 campaign).

Tel Halif
Settlement at the site resumed after the Assyrian destruction, but was then abandoned, probably during the first half of the seventh century b.c.e. (Seger 1993, 558; Finkelstein and Na'aman 2004, 64; note that Blakely and Hardin 2002, 24 attribute this phase to the late-eighth century).

---

3. The data regarding Sennacherib's campaign is based on Faust (2008b). The discussion there is more detailed, but the information in this chapter is more updated.

4. Many of which were already discussed above, when I examined the finds in the late Iron Age in comparison to those of the Persian period.

Tel Batash

The site recovered after the destruction of 701 (probably as part of Philistia), and seems to have prospered until the Babylonian destruction in the late-seventh century (Mazar and Panitz-Cohen 2001, 281–82).

Tel Beth-Shemesh

The last Iron Age city at this location was destroyed by Sennacherib. The site was deserted during the seventh century, though some pottery unearthed in the blocking of the water system might indicate a small-scale (failed) attempt at resettlement (Bunimovitz and Lederman 1997; 2003; see also Fantalkin 2004).

Tel 'Eton

Though salvage excavations in some tombs appeared to have produced possible seventh century-sherds, the excavations carried out at the site did not produce seventh-century pottery. It appears that the last Iron Age city at this location was destroyed by the Assyrians during the eighth century (Faust 2009; 2011a, Katz and Faust 2011; see also Ayalon 1985; Zimhoni 1985).

Tel Goded

Dagan (2000, 91–93) and Lipschits (2005, 220) believed that the late Iron Age settlement existed until the early-sixth century. However, according to Gibson's study, which gives the most detailed research on the data provided by the century-old excavations, the city ceased to exist in 701 B.C.E. (Gibson 1994). The data from this site should, therefore, be treated with caution (see also Broshi 1993; Manor 1997).

Maresha

The original excavations were carried out over a century ago, and the published report is problematic to use today. Comparisons of the findings suggested that there was settlement at the site during the ninth to eighth centuries, though not during the seventh century B.C.E. (Vaughn 1999, 27; Dagan 1992, 47). Still, recent excavations have revealed some remains from this period (Kloner and Eshel 1999).

Khirbet el Qom

It appears that Kh. el Qom was also destroyed in the late-eighth century B.C.E., and did not recover (Defonzo 2005, contra previous summaries, and see ch. 1).

Our data show that the sites of the Shephelah were destroyed by the Assyrians. A number of towns began to recover, but most of them did not reach their eighth century status and population. Many other sites did not recover (or hardly recoved). Yehuda Dagan surveyed the Shephelah and estimated that the number of eighth century sites was about 3.3 times larger than that of the seventh century, and the population was larger by a factor of 3 (Dagan 2000, 210). Although such calculations and comparisons are problematic on several levels, Dagan's estimations give us an impression on the data which produced the "consensus." Despite the reservations, it is clear that the Shephelah in the eighth century was much more settled than in the seventh century. The Shephelah was not empty in the seventh century, but the decline in relation to the eighth century was significant.

THE JUDEAN DESERT

As noted above, the consensus is that the Judean Desert was not settled (or was hardly settled) in the eighth century (Stern 1994, 406–7; 2001, 137).[5] Scholars agree that the settlement and demographic peak was in the seventh century. The following list includes mainly small sites.

Ein Gedi

The settlement at Tel Goren (the early settlement at the Ein Gedi oasis) was the central settlement in the Judean Desert. Excavators attributed the site to the seventh century B.C.E. (Mazar, Dothan, and Dunayevsky 1966; Yezerski 2007, 107). It was most likely founded in the eighth century (see, e.g., Finkelstein 1994, 175; Vaughn 1999, 72–74), but prospered in the seventh century until the Babylonian campaigns.

Rugm el-Bahr

A late Iron Age fort was excavated at the site (later remains included the Hellenistic and Roman periods), located on the northeastern shore of the Dead Sea (Bar Adon 1989, 3–14)

Qumran

The earliest settlement at Qumran was during the late Iron Age, and the finds included pottery forms which are not earlier than the eighth century, and not later than the early-sixth century, including a *lmlk* stamp. Other Iron Age remains were found nearby (De Vaux 1973, 1–3, 58–60, 91–93; 1993, 1236).

---

5. A notable exception from this consensus was Vaughn (1999, 71–78; more below), but even he agrees that the peak was during the seventh century.

Khirbet Mazin/Qasr el-Yahud

Another late Iron Age fort was excavated near the outlet of the Qidron to the Dead Sea. The findings included pottery from the seventh century B.C.E., although the relative frequency of burnished bowls might hint that the site was established already in the eighth century (Bar Adon 1989, 18–29). It is likely that it was related to a nearby village (Bar Adon 1972, 126 [site 114]; Ofer 1999, 25).

Ein el-Ghuweir

A structure, part of a nearby settlement, was excavated. The findings indicated that the site existed in the late Iron Age. An eighth century date for the establishment of the site cannot be precluded (Bar Adon 1989, 33–40). South of the site, a long wall with rooms and houses that were built adjacent to it was discovered. The rooms and houses were found on the way to the nearby site of Ein et-Turaba, and it is possible that both sites were actually one (Ofer 1999, 20, 29).

Ein et-Turaba

A large and well–built structure with a courtyard was excavated. The site seemed to have existed in the eighth to seventh century B.C.E. (Bar Adon 1989, 41–48). As mentioned, it is likely that this was part of a larger site, which spread along the coast to Ein el-Ghuweir.

Rujm esh-Shajra

This is a small late Iron Age fort (?) near the coast of the Dead Sea (Bar Adon 1989, 86).

The Boqeʾah Valley Sites: Khirbet Abu Tabaq, Khirbet es-Samrah and Khirbet el-Maqari

According to Stager (1976, 145), this group of sites in the Boqeʾah valley were "paramilitary outposts," which were supposed to guard the road(s) leading from the Dead Sea to Jerusalem. The sites, along with "outliers and nearby desert farms," were "established in the Buqeʾah wasteland in the seventh century B.C.," and were destroyed in the early-sixth century (Stager 1976; see also Cross and Milik 1956). Note that Vaughn (1999, 75–78) dates their foundation to the eighth century B.C.E.

Vered Yericho

The site of Vered Yericho was discovered to the north of the Judean Desert, near Jericho. A well-built structure was discovered. The nature of the site is not clear (e.g., Stern 1994, 400), but it is dated to the late-seventh to early-sixth centuries (Eitan 1983).

Wadi Qelt
Approximately 3 kilometers north of Vered Yericho, a large site (about 30 dunams) was unearthed on the southern bank of Wadi Qelt, near Jericho (about 3 km south of biblical Jericho [Tell es-Sultan]). It appears that this site was also dated to the seventh to early-sixth centuries (Eitan 1983; also Stern 2001, 134).

Jericho (Tell es-Sultan)
The city seems to have flourished during the last phase of the Iron Age (Stern 1994, 400, and many references).

While it is clear that in the Judean Desert, the seventh century was more densely settled, we concur with Vaughn (1999, 71–78) that the settlement wave already started in the eighth century (note that Bar Adon usually referred to the eighth–seventh centuries, and not only to the seventh, e.g., 1989, 19). In any event, the region was regarded as demographically unimportant, and its settlement as a rare phenomenon that did not reflect the situation at large.

THE NEGEV

The seventh century was the peak of settlement in the Negev (Finkelstein 1994, 176; 199, 144–49; Herzog 1997a, 239–42; Na'aman 1987, 4–6). While some eighth century sites were destroyed and abandoned,[6] others continued to exist, and additional sites were established only in the seventh century B.C.E.[7]

Arad
The Iron Age fort, which was erected earlier in the Iron Age though rebuilt several times, continued to exist until its destruction in the early-sixth century (M. Aharoni 1993, 85; Herzog 1997a, 242, 244, 245).

Tel Malhata
The eighth century city continued to exist in the seventh century, until its destruction in the early-sixth century (Kochavi 1993a; 1998),

---

6. For example, Tel Beersheba and perhaps the settlement near the Beer-Sheva market.
7. Tahareani Sussely (2007) suggested that the settlement in the eighth and seventh centuries was similar. While many of her arguments are feasible, the data suggest that seventh century settlement was somewhat larger. Since she agrees that the settlement of the seventh century was not smaller than that of the eighth, this has no real impact on the current discussion.

Beer-Sheva, near the Old Market

A large Iron Age site was revealed in the modern city of Beer-Sheva below the Beduin market (e.g., Gophna and Yisraeli 1973, 115–18). According to some, this could have been the location of the seventh century city (but see Panitz–Cohen 2005; Fabian and Gilead 2007).

Tel Ira

The earlier Iron Age city continued to exist. The last Judahite city (Stratum 6) at this location was built in the mid–seventh century B.C.E., and existed until the violent destruction by fire at around the year 600 B.C.E. or the early phase of the sixth century (Beit Arieh 1997, 176–77; Beit Arieh 1993a, 644).

The sites listed above continued to exist from the eighth century to the seventh century. In the Negev, there were also a number sites that were established only in the seventh century, exemplifying the period's prosperity.

Tel Masos

After a gap of a few hundred years, a new settlement was erected at Tel Masos (though not exactly on top of the Iron I settlement). The seventh century site was quite small and was perhaps a fort or a road station (e.g., Kempinski 1993, 989).

Aroer

The excavator dates the three Iron Age strata at the site to the seventh century B.C.E. (Biran 1993), although it is possible that the settlement started already in the eighth century (see also Thareani Sussely 2007).

Khirbet Uza

A fort and a nearby village were established in the seventh century at Kh. Uza, about 10 km south of Arad (Beit Arieh 1993c; Beit Arieh and Cresson 2007b).

Khirbet Radum

A small fort from the seventh century was excavated south of Kh. Uza (Beit Arieh 1993b; Beit Arieh and Cresson 2007b).

Qitmit

A small unfortified site was excavated in the southeastern part of the biblical Negev (Beit Arieh 1995). The site was not a settlement, and was more likely a road-shrine or something of the sort. It is usually attributed to Edomite presence (e.g., Beit Arieh 1991; 1995), but it is more likely that it was used by various peoples, mainly those involved in the Arabian trade (e.g., Finkelstein 1992; 1996, 139–53; cf. Beck 1995; 1996).

Khirbet Tov

A seventh century B.C.E. fort was excavated in the northern Negev (Cohen 1995, 115–16).

The seventh century peak of settlement in the Negev was a well-known phenomenon. This, however, was attributed to unique geopolitical circumstances (e.g., Finkelstein 1994); like the settlement in the Judean Desert, settlement in the Negev was not regarded as demographically important.

THE REGION OF BENJAMIN

A large number of Iron Age sites were excavated in Benjamin, just north of Jerusalem. It appears that the peak of settlement in this region was also in the seventh century.

Tell en-Nasbeh (biblical Mizpah)

The site was a relatively central town in this region at the time. The stratigraphy of the site is not clear, but it seems that the town was established in the Iron Age IIA (probably in the tenth century), was heavily fortified in the ninth century, and continued uninterruptedly until the sixth century B.C.E. (Zorn 1993a; 1993b; 1997a; 1997b; 1997c; see more below). There is no reason to believe that the town of the seventh century was smaller than that of the eighth century (see also Vaughn 1999, 34–37).

Gibeon

At Gibeon, too, the stratigraphy is unclear, but it seems that the town existed throughout the Iron Age II without interruption (Pritchard 1962; 1964; see also Vaughn 1999, 37–38). Pritchard explicitly wrote (1962, 161–62) that the site was not destroyed during the Iron Age, adding that "the frequent invasions of the Assyrian kings in the eighth and seventh century apparently bypassed the city." Despite many problems with the excavations, this observation seems correct, and it is unlikely that the excavators would have missed the Assyrian destruction layer should they have encountered it. It is likely that the settlement's peak was during the seventh century B.C.E. (e.g., Pritchard 1962, 162–63).

Notably, it is likely that one reason for the lack of clear stratigraphy at both sites was the lack of destruction layers during the Iron Age. This further supports the view that nothing of importance occurred at the sites in the late-eighth century.

Tell el-Ful

Following the 1964 campaign, Lapp suggested that the last Iron Age settlement at this site was established in the second half of the seventh century, after a gap of a few centuries (Lapp 1978b; 1978c, 81–101). It appears that this occupation started already in the eighth century, as evident by the existence of eighth century pottery that includes *lmlk* handles (Lapp 1978a, 111–12; see also plates 41, 42, 67, 70; Gibson 1996, 17*),[8] but it is clear that the peak was in the seventh century.

Nebi Samuel

Many Iron Age finds—mainly pottery, but also *lmlk,* and rosette handles—were reported. These finds indicated settlement in the eighth–seventh centuries B.C.E. (Magen and Dadon 1999, 62–63). Nothing can be reconstructed on the nature of the settlement, but it obviously existed during the seventh century.

Ras el Kharrûbeh

Very little Iron Age pottery was unearthed in the excavations, indicating the site was of little importance. These limited finds, however, are dated to the seventh century B.C.E. (Biran 1985, 209–210).

Khirbet es Sid

This is a fairly large site (over 30 dunams) which was excavated by Biran and identified with biblical Anathoth. The finds were dated almost exclusively to the seventh and early-sixth centuries B.C.E. (Biran 1985, 211–13).

---

8. Lipschits, Sergi, and Koch (2010, 2011) recently suggested dating some types of *lmlk* impressions, esp. those found in the highlands, to the seventh century B.C.E. This suggestion has already been rejected by some (Ussushkin 2011; Barkay 2011) and does not stand up to scrutiny. While this note is not the place for a detailed discussion of this suggestion, it must be pointed out (in addition to the objections of Ussushkin and Barkay) that they confused geographical patterns of distribution with chronological ones. It is likely that the impressions should be dated to the eighth century, as the scholarly consensus holds. The differences they observed are largely regional differences between highland (where the sites were not destroyed in the eighth century, and the impressions are therefore found along with seventh century pottery) and lowland (where sites were destroyed, and the impression are found within the 701 destruction layer), and not between the eighth and the seventh centuries (the issue will be addressed in more detail elsewhere).

Khirbet Shilhah

A small farmstead or an estate was found in the desert fringe of Benjamin, on route to Jericho. According to the excavators, the site was established in the seventh century (Mazar, Amit, and Ilan 1996).[9]

Mezad Michmas

An isolated structure was unearthed in eastern Benjamin. The site is dated to the seventh century B.C.E. (Riklin 1995).

Other rural sites, unearthed north of Jerusalem, will be discussed below. They also exhibit a settlement peak in the seventh century. The same can be said of the few sites near Jericho, discussed in the Judean Desert section. Notably, it appears that the seventh century was the peak of Iron Age settlement in this region, as represented also in the surveys (e.g., Finkelstein 1993b, 27). Clearly, all lines of evidence indicate that the settlement and demographic peak in the region of Benjamin was in the seventh century B.C.E. (see also Magen 2004, 1–2).

JERUSALEM AND ITS ENVIRONS

Jerusalem

We have seen that while the consensus holds that in the wake of Sennacherib's campaign, Judah experienced a political and demographic decline in the seventh century, most scholars agree that Jerusalem was an exception and flourished at the time (for a more detailed discussion, see also Faust 2005b; but see Na'aman 2007; Faust 2008b). Some scholars even suggested that the population of Jerusalem and its surroundings was equal to that of the rest of Judah. They believed this was the demographic reality behind the term "Judah and Jerusalem," which is mentioned sixteen times in biblical sources from this period (modified from Barkay 1988, 125; as for the biblical sources, see, e.g., 2 Kgs 23:1; Isa 1:1; 2:1; Jer 19:7; 29:2).[10]

---

9. Even if the *lmlk* stamp found, which dates to the eighth century, will be taken as evidence of an earlier establishment date (contrary to the view of the excavators, with which I concur, Mazar, Amit, and Ilan 208–9), the site still prospered in the seventh century.

10. Geva claimed that the overall decrease in settlement that was observed in most parts of Judah during the seventh century B.C.E. can also be seen in Jerusalem, and that the settlement in the Western Hill declined (Geva 2002, 23–24; 2003a, 522–23). He estimated, though, that Judah's settlement decrease was less significant near Jerusalem, and accepted the idea that Jerusalem was equal to the rest of Judah at the time (see also De Groot, Geva, and Yezerski 2003, 16). The issue was dealt with in more detail elsewhere (Faust 2005b), but a few words are in order here. Geva's

Jerusalem was a metropolis of some 650 dunams of walled neighborhoods, and some 300 dunams of extramural neighborhoods. The city was the primary city in Judah of the seventh century (Barkay 1988; Faust 2005b and references). Seventh-century pottery was found throughout the western hill, indicating continued occupation from the eighth century.[11] The dense nature of the settlement within the city is also supported by its countryside, which peaked at the time.

Jerusalem Countryside

The evidence from Jerusalem's environment indicates that settlement intensified in the seventh century in comparison to the eighth century. Jerusalem's hinterland was more densely settled in the seventh century than ever before (even Na'aman 2007). While survey data cannot be sufficiently detailed,[12] a wealth of excavated sites in Jerusalem's environs exists (also ch. 2), enabling a detailed discussion. These sites include two farmsteads at Kh. er-Ras, Manahat, Nahal Zimri, the French Hill, Ketef Hinnom, Pisgat Zeev A, Pisgat Zeev D, Givat Homa, Kh. 'Alona, Mevasseret Yerushalayim, the Ramot farmsteads (five isolated buildings), the Ramat Beit Ha-Kerem farmstead, Beit Ha-Kerem, Mamilla, Talpiyot East, and a settlement near the Rambam Cave, and more.[13] Well over twenty excavated Iron II rural sites are reported to have existed at the end of the Iron Age; according to the excavators, all the sites seem to have existed during the seventh

---

estimation resulted from the absence of cooking pots with a thin out-turned grooved rim in the Western Hill (De Groot, Geva and Yezerski 2003, 9, 16; but see Tushingham 1985, e.g., plate 18 and fig. 8: 22). This absence, however, could result from other reasons (regional variation?), and does not indicate a decline in settlement. Other types of seventh-century pottery were found in the Western Hill, e.g., lamps (De Groot, Geva and Yezerski 2003, 13) and certain types of cooking pots (9). Moreover, the authors stress that the nature of the data precludes any quantitative conclusions (1–2; and such an analysis was not even attempted), so the relative presence or absence of forms is a problematic tool. For the dating of Iron Age pottery in the western hill, see also Tushingham 1985. Notably, in his rejoinder, Geva (2006) did not challenge my evaluation of the situation in the seventh century (see also Faust 2008b).

11. Na'aman (2007) recently questioned this. The issue will be discussed in more detail elsewhere (see also Faust 2008b).

12. The surveyor (e.g., Kloner 2003, 20) referred to the eighth to seventh centuries as the peak of Iron Age settlement, and treated both centuries as one.

13. Kh. er-Ras: Edelstein 2000; Feig and Abd Rabu 1995; Feig 1996; Manahat: Zehavi 1993; Nahal Zimri: Yogev 1985; the French Hill: Mazor 2006; Ketef Hinnom: Barkay 1995; Pisgat Zeev A: Seligman 1994; Pisgat Zeev D: Nadelman 1993; Givat Homa: Mai 1997; Kh. 'Alona: Weksler–Bdolah 1997; see also Faust 2003b, 40; Mevasseret Yerushalayim: Edelstein and Kislev 1981; the Ramot farmsteads: Davidovitz et al., 2006, 68–79, 91–93; the Ramat Beit Ha-Kerem farmstead: Davidovitz et al., 2006, 80–82, 86–87, 93–94; Beit Ha-Kerem: Billig 2007; Mamilla: Amit 2009; Talpiyot East: Solimany and Barzel 2008a, and a settlement near the Rambam Cave: Zissu 2006.

century. It is not certain how many were established earlier, as the date of establishment of about half of the sites is not clear; at least five sites appear clearly to have been established only in the seventh century, while some six sites were probably erected already in the eighth century.[14] It is quite clear, therefore, that the peak of settlement in Jerusalem and its surroundings was during the seventh century B.C.E.

THE HIGHLANDS OF JUDAH

The highlands of Judah, along with the area of Jerusalem, formed the core of Judah. Relatively few sites were excavated from this region (though parts of it were surveyed by Ofer 1993b; 1998, see more below). Most of the urban and rural sites existed in the seventh century. First we will look at the urban sites.

Ramat Rahel
Following Aharoni's excavations and an additional season led by Barkay in the 1980s, it appears that the earlier fort/palace that was discovered was destroyed in the late-eighth century, probably by Sennacherib. Later in the seventh century, a new palace was built (Aharoni 1993; Barkay 2006). The recent excavations conducted by Lipschits et al. also showed that regardless of the nature of the transition from the first phase of construction to the second, there were major architectural differences between them (2009, 61–70).

Beth Zur
The excavators identified a large gap in the settlement of the site during the Iron Age II, and concluded that resettlement occurred only in the seventh century B.C.E. (Funk 1968, 8; 1993). Still, the discovery of eleven *lmlk* stamps (Funk 1993, 261) indicates that the settlement was founded already in the eighth century B.C.E.

Hebron
An eighth-century destruction layer was observed in the excavations (Eisenberg and Nagorski 2002, 92*; Emanuel Eisenberg, personal communication).

---

14. Khirbet er-Ras II, the French Hill, Ketef Hinnom, Mamilla, and Mevasseret Yerushalayim are very likely to have existed already in the eighth century. Khirbet er-Ras I and Pisgat Zeev A exhibit some eighth-century pottery, but could have been established in the early-seventh century. The data from Malaha is not clear. The five structures at Ramot exhibited some eighth-century forms, although the overall assemblage seems more seventh century. Other sites (e.g., Bet Ha-Kerem and the Rambam Cave) were probably established only in the seventh century.

A seventh century occupation was unearthed in the excavation area (which is located down the slope), indicating that the settlement at the time was fairly large.

Khirbet Rabud
The eighth century city was destroyed, probably by Sennacherib, but settlement resumed and even expanded in the seventh century. Kochavi wrote: "The wall was rebuilt ... and it was even widened in places to 7 m. ... An unwalled settlement was also established in this period on a lower terrace northeast of the mound" (1993b, 1252; see also 1974).

All the urban sites in the highlands of Judah existed in the seventh century, and most of them reached a settlement peak during this time. The data from the rural sector is similar.

Farmsteads and Villages in the Gush Etzion-Bethlehem Region
Late Iron Age rural settlements, mainly farmsteads, were reported at Kh. Abu Shawan, Kh. el-Qatt, Har Gillo (West), southeast of Wadi Fukin, R.P. 1618/1239 (with another farmstead nearby), Kh. Jarish, Fajer-South (a wine press—probably representing agricultural usage of the area), Kh. abu et-Twein, el-Id, and Kh. Hallel.[15] Many of these sites existed from the eighth century to the Babylonian destruction, while a few were established only in the seventh century. None, however, ceased to exist after the eighth century, hence indicating the strength of the seventh century settlement also in this sector (for a detailed discussion of rural settlements, see ch. 2).[16]

---

15. Kh. Abu Shawan: Baruch 2001b; Kh. el-Qatt: Amit 1989–90a; Amit and Cohen-Amin in press; Har Gillo (West): Peleg and Feller 2004b; southeast of Wadi Fukin: Amit 1991, 77; R.P. 1618/1239: Amit 1991; Kh. Jarish: Kochavi 1972, 38; Amit 1989–90b; Ofer 1993b, 2, 88–89; and see now Amit and Cohen-Amin in press; Fajer-South; Ofer 1993b, 2, 87–88; Kh. abu et-Twein: Mazar 1982; el-Id: Baruch 1997; below the fort; and Kh. Hallel: Amit 1991.

16. The only exception might be Beitar 'Ilit (west) (RP 15972/12250), where Har-Even (2009) recently reported an Iron Age IIB farmstead (near the above mentioned field towers, spelt as Betar Illit [west]), which according to him did not exist in the seventh century. By examining the publication, however, it appears more likely that the farmstead existed in the eighth–seventh centuries B.C.E., and that Har-Even was misled by the assumption that the eighth–seventh-century forms should be dated to the eighth century only, unless proven otherwise. Notably, some of the forms unearthed are much more typical in the seventh century than in the eighth, but real fossiles directeurs of the seventh century, which are very limited in number, were not found (cf., Finkelstein 1994, 174–75; Ofer 1993b, part 3, 153; Faust 2008b; see also the discussion of Batz's interpretation, below).

Farmsteads in the Southern Hebron Hill Country

The settlement at Kh. Anim seems to have been a rural site during the seventh century, after the earlier fort ceased to exist (David Amit, personal communication). The settlements at Kh. Sansanna (Peleg and Feller 2004c, 65*) and Kh. Be Shim'a (Peleg and Feller 2004d, 64*) seem to have been established only in the seventh century, and although an earlier establishment date cannot be ruled out, they clearly existed in this century.

Interestingly, Batz published recently, in a preliminary fashion, an article about a group of farmsteads in the southern Hebron highlands which seem to deviate from the norm above (Batz 2006). According to him these farmsteads existed only at the end of the eighth century. While it is possible that this micro-region is an exception, it is more likely that his interpretation is problematic and that the sites existed also in the seventh century. This can be seen in some of the pottery forms he discusses. It appears that Batz dated the sites to the eighth century due to the general lack of "clear" seventh century forms (although a few do appear). He dated the "general" eighth- to seventh-century pottery assemblages to the eighth century by default. As noted above, this is a very problematic procedure. It seems as if those farmsteads also existed in the seventh century B.C.E. Whether or not those few farmsteads form an exception to the rule, however, it is clear that in most parts of the Judean highlands the settlement peak was in the seventh century.

In summary, it is clear from the above that whenever there is sufficient information, it appears as if the seventh century settlement in the highlands was at least similar to that of the eighth century, and in most cases it was even larger.[17] While the number of large excavated sites is not very large, the accumulated data are significant. The excavators of almost all urban and rural sites indicate that the seventh-century settlement was at least as large as that of the eighth, and in many cases the seventh century represents the settlement peak of Judah.[18]

---

17. The data from the excavations of both major tells and small rural sites (the only possible exceptions are Batz's sites) seem to be contradicted by the data from the survey. On the basis of his survey, Ofer (1998, 46–47; 2001, 28–29) concluded that the region did not fully recover after Sennacherib's campaign, and that the settlement was significantly reduced (see also his estimates of Kh. Rabud; Ofer 1993b, 2, 64). Indeed, this is in line with the common view of seventh century Judah mentioned above (which is to some extent based on this survey), but it contradicts the picture that emerges from the excavations in this region. It seems as if his conclusion resulted from treating the typical eighth to seventh centuries ceramic assemblage as representing the eighth century only, when no "clear" seventh-century forms were unearthed (above).

18. Vaughn (1999), in what is generally speaking the most sophisticated and updated treatment of the question of the highland prosperity during the eighth and seventh century B.C.E., reached a different conclusion, and he cautiously accepted Ofer's notion of a certain decline. It

Notably, already in the early 1990s, Finkelstein challenged the "consensus" that the eighth century was the demographic peak, pointing to the discrepancy between the surveys and the few excavations. He concluded:

> I therefore assume that the seventh-century occupation in the Judean hills south of Jerusalem was no less dense than in the eighth century. Farmhouses and small settlements that have recently been surveyed and excavated in the region may even hint at a settlement and demographic growth at the late Iron II (Finkelstein 1994, 174–75; see also Finkelstein 1993a, 59, for even higher estimations regarding seventh century Judah).

Finkelstein was right in pointing to this direction; however, his argument was not followed, and therefore the prevailing view of the seventh century was still one of weakness and decline.[19]

Summary

In five out of six regions, settlement of the seventh century exceeded that of the eighth century. Therefore, most parts of Judah prospered in the seventh century and were demographically denser than in the eighth century. Only in the Shephelah did we observe the expected pattern, in which the seventh century was a shadow of the eighth. Despite the upheavals caused by Sennacherib's campaign, the destruction was not complete and the recovery significant. It is likely that the campaign concentrated on the Shephelah (Faust 2008b), and hence other regions were only partially destroyed (or not destroyed at all) and recovery was fast (see now also Greenhut and De Groot 2009, 227).

---

should be noted, however, that Vaughn did not discuss all the sites; therefore he missed additional data that contradicted Ofer's conclusions. In addition, in all the sites Vaughn discussed, his own bottom line was at odds with Ofer's conclusion that there was a decline in the highlands, with one exception—Beth Zur. This is simply insufficient to support Ofer, and moreover, even this site contradicts Ofer's results. Whether discussed by Vaughn or not, the sites support the fact that the seventh century was the peak of settlement in the highlands of Judah.

19. Mazar (1990, 438) also expressed the view that "the seventh century was a period of great prosperity in Judah," but did not develop the argument (he devoted only a brief paragraph to it) and referred only to the well-known examples of Jerusalem, the Judean Desert, and the Negev, which most scholars considered to be exceptions. Note that a few scholars who expressed such sentiments (that the seventh century was the settlement peak in Judah) in the past, based their views on the wrong dating of Lachish III and similar assemblages (e.g., Stern 1975).

SENNACHERIB'S CAMPAIGN AND NEBUCHADNEZZAR'S
CAMPAIGN COMPARED: CONCLUSIONS

Neither the exact extent of Sennacherib's campaign nor the list of destroyed sites is important for our purposes. What is important is that the Assyrian campaign of 701 B.C.E., whose consequences for Judah were viewed as disastrous by practically all scholars, and rightly so, did not leave a mark which was even close to the consequences of the 586 B.C.E. war. Most areas increased in settlement after Sennacherib's campaign, and the destroyed cities were resettled. Even if one were to believe that most settlement declined in size and importance (cf. Ofer 1993b, above), the overall estimation would not be changed. Most regions of Judah recovered relatively quickly after the destruction. Even in the Shephelah, which was indeed devastated, new settlements were erected and a limited recovery was still noticeable.

In contrast, nothing of the like can be seen after the 586 B.C.E. Babylonian campaign. All areas were practically devastated, even if a number of villages continued to exist. The area reached a settlement and demographic recovery only in the Hellenistic period.

The differences between the outcomes of the 701 B.C.E. and 586 B.C.E. campaigns are, therefore, striking. The former had horrible consequences (although more limited than is commonly thought), but the latter was many times worse. When viewed in context, it is very difficult to speak of continuity and prosperity in Judah after the Babylonian campaigns.

CHAPTER 7
SIXTH-CENTURY JUDAH AS A POST-COLLAPSE SOCIETY

Previous chapters have shown that Judah was devastated during the Neo-Babylonian campaigns of the early-sixth century B.C.E. But is it possible that devastation was so widespread? And what was expected after such destructions?

This chapter will review the reality in the sixth century and examine the processes Judah experienced after the Babylonian destructions, in light of similar processes in other parts of the world, where "post-collapse" societies were studied. We will see that almost every aspect of the situation in Judah in the sixth century is in accordance with the reality in other such societies. Furthermore, the detailed information on Judah can, and should, supplement studies of processes of post-collapse elsewhere and enhance our information on such processes.

BACKGROUND

Until twenty years ago, practically all scholars described sixth-century Judah as desolate. However, scholars who support the continuity theory argued that it was unlikely that the land would be so empty, adding that "emptying" the land was against Babylonian interests. For example, Barstad claimed,

> it would have been nonsensical of Nebuchadnezzar to destroy Judah. As his imperial system depended on the accumulation of wealth based on the production outside his own country, the total annihilation of a conquered territory would in fact be an act against his own interest ... it would rather be in his interest to maintain, or even increase, the existing modes of production (1996, 67–68).

More recently, Barstad wrote in a similar vein that "it would have been unwise of Nebuchadnezzar to destroy Judah" (2003, 11). Lipschits (2005, 69) also wrote that "total devastation of the entire region would have been contrary to Babylonian interests because the Empire needed the population of Judah as the human nucleus for the new province it had established."[1] Blenkinsopp also claimed that "it is difficult to see what point would have been served by wholesale devastation of the country" (2002b, 187; see also Albertz 2003, 91–92).

These views are problematic (cf. Stern 2000b; 2001; Vanderhooft 2003a; more below). Common sense, as seems to have been applied by the above scholars (i.e., Barstad, Lipschits, Blenkinsopp, and others) in their criticism of the traditional view, is essential but is culturally laden and can be very misleading (Deutsch 1959). In chapter 5, we have seen that destroying the enemy's settlement, even after the victory, made sense in Mesopotamian perception of warfare (psychological warfare, see Saggs 1984, 248–50; see also Kern 1999). In chapter 8, we will see that the above quotations are also based on what appears to be a misunderstanding of the place the region had in ancient Mesopotamian imperial economic systems (compare also the fate of Tyre, for example in ch. 3). Here, however, we would like to examine the issue from a broader, cross-cultural perspective.

THE ARCHAEOLOGY OF POST-COLLAPSE

Over the last two decades, significant archaeological attention was devoted to the processes of collapse (e.g., Tainter 1988; Yoffe and Cowgill 1991). However, the processes that succeeded collapse, termed "post-collapse," received far less attention. Still, Tainter devoted a detailed cross-cultural study into the state of post-collapse societies (1999), and others have made an effort to study regeneration after collapse (Schwartz and Nichols 2006). According to Tainter, "collapse is a rapid, significant, loss of an established level of socio-political complexity" (1999, 989). A society can collapse as a result of internal processes (as emphasized in many recent studies), as a result of external forces, or a combination of the two (e.g., Tainter 1999; Fagan 1999, 193–95; Liverani 2001). Frequently, the consequences of collapse were seen in diverse areas such as art, architecture, and literature. Tainter's study is relevant for our discussion, and almost all of his characteristics of post-collapse societies, for example, population decline, end of monumental construction, political fragmentation, etc., can be seen in sixth century B.C.E. Judah.[2] The next section will review the main characteristics as outlined by Tainter (and others), and their application to sixth-century Judah.

---

1. It should be noted that the mere establishment of such a new province is doubted by many scholars (e.g., Oded 2003; Vanderhooft 2003b, 227–29).

2. It should be noted that while the study of "post-collapse societies" tended to concentrate on empires, "any kind of society can collapse" (Tainter 1999, 991).

POPULATION

Tainter first focused on population:

> Whether as cause, consequence, or both, depopulation frequently accompa-
> nies collapse. Not only do urban populations decline, so also do the support
> populations of the countryside. Many settlements are concurrently aban-
> doned. The levels of population and settlement may revert to those of centu-
> ries or even millennia before (1999, 1021).

This description depicts the way most scholars view Judah in the sixth century.
Tainter showed that depopulation could reach 75 to 90 percent (Tainter 1999,
1010) and even as high as 94 percent (1016). The data Tainter presented do not
prove that this is what happened in Judah, but they clearly showed that it is possible. Tainter provided various examples to such depopulation, ranging from
Rome, to Ur, to the lowland Maya.[3] While not part of his comprehensive study,
we can also use the Intermediate Bronze Age in the southern Levant as another
archaeological example. The urbanized Early Bronze Age is usually regarded as
a settlement peak of 140,000 people (e.g., Broshi and Gophnah 1984).[4] The succeeding intermediate Bronze Age, however, presents us with one of the lowest
periods in the settlement and demography of the region. Not only were the urban
centers destroyed or abandoned, but the estimated population was about 10,000–
15,000 people, which was a mere 10 percent (or even less) of the preceding and
succeeding period (for the Intermediate Bronze Age, see for example, Gophna
1992, 155–56, and for the Middle Bronze II, see Broshi and Gophna 1986).

The estimates of Judah's population in the sixth century as some 10 percent
or slightly more (twenty percent at the utmost, see above) of that the seventh
century B.C.E. on the basis of the archaeological evidence is in line with the situation in many other post-collapse societies. Interestingly, similar conclusions were
recently reached by Liverani (2005, 195–96), who referred to "a severe demographic and cultural crisis," adding that "all the archaeological indicators point
to a real collapse." Liverani estimated "a population collapse of 85–90 percent"
(195), and the remaining "peasant population (in Judah is) estimated at between
10,000 and 20,000 people" (196).

---

3. For another case of extreme abandonment, where "almost all existing settlements were
abandoned," see Conlee 2006, 106–7.

4. See the reservations in ch. 5 regarding population estimations. In the following, I refer to
the trends, which are clear-cut.

ARCHITECTURE

From an architectural perspective, in post-collapse societies "there is an end to monumental construction" (Tainter 1999, 1024). In many cases, people reuse older structures, or even "mine" them for building material. Such processes are witnessed in Rome, in Maya sites, and Teotihuacan (1024–25). The rarity of finds in the sixth century was already discussed. The reuse of the fort (or estate) at Kh. Abu et-Twein (Mazar 1982, 105), at whatever capacity, is a good illustration of the reality in Judah, and how nicely it fits with that of other post-collapse societies (for the reuse of structures, see ch. 10). Notably, even the Persian period in Judah is characterized by the rarity of structures, and the number of monumental buildings was very small even then (ch. 5). The scarcity of architectural finds from the sixth century is neither impossible nor unique.

COLLAPSE, SIMPLIFICATION, AND FRAGMENTATION

Collapse is also accompanied by political and territorial fragmentation (Tainter 1999, 1026; see also Schwartz 2006, 5; Conlee 2006, 105). According to Tainter, "simplification of the political hierarchy is almost by definition an attribute of collapse" (1999, 1023). Many ranks simply disappear, and the entire political structure changes in make up by becoming much simpler. So does society in general (Tainter 1999, 1024). Specialization also decreases, trade is reduced, and the economy becomes simpler. In Mycenea, for example, craft workers and artisans disappeared after the collapse.

This description depicts the situation in Judah, as exemplified by the later emergence of the Yehud province. The area covered only a limited part of the former kingdom of Judah, which was divided between several polities. The economy was simplified (ch. 10) and trade almost disappeared in the sixth century (ch. 3).

Interestingly, when studying the collapse of Ur, Tainter (2000, 12) wrote, "when the administration apparatus collapsed it took the countryside with it." The situation in Ur was more complex than in Judah because the administration managed the canals which were crucial for agriculture. Nevertheless, this statement is important because the countryside is precisely where supporters of the continuity school look for continuity. While less complex than Ur, the economy of Judah (and Philistia) in the seventh century was quite advanced and dependent upon many factors (Faust and Weiss 2005; 2011, and references). This economic system could not have existed without a complex system of arbitrators, middlemen, transportation, and so on. While probably not intentionally created by any government, the complex network could not have existed without administration. Tainter's example clearly shows that the countryside was dependent on the central administration. The more complex the economy, the less chances the countryside stands to exist without such administration. Once the administration collapsed, so did the countryside.

Interestingly, a similar explanation was raised by Jamieson-Drake (1991, 75–76, 145–47) for the collapse of Judah in the sixth century B.C.E. Admittedly, Jamieson-Drake's work was very problematic in many respects, but he correctly identified the collapse, and brilliantly described the processes. According to him, the regional administration system became gradually more and more complex. But, "a heavy price was apparently paid in terms of adaptability and survivability" (Jamieson-Drake 1991, 147). The Babylonian destruction, along with the removal of the central administrative systems which sustained the complex economic systems (76), as well as the loss of the administrative system of communication "doomed the regional social system to almost complete dissolution" (146). Without the administrative system, other problems, such as famine and "voluntary" migration to other regions, reduced the population even further (75–76).

Emic Perspectives on the Pre-Collapse Past and on the Present

Tainter (1999, 1028) also noted that a feature of many post-collapse societies was that they treat their past as "a paradise lost, a golden age of good government, wise rule, harmony and peace." Such perspectives or mythology are evident, for example, in the Roman world, the western Chou, and the Mauryan of India. This could also be the background for the development of epics like the *Iliad* and *Odyssey* and the emergence of the hero-cult in ancient Greece (Tainter 1999, 1028–29).

This phenomenon is also seen in Judah. Lamentations' opening words, for example, refer to Jerusalem prior to the destruction as "she that was great among the nations; she that was a princess among the provinces" (Lam 1:1). Later, Jerusalem is referred to as "the city that was called the perfection of beauty, the joy of all the earth" (Lam 2:15).

Views of the Present, in Light of the Past
    The grave situation in Judah was reflected in the period's sources (cf. Tainter 1999, 1022, 1028–29). This can be seen in Neh 7:4, "The city was wide and large, but the people within were few and no houses had been built." The exact dating or historical reality behind the verse is of less importance. The significance is conveyed by the words that describe the density of the population, especially when compared with the ruins that dominated the City of David and the Western Hill (see also Eshel 2000, 341). Moreover, various prophecies in Zech 9–14

(second Zech) give the same impression (Meyers and Meyers 1994). The lower demographic density of Judea had a strong impact on Zechariah. Meyers and Meyers wrote:

> the eschatological setting of a divinely effected in-gathering in chapter 10 emerges from the sense that the population of Yehud is extraordinarily limited in size. ... The sense that the prophet is speaking from the context of a weak and much reduced population is highlighted by the eschatological emphasis on population growth and of expansion (1994, 271).

Meyers and Meyers (1994, 273) summarized, "The eschaton, in military-political matters and also in demography, will be a dramatic reversal of the dismal situation of the first half of the postexilic period" (see also their discussion of Zech 13 and 14; 273–78). The above examples show that the inhabitants of Judea felt they were few and weak (see also Schniedewind 2004, 168–69).

EMIC PERSPECTIVE ON COLLAPSE

Tainter also pointed out that as societies become vulnerable to collapse, there are differences in opinions as to what went wrong (1999, 1022). He presents literary evidence common to many such societies, from diverse cases like China at the end of the Western Chou, Rome in the third century, and the Old Kingdom of Egypt. Literary evidence from late-seventh and sixth-century Judah fits this pattern. Lamentations 4:13, for example, blames, "it was for the sins of her prophets, and the inequities of her priests who shed the blood of the righteous in the midst of her" (see also Lam 2:14; Jeremiah 3:6–11, and many others; for an extended discussion with many references, see now Rom-Shiloni 2009; see also Middlemas's 2007, 47–49 theological analysis; especially worthy of mentioning in this context is the Deuteronomistic History [pp. 52–63]). Again, the information from Judah, while not surprising, is in line with other post-collapse societies.

RECOVERY FROM COLLAPSE

Tainter also noted that recovery is a long process—usually lasting three to five hundred years, but sometimes even longer (1999, 1026–27). This is indeed in line with our understanding of the demographic reality in the Persian period Judea as discussed in chapter 5. While the sixth century B.C.E. reflected the lowest point in the region's social complexity, demography, and so on, the effects of the collapse remained long after the sixth century. Therefore, both the sixth century and the Persian period lie in the shadow of the collapse. As in many other instances, the recovery of Judah took hundreds of years, and only in the Hellenistic period (and probably even in the late Hellenistic period) did Judah fully recover (see also Smith 1990; Berlin 1997; cf. Kloner 2003, 26; Magen 2004, 5, 7). Judah during the entire Persian period should therefore still be viewed as a post-collapse society.

Terminology and Sources of Information

The lack of concrete data regarding the sixth century has led many scholars to stress the gloomy reality in the region during this century, to speak about the great decline, and to refer to the relative emptiness of the area (though they did not literally speak of an "empty land"—see ch. 8). Sometimes the period has even been regarded as a "dark age." Barkay, for example, wrote in his oft-quoted work on the periodization of the Iron Age (after describing the lack of finds from this period), that "as a consequence, it is a *dark period* for archaeological stratigraphy" (Barkay 1993, 108; emphasis added; cf. Weinberg 1969, 28).

Interestingly, Tainter (1999, 1025) noted that in many cases the term "dark age" is applied to post-collapse societies. While he suggested that the term should be used with care, suffice it to show that situations similar to Judah were frequent (and could indicate something on the nature of the period itself).

More important for the present section are the usual sources of information on this "dark age" and for what Tainter labeled "post-collapse archaeology" (Tainter 1999, 1029–30). Tainter lamented the lack of data from settlements, and wrote, "the extent to which post-collapse archaeology relies on burials is striking. ... Much of what we know of these post-collapse societies comes from a very small number of graves" (1029). He added, "archaeologists who study these periods are not averse to excavating settlements, but they are able to locate surprisingly few." Furthermore, "while this is deplorable from the perspective of representative data, it does reflect the nature of post-collapse societies" (1030). Again, this description fits well with the traditional view of the sixth century B.C.E. in Judah. Here, the limited data was derived to a large extent from a few tombs, and no real settlements were excavated. The following quotations exemplify the phenomenon.

In his summary of the Iron Age II, Barkay wrote, "the material culture of the Babylonian period in Judaea is known chiefly from surveys and burial caves found in Beth-Shemesh, Gibeah (Tell el-Ful) and Jerusalem" (1992, 372). And elsewhere he explicitly wrote, "most of the information on this period comes, in the meantime, from tombs" (1998a, 25; my translation; and he added that the reanalysis of Tell en-Nasbeh and Tell el-Ful also clarified the picture; for the latter; see ch. 9). After lamenting the lack of stratigraphic finds, he wrote, "ceramic assemblages from this period are primarily from burial caves" (1993,

108). Recently, in his monumental work on the Assyrian, Babylonian, and Persian periods, Stern wrote, "We have already seen that the most prominent evidence for the existence of the sixth century B.C.E. pottery comes from a small number of tombs at Tell en-Nasbeh, Tell el-Ful, Abu Ghosh, and especially Tomb 14 at Beth-Shemesh" (2001, 342). This is no accident, and Judah follows the trends of other post-collapse societies. This is important not only because it shows that Judah fits the patterns of post-collapse societies so nicely, but also because it indicates the scarcity of settlement at the time. We simply have not found it yet.

SOCIAL MOBILITY

Collapse of the social order also allows for social mobility. When a society loses its "fabric" and experiences drastic change, there is movement between the social classes. Individuals once of low status might have the opportunity to acquire symbols of higher status, such as better quality lands, and with them a higher social position. Meanwhile, members of the higher classes might lose their positions of wealth (e.g., Schwartz 2006, 9; Morris 2006, 66–67; see also Conlee 2006, 107–8, 113). Such drastic shifts in a society further escalate the process of social change and societal collapse.

ADDITIONAL CHANGES (CH. 4 REVISITED)

Chapter 4 has already discussed transformations that occurred in family and kinship ties, architecture, burial practices, language, cosmology, and so on; this chapter will not repeat those arguments. It must be stressed, however, that those social changes were clearly the result of the collapse of the Judahite society in the sixth century.

DISCUSSION

JUDAH AS A POST-COLLAPSE SOCIETY

The characteristics mentioned in this chapter show that sixth-century Judah should be viewed as a post-collapse society. Moreover, the above shows that the traditional view of Judah cannot be ruled out, even though some scholars claim that it simply does not make sense. As Barstad wrote "it would have been unwise of Nebuchadnezzar to destroy Judah" (2003, 11). Even if the Babylonians did not want this to happen, as claimed by Barstad (1996, 67–68; 2003, 11) and Blenkinsopp (2002b, 187), and this is doubted by many (Stern 2000b; Vanderhooft 2003a;

and Stager 1996, 71*–72*; see also ch. 5), then not everything was in their hands. Once in motion, the processes of collapse continued, to a large extent indifferent to Babylonian imperial intentions.

Not only did people die in the war, the executions that followed, the famine and epidemics that occurred during the war and after it, and others were exiled or "voluntarily" fled to other regions (ch. 5), but the collapse of the state and its apparatus made the above mentioned problems even more severe. Coupled with the growing insecurity, the population of Judah shrank dramatically in the first years following the destruction. Notably, we have already discussed the relevant population estimations, but the present chapter addressed something more important: not only was there a great demographic decline, but society simply collapsed and crushed. Regardless of the exact number of inhabitants, life did not go on as usual following the collapse of the kingdom of Judah (cf. Reviv 1993, 196). Even Albertz (2003, 96), who generally speaking accepts the basic tenants of the continuity theory, claimed that the remaining inhabitants had "largely lost their territorial social integrity."[5]

Such post-collapse societies are common throughout history (see also Price 1978, 176), and we should try to understand them instead of ignoring the evidence and claiming that they are "illogical." The situation in Judah was not unique or unheard of, but fits nicely into the category of a post-collapse society. This supports the traditional view of sixth-century Judah and shows that collapse is a process involving fragmentation, disintegration, and social change. The cessation in the use of cultural features (i.e., the Judahite tomb and the four-room house in our case; see ch. 4) is therefore expected.

A COMMENT ON THE SITUATION IN JUDAH AND THE STUDY OF POST-COLLPASE

While collapse and cultural break can be almost total (e.g., Manahan 2004; see also various papers in Schwartz and Nichols 2006), it is clear that this is not necessarily the case (e.g., Schwartz 2006, 6). As far as Judah is concerned, we have stressed the "break" with the Persian period, but there were also some patterns of cultural and religious continuity (though less apparent; and, to stress, with almost no patterns of settlement continuity), for example, negative views of imports and trade (e.g., Faust 2006b, 49–64; 2006c, and references).

---

5. Albertz also wrote about a collapse after the attempts to stabilize Judah at the time of Gedaliah failed, so it appears that (in relation to most of the sixth century) he should not be counted as supporter of the continuity school.

I believe that those patterns should be incorporated in studies that examine the society in the Persian and Hellenistic periods. While naturally concentrating on the Judean contexts, it would probably be worthwhile to conduct such studies also within the framework of more general studies of regeneration (Schwartz and Nichols 2006) which can provide useful conceptual tools and research questions.

I believe that such studies would be the appropriate place to examine lines of real and imagined continuity with the Iron Age. Such lines are apparent in the Hasmonean period—the time in which Judea and its environs finally recovered (demographically) from the collapse (the time when "regeneration" occurred).[6] While the issue of Jewish identity in the Second Temple period has already received more attention and sophisticated analysis (e.g., Mendels 1992; Schwartz 2001; Goodblatt 2006, and references), I think that the "framework," or concept of regeneration might be useful for future studies.

As mentioned above, processes leading to collapse have received much attention in the recent past. I should therefore note that I did not deal with these processes in the present monograph, as those processes preceded the period discussed here.

While it is quite clear that the collapse of the various southern Levantine states in the late Iron Age can be studied within an examination of large-scale, long-term processes involving the position of the region within the greater ancient Near East, I believe the present case study can also demonstrate the importance of more traditional lines of explanation, e.g., military campaigns. The various lines of evidence are not mutually exclusive, of course, and the latter can be examined within the framework of the former, but since traditional explanations (e.g., war) are sometimes disregarded nowadays, I believe the present study demonstrates that they are also important.

SUMMARY

Collapse is an integral part of social complexity, and many societies collapse as a result of either internal of external factors, or a combination of both. Collapse might have severe consequences affecting all spheres of life, and the recovery usually takes centuries. We have shown that Judah in the Neo-Babylonian period, and even during the Persian period, was a post-collapse society. An examination of additional such societies show that Judah has many parallels worldwide. Therefore, the traditional view is very reasonable when examined within a broader anthropological perspective.

---

6. See comment above regarding the reuse of Iron Age burials at the time (above, ch. 4).

Postscript: Northern Israel (and the Coastal Plain) in the Seventh and Sixth Centuries b.c.e. and the Archaeology of Post-Collapse

A similar process of collapse, even if somewhat weaker, took place in northern Israel following the Assyrian destructions of the eighth century b.c.e. The former kingdom of Israel was devastated following the Assyrian campaigns. For example, according to Gal, the Galilee was almost empty following the Assyrian destructions and deportations,[7] and the same was true for the Northern Valleys (Cohen-Tavor 2011, 18) and other regions, both in Israel and in the coastal plain.[8] Almost every excavated settlement in those regions was destroyed by the Assyrians—or, at least, there is evidence that its occupation stopped—such as Dan, Hazor, Kinrot, Tel Hadar, Bethsaida, En Gev, Beth-Shean, Tel Rehov, Tel Zira'a, Kedesh, Megiddo, Jokneam, Tel Qiri, Acco, Tel Keison, Shikmona, Dor, Taanakh, Dothan, Samaria, Tell el-Far'ah (N), Shechem, Bethel, Gezer, Rishon Leziyon, Tel Mor, Ashdod, Ashdod Yam, Tell el-Hesi, Kh. Huga, Tel Haror, and Tel Sera.[9] While the issue deserves a more detailed discussion, and the destruction was not the same throughout the area (cf. Knoppers 2004; see also Dever 2007), recovery was extremely limited and took a very long time—perhaps even longer than in Judah.

Economic Setback

Perhaps the best evidence for this gloomy situation in the area of the former kingdom of Israel in the seventh century is economic. The seventh century was a peak of economic activity in large parts of the land of Israel, as seen by the large port town of Ashkelon, the giant olive oil production center at Ekron, the settlement and finds in the Negev and the Judean Desert, and the dense hinterland of Jerusalem.[10] In contrast, the new Assyrian provinces were left out of this prosperity (ch. 8). Phoenicia, Philistia, and even Judah were part of the flourishing economic

---

7. (1992, 108–9). For the limited settlement that existed there, see Gal 2009.

8. See also Pakkala, Munger, and Zangenberg 2004, 25; Gilboa 1996, 122; Herzog 1997b, 278; Vieweger and Häser 2007.

9. A partial list of sites outside Judah, based on Stern 2001, 7, 9; see also Mazar 2011; Stern 2004, 274–75; Gal 1992, 108–9; Vieweger and Häser 2007.

10. Ashkelon: e.g., Stager 1996, Master 2003; Ekron: Gitin 1989; 1995; 1997; the Negev and the Judean Desert: Finkelstein 1995a; Bar-Adon 1989; Liphschits and Biger 1991; Jerusalem: Feig 1999; Faust 2007a; for the entire phenomenon, see Faust and Weiss 2005; 2011, with many references.

system, but the territories that were previously part of the kingdom of Israel and were now Assyrian provinces did not. The area still lay in ruins to a large extent (see also Faust 2011b; Faust and Weiss 2011).

This is even more striking when looking at the role of olive oil in the new economic system of the seventh century B.C.E., probably because nothing of significance was produced there (cf. Ekron; Gitin 1989; 1995; 1997). During the eighth century, the regions of Samaria and the Galilee were the largest centers of olive oil production in the region (e.g., Eitam 1980; 1992; Gal and Alexandre 2000; Gal and Franker 1993; see also the detailed discussion in Faust 2011b). After the Assyrian conquests, however, the centers of olive oil production moved southward (e.g., Gitin 1998; see also Eitam 1987; 1996), and the territories of the former kingdom of Israel did not participate in the seventh-century economic system.

SETTLEMENT RECOVERY UNDER ASSYRIAN RULE?

Stern wrote that after a while the Assyrians attempted to resettle the country, to bring new populations to the region, and to conduct public building operations (2001, 50). He even concluded that some regions reached settlement explosion at the time of Assyrian hegemony. However, this latter observation was based on the identification of settlements in a fringe area that had not been settled before—Samaria's western foothills. Stern believed this could have only resulted from population explosion (50–51). This settlement wave, however, was not a result of settlement explosion in Samaria. It was rather a result of relative flourishing in the coastal plain and the international highway that passed along the trough valley, together with the settlement of exiles—probably from Mesopotamia—that resettled in the region (Faust 1995b; 2006a; Na'aman and Zadok 2000). There is no need, therefore, to postulate population explosion anywhere within the Assyrian Provinces in the seventh century.

Stern's lists also show that many of the sites that were destroyed by the Assyrians did not recover at all, while many that were resettled after the destruction did not reach the same density and size (e.g., Stern 2001, 7, 9, 312–15; 2004, 275). This is inevitable. The population that was transferred to the region by the Assyrians[11] must have been much smaller in size than the one that existed prior to the Assyrian conquest. This was not just a peaceful "exchange" of populations. Many people died in the wars, famine, epidemics, and so forth; those that were exiled

---

11. The Assyrians, unlike the Babylonians, also transferred people to the region (e.g., Oded 1979), whereas, the Babylonians only transferred populations from the region.

(and stayed alive during the long march to their new homes) in both regions could not have made up for the loss of population. Furthermore, the exiled were not familiar with the local terrain, ecology, and economy, and could not have brought real prosperity. The Assyrians insured that the resettled populations would not rebel ("creating a less homogenous population that was more docile"; Van de Mieroop 2007, 251), and would perhaps bring some limited "income," but no more than that.[12]

Almost every region of the country that was under Assyrian rule experienced severe decline (also Herzog 1997b, 278). The only exception was the coastal plain (see also Gilboa 1996), partially due to the importance of the international highway for the Assyrians, and partially due to flourishing maritime trade (Frankenstein 1979; Bedford 2005, 72–73; Faust and Weiss 2005; 2011, and references). Economically, Samaria and other regions were quite "backward" during the seventh century. Coupled with the data regarding settlement, "recovery" under Assyria was very limited at best.[13]

The Nadir

The Assyrian period, while representing a severe decline, does not necessarily present us with the demographic and economic nadir. Many of the seventh-century settlements—those that recovered (partially at least) after the Assyrian campaigns—simply ceased to exist during the transition to Babylonian rule (e.g., Stern 2001, 312–21; 2004, 275). The sites that recovered during the seventh century but were destroyed in the late-seventh century B.C.E. include Megiddo III,[14] Jokneam (Ben Tor 1993), Dor (Stern 2000a, 131–45), Tel Batash (Mazar and Panitz-Cohen 2001), Tel Sera (Oren 1993b), and Tel Haror (Oren 1993a). The exact agent of destruction (cf. the claims of Bleninsopp 2002b, 183) is irrelevant for the present discussion, but what is important is that the sites were destroyed in the upheavals that accompanied the demise of the Assyrian Empire. The sixth century represents the lowest point in the history of some of those regions, which

---

12. For the Assyrian policy and its rationale, see Oded 1979; Kuhrt 1993, 532–34; Smith 1989, 29–31; Van de Mieroop 2007, 251.

13. For various sites that existed at the time and perhaps served as Assyrian administrative centers in the new provinces, see ch. 8. Those sites, however, were insignificant demographically. Furthermore, even if their interpretation as Assyrian administrative centers is correct (and in many cases this is doubted), they only show that the Assyrians did build specific structures in order to rule the devastated provinces.

14. At Megiddo, the central Assyrian provincial city (and probably the only one built by the Assyrians) ceased to exist in the late-seventh century B.C.E. (e.g., Kempinski 1989).

did not have an opportunity to recover from one catastrophe before suffering another one. Generally speaking, those regions took centuries to recover. This explains why the Persian period was a period of minimal settlement in some of the regions that were also part of the Assyrian Empire, and did not suffer from the Babylonian military campaigns to the same extent as Judah (ch. 5). The country was just beginning the long process of recovery. A similar nadir is seen in other aspects of the archaeology of the sixth century, for example, the lack of Greek pottery (ch. 3) and evidence of "Neo-Babylonian administration" (ch. 8).[15]

Implications

This has clear implications for our study, even beyond supplying additional examples for the effects of collapse. It shows that we are not discussing a "myth of empty land" in Judah created by biblical writers, and perpetuated by naïve scholars. There was indeed a huge demographic and economic decline in the sixth century throughout the region (and it was even more than the decline during the Assyrian period). If the Bible was "responsible" for scholars' failure to identify the expansive settlement of Judah in the sixth century, there was nothing to prevent scholarship from identifying the large and dense settlement in the rest of the country. That Judah is but one component of a larger phenomenon (see also Stern 2001; Liverani 2005, 231; Herzog 1997b, 278) proves that it is not the "myth of the empty land" and an uncritical reading of the Bible that are responsible for creating this perception.

More importantly, however, is the fact that the above shows that processes of collapse have grave impact on large regions, and that the processes of recovery take hundreds of years. Judah was but one component of this large-scale process.

---

15. The situation in the former territories of the kingdom of Israel is worthy of a detailed examination, which is well beyond the scope of the present work.

CHAPTER 8
CONSEQUENCES OF DESTRUCTION:
THE CONTINUITY THEORY REVISITED

D ue to the debate that arose in the last decade over the reality in Judah during the sixth century B.C.E., I have attempted in previous chapters to decipher the "reality on the ground" at this time. Throughout the investigations, various aspects of the debate between the traditional view of the sixth century in Judah and the supporters of the continuity theory have been examined, but only as part of a larger attempt to reconstruct settlement, social, and cultural patterns. Those investigations have led us to conclude that it is the traditional view, albeit in a somewhat more sophisticated and complex way, that fits the archaeological and historical data. Over the course of the discussion, we discussed and refuted various aspects of the theory that the Babylonian destructions were partial and that life in most settlements in Judah was not affected by them. While the above is clearly sufficient to disprove this theory, this chapter will discuss the continuity theory in more detail. The discussion will focus on aspects of the continuity theory that were not discussed in earlier parts of the book or that received only scant attention (see also Oded and Faust 2006). I will begin with an examination of the arguments raised by supporters of the continuity theory and will proceed by scrutinizing them.

THE INVENTION OF A LITERARY "EMPTY LAND"

The theory of continuity in Judah after the Babylonian destruction was developed with the explicit aim to "free" research from the biblically derived conception of an "empty land," to which the exiles returned in the Persian period.[1]

---

1. For the "biblical myth," see, e.g., Caroll 1992; Barstad 1996; 2003; Blenkinsopp 2002a; 2002b; 2002c. It should be stressed that this will to "liberate" archaeological research from the

The initiators of the theory, therefore, strove to prove that the land was not liter-ally empty, and concluded that most of the inhabitants remained in the land.

Barstad, in the first sentence of his influential work wrote (Barstad 1996, 13), "I shall rather occupy myself with the widespread belief that Judah during this period was a *tabula rasa* where no activity to speak of took place." Later, for example, he referred to the idea "that Palestine was *completely* depopulated and in ruins after 586 B.C.," and adds: "This idea of an uninhabited and uninhabit-able Palestine ... was deeply rooted, and its after effects may be felt strongly even today" (15, emphasis mine) Then he referred to "the notion of a *total* exile, with the carrying away of the *entire* population" (15; see also page 77; the same sen-tence is repeated in Barstad 2003, 3; emphasis mine). In the opening sentence of his 2003 paper he refers again to "the idea of uninhabited and uninhabitable Palestine following Nebuchadnezzar in 586 B.C.E.," which was rooted deeply in the mentality of nineteenth century scholarship, and whose aftereffects are felt even today (3). Elsewhere, again, he counters the view of a *"total annihilation"* of a conquered territory (1996, 67–68). In the conclusions he writes, "in particu-lar I have attempted to demonstrate that the belief that the land of Judah was in ruins and *uninhabited...* is highly improbable" (77). Notably, in his 1996 book he admits that there are many other voices (1996, 15–16, 18, n. 19), but basically confronts the idea of a *totally* and *completely* destroyed and empty land. Lipschits, too, rejects the idea "that *all* of the kingdom's territories were destroyed or that the population in its *entirety* was deported. ... *Total* devastation of the *entire* region would also have been contrary to Babylonian interests" (2005, 69). And Blenkinsopp (2002b) wrote:

> More than half a century ago William Foxwell Albright, one of the icons of biblical scholarship in the twentieth century, gave a characteristically cat-egoric answer to the question. Between the fall of Jerusalem in 586 B.C.E. and the fall of Babylon in 539 B.C.E., "All, or virtually all, of the fortified towns in Judah had been razed to the ground. There is not a single known case where a town of Judah was continuously occupied through the exilic Period." We can hardly avoid a sense of *déjà vu* (or *déjà lu*) on reading the opinion of Ephraim Stern, one of the leading Israeli authorities on the archaeology of the period (Iron IIIB), stated in the November–December 2000 issue of *Biblical Archaeology Review* and more fully in the second volume of his *Ar-chaeology of the Land of the Bible*. He concludes as follows: "A review of the

---

biblical burden resulted from interests that had nothing to do with archaeology or with history, but rather with debates over the dating and/or place of writing of the various texts (see more below in this chapter); it even had some connection with modern politics (the issue is touched upon briefly in the summary).

archaeological evidence from sixth-century B.C.E. Judah *clearly* reflects the literary (i.e., biblical) evidence for the *complete* destruction of *all* the settlements and fortified towns by Nebuchadnezzar II's armies in 586 BCE." Or, again: we are told that the archaeological data attest to "the *total* destruction and devastation of *all* the main cities that had flourished during the Assyrian period. ... *All* its cities lay in ruins by the end of the Babylonian period" (177–78).

Judah was not literally empty. But, in contrast to Barstad's, Blenkinsopp's, and Lipschits's claims, such was never the common view.

Almost all scholars who have dealt with the sixth century referred to those who remained in the land. Kenyon (1965, 298), for example, wrote that "the remnant of the population must have continued to live in such villages as had survived destruction," but added that they "contributed little toward their structural history." Even Albright stressed, in contrast to the impression one might get from Blenkinsopp's quotation of him, that there was population in ruined Judah. Indeed, he writes against the views of Torrey and others that there "was no drastic break in the continuity of life in Judah as a result of the Chaldaean invasion" (Albright 1960b, 140–41). But even he refers to the phenomenon in which strata that were destroyed in the sixth century were followed by "use for non-urban purposes" (141–42; whether he is right in attributing those phases to the sixth century is irrelevant for the present discussion). Elsewhere, he attributed settlement to the Negev and Benjamin (Albright 1940, 247; see also 1963, 86). Notably, Albright (1963, 87) even attempted to calculate the number of those who lived in small Judea (from the area of Benjamin to Beth-Zur) in 522 B.C.E., and reached the figure of twenty thousand people. This is in line with relatively high modern estimations (ch. 5).[2]

It is clear that nobody could blame Albright in believing that the land was completely void of population (contra, e.g., Blenkinsopp 2002b, 177, above).[3] Following Albright, Bright (1972, 344) also believed that the population in Judah when the first returnees arrived was over 20,000, and before that it was "sparse indeed." Aharoni (1979, 409–10) also referred to the remainders and, on the basis

---

2. Actually, this is a high figure, but one should remember that demographic estimation of the time tended to be much higher than those of today (though Albright's estimation for seventh-century Judah [Albright 1963, 84] is also not too far apart from Lipschits's estimation, above).

3. Albright (e.g., 1963, 86; quoted above by Blenkinsopp) wrote about the destruction of "all, or virtually all, of the *fortified towns* in Judah had been razed to the ground" (my emphasis). This view is accepted by most supporters of the continuity theory, so the way Blenkisopp used this quote is somewhat misleading.

of the texts, assumed that they were relatively concentrated "in the border regions of Judea, viz. in the Negeb, the Shephelah and the district of Benjamin." Mazar, while addressing the scarcity of information on the Babylonian period (1990, 549) and the destruction of many sites (1990, 458–60, 548), still stressed that there was settlement in Benjamin (460, 548). He wrote that not all the population was exiled and the poorer people remained in Judah (548). The same can be seen in Barkay's works (e.g., 1992, 372). King and Stager (2001, 257) also wrote, "of course, there must have been some 'am ha'ares[4] who remained," adding that the widespread destruction did "not imply that the countryside was totally uninhabited between 586–538" Almost every archaeologist[5] stressed that there were people in the land (see also Dever 1971, 469–70, n. 16). Even Stern (e.g., 2000b, 51), the archaeologist who is most accused of forwarding the myth of the empty land (e.g., Blenkinsopp 2002b, 177–78, above) wrote "there were undoubtedly some settlements" (but added, "but population was very small"; see also Stern 2001, 350).[6]

Not only were balanced views regarding settlement in the sixth century quite common (see also Dever 2005, 291–94), but many scholars had even explicitly stated that the land was not literally empty. Bright (1972, 343–44), for example, wrote that "the popular notion of a total deportation which left the land empty

---

4. The term refers to the free, probably land-owning, population of Judah (e.g., Reviv, 1993, 149–56, and many references).

5. Many non–archaeologists also stressed this point. See the quote from Bright above; see also Smith (1989, 31–32).

6. It must be admitted that in some places Stern and others have used terminology that stressed the emptiness of the land (e.g., Stern 2001, 323). However, many of the quotes that were brought forth by Blenkinsopp refer to the total destruction of the urban centers—a view which is supported also by Barstad, Lipschits, etc. (see also above), so the quotes are misleading. At any event, a close reading of Stern's (and others') work will usually show reference to the population that did live in sixth-century Judah.

Notably, many of Blenkinsopp's arguments are problematic. For example, he debates Stern's attribution of some destructions to the Babylonians (Blenkinsopp 2002b, 181–87). But when discussing the "empty land," it is immaterial who destroyed each and every site; whether all or most of the sites were destroyed by the Babylonians (as suggested by Stern), or that some or even many were destroyed by the Egyptians, Edomites, etc., does not change the fact that the sites were destroyed, and this is the real issue. Blenkinsopp's writing is problematic in other aspects as well, but given the overall evidence, there is no need to discuss each point he raised in his paper. Finally, I should note that I sympathize with Blenkisopp's (2002a, 13–14) claim that one need not be an archaeologist in order to express a view on archaeological matters; the academic degree should not count, but whether one knows the data one is writing about does.

and void is erroneous and to be discarded."[7] However, he stressed that "the catastrophe was nevertheless appalling and one which signaled the disruption of Jewish life in Palestine" (1972, 344). In a similar vein, Schniedewind wrote that "the land was not emptied," adding "but it was depopulated" (2004, 143). Oded also wrote that "all lines of evidence converge to the conclusion that Judah was not an empty land, a tabula rasa, during the exilic period" 2003, 71). He added, however, that "the population was very small," noting "continuity yes, but with a marked decline in quality and very limited in quantity" Such balanced views match the archaeological evidence, as discussed above.

So why did Barstad, Blenkinsopp, and Lipschits attempt to stress that the land was not completely empty (note that since the remnants in the land are even mentioned in the Bible, even the most fundamentalist readers are not expected to deny their existence)? The views presented by Barstad and advocated by Lipschits and Blenkinsopp regarding the settlement in the sixth century B.C.E. are indeed extreme, but there was quite a wide spectrum of views in existence before that. When compared to many of the works quoted above, the continuity theory is not convincing and is seen as extremist. Therefore, Barstad, Blenkinsopp, and others created a straw man. The straw man claimed that the land was literally empty— totally; and that the entire population was carried away. Now, when supporters of the continuity theory contrasted their views with that of the straw man, their views were seen as the more reasonable, while their opponents were ridiculed.[8] We should remember, however, that the unreasonable claims they are disproving are simply those of the straw man. In this way, the continuity theorists invented the theory of a completely empty land.

THE CAUSES OF THE DEMOGRAPHIC "EMPTINESS"

Another problem with the continuity theory is its representation of the reasons behind the "emptiness" of the land, as supposedly viewed by other scholars. Supporters of the continuity theory systematically suggest that the "complete emptiness" of the land was a result of the "total" exile of the entire population by the Babylonians.[9] Thus, Barstad wrote:

---

7. Noth (1960, 296) also wrote "the Babylonian group represented a mere outpost, whereas Palestine was and remained the central arena of Israel's history, and the descendants of the old tribes who remained in the land, with the holy place of Jerusalem, constituted not only numeri- cally the great mass but also the real nucleus of Israel."

8. See also Lipschits 2004.

9. E.g., Barstad 1996, 18, 30, 33–34, 37–38, 40, 42–43, 62–63, 68, 79–80; Lipschits 2003b, 219; 2005, 59–62, 69, 187, 367–72. This seems to be part of Torrey's heritage, e.g., 1910 [1970].

Obviously, we should not deny that several deportations took place. What we must renounce, however, is the claim that these deportations affected life in Palestine in the way that much scholarly consensus appears to believe they did. The land left by the Babylonians was not a desolate and empty country lying in ruins" (1996, 79).

And later he wrote, "the view that the Babylonians brought into exile 'the whole of' the Judean people is preposterous on any account" (80) and that only the royalty, the elite, and skilled labor were exiled. Lipschits (2005, 69) also wrote that "there are no signs … that the population in its entirety was deported."

However, the claim that it was only the exiles who went to Mesopotamia that caused the demographic decline of the sixth century B.C.E. is just another straw man. It enables Barstad, Blenkinsopp, and others to present their views as reasonable, and their opponents' as unreasonable.

As seen in ch. 5, there were many mechanisms for demographic decline, exile being only one of them (cf. Weinberg 1969, 84; Stern 2001, 323; Schniedewind 2004, 143). Those mechanisms included death from war, executions following sieges (see, e.g., Eph'al 1996, 37–39; Kern 1999; see also Bright 1972, 344), epidemics and famine (Eph'al 1996), and movement of populations who fled to other regions (Liverani 2005, 218–20; Jamieson-Drake 1991, 76).

Clearly, a demographic decline following the Babylonian destruction is logical and feasible. Supporters of the continuity theory have therefore misrepresented the traditional view, in an attempt to make their view more reasonable. Notably, already Bright wrote that, "aside from those deported to Babylon, thousands must have died in battle or of starvation and disease (cf. Lam. 2: 11f., 19–21; 4: 9f.), some—and surely more than we know of (II Kings 25: 18–27)—had been executed, while others (cf. Jer., ch 42f.) had fled for their lives" (1972, 334).

By referring to the "notion of a total exile, with the carrying away of the entire population" (Barstad 1996, 15, and the same sentence is repeated in Barstad 2003, 3; emphasis mine), Barstad practically created two straw men in one sentence: the first was the view that the land was totally devoid of population, and the second was that it was only the exile that was responsible for it. The demographic decline of the sixth century, however, resulted from many factors, exile being only one of them (and probably not an important one).

Due to the (natural) biblical bias of biblical scholars, they have spent a greater time studying the exile. This can be demonstrated by the historical discussion in Albertz (2003, 74–111), where almost the entire discussion is devoted to exile/s, and only a few pages to the situation in Judah. This bias, however, influenced biblical scholars and theologians more than anyone else (i.e., more than archaeologists, see more below).

Finally, on the issue of exile, the supporters of the continuity school claim that the exiles were minimal, and only included the elite. However, it is well known that Babylonia was short of manpower at the time (see even Lipschits 2003b, 404–6; 2005, 59–60, 364–66). The exiles from the region were probably extensive, and included many members of various ethnic groups, including Judeans (Oded 1979; see also Oded 1995; 2000; 2010; Pearce 2006). Many settlements were even named after former settlements in the west, from which the exiled to Mesopotamia apparently came (Eph'al 1978; Vanderhooft 1999, 110–12; see also Pearce 2006; Oded 2010, 94–95). So why did supporters of the continuity theory claim that the exile was not that significant? Clearly this was not the only mechanism, and it was demographically far less important than death, but it could have still been an important one—more than some scholars care to admit.

The "Extent" of the "Empty Land" and Its Possible Biblical Origins

A basic claim of many supporters of the continuity theory was that the myth of the "empty land" was invented by those who returned from Babylonian in the Persian period, in order to legitimate their claims to the land (e.g., Lipschits 2005, xiii, 374–75; see also Caroll 1992; for a different scenario, see Barstad 1996, 14–15). They argued that modern scholarship was influenced by this myth, and "forced" it upon the finds, as they were interpreted through a biblically influenced lens (e.g., Barstad 1996, 77–79; Blenkinsopp 2002b; 2002c). There is logic behind this claim. Scholarship was indeed biblically driven, and to a large extent still is. Ironically, as we will see below, it is the supporters of the continuity theory who are driven much more by the biblical agenda.

But is the archaeological "myth of the empty land" biblically driven? It appears that contrary to those claims, this is not the case. Archaeologists who maintain that the land was relatively empty in the sixth century, that is, in a great demographic decline, speak about most of the country, including Judah of course, but also Samaria, and even the coastal plain and other regions. The following quote from Stern (2001, 350) is most revealing. After describing the gloomy reality throughout the country, he claimed that "large parts of the towns and villages were either completely or partly destroyed, and the rest was poorly functioning," adding, "(O)nly two regions appear to have been spared this fate, the north of Judah, i.e., the region of Benjamin …, and probably the land of Ammon." The same can be seen in Stager's words: "From an archaeological perspective, not only Judah but also Philistia and most of Palestine west of the Jordan River 'lay desolate' for 70 years, a veritable wasteland resulting from Nebuchadrezzar's 'scorched earth' policy in the west" (1996, 72*).

This archaeological view of large-scale desolation is supported, as we have seen, also by the lack of sixth-century imports throughout the country—even in the coastal plain (ch. 3)—as well as by the fact that the northern parts of the country were already devastated by the Assyrians and did not flourish even in the seventh century. These regions reached an even lower demographic nadir in the sixth century, as seen in chapter 7 (this fits well with the reality throughout the Levant; cf. Liverani 2005, 231).

This is another major problem for the continuity theory. If the "empty land" was just a biblically driven myth, it should have related to Judah only. There was no biblical motivation to speak about "empty" Philistia, or "empty" Samaria, or the "empty" coastal plain. Archaeologists claimed Philistia was "empty" (again, not literary empty) because of archaeological evidence. Their analysis might be wrong, but to blame them with blindly following a biblical narrative is irrelevant.

The mere fact that the same fate was attributed by archaeologists to almost the entire country, and not simply for Judah, attests that it was archaeological evidence and not biblical data that drove them to this conclusion. Would it have been a biblically driven archaeological construction, one would have expected archaeologists to construct, beside the empty Judah, a populated and flourishing Samaria and coastal plain.[10] That this is not the case suggests that we are not witnessing biblically driven archaeology, but a reconstruction based on the best available data.

The Nature of Babylonian Economic Interests in the Region

One of the main arguments of the supporters of continuity is economic, as seen in many of their arguments (e.g., the first page of Barstad's 2003 paper, as well as pages 9–13). For example, Barstad wrote that due to Judah's importance and potential, "it would have been unwise of Nebuchadnezzar to destroy Judah" and that it was in his interest to "maintain, and even increase," Judah's means of production (2003, 11; see more below). Lipschits also wrote that "total devastation of the entire region would also have been contrary to Babylonian interests, because the Empire needed the population of Judah as a human nucleus for the new

---

10. Note that Albright (1957, 322; 1960b, 142) had indeed contrasted Judah with the finds at Bethel in order to stress the break in the former (Albright identified continuity in Bethel during the sixth century B.C.E.). But this did not lead him to reconstruct sixth century settlement throughout the country. He still treated most of the country as in great decline (see his entire treatment of the Persian period, e.g., Albright 1960b, 142–45).

province it had established."[11] Interestingly, Lipschits was aware of the economic decrease under Babylonian rule (2003b, 218; 2005, 186), but he still wrote (2005, 69) that "the Babylonians also needed the settlements and their annual agricultural production in order to be able to collect annual taxes and to provision the Babylonian troops stationed in the country." Lipschits added:

> The Babylonians definitely had an interest in permitting the rural population to continue. The Benjamin region … could have served as a source for essential products during the siege years. Dry-farming crops from the region, particularly the orchards and in the wine and oil industries, released the Babylonian government from concern about long supply lines with regard to these essential commodities.[12]

This view was followed by others, who stressed the importance of the region for the Babylonian economy (e.g., Middlemas 2007, 17). Barstad summarized that "After the fall of Jerusalem, Judah made up another cog in the great economic wheels of the Neo-Babylonian Empire and life went on after 586 pretty much in the same way as it did before the arrival of Nebuchadnezzar's armies" (2003, 14).

---

11. 2005, 69. Note that the mere establishment of a new province is an estimation which is based on the overall understanding of the historical process, and is not supported nor hinted at by any textual or archaeological evidence.

12. 2003b, 126; 2005, 104. Note that the entire idea about "long supply lines" is modern. Van Creveld (2004, 36) noted that even "eighteenth-century armies lived off the country as a matter of course." It is clear that some form of logistics and transportation existed earlier, and certainly during the Roman period (e.g., Erdkamp 1998; Roth 1999), but significant transportation could have been carried out mainly by sea or rivers. Roth (1999, 221) noted that "the difficulties and expense of land transportation given ancient technologies are real enough, but the Romans could move large amount of supplies over one hundred, or in rare cases, up to two hundred, kilometers over land." If this is the most the Roman legions could do over Roman roads, it appears that the idea of "long supply lines" for the Babylonians is out of place. Moreover, the mere idea that the Babylonians would supply the conquering army is modern in the sense that it misses the point of what war was about. As van Creveld (2004, 39) wrote (regarding Fredrick II): "To imagine that rulers … ever took away from their own country a single thaler that could possibly have been stolen from another is to misunderstand, not merely the eighteenth century but the very nature of that horrible and barbaric business, war."

BABYLONIAN POLICIES AND THE PROCESSES OF COLLAPSE

We have seen in chapter 7 that whether it was in the interest of the Babylonians or not, the processes of collapse were operating, oblivious to the empire's wishes.[13] So, whether it had been "unwise" of Nebuchadnezzar or not, is not necessarily the issue.

BABYLONIAN INTERESTS?

However, we would like to advance a step further, and to show that the entire common-sense assumption that the Babylonians had important economic interests in the region and that these interests prevented the destruction of Judah is naïve. This view is based on a misunderstanding of the Babylonian economic interests.

If the Babylonians were driven by modern concepts of economic maximization, they would be expected to reinstitute the impressive economic system of the seventh century in Philistia, and only to a lesser extent in Judah (e.g., Gitin 1997; Master 2003; see also Faust and Weiss 2005; 2011 and references): Ashkelon and Ekron were the most important economic centers in southern Israel during the seventh century. Both the huge olive-oil production center in Ekron and the wine-production center and major port city at Ashkelon were destroyed by the Babylonians, and were not renewed in the sixth century (e.g., Stager 1996; Gitin and Dothan 1993). The same is true for the secondary center of Timnah (Tel Batash; Mazar and Panitz Cohen 2001).[14] If indeed the Babylonians were motivated by economic considerations, as suggested by the continuity school, they would have reestablished these flourishing economic centers in the coastal plain. The mere fact that they did not bother to restore the major economic centers is evidence that the Babylonians were not driven by economic interests, as postulated by Barstad and Lipschits.

Moreover, chapter 3 illustrated that the coastal plain was outside the scope of the Mediterranean trade system of the sixth century. The Babylonians could

---

13. Cf. Barstad's (2003, 4) assertion that the economic production was not harmed, with Tainter's work.

14. Ashkelon was completely destroyed by the Babylonian destruction (Stager 1996). The fate of Ekron was similar (Gitin and Dothan 1993; but see Mazar and Panitz-Cohen 2001, 282, who claim that a few houses might have been built there at the time). At Timnah (Tel Batash) an agricultural installation was found, indicating some sparse rural population or squatters, but no more (Mazar and Panitz-Cohen 2001, 282). For all practical reasons the site ceased to exist, and was no longer a town (and this is not contradicted by supporters of the continuity theory).

have received more taxes (or tribute) by encouraging this extremely important maritime trade. But they did not, and the coasts of the southern Levant remained outside the realm of the trade network during most of the sixth century.

Furthermore, not only was Philistia destroyed in the sixth century, hence showing that the Babylonian Empire did not act in order to maximize its economic gains, but so was Tyre. Probably the strongest economic engine of seventh-century Mediterranean prosperous trade, Tyre lost its position as a result of Babylonian activity (ch. 3). Tyre was much more important than Judah, and if the Babylonians were interested in maximizing profits, this would have been the first place they should have wanted to build and support, let alone destroy and damage. The reality in Tyre, which influenced settlement throughout the Mediterranean, should warn us against attributing modern economic considerations to the Babylonians: they killed the goose which laid the golden egg (Tyre), so they had no reason not to destroy an impoverished and unimportant region like Judah.

It appears that the Babylonians came to the west to sack, not to invest. They took what they could and planned to take their share of anything that the area would produce in the future–from what it would produce and no further. They had no intention of investing in order to increase this productivity. Such concepts are modern. There is no evidence that a society worked in this way in the past. Therefore, it is impermissible to assume it, let alone to force the assumption, on the unwilling data.

Indeed, this is the way most scholars view the Babylonian economic involvement (e.g., Stern 2001; Betlyon 2003, 269, 271, 278–79). Na'aman observed:

> the Babylonians neither tried to develop their new provinces, nor tried to defend them. … The trade network in southern Palestine and Transjordan was neglected. … Archaeological excavations and surveys … indicate a drastic reduction during the sixth century in the number of settlements and their size, in *economic activity* and in material culture (1995, 114–15; emphasis mine).

Na'aman explicitly attributed this decline to the "overall" policy of the Babylonian empire (115; see also Na'aman 2000).

It was not only the Babylonians that did not invest. It seems that even the Assyrians, who were usually attributed with being much less destructive (even Stern 2001; also Na'aman 1995), did not invest. The entire prosperity of southern Israel in the seventh century B.C.E., of which Ekron was but one part, took place in semi-independent areas and not in the Assyrian provinces in the north of the country (e.g., Finkelstein and Ussishkin 2006, 2002, 602; see also Herzog 1997b, 278; for more details see ch. 7). The Assyrians also took what they could, but they did not invest and initiate prosperity. Hence, the economic insignificance of Samaria and the Galilee in the seventh century, the very same region that a century earlier was the center of olive oil production, lost its importance under Assyrian rule, and the new center was established just outside the Assyrian province (Faust 2011b; Faust and Weiss 2011, with references).

If there were no large-scale olive oil production installations in Philistia in the sixth century—and as we have seen this should not have been a surprise—there is no reason to look for them in a less suitable area, that is, in Judah.

Furthermore, Barstad[15] and Lipschits (2003b, 126; 2005, 104) believed that the Babylonians wanted the oil and wine in the land of Israel. As Barstad wrote, "as Palestine always produced more than it could consume, wine represented a major export article and would, together with olive oil, be of considerable economic interest to the *biltu*-hungry Neo-Babylonian empire" (1996, 74). But Mesopotamia was simply too far away, and no export of such products was likely to have reached it. The Mesopotamian empires received their wine and olive oil from closer regions (e.g., Oppenheim 1967, 243–44; see also Liverani 1992, 158, and fig. 22). Exporting these commodities to Mesopotamia was practically impossible given the distance and the costs involved in antiquity (Machinist 1992; 76; see also Faust and Weiss 2005, and references). A detailed discussion of the Mesopotamian imperial economy is beyond the scope of the present chapter, but it appears that while the Mediterranean coast was of great importance for luxury objects and expensive commodities (mainly imported to this region), it was probably less important for its agricultural potential for Mesopotamia (Postgate 1979, 198–99; see also Elat 1978, esp. 30–32).

Furthermore, even Barstad (2003, 13) admitted that there was no evidence for this "import" in Mesopotamia, nor for its production in Judah in the sixth century (14; though he tried to find "excuses" for this lack). It appears that Barstad did not grasp the way the economic system in the region worked. From the west, the empires of Mesopotamia wanted luxuriant commodities, not necessarily products produced in the region. The local rulers got such items through trade, to a large extent in exchange for agricultural surpluses. However, surpluses were not sent to Mesopotamia (and contrary to Barstad, the Mesopotamian empires did not "need" the Southern Levant for those products). There is plenty of evidence for transporting (as tribute) luxury goods from the land of Israel to Mesopotamia on the one hand.[16] On the other hand, there is no evidence for the

---

15. 1996, 70–74; most of the discussion of Barstad 2003, 9–13, is based also on this premise; but see below.

16. E.g., Tadmor 1975, 37; Elat 1978, 30–31; 1991, 21–22; Mitchell 1997, 187; Schloen 2001, 146–47, n. 17; Cogan 2003, 36–43; see also Beford 2005, 72–73.

import of wine and oil from this region (as admitted by Barstad).[17] Again, the entire system reconstructed by Barstad on the basis of his expectations is wrong, as even the expectations (let alone the finds which are missing) are based on a misunderstanding of the imperial economy.

Finally, Barstad suggested that "When Ekron was destroyed …, olive presses elsewhere *had* to take over the production of the valuable oil" (2003, 12; emphasis mine). After assuming that Judah must have been a great producer of agricultural products, he wrote, "It will be the task of archaeology in the future to look for other olive installations that were prospering during the Neo-Babylonian period." And if they did not exist? From an "archaeological" perspective, the vast installations imagined by Barstad to have existed in Judah during the sixth century were simply not found. Instead of abandoning the theory in face of the data, Barstad encourages archaeologists to look harder.

Causes for the Devastation of the Economy
The causes for the destruction are related mainly to the consequences of the war, and especially the devastation brought about by siege warfare. The causes for the devastation of the countryside were dealt with in some detail in chapter 2, and here I would like to reiterate that siege warfare not only left the besieged cities in desolation, but also their surroundings (regarding death, flight, etc., see ch. 5).

This can be exemplified by the following quotation from Van Creveld (2004). After explaining the insignificance of supply lines even in the early-modern era (since the armies lived off the land; see above), he added,

> The only case I have been able to discover when a commander actually ex-plained his inability to carry out an operation by the size of the supply col-umns occurred in 1705, when Houssaye told Louise XIV that, to besiege Landau, a train fifty-four miles long would be needed. Nor was this due to any weak-heartedness or reluctance to live off the country; rather, Landau had already been besieged twice in previous years so that the surrounding was thoroughly devastated (37).

This clearly shows that the consequences of war were grave. The Babylonian policy of "neglect" (e.g., Naʾaman 1995, 115, see more below) only exacerbated the devastation caused by the war.

---

17. The evidence for importation of wine and oil to Mesopotamia directs us toward much nearer places, see Oppenheim (1967, 244), Liverani (1992, 158, fig. 22) and Yamada (2000, 270–71, 416).

In summary, not only do the archaeological data suggest economic collapse, but this is to be expected. Scholars that assume otherwise appear to misunderstand the relative (un)importance of Judah in the economy of the region and in the "grand" economy of the Babylonian Empire; we should reiterate the fate of Philistia and even Phoenicia. Those were regions far more important economically than Judah, but this did not save them. Modern, rational economic considerations did not play a role in Babylonian policy.

An Additional Note on Economic Continuity: Weights

The weights system that evolved in the eighth to seventh centuries in Judah has received a great deal of scholarly attention (fig. 15). The Judaean inscribed limestone weights (JILs, in Kletter's 1998 terminology), are mentioned in biblical references and were therefore of great interest to scholars, and are important for the study of the ancient economy (e.g., Kletter 1991; 1998; Barkay 1992, 360–61; see also Dever 2001, 221–28). More than 350 such Iron Age weights were collected and analyzed by Kletter (1998). What is important for our purposes is the chronology of the weight system. Whenever the system evolved (see discussion in Kletter 1998, 42–48), it is clear that the system "went out of use after 586 B.C.E." (42). Dever also agreed that the system "went out of use completely with the fall of the Judean kingdom in 587/586" (Dever 2001, 227).

The cessation in the usage of this system was caused by the drastic economic decline of the sixth century B.C.E. No significant trade took place in the region, and there was no institution that could have organized such trade. The system was not used and fell into oblivion. When trade was resumed in the Persian period, coins were already becoming widespread, and the entire economic system was different (e.g., Kletter 1998, 43). The Judean weight system indicate that the economy of Judah in the sixth century B.C.E. was basic and rudimentary.

Continuity in Mesopotamian Rule in the Southern Levant

Various studies have claimed that the Babylonians merely replaced the Assyrians, and that the administration of the former simply continued that of the latter.[18] Moreover, even regarding Judah, which was semi-independent before the Baby

---

18. For Mesopotamia, see, e.g., Van de Mieroop 2007, 277; Dalley 2003; Grayson 1991, 161; for the current debate, see Barstad 2003, 4; Lipschits 2005, 36, 364; Blenkinsopp 2002b, 180; James 2004, 51.

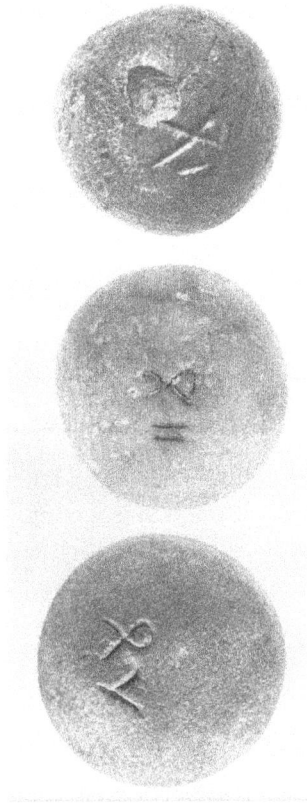

Fig. 15. Iron Age inscribed weights (Meshorer 1976, 54;
courtesy of the Israel Exploration Society).

lonian conquest, Barstad (2003, 4) claimed that the Babylonian imperial system
simply replaced the local jurisdiction, and there should not have been any significant change in daily life.

Generally, speaking, the arguments seem convincing and the present author
is in no position to judge the situation in most parts of the Assyrian Empire after
its collapse. However, there are too many elements that cast doubt on the truism
of this view, at least regarding the transition of power between the empires in
the land of Israel. There are very limited historical data about the Babylonian
administration (Dandamayev 2006, 373), so the entire debate revolves around the
archaeological evidence. Therefore, we must first examine the archaeological data
before explaining the patterns observed.

Lack of Evidence for Babylonian Administration

The lack of direct evidence for *any* Babylonian imperial administration in the region was stressed by many, and stands in sharp contrast to the reality in the Neo-Assyrian period, when finds attesting Assyrian imperial administration were well-known (e.g., Stern 2001, 307–11, 348; Vanderhooft 2003a, 243–48; 2003b, 227–29; Betlyon 2003, 269, 271; see even Lipschits 2003b, 218–20; 2005, 186–88). This sharp contrast in the nature of the finds attests to a different imperial system of control.

Examining Continuity "On the Ground"

Not only we do not have any evidence for Babylonian administration in the region, but the existing data suggest that there was no real continuity between the administrations of the two empires (see already Vanderhooft 1999, 64–68).

Strong archeological evidence suggests that quite a few strata or structures were Assyrian forts or administrative centers, and those are the focus of the following section. The following discussion is not meant to be conclusive, but is only meant to show that the assumed continuation in administration and control is dubious.

Megiddo

Megiddo III appears to have been the only city the Assyrians built in the region (Stern 2001, 48). This Assyrian administrative center was destroyed during the late-seventh century (Herzog 1997b, 255–57; Stern 2001, 27–29). In the Persian period, a fort (with two phases, according to Stern, 2001, 313–14) was built on top of the destroyed city, and it appears that the site was deserted during the Neo-Babylonian period (Herzog 1997b, 255–57; Stern 2001, 312–14). Even if one wishes to claim that the fort was built earlier and should be dated to the sixth century (and this is not supported by any evidence), we still face the destruction and abandonment of the Assyrian city and administrative center.

Kabri

Evidence suggests that during the period of Assyrian rule a large fortress was built at the summit (area E). The finds include Assyrianized pottery, though the excavator writes that "whether this pottery reflects Assyrian presence or local imitations of Assyrian pottery remains uncertain" (Lehmann 2002, 86). While the exact function and detailed history of the fortress during the seventh century B.C.E. are not certain, its "destruction was most probably a result of the campaigns of Nebuchadnezzar against Syria and Palestine and occurred either as early as 604 B.C.E. or later in 585 B.C.E., when the Babylonians laid siege to Tyre" (87). Notably, the Iron Age fortress was not rebuilt. While graves were dug into its ruins in the Hellenistic period, the site was resettled only in the Ottoman period.

Ayyelet HaShahar

The site, just below the tel of Hazor, was excavated by Guy and Dothan and was identified as an Assyrian residency. In the 1970s, Reich (1975) identified Ayyelet HaShahar as an Assyrian administrative center. Lipschits (1990) agreed, and even attempted to give a more precise date to its establishment in the early years of Assyrian rule (parallel to Stratum 4 on the tel itself). Recently, in the final publication of the excavations, Kletter and Zwickel (2006) argued on the basis of architectural features that the site was indeed established during the time of Assyrian rule. As of yet, no evidence for sixth century occupation has been unearthed, and the fort's final phase of use was in the Persian period (also Reich 1992, 215; Stern 2001, 24–25). Still, if one wishes to claim continuity, on the fort itself, this is not an impossibility (although there is no evidence to support such a claim).[19]

Hazor and Kinrot

A fort was unearthed near the upper part of the mound of Hazor (Yadin et al., 1958, 64–65; Yadin 1972, 191–95). The post–Iron Age structure had two phases. Yadin dated the first to the Neo-Assyrian period[20] and the second to the Persian period. Stern, however, tended to date both of them to the Persian period (e.g., 2001, 312–13). Stern also dated the fort unearthed at Kinrot to this period (Fritz 1990; 1993, does not give a specific date, only that it is the seventh century or later, see, e.g., Fritz 1993, 193). If Stern is correct, there is no need to discuss these structures. Since others date the first phase to the Neo–Assyrian period (see, e.g., Kletter and Zwickel 2006, 175–78, and references), however, it can be suggested that the site(s) could have been occupied continuously. Currently we have no positive evidence for this, and the mere dating of the early phase to the Iron Age (Assyrian period) is not secure.

Rishon Leziyon

It was suggested that this fortress was built by the Assyrians (Wolff 1996, 744). The excavators noted that while this was possible, a fort of a more local nature could not be ruled out (Levy et al., 2004, 94; see now also Levy and Peil-stocker 2008, 2022). The fort was destroyed at some point during the seventh

---

19. Here we have "continuity" in usage. Since this was a central site, and not a rural settlement, it cannot be taken for granted that this indicates continuity in the sense examined in ch. 2.

20. Yadin (1972, 194) also considered a Neo-Babylonian date, but preferred to date it to the Neo-Assyrian period.

century (Levy et al., 2004; Wolff 1996, 744). The site was reused at the beginning of the Persian period.[21]

The Assyrian Palace at Ashdod

Elena Kogan-Zehavi excavated an impressive building, interpreted as an Assyrian Palace (2005; Shanks 2007). Notably, this is one of the only "secured" Assyrian structures in the region. The structure had two seventh century phases (Kogan-Zehavi 2005), but was destroyed during this century in "an intense fiery conflagration" (Shanks 2007, 60). The pottery, both the local and the few imported Greek sherds, was of the same nature as that of seventh century Ekron and Ashkelon. Later, in the Persian period, flimsy walls were built on top of the palace, indicating that it went out of use. Clearly, the Assyrian palace went out of use in the seventh century, and was not used again.

Ramat Rahel

Scholars have claimed that the palace at Ramat Rahel was an Assyrian palace/fort (e.g., Na'aman 2001). I do not agree and believe the evidence clearly disproves this suggestion (see also Kletter and Zwickel 2006, 178). Should this be true, however, there is no continuity in the sixth century (above). Recently, Lipschits et al. (2009, 70; 2011, 34), on the basis of large-scale excavations at the edge of the site, claimed that the situation from this period was not clear, but even they did not suggest continuity.

Tell Qudadi

It has been suggested that the Assyrians built the Iron Age fortress at Tell Qudadi (Fantalkin and Tal 2009). While this interpretation is far from certain and there is strong evidence against it, it must be stressed that the fortress ceased to exist at some point in the seventh century, and did not continue to exist into the sixth century .

Several other sites in the southern coastal plain were regarded as Neo–Assyrian centers of "of pure Assyrian type" (according to Stern 2001, 25).

Tel Sera

The site probably served as a military fort during the seventh century B.C.E., perhaps Assyrian (Oren 1993b, 1333–34; Stern 2001, 26). The fort (Stratum 5) was destroyed in the second half of the seventh century (Oren 1993b, 1334; Stern

---

21. Wolff 1996, 744–45; also Stern 2001, 26–27, 371. Note that the excavators, in their brief reports (Levy et al., 2004; Levy and Peilstocker 2008), do not mentioned Persian period pottery at the site and only discuss Persian period pottery at similar sites.

2001, 318), though the agent of the destruction is not clear. After the destruction, a few pits were dug into the destroyed fort (Stratum 4) and they date to the same period, or to the late-seventh century and perhaps early-sixth century B.C.E. (Oren 1993b, 1333–34). During the Persian period a new building, perhaps a fort, along with many silos and pits, was erected at the site (Stratum 3; Oren 1993b, 1334; see also Stern 2001, 371). Clearly, the seventh century building went out of use, and there is no continuation with the Persian period building. The difference is attested architecturally, but is also evident by the existence of the intermediary Stratum 4.

Tel Jemme

The site is usually regarded as an important Assyrian center on the empire's southern border. According to Van Beek (1993, 672), "the typical Assyrian plan, the style of vaulting, and the great quantity of palace ware suggest that the building was built by Assyrians as the residence of the Assyrian king, military governor, or other ranking official" (see also Stern 2001, 25–26). Later, probably during the sixth century, a few buildings were erected, and they are represented "by only a few walls" (Van Beek 1993, 672). In the later part of the Persian period (fourth century B.C.E. only), a huge fort (29 × 38 m) was built at the site (Van Beek 1993, 672; see also Stern 2001, 371). In this case, too, the major differences between the Assyrian building and the Persian one indicate that there was no continuous use of the administrative center. This is further supported not only by the almost two-hundred-year gap between the two, but also by the existence of another stratum in between—a stratum with meager remains that appears to represent the Neo-Babylonian period.

Discussion

Before assessing the data,[22] it should be stressed that the above survey does not prove anything regarding other parts of the empire. The data do show that there is no positive evidence for continuity in imperial administration in the land of Israel or for the mere existence of Babylonian administration (see already Stern 2001, 309). The Babylonians did not continue to rule the region through the structures that were used by the Assyrians, and this casts grave doubts on the claim of administrative continuity.

---

22. Tell el-Sheik Zuweid, too, is regarded as a Neo–Assyrian center in the south (Stern 2001, 26), which was reused in the Persian period (371). The site, therefore, fits the pattern discussed above. The data (Petrie 1937), however, are limited and do not allow for a more detailed discussion.

Notably, the complete cessation in use of those centers after their destruction and until the Persian period (e.g., Stern 2001, 23–29, 316–19) can be doubted. Could there have been continuity from the seventh century to the Persian period, and hence Neo-Babylonian occupation, that archaeologists have not yet identified? This is tempting, given the debated nature of the period's pottery (above, ch. 2). However, there is evidence that this is not the case, and there was at least a severe decline in the use of those sites.

1. The "disappearance" of the Assyrian "capital" at Megiddo is instructive. Even the major Assyrian center did not continue as before.

2. Almost every site contains a late-seventh century destruction layer. The sites were destroyed, and administration could not have continued without interruption.

3. In most cases when Persian occupation is present and the stratigraphy is obvious, there does appear to be a gap or an intermediate stratum of ephemeral nature between the Persian period and the previous occupation (seventh century, which usually ended in destruction). Before suggesting that the gap is a scholarly construction, one should refer to cases like Ashkelon, where a gap was undeniable. Therefore, a "gap" is indeed an option, whether it seems "logical" to our modern mind or not (see more in point 7, below).

4. There are cases in which we do not even have a Persian fort/palace, such as at the Assyrian fort/palace near Ashdod. In this case, the Persian period occupation was of a different nature and appears to have nothing to do with the Assyrian administrative building that existed previously. Notably, such situations are rare, as most sites were located on or near tells and were therefore used in most periods (i.e., resettlement, or resumed human activity at the same site, is therefore expected even if there was no continuity, above ch. 2).

5. In most cases of sites with both late Iron Age and Persian period occupations, the nature of the finds and the architectural plans were different. This shows that we are not discussing "unseen" continuity, and indicates that the phenomenon is a result of resettlement at a suitable location.

6. Moreover, in many cases there is even a stratum—with meager remains—between the strata from the Iron Age and Persian period. This precludes continuity altogether, and reveals the ephemeral nature of the Neo-Babylonian occupation.

7. Since many sites were located in the coastal plain, the absence of sixth century imported Greek pottery should be taken into account, hinting at the abandonment of those structures at the time discussed here, or their

significance (imported Greek pottery is found in the Persian period and usually also in seventh century strata in the coastal plain; ch. 3).

The archeological evidence shows that any claim for continuity in administration is problematic. If the Neo-Babylonian Empire simply continued Assyrian rule in the region, why didn't it use the well-established administrative centers? Even more striking is the absence of Neo-Babylonian centers from the archaeological record. From where did they rule? Notably, nobody would deny that the region had some form of Babylonian administration. But when compared to the Assyrian one, it was of an ephemeral nature. In some cases the Assyrian centers were reused, but not always. Overall, it seems as if the Babylonians did not care about the provinces in this region. They sacked what they could during the war and later taxed the remaining population. They did not try to continue administration in the areas they sacked, especially if the region was already in ruins.

The transition of power in the southern Levant was different from that in other parts of the former Assyrian Empire. During the final years of the latter, the region was ruled by the Egyptians (e.g., Lipschits 2005). Therefore, either the Egyptians used the Assyrian centers, and the centers were destroyed during the Babylonian conquests, or the Egyptians destroyed the Assyrian centers and did not use them. This might also explain the lack of continuity. The structures were simply destroyed, perhaps even before the Babylonians took over. Since the region was of little economic importance, the Babylonians did not bother creating (or recreating) the entire administrative infrastructure, and managed with a governing apparatus on a much smaller scale.

Whatever the correct scenario, it is clear we are looking for an explanation for the (unique?) reality in the region. The reality is that there is currently no real archeological evidence for continuity between the Assyrian and Babylonian administrations. Furthermore, we have hardly any evidence for Babylonian administration whatsoever. While there is no doubt that it did exist, the lack of evidence probably indicates its ephemeral nature.[23] Finally, the above survey examined sites within the Assyrian provinces, or places where Assyrian presence is expected (due to their location), and hence continuity is to be anticipated if the Babylonians continued Assyrian administration. Judah, however, was not an Assyrian province, and no Assyrian administration existed before the Babylonian conquest. Hence, even if continuity in administration would have been observed elsewhere, it is not clear that continuity should be expected in Judah.

---

23. I believe that as research progresses, evidence will be found. It will always be necessary, however, to check this evidence quantitatively, in comparison to that of the Assyrian administration.

WHAT SETS THE AGENDA?

Supporters of the continuity theory claim that the common view of the sixth century is based on a biblically derived myth. Ironically, however, it is the continuity
school which bases many of its arguments, and its entire agenda, on the Bible.
For example, the entire reconstruction of the early years after the Babylonian
conquest is based not on archaeology, but on the biblical story of Gedaliah,[24]
which scholars accept almost uncritically (ch. 9). Moreover, their preoccupation
with "the exile," and whether it is possible that the entire population was exiled,
is derived from the biblical texts, and to a large extent even from the discourse
of biblical scholarship and theology, where "the exile" is of paramount importance (the number of possible references is of course almost endless, from Torrey
onward; see more in the summary).

Even when they "discredit" the Bible, the agenda of many of the supporters
of the continuity theory is biblically, not historically, driven, and the supporters
want to prove or disprove biblical issues. They do not wish to know the "reality"
in the sixth century—they want to prove or disprove theories and assumptions
on the date and place of authorship of some biblical texts (see more in the summary).

Barstad, for example, acknowledged that "(M)y present interest in the exilic
period was caused primarily by the claim ... that no economic, cultural or religious activity could have taken place in Judah during this period" (1996, 45). And
elsewhere he added: "One very important question is whether Neo-Babylonian
and Persian period Judah had the necessary population or infrastructure to
produce the literature that we now find in the Hebrew Bible" (2003, 4; and he
concludes, "I do believe that it did"). Blenkinsopp added:

> The issue is important enough to historians and Biblical scholars to warrant
> close scrutiny. After all, Judaism itself emerged in this period, after the liqui-
> dation of the Judahite state. Many Bible books of first importance—much of
> Isaiah 40–66 and the final version of Deuteronomy, for example—are dated
> by many scholars to this time. If Albright and Stern have it right, it is dif-
> ficult to see how anything of consequence could have happened in this "gap"
> (2002a, 37).

Indeed, understanding the archaeology of the exilic period in Judah is significant for biblical scholars' reconstruction of the authorship and editing processes

---

24. This biblical story influenced the archaeological interpretation of the finds in Benjamin
(e.g., Vanderhooft 2003a, 254, n. 18.)

of the texts. In reality, however, biblical scholars, historians, and theologians are divided. Some prefer to view the sixth century as desolate (e.g., Oded 2003; Vanderhooft 2003a), while others view it as relatively settled and prosperous (e.g., Barstad 1996; 2003; Middlemas 2005; Lipschits 2005). For many of those scholars, however, the agenda is not to understand the actual historical events, but rather their implication for understanding the authorship of the biblical texts. In most instances, these scholars simply "know" what the reality "should be."

While it is legitimate to work with assumptions (and certainly with those interests!), there are dangers to this approach. Some biblical scholars and theologians who view the sixth century as settled and prosperous attempt to force the archaeological record to suit their thesis. Most of them suffer from both a (not always) hidden agenda and a misunderstanding of the archaeological record. Archaeologists simply "know" that the continuity theory is impossible[25]—a functioning society or polity did not exist in sixth-century Judah. If the reality on the ground during the sixth century bears importance for the creation of the various texts, then biblical scholars should correct their views on the basis of this reality, not vice versa.

The agenda led to the "desired" results. Barstad (1996, 18–19; my emphasis) assumed there must have been many people in Judah: "If, in fact, 'most of the population' remained in Judah, *as it must have done* ... this society must have consisted *not only* of peasants. . ., but also of artisans, traders, village and town elders, scribes, priests and prophets. In other words, ... a functioning society, with many of its political institutions still intact." This is what Barstad *wants to find*, and it has nothing to do with the available data, which does not support such a reality. Barstad needs a functioning society, prophets, scribes, and priests because his dating of various texts is dependent on it. As Middlemas commented, "seemingly, as part of this wider desire to locate Deutero-Isaiah in Judah rather than Babylon, Barstad sought to redeem Judah from the wasteland to which it had been relegated by historians" (2005, 20; the problems into which such an approach might bring us will be discussed in more length in the summary of the book). In conclusion, the continuity theory is driven by the biblical agenda to a far greater extent than the traditional view, which is much more empiricist.

---

25. There is almost a consensus on the matter among archaeologists. For references and additional discussion, see the summary.

ADDITIONAL PROBLEMS

This section will address a few specific issues related to problems with the continuity school's reconstruction of the Neo-Babylonian period.

Mwsh (Moza) Impressions

Lipschits suggested that the distribution of the *mwsh* impressions reveals the concentration of the remnants in the land, and that the impressions were used by the administration of the sixth century Babylonian province (2003b, 284; 2005, 149–52). Dating the impressions to the Neo-Babylonian period is only a speculation.[26] There would not have been any need to address the issue any further, but Lipschits's own assumption seems to contradict his theory that there was significant population in northern Judah.

The *mwsh* impressions are concentrated almost solely in a small stretch of land, from Jerusalem[27] northward (Lipschits 2005, 149). South of Jerusalem, there is only one impression at Ramat Rahel. Such an exception should be seen as incidental, and it does not allow us to extend the distribution map of the discussed impressions to the south of Jerusalem, let alone to northern Judah (which is even southward of this single example). If indeed the impressions should be dated to the Babylonian period, then they show that settlement was concentrated in the area to the north of Jerusalem and Benjamin, and not both in this area and in northern Judah as Barstad and Lipschits repeatedly claim (more below). While Lipschits may be correct in rejecting previous interpretations of the impressions as correlating to the Benjaminite inheritance, his claim that the distribution deviated from the area of Benjamin is wrong, and northern Judea is practically excluded.

Hence, if the suggestion that the impressions represent the remnants in the land or even the Babylonian province is correct, there were no remainders in northern Judea, nor was it part of the Babylonian province. And this brings me to another minor issue.

---

26. Rejected by many, see, e.g., Naveh 1970, 61–62; Carter 1999: 266–67; see also Schniedewind 2004, 146.

27. About ten percent of the impressions were found in Jerusalem, and this seems to indicate that it was inhabited at the time. It is therefore not clear why Lipschits consistently claims that "the city and its environs remained *completely* empty" (e.g., Lipschits 2005, 367; emphasis mine; see also ch. 10). This piece of evidence clearly contradicts this claim (if the sixth-century date for the impressions will be sustained of course).

Where Is the Evidence and What Is the Heading?

Barstad, Lipschits, Middlemas, and others speak about continuity in both Benjamin and northern Judah; the latter referring mainly to the area between Beth Zur and Bethlehem (e.g., Barstad 1996, 47; 2003; Lipschits 2003b, 222; 2005, 190–91, 196, 258, 374; see also Middlemas 2005, 46; and see already Stern 1983, 120). In most cases, the evidence those scholars cite relate only to Benjamin, although their "heading" relates to both regions. This can be seen throughout Lipschits's work, for example, when he addresses the archaeological digs that (according to him) show continuity from the Iron Age to the sixth century, which are practically all from Benjamin;[28] when he discusses the *mwsh* impressions (above), and in many other places, when this is simply repeated (e.g., 2003b, 223, 224, 229, 291, 412; 2005, 191, 192, 196, 258, 374; cf. Lipschits 2005, 356; see also Barstad 1996, 47–50). Not only Lipschits titles the region "Benjamin and Northern Judah" when his evidence only comes from the Benjamin region. Middlemas also writes about populations that lived both south and north of Jerusalem, but all of the evidence she refers to is from the area north of Jerusalem (e.g., Middlemas 2005, 46; see also Barstad 2003, 6).[29]

It appears that the source of this error can be traced back. In his highly influential paper, Malamat (1950, 226–27) showed that the fate of the area of Benjamin was different from other parts of Judah (ch. 9). In the final part of the paper, he briefly suggested, on the basis of a few "implicit" texts, that perhaps the area around Bethlehem was also spared (Malamat 1950, 227). It appears that this suggestion was followed by Stern (e.g., 1983, 120), although he did not provide any archaeological evidence for that observation. All of his evidence was also from Benjamin (ch. 9). Barstad, Lipschits, and others simply followed these observations uncritically.[30] To his credit, it should be noted that Lipschits at least attempted to prove this assumption.

---

28. Note that when he is discussing the excavations in northern Judah, he is on the defensive, and is only trying to claim that they are inconclusive, e.g., 2003b, 283–85; 2005, 250–51. See also above.

29. Note that the archaeological errors in the works of scholars like Barstad, Blenkinsopp, and others, are numerous, and will not be dealt with here. As an example, see Barstad's (1996, 80; 2003, 14) attribution of continuity to the Negev. Barstad does not provide references, but probably bases them on old works, which were themselves based on texts (e.g., Aharoni 1967, 409–10, on the basis of Nehemiah 11: 25–35). To reiterate, one cannot treat the Negev as an area in which sites continued to the Persian period (see even Lipschits 2005, 224–30, 237, 262–63). The dating of the various sites is also wrong (e.g., Barstad 2003, 6).

30. It is ironic that the data is based on biblical assumptions and not on archaeology.

A Note on Settlement Continuity in Judah

Despite claims for continuity, the archaeological evidence clearly indicates that there was a break in settlement in northern Judah at the end of the Iron Age.

Interestingly, it appears that Lipschits is aware of the fact that continuity in this region was limited. In discussing the finds from Samaria's foothills, Lipschits wrote,

> This is a very limited and defined area, part of the Samaria province since the end of the 8th century BCE, *and one of the most stable regions in demographic and political terms* from the 7th to the 4th centuries BCE, *with clear continuity between the end of the Iron Age and the Persian period.* The Samaria data, thus, provide no control for assessing processes in Judah (2007, 46; emphasis added).

This quote and the problems behind the logic Lipschits applies were addressed in chapter 2. Here I will only stress that even according to Lipschits, the patterns of continuity observed in Samaria's foothills were different from what he was familiar with in all parts of Judah—so different that he believed that it was impermissible to compare both regions. In writing the above, Lipschits admitted that continuity in Judah was at best very limited. There was nothing that resembled straightforward continuity, similar to Samaria's foothills.

Successful Cultic Reforms in the Sixth Century B.C.E.?

Lipschits maintained that during the sixth century, cult in traditional Israelite places of worship prospered, and he mentioned Bethel, Mizpah, Gibeon, and Shechem (e.g., Lipschits 2005, 113, 371). If the remnants were so many and the returnees were so few, (e.g., Lipschits 2003b, 411; 2005, 372) then how did the returnees manage to eliminate all cult places that flourished at the time? This is unlikely (though not impossible) and would at least require a more detailed discussion and explanation of the processes involved.

Other problems have already been discussed, such as the fate of the rural sector (ch. 2), Lipschits's failure to account for his own demographic data (ch. 5 graphs), and the continuity school's contention that the demographic decline is illogical. In all these, the continuity school's arguments were shown to be unfounded.

SUMMARY

Previous chapters have given evidence for the great demographic decline in the sixth century B.C.E., in accordance with the traditional view. While most tenants of the continuity theory have been disproved, this chapter examined the continuity school in a more systematic way.

Notably, we have seen that supporters of the continuity theory created straw men, which were presented as the "traditional view," and were then attacked. Supporters of the continuity theory claimed that it was impossible that the land was totally empty, and that the entire population was exiled. Both views are indeed an impossibility, but were not really held in previous scholarship. By creating these straw men and equating scenarios to them, the continuity theory was seen as more reasonable and convincing.

However, most scholars rejected the claims that the land was literally empty and, moreover, did not consider exile as the only mechanism for population decline. There were additional causes of demographic decline, such as death, executions, famine, epidemics (during the war, and afterward), as well as migration. Exile was just one cause out of many. (Interestingly, it appears that the continuity school's fascination with exile derived from its biblical and theological agenda.)

We have also brought additional evidence that the "empty land" was not just a biblically driven construct. After all, archaeologists identified (relative) "emptiness" in various regions and not only in Judah (as could have been expected from a biblically driven agenda or theory).

Many of the continuity school's hypotheses, such as Babylonian economic interests in the region, were shown to be wrong. Supporters of the continuity theory have also ignored the drastic cultural and social changes that occurred during the transition from the Iron Age to the Persian period, such as the disappearance of the Judahite tomb, the four-room house, the figurines, etc.

It is therefore not surprising that supporters of the continuity theory have failed to show where the presumed continuity is to be found. While extensively discussing the well-known sites in Benjamin, they have not added sites to our possible sixth-century B.C.E. inventory of settlements.

Notably, there were people in the land, and it was not completely empty. And the population was not exiled in its entirety (exile was probably very limited when compared to the seventh-century population estimates). There were thousands of people in ruined Judah. But the catastrophe was great, and the consequences grave. Not only was there a major demographic decline, but the society was also crushed. Nothing seems to have continued as before.

CHAPTER 9
THE LAND OF BENJAMIN REVISITED

As we have seen, there is practically a scholarly consensus that the region of Benjamin was not devastated during the Babylonian campaigns. According to the Bible, this is the region which served as an area into which many people fled for their lives before the destruction of Jerusalem (e.g., Jer 37:12–13). After the fall of Jerusalem, the area became a new center (e.g., 2 Kgs 25:22–26; Jer 40). Settlement continuity after 586 B.C.E. and the lack of Babylonian destruction were observed in the various excavations in the major sites in the region, e.g., Gibeah (Tell el-Ful) and Bethel, as well as Mizpah (Tell en-Nasbeh) and Gibeon.[1] This was usually explained by an earlier annexation of the region by the Babylonians in 597 B.C.E., and hence there was no need for them to destroy it. Whatever the reasoning, the view that the region of Benjamin was not harmed in the 586 campaign is widely accepted.[2]

This chapter suggests that this consensus needs reexamination and modification. The arguments raised will inevitably attract "fire," and I therefore stress that even if one does not accept the conclusions of the present chapter, it does not have any necessary implications on the assessment of the overall conclusions of the book. Whether settlement in Benjamin in the sixth century was significant or not can be discussed separately, and this monograph can be complete even if one chooses to skip this chapter.

In the following, we will address the differences between the results of the surveys and excavations, as presented above. This will be followed by an examination of the settlement history in the land of Benjamin at the time discussed,

---

1. Gibeah (Tell el-Ful): Lapp 1978b; 1978c; Bethel: e.g., Albright and Kelso 1968, 37, 51; Kelso 1993, 194; Mizpah (Tell en-Nasbeh): Zorn 1993a; 1993b; 1997a; 1997b; 2003; see also Stern 2001, 322; Gibeon: Stern 2001, 321, 336–38; Lipschits 2005, 243–44.

2. E.g., Malamat 1950, 226–27; Stern 1975, 35; 1982, 31–34, 229; 1983, 120; 2001, 321–23, 350; Mazar 1990, 548; Barstad 1996, 48–50; Lipschits 1999; 2003a, 347–51; 2003b, 272–83; 2005, 237–49.

according to the scholarly consensus. In this section we will especially address the significance of the scarcity of settlement during the Persian period. Finally, we will reexamine the scholarly consensus regarding settlement in Benjamin in the sixth century.

DIFFERENCES BETWEEN THE RESULTS OF THE EXCAVATIONS AND THE RESULTS OF SURVEYS AND SALVAGE EXCAVATIONS

While there is an agreement regarding the reality on the ground during the sixth century b.c.e. in Benjamin, it appears that this scholarly consensus is based on the common interpretation of the results of the excavations in the major mounds in the region, but it is in contrast to the situation that is revealed by both surveys and salvage excavations.

Surveys

The land of Benjamin was surveyed extensively by a number of teams, and the results were analyzed by many scholars.

Finkelstein, one of the directors of the major survey of Benjamin, mentioned a major change that occurred throughout the highlands in the Persian period (1993b, 27); there was a significant decrease in the number of sites at the time. He added, "moreover, the Persian period sites are mostly small, and this means that demographically, the crisis was even more significant" (my translation). Finkelstein connected this decline to the fall of Judah, and noted that the crisis was even larger, since "the settlement picture of the Persian period actually reflects the situation in the fifth century, when the region had somewhat recovered" (my translation).

Magen, the second director of this survey, also wrote that "archaeological surveys show that the large-scale settlement of the Iron Age II in the Land of Benjamin shrank significantly in the Persian period" (2004, 2). He, too, attributed it to the destruction of Judah, and added (3), "very few settlements from the Persian period have been discovered, and the ceramic finds at these sites are meager, an indication not only that the settlements were few, but that they were small in size." Later, he wrote, "archaeological finds prove that it [settlement in Benjamin; A.F.] declined drastically in the Persian period. Few, if any, settlements continued during the Babylonian period. The extensive late first Temple period was revived only during the Hellenistic period" (5), and he noted that even then settlement was smaller than that of the Iron Age (6).

Decline was also noted by Gibson (1996, 17*) in the northeastern Jerusalem survey, and he wrote that "settlement diminished considerably." Milevski's (1996–97) analysis reached similar results.

Indeed, as we have seen in chapter 5, the surveys exhibited a decline from 101 sites in the Iron Age to 34 sites in the Persian period, and a recovery to 115 sites in the Hellenistic period.[3] Carter (1999, 235) reanalyzed the results of the survey (though of the entire area). He found a similar trend, with an even sharper decline, 157 Iron Age settlements, 39 Persian period settlements, and 163 Hellenistic settlements.

Since the number of Persian period sites represented the peak of this period, the contrast between the settlement of the Iron Age and Hellenistic period and the nadir of the Persian period was even larger (see, ch. 5).

Salvage Excavations

A similar picture can be seen in the results of the salvage excavations. Small and rural Iron Age sites in Benjamin did not continue to exist in the Persian period, and most probably ceased to exist in the sixth century. Out of sixteen rural sites north of Jerusalem (Mezad Michmas, Khirbet Shilhah, Khirbet Kharruba Anata, Nahal Zimri, the French Hill, Pisgat Zeev A, Pisgat Zeev D, Kh. 'Alona, Mevasseret Yerushalayim, the five Ramot farmsteads, and the settlement near the Rambam Cave), only two exhibit possible continuity into the Persian period (Kh. 'Alon and Khirbet Kharruba, see detailed discussion in ch. 2).

While any date in the sixth century can be given to the abandonment of the sites, a date closer to the beginning should be our default. Only with substantial evidence can we push this date down. In any event, the abandonment was during the sixth century and not during the Persian period (as no Persian period pottery was reported).

Intermediate Summary

While data from surveys are problematic, the decline noticed in the Benjamin surveys is too sharp to be a mistake. More importantly, it is also supported by the results of the salvage excavations. Surveys and salvage excavations relate to the rural sector, and they hint that the rural sector in Benjamin was devastated in the sixth century.

Possible Differences between Urban and Rural Settlements

It is important to stress that the discrepancy between the data from surveys and the data from (planned) excavations, as understood by Lipschits, led him to cor-

---

3. On the basis of three maps: Ramallah and el-Bireh (North) (Finkelstein 1993b), Ramallah and el-Bireh (South), and Wadi el-Makukh (Goldfus and Golani 1993).

rect the data from surveys to conform to the data from the excavations (Lipschits 1999, 180–84; 2005, 245–48),[4] which he accepts uncritically.[5]

When discussing the results of the surveys, which showed drastic decline, Lipschits wrote, "the finds of the Persian period discovered in the survey reflect this low point, rather than the peak of settlement activity or a stage of rebuilding" (2003a, 349). Lipschits claimed that the decline was gradual and the small number of Persian period sites in Benjamin reflected the end of this gradual decline, that is, the data represents the nadir of the Persian period. Not only is this suggestion arithmetically impossible (the finds reflect the peak of the period, as all the Persian period sites would provide Persian period pottery, including those that were supposedly abandoned before Lipschits's "low point"; the issue was discussed in detail in ch. 5), but it is also methodologically unsound. The assumed discrepancy between the two sets of data should not be forcibly harmonized. The two sets represent different settlement sectors that could have had different settlement histories. The fact that excavations in rural sites produced results similar to those of the surveys seems to prove that the data from the rural sites should not be forced to be in line with the results of the "large" excavations.

It is possible that the urban sector of Benjamin flourished (or at least continued to exist), while the rural sector was devastated. This is the simplest explanation for the discrepancy between the data from surveys and salvage excavations on the one hand and planned excavations in tells on the other hand. The former tend to quantitatively overemphasize the rural sector, whereas the latter represent almost exclusively the urban sector.[6]

---

4. Although the data from surveys is less reliable than that of excavations (above), one should note that the (almost) total lack of Persian period pottery in the Benjamin survey should be accounted for. The most logical explanation is the dearth of settlements. Methodologically, surveys tend to flatten graphs and to not present periods of decline as clear as they really are (Faust 2007b, 5–6; Faust and Safrai in press a), but here the situation is the opposite (the decline is clear). Therefore, it is difficult to blame the shortcomings of surveys for the phenomenon. In this case, the data from surveys should be given consideration. In addition, the surveys represent mainly the rural sector, and will not necessarily be in accordance with excavations of large sites. Finally, the data from excavations in rural sites supports the surveys in this regard (below).

5. Contrary to his treatment of north Judah, where he accepted the data from surveys and corrected the data from excavations to fit into his interpretation of the former (2003a, 284–85; 2004; 2005, 250–52). While such exercises might be legitimate, they require very detailed reasoning (which was not supplied).

6. The fact that the rural settlements in the region of Benjamin show exactly the same patterns as elsewhere in Judah supports the view that they, too, were abandoned or destroyed in the 586 B.C.E. campaign or during its aftermath. They did not prosper throughout this century, in contrast to what was suggested regarding the fate of the urban sector.

Such a reconstruction, which is supported by both the data from excavations and surveys, is extremely plausible. Devastation of the rural sector in tandem with the existence or even prosperity of central sites happened many times in history, and is not something unique.

For example, the Iron I rural sites, which received so much attention in the research and debates regarding the Israelite settlement in Canaan, were either abandoned (or destroyed) or evolved into towns and central settlements during the transition to the Iron Age II. The number of rural sites in the Iron Age IIA was greatly reduced when compared to that of the Iron Age I or later Iron Age II (Faust 1999b; 2003a; 2007b; 2012; contra Finkelstein 2005). The explanation suggested for this phenomenon was that the rural sector suffered initially due to security problems, which caused the population to concentrate in larger settlements and develop stronger leadership. Later, the process of population concentration in larger sites continued due to the advantages such a process had for the "state."

A similar decline in the rural sector was observed in Iron I Philistia, where Finkelstein referred to "an almost complete abandonment of the countryside" (Finkelstein 1995b, 232) and "an annihilation of the countryside" (2000, 169; see also Shavit 2003). Bunimovitz explained this phenomenon by forced settlement by the Philistines (1998). Whether the explanations offered are to be accepted or not, these examples clearly show that such a dichotomy between central, urban settlements and small, rural sites is well known. Similar situations, in which rural sites went through different (and even opposite) processes than their urban counterpart is a well known phenomenon throughout history and all over the world (e.g., Demand 1990; Marcus and Flannery 1996; see also Faust 2003a, and references).

It is more than likely, therefore, on the basis of the data available from the surveys and salvage excavations, and in light of the available information from the excavations of central sites in Benjamin, to reconstruct a settlement reality in which the urban sector continued to exist in the Neo-Babylonian period, while the rural sector was devastated. While contrasting recent claims for prosperity in the rural sector of this region, such a reconstruction might also be in line with the historical sources which stand at the heart of the "Benjaminite prosperity" scenario. However, before developing this line of reasoning, the data from the major excavations in Benjamin should be reexamined.

Excavations in Central Sites in Benjamin: A Reexamination

The data from the major excavations in the region lie at the base of the commonly held view that the region of Benjamin prospered in the sixth century. The consensus is so strong that it led scholars, such as Lipschits, to correct the results of the surveys to conform to the excavations. Not only is that a problematic procedure, as we have seen above, but it is even possible that this "secure" data from large scale excavations should be treated with extreme care.

Below is a short summary of the data from the major sites excavated in the land of Benjamin.

Bethel

The site is located in southern Samaria, just to the north of the discussed region. Following the result of the excavations (e.g., Kelso 1968, 37, 51; 1993; Sinclair 1968), many agree that the site probably flourished during the sixth century (Albright 1960b, 142; Stern 2001, 321; Lipschits 2005, 242–43). It should be stressed from the outset, however, that the importance of the data for the present discussion should be doubted, as the site was north of Benjamin. In the earlier part of the Iron Age, Bethel was part of the Kingdom of Israel, and later of the Assyrian province, and was not part of Judah. Moreover, even the excavators dated the end of the occupation to the mid–sixth century or somewhat later (Kelso 1968, 37, 51; Sinclair 1968, 76), and the continuity after the Babylonian conquests was therefore very limited. The importance of the site declined in the Persian period (e.g., Kelso 1968, 38) and Sinclair (1968, 75) explicitly wrote about the "lack of characteristic Persian period forms," concluding that it "means that we cannot date the destruction of Bethel beyond the end of the 6th century B.C. when such forms presumably began to make their appearance." Whether this "lack" is complete or not[7] is of less importance. It is clear that Bethel was, at best, a very small site at that time. Dever (1971, 468–69), in reviewing the report, explicitly wrote that the sixth century date was based on an out-of-context corpus, and that the occupation at the site ended in the early-sixth century B.C.E. (Dever 1997a, 301). A similar view was expressed by Finkelstein and Singer–Avitz (2009, 42), who claimed that most of the pottery associated with the sixth century should be dated to the Iron Age IIB. Finkelstein (2011a, 364–65) had recently expressed the view that the site did not exist in the sixth century.

Gibeon

It is generally agreed that the site ceased to exist around the end of the Iron Age, as very little Persian period material has been found (e.g., Pritchard 1962, 163; Hallote 1997; Finkelstein 2008a, 8–9; 2010, 42). During the late Iron Age, the site was a major center for wine production and storage (Pritchard 1962; 1964),

---

7. It is not, and in the report there is reference for limited finds from this period; see also Stern (1982, 31), and references.

and some scholars suggested that the site also prospered in the sixth century, like other sites in the region, and that the above facilities continued to function (e.g., Stern 2001, 321, 336–38; Lipschits 1999; 2005, 243–44). This is based either on a brief pottery analysis (e.g., Wright 1963) or on the paleography of the inscriptions on the jar handles, found out of context (Cross 1962; see also Avigad 1972).[8] The issue will be further elaborated below. While the reality in the sixth century can be debated (more below), it is clear that there were very few finds from the Persian period at this site (Pritchard 1962, 163; Hallote 1997, 404; Finkelstein 2007, 53; 2008a, 8–9).

Gibeah (Tell el-Ful)

It has been assumed that the site was destroyed in 586 B.C.E. (Sinclair 1975), but further analysis of the finds indicate that the site (Stratum 3B) existed until the end of the Babylonian period, although it declined in size. After the sixth century, the site was not resettled until the Hellenistic period (e.g., Lapp 1978b, 39–40; 1993, 447–48), and Lapp (1978b, 40) stressed that "common Persian pottery forms do not appear."[9]

Tell en-Nasbeh (biblical Mizpah)

The results of the original excavations led scholars to conclude that the site was destroyed at the end of the Iron Age, and that there was relatively little later material (e.g., Broshi 1992). The original report suggested that later settlement "was a mere unwalled village" (McCown 1947, 63). In the 1970s, Aharoni (1978, 279) suggested that Mizpah, "to which the seat of the government was transferred with the destruction of Jerusalem," was excluded from the overall devastation in Judah, although he did not supply any data for this statement. Recently, Zorn (1997a; 1997b; see already Albright 1963, 86) tried to reanalyze the finds, and claimed that there was a significant Babylonian-Persian stratum at the site. While he attributed the new city to the Neo-Babylonian period (the time of Gedaliah), he admitted that the finds from the Persian period were limited. After listing the late finds (from the Persian period or afterward) he defined them as a "more-

---

8. For the *mwsh* impressions, see discussion above (ch. 8).

9. Similarly, Lapp (1978b, 40) suggested that the abandonment of Tell el-Ful 3B was "before" the period of the Shechem (Balatah) 5. While the date of the latter is not easy to establish, its beginning appears to have been during the sixth century B.C.E. (e.g., Campbell 2002, 8), probably toward its last quarter (Campbell 2002, 307; Lapp 2007, 221; 2008, 4, 33–36). This clearly indicates that, on the basis of the relative chronology observed by Lapp, the abandonment of Tell el-Ful was before the end of the sixth century. See now also Finkelstein 2011b, 113, who claimed that there are very few sixty-century finds at the site and practically no finds from the Persian period.

than–passing" occupation (Zorn 1993a, 1102). Still, the Persian period finds from this site, although limited, seem to be more significant than in other sites in the region.

Khirbet Es-Sid

A relatively large site in eastern Benjamin (near 'Anata). Limited scale excavations were carried out at the site by Biran (1985), who found many late Iron Age remains, but nothing that he dated to the Persian period.

It is clear that all sites prospered in the Iron Age, but declined or even disappeared in the Persian period. While some of the sites might have existed during most of the sixth century, this is not clear for all of them. Even those which appear to have existed at the time were probably in decline (e.g., Lapp 1997, 346). Since Persian period material is scarce or missing from all sites, there can be no doubt that the decline occurred before the Persian period.

Discussion: When Did Settlement in Benjamin Decline?

Clearly, the major sites discussed above exhibit decline during the sixth century. Since we can at best (more below) identify sixth century occupation at some of these sites (and even this is usually limited, see, e.g., Finkelstein 2007, 53; 2008b, 513, regarding Gibeon), there is no way to distinguish the exact dates within this century (i.e., 538, 549 or 575 B.C.E.). Even if we find pottery that should be dated to the sixth century B.C.E. (something that is currently impossible), with the absence of Persian period pottery, there is simply no way to ascribe it to the later part of the Neo-Babylonian period.[10] It is much more likely that the "sixth cen-

---

10. Archeological evidence that Iron Age prosperity did not continue into the Persian period posed a problem for Lipschits (e.g., 1999, 2003a; 2005). Therefore, he developed a sophisticated, but arithmetically impossible, scenario where the Iron Age population continued to live in the region, and left only during the beginning of the Persian period to other regions, including the valley of Lod (Lipschits 1997b). This reconstruction suffers from a severe problem: if the people still lived in the region of Benjamin during the early Persian period, there should be more significant Persian period pottery remains, unless someone would claim that this pottery appeared only later. Such a claim is not only against what most archaeologists think (i.e., that the transition from the Iron Age horizon to that of the Persian period was within the sixth century [see e.g., Barkay [1992, 373; 1993, 108–9; Lapp 1978b, 40; Sinclair 1968, 75, and even Lipschits himself, e.g., Lipschits 2005, 197–203]), but will also render the entire archaeological study of the late Iron Age and Persian period meaningless as there will be no way to distinguish those sites.

The lack of Persian period pottery, at least in the small sites, means that the area was deserted by the majority of its settlers before the appearance of this pottery (or in the very first years of its appearance). One must therefore conclude that the small sites (both surveyed and excavated) were deserted during the sixth century, and so were the major excavated sites. Moreover, Lip-

tury pottery" that was identified, for example, by Lapp (even if indeed it belongs
to the Neo-Babylonian period, below), represents the early part of the Neo-Babylonian period, rather than its end.

   If the biblical narrative of Gedaliah has any historical value,[11] then it is likely
that the region survived the 586 B.C.E. events better than other regions. However, the situation gradually deteriorated after Gedaliah's assassination (as indeed
depicted in the Bible: 2 Kgs 25:22–26; Jer 40–41; those narratives are the basis of
the continuity theory), and the population, even in Benjamin, declined during
the Neo-Babylonian period. Demography reached a nadir during this period
before recovering to a very limited extent in the Persian period.

   All three types of archaeological data—major excavations, salvage excavations, and surveys—support such a reality. Excavations in the major sites, which
gave rise to the concept of continuity in Benjamin, show that at least in the Persian period settlement was in great decline. Salvage excavations and surveys
further show a lack of settlement during this time.

   By default, and until another explanation is provided, we should treat
these sites as being abandoned in or just after 586 B.C.E. If the biblical narrative
of Gedaliah has historical value, the region might have fared better during the
586 B.C.E. destruction (2 Kgs 25:22–26; Jer 40–41), but only for a short time. In
reality, many small sites were probably destroyed or abandoned, when the Babylonian army exploited and sacked the region during the siege of Jerusalem. Large
sites did continue to exist after 586, as they were not destroyed in punitive acts
like their counterparts in the south. The decline in Benjamin was more moderate
also because the region attracted refugees from Jerusalem and its environs, hence
increasing its demography to some extent. However, the remaining system collapsed after Gedaliah's assassination.

   The reconstruction of continued settlement in the land of Benjamin is based
mainly on the biblical narratives, but it is possible that there is some supporting evidence for it in the archaeological finds, that is, perhaps some later pottery
forms and mainly the lack of clear destruction layers in most of the sites (although
it is unlikely that this in itself would have been sufficient to proclaim continuity).
As Pritchard (1962, 161) wrote about Gibeon, "no evidence has appeared thus
far for a general destruction by fire within either the Iron I or the Iron II periods.
Apparently the city continued to grow and develop throughout these two ages
of its history without any marked disruption of its normal life." This means that

---

schits's demographic trends are based on a misunderstanding of the nature of the archaeological
data, and as we have seen in chs. 5 and 7, are arithmetically impossible.

   11. Along with the supporters of the continuity theory and most other scholars, I believe
the narrative has some historical value.

the central sites were not destroyed in a military campaign. However, they were gradually abandoned and deserted during the sixth century, probably following Gedaliah's assassination. Whether this was in tandem with the abandonment of the rural sites or slightly afterward will be discussed below, but it seems that all forms of settlements in Benjamin declined dramatically in the sixth century, and not only toward its end.

THE SIXTH CENTURY IN BENJAMIN: A MYTH?

The following section will show that the current "consensus" regarding the sixth century dating of many sites in Benjamin is far from secure, and appears to be a scholarly construction.

Notably, we have not discussed the pottery itself at any length so far, and we have not reexamined the dating of the various Benjaminite sites independently; this issue is well beyond the scope of the present chapter. It is quite clear from the brief discussion (above and in the introduction) that the specific dating of pottery to the sixth century cannot be sustained, is based on erroneous dating of other sites (see also more details below) and is to a large extent an archaeological mirage. It is interesting, therefore, to examine the development of the "consensus" regarding the prosperity of Benjamin in the sixth century B.C.E. I will first inspect the "history" of the dating of the major sites in Benjamin.

Bethel[12]

Albright wrote,

> In the sixth century Bethel was destroyed by a great conflagration, followed by a period of abandonment. In part the pottery from the burned houses is identical with that of the latest strata of Tell Beit Mirsim, Beth-shemesh and other towns of Judah which were destroyed by the Chaldaeans shortly before 587 B.C. In part the types here represented were new to us, presumably local. Probably the town was destroyed by the Chaldaeans at the same time as the other towns of Judah ... A destruction somewhat later in the sixth century is not, however, excluded, and would perhaps explain some strange features about the pottery (1934, 14).

---

12. As mentioned, the site is located to the north of Benjamin. Despite its actual location, the site is an integral part of any discussion of Benjamin in the sixth century because it is commonly mentioned with other sites in the region.

The later date was quickly adopted.[13] In the final publication of the Albright-Kelso excavations (Kelso 1968), the excavators preferred the lower date, and identified a sixth century occupation at the site (Kelso 1968; Sinclair 1968). This was followed by many others (e.g., Lapp 1978c, 84; Stern 1983; 2001; Lipschits 1999; 2005).

The dating of the pottery to the sixth century was based on the fact that the pottery appeared to have been later than that of the late Iron Age at other sites. Kelso (1968, 37, n. 6) wrote, "it became steadily clearer that the pottery from the burned Iron II houses is to be dated well after the destruction of TBM [Tell Beit Mirsim; A.F.], Beth-shemesh, Lachish, Gibeah, and other towns of Judah by the Challdeans" (this was initially based on the reanalysis of the pottery from the 1934 season, and "had been confirmed by subsequent excavations and study"). While considered at the time to have been destroyed by the Babylonians (Albright 1943; see also Stern 1975), it is clear today that the Iron II destruction at Tell Beit Mirsim, Beth-Shemesh, and Lachish III, was carried out by the Assyrians in the late-eighth century (e.g., Ussishkin 1977; 2004; Aharoni and Aharoni 1976; Finkelstein and Na'aman 2004, and many references), and not in the early-sixth century. That the pottery at Bethel is later does not necessitate down-dating the site to the mid-sixth century or later (for problems with "fine" dating in the sixth century, see also above, in the introduction, and below in this chapter). Further-more, as Dever noted (1971, 468–69, 1997a, 301), the sixth century corpus was without clear context, and the comparison to tomb 14 at Beth–Shemesh (which served as the "secured" assemblage to which the pottery was compared) was par-tial. Dever concluded that it is likely that "occupation at the site ends with the Babylonian destructions in the early sixth century BCE" (Dever 1997a, 301). Fin-kelstein and Singer-Avitz (2009) concluded that the "later" forms should actually be dated to the Iron Age IIB (see also Finkelstein 2011a, 364–65).

Gibeon

Pritchard initially dated the end of the Iron Age settlement to the beginning of the sixth century. Thus, in his 1962 popular book, Pritchard wrote, "There is every indication that the prosperous era for Gibeon came to a sudden end at the beginning of the Babylonian exile" (1962, 163; note that only a few remains were dated, as we have seen, to the Persian period). Accordingly, he dated the finds

---

13. See the various editions of Albright's *The Archaeology of Palestine*, e.g., Albright 1960b, 142, and of Albright's *From the Stone Age to Christianity*, e.g., Albright 1957, 322; see also Al-bright 1948, 205. It is likely that it was "convenient" for Albright to accept the late date, since it created a contrast between the situation in Judah and in the province of Samaria (where Bethel was located)—a point that was stressed by Albright 1957, 322; 1960b, 142.

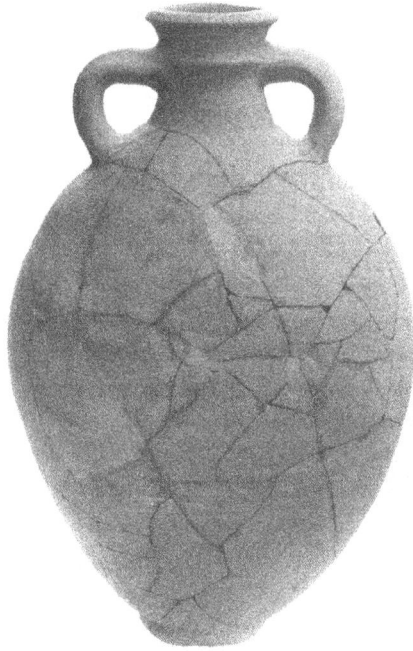

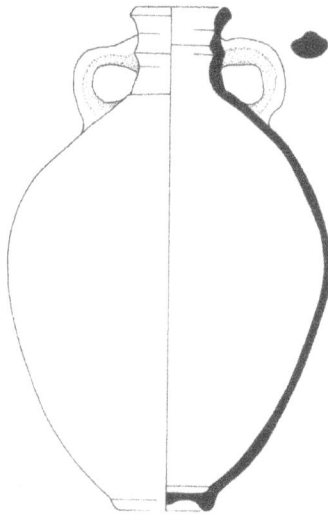

Fig. 16. A Gibeon jar from Tel Batash (Mazar and Panitz-Cohen 2002, 79; courtesy of the
Institute of Archaeology, the Hebrew University of Jerusalem, and Amihai Mazar).

of the stamped handles to this period (Pritchard 1959, 15; more below), and he expressed a similar view in the original publication in the first Hebrew edition of the *Encyclopedia of Archaeological Excavations in the Holy Land*. Pritchard (1972, 108) wrote that "from the 6th century to the 1st century B.C.E. only scant remains were unearthed in the excavations." In the later English version, however, Pritchard said that "there is but scant evidence for occupation from the *end* of the sixth century until the beginning of the first century B.C" (1975, 450; my emphasis). The summary in the *New Encyclopedia of Archaeological Excavations in the Holy Land* is similar (Pritchard 1993, 513).

The new dating was apparently a result of criticism of Pritchard's earlier conclusions. The criticism was based on both pottery analysis of the Gibeon jar handles (all found broken and out-of-context) and paleographic analysis of these handles. Already in 1960 Albright wrote that "judging from both script and pottery the reviewer [i.e., Albright] feels certain that most—probably all—of these graffiti belong to the Babylonian exile or immediately after it in the sixth century B.C." (1960a, 37). Albright was immediately followed by his students. Wright commented on the pottery, and although no good parallels were known at the time for the Gibeon jars, he (1963, 211, n. 1) briefly discussed the possible development of similar forms and dated the jars to the sixth century. At the same time, Cross (1962) questioned the original dating of the handles to the Iron Age, and concluded that "in light of the evidence, it does not appear feasible to date the group before ca. 600 B.C. ... perhaps we can do no better than to date the Gibeon handles broadly to the sixth century." Later, Albright (1966, 33) wrote "that they date from the sixth century B.C. appears certain" (see also Avigad 1972). It appears that the above criticism and reanalysis lie behind the re-dating of Gibeon, and the sixth century occupation at Gibeon had since become accepted by many (e.g., Stern 2001, 321, 336–38; Lipschits 1999; 2005, 243–44).

A reevaluation of the data, however, questions the low date of the Gibeon handles. As far as the jars are concerned, it appears that closest parallel came to light at Tel Batash (fig. 16),[14] where a complete jar was found (this is the only known example of a complete jar of its type; in other sites, Gibeon included, only sherds were found). At Batash, however, the jar clearly dates to the late-seventh century (e.g., Kelm and Mazar 1985, 114–16; Mazar and Panitz-Cohen 2001, 79; see already Amiran 1975; for the Iron Age date of the additional pottery which some date to the sixth century, e.g., the "carrot shaped" bottles, see now Kelm and

---

14. Kelm and Mazar (1985, 114) note that the parallel supplied by Pritchard (1959, 12, 13) was somewhat different from the Gibeon jars.

Mazar 1985, 114–15; Mazar and Panitz-Cohen 2001, 131). Therefore, it is much more likely that the pottery should be dated to the late Iron Age.

As for the inscriptions, Cross suggested they could not be earlier than 600 B.C.E., but did not flatly reject a date in the early-sixth century. The arguments for a later date were inconclusive.[15] A date later in the sixth century is therefore not a necessity even according to Cross's considerations. It is more likely to combine the paleographic consideration and the pottery analysis, and date the jar handles to the first decades of the sixth century B.C.E.[16] Interestingly, Finkelstein (2007, 53) referred to these finds as only representing "some activity in the Babylonian period."

Tell el-Ful/Gibeah

Earlier summaries tended to date the destruction of the Iron Age settlement to the early-sixth century. Hence, Sinclair (1975, 446) wrote, "the Chaldeans probably brought this phase to an end in 597 or 587 B.C." He added, "after a short period during which the site was abandoned, the mound was reoccupied in the late sixth century B.C."—this was the Persian period settlement (see also the table in Sinclair 1975, 444). Later, however, following the analysis of the new (1964) excavations, Lapp changed the dating of the Iron Age settlement (see mainly Lapp 1978c; see also Lapp 1965, 6). While the destruction of late Iron Age fortress destruction is still "attributed to Nebuchadnezzar's campaign in 588–87 BCE," the settlement itself is considered to have continued to exist—perhaps because "once the fortress was useless, the Babylonians may have been unconcerned with the remainder of the town's inhabitants and allowed them to live in peace" (Lapp 1993, 447; it should be noted that this is based on finds within a cistern, and not

---

15. Even without taking into account that paleography is not an exact science, and it is difficult to treat it as much more accurate than Carbon 14.

16. Interestingly, more recent treatments of the handles discussed them as part of the Iron Age, but still maintain the sixth century dating. Ahituv (1992, 108) for example, wrote, "The Inscriptions are from the sixth century B.C.E.," but added that the individuals mentioned were "probably officials in the local administration in the last days of the Judean monarchy." It appears, therefore, that Ahituv views the jars as dating to the late Iron Age. The same can be seen in Dobbs et al.'s discussion (2005). Dobbs et al. (2005, 167) wrote that "the city reached its zenith in the eighth and seventh centuries when it became a major center for the production of wine. From this period come the sixty-two inscriptions on handles of storage jars that are included below." But later they write (same page): "These inscriptions are all dated to the sixth century on the basis of its script and pottery type." Clearly the handles are discussed within the Iron Age context, but are they dated to before the Babylonian conquest? This is not clear, and since Dobbs et al. quote Albright (1960a, above) as the source for the sixth century date, it appears that this is not the case.

on a well-stratified occupation). Lapp (1993, 447) believed that the Stratum 3B settlement existed "probably throughout the exilic period" and was then abandoned. The stratum is attributed to the years 587–538 B.C.E. (e.g., Lapp 1978c, 84, 88, 100, and elsewhere). This dating is followed by many today (e.g., Stern 1982, 33–34; 2001, 321–22; Lipschits 1999, 178; 2005, 204; but see Finkelstein 2011b, 113).

Tell en-Nasbeh

The major settlement was attributed to the Iron Age, with only a limited occupation dated to the Persian period (587–400 B.C.E.; e.g., McCown 1947b, 63; Broshi 1975, 917–18; but see Malamat 1950, 226–27). Like other sites, a sixth century destruction at Tell en-Nasbeh was questioned by many as time progressed (e.g., Aharoni 1978, 279; see also Albright 1963, 86).

The findings at the site were subject to unique scrutiny by Zorn, in his Ph.D. thesis and subsequent publications. He wrote that "if the identification of Tell en-Nasbeh with Mizpah is accepted, it is natural to expect to find remains associated with the Babylonian period, the era of the site's greatest importance" (1993a, 1101; for the importance of the biblical narrative on Gedaliah, see already Muilenburg 1947). He also noted that "the excavators, however, failed to distinguish buildings from this period." It is indeed natural to expect sixth century pottery at the site, which is identified as biblical Mizpah and was the governing city of Gedaliah after the fall of Jerusalem. While the earlier excavators failed to find it, Zorn's restudy (and Zorn was searching for it), claimed to have identified a stratum with impressive remains, which he dated to this period (1993a; 1993b; 1997a; 1997b; 1997c; 2003). However, he admitted that no sixth-century assemblages were found and the reconstruction was artificial (Zorn 2003, 416–17, 445, see above).

Zorn's enterprise is legitimate, and perhaps required. However, it cannot be used to prove the existence of a sixth century city at Tell en-Nasbeh, let alone in other sites in Benjamin. Zorn's level II is a biblical construct. While such a construct might be true, it cannot be used to prove other sixth century levels—this would be cirucular argumentation, especially since it is artificial and Zorn was not able to locate a single locus from this period. Moreover, the Bible does not say much about the site in the "Neo-Babylonian period"—only about its initial years. Even if Zorn is right, it is still possible that the site was abandoned a few years after the fall of Jerusalem,[17] and does not represent the sixth century at large.[18]

---

17. Lipschits (2006, 34–35) suggested that Mizpah was the capital for 141 years (until 445 B.C.E.), but this was based only on his interpretation of the biblical evidence (which is indirect).

18. The identification of a new "city" is problematic. First, its dating is based on the assumption that Gedaliah built a new city. This is probably wrong; there is no evidence that Gedaliah

Interestingly, when reviewing the Tell en-Nasbeh report, Albright (1948, 205) noted that there was no sixth century pottery at the site (nothing similar to the one identified at Bethel was found there).[19] While this is only a relative chronology, it does show that these sixth-century forms are missing either here or there (see the discussion on the problematic nature of the pottery analysis, and in the introduction to the book). This observation on the relative chronology of the sites, made by someone who knew the relevant pottery very well, runs against many recent studies which simply accept, uncritically, any sixth century dating that was suggested in the past.

---

established a new city or that the Babylonians built any new city in the region (the mere suggestion that the Babylonians built a new city sounds fantastic and is not supported by any piece of evidence). It is more likely that Gedaliah used the Iron Age city that was not destroyed. That the buildings attributed to the sixth-century strata are later than the original ring road (e.g., Zorn 2003, 428) does not say anything about their exact date other than that they were later than the road. They could have been built during the Iron Age, and were probably built when the city was enlarged (during the Iron Age; cf., Herzog 1997b, 239). Furthermore, the city was probably abandoned gradually after the assassination of Gedaliah (it should be stressed that whether or not a new city was built by the Babylonians is immaterial to the fate of the settlement after the assassination). Notably, Zorn did not find any pottery assemblages from this period, and there is nothing whatsoever in the finding that hints at a construction date later than the Iron Age (see also Herzog 1997b, 237; Faust 2005a, 81–83, n. 148; 2012: 74). While Zorn admits the lack of any clear assemblage from the sixth century (Zorn 2003, 416–17, 445, and above), there is discrepancy in the pottery found in the large four room houses which led Zorn to claim that the buildings were late (cf., Zorn 1993a, 1101; 1997a, 65). Thus, one of the buildings (110.01) contained in situ pottery indicating that the building ceased to be used in the fifth century B.C.E. (i.e., the Persian period, which suits Zorn's analysis, 1999, 61), but in a neighboring building (125.01) the pottery was identical to pottery from the destruction levels of Jerusalem and Lachish (in 586 B.C.E.). Zorn tried to argue that the use of large Iron Age storage vessels lasted a very long time and that the structure with the Iron Age pottery was built immediately after 586 B.C.E., and lasted until the Persian period. This Iron Age pottery, however, does not indicate the construction time of the building where it was found, as Zorn argues, but rather its destruction time, as is the case in the equivalent sites that Zorn refers to. Furthermore, if Zorn was correct and the Iron Age storage vessels were used in the Persian period, why was not any Persian period pottery found in association with it? The finding of this Iron Age pottery, therefore, simply shows that the house it was found in was destroyed in the late Iron Age (as was claimed in the past). The exception is of course the house in which Persian period pottery was found, and this late pottery most likely arrived at the house when it was reused during the Persian period (reuse of buildings was very common in the Persian period; see, e.g., the reuse of Iron Age houses during the Persian period at Tel Eton and Kh. el-Qom; Faust 2011a: 204, 214; Dever 1997b: 392, respectively).

19. Note that later Albright (1963, 86) suggested that there was sixth-century occupation at Tell en-Nasbeh, but this seems to have resulted from his overall new understanding of the situation in Benjamin (see below).

Discussion

Although not always explicit, the interpretation of the dating of the late Iron Age settlement in all the discussed sites went through a similar process. Originally, the sixth-century occupation was not identified in any of the settlements in Benjamin. Only after a reanalysis of the data mainly from the 1960s and 1970s onward, did the sites receive different dating.

At Gibeon, for example, sixth-century occupation was not observed in the excavations and the date of the last Iron Age settlement was gradually (from the early 1960s onward) pushed toward the late-sixth century, rather than the early-sixth century. While the situation at Tell el-Ful was more complex, the dating process was similar. No sixth century level was identified there until Lapp's work in the 1960s, and since then it has become a "type–site" for the sixth century B.C.E. The same is true for Tell en-Nasbeh (biblical Mizpah), which joined in mainly during the early 1990s (but see already Aharoni 1978, 279; Albright 1963, 86; in contrast to Albright 1948, 205).[20]

This is not to deny that in some cases the new datings were based solely on pottery (or paleography). In most cases, however, the low dates were not founded on enough data, and should be revised and pushed back a little. For example, Zorn (1993a, 1101) had explicitly been looking for the sixth century (see also Barstad 1996, 47), but was unable to base his claims on pottery. In addition, the exact dating of Tell el-Ful's Stratum IIIB to 587 to 538 B.C.E., that is, the exilic period, is also not purely archaeological. It should also be noted that given the archaeological considerations for parallels (above), it appears that a "reanalysis" of the pottery from Bethel, on the basis of the new knowledge on the dating of Lachish III (and subsequently on the destruction of Tell Beit Mirsim and Beth-Shemesh), should change the low date of Bethel.

We must conclude, therefore, that the sites in the region of Benjamin that were dated to the sixth century B.C.E. had not been dated to this period in the past. Only in recent decades were the relevant strata "rediscovered"—at times after explicitly assuming their existence on the basis of biblical data (for Gibeon, see the reference to Malamat in Avigad 1972, 9).

This archaeological trend can be traced back to the 1960s, with Albright's (re)dating of the Gibeon handles, and the subsequent studies of his students. Interestingly, in most of his writings (e.g., the various editions of *The Archaeology of Palestine* [e.g., 1949a, and even in Albright 1960b, 142] and *From the Stone Age to Christianity* [Albright 1957, 322]), Albright did not write about settlement

---

20. Bethel, located outside of Benjamin, is an exception in that the late date of abandonment/destruction became widely accepted before that of the other sites (see above).

in Benjamin proper. He only mentioned Bethel, but stressed that it was part of Israel (and now an Assyrian province), and not of Judah. However, in *The Biblical Period from Abraham to Ezra* (Albright 1963, 86), Albright spoke of continuity in Tell en-Nasbeh (but see Albright 1948, 205). Perhaps this work is an indication of his new understanding of the settlement processes in Benjamin, as this is approximately the time in which he wrote his reviews on the date of Gibeon (Albright 1960a, 37). It is important to stress that in the earlier version of *The Biblical Period* (which was published as an article in 1949), Tell en-Nasbeh was not mentioned (see Albright 1949b, 48). It is not clear what led Albright to change his view. While his reanalysis was based on the interpretation of the archaeological data, it is also likely that it was combined with a broader understanding of the settlement process that included his understanding of the biblical texts.

Interestingly, it appears that the first to suggest that the region of Benjamin was not devastated was Malamat. He noticed the lack of destruction in Benjamin, and brilliantly discussed the archaeological finds in light of the biblical texts. Malamat (1950, 26–27) noted that there was no real reason to date the end of the Iron Age settlement in the region to the Babylonian destruction. He contrasted the finds at Tell en-Nasbeh with those at Lachish, and suggested that they had a different fate, because the former surrendered to the Babylonians, and was therefore not "punished." Malamat then showed that there was plenty of biblical evidence for continuation of life in this region after the destruction of Jerusalem, and this is where the Babylonians appointed Gedaliah—probably because it was not destroyed. (Malamat then noted, on the basis of textual analysis, that perhaps the area around Bethlehem was not destroyed either; Malamat 1950, 227;[21] see ch. 8).

Malamat's analysis was influential, and this could be the reason why the sites in Benjamin were redated and why the consensus became that Benjamin was not destroyed by the Babylonians (see Lipschits 2005, 237, n. 190 for many references). Malamat was followed by Albright's (1960a, 37; 1966, 33) reviews of the Gibeon reports, Wright's (1963, 211, n. 1) comment on the Gibeon jars, and then with Cross's (1962) more detailed discussion of the paleography of the handles. In "pure" archaeological literature, the redating can be seen in the preliminary report of the new salvage excavations at Tell el-Ful, where Lapp (1965, 6–7) reported the continuation of the settlement in the sixth century, after the Babylonian destruction (attributed to Nebuchadnezzar's 597 campaign), until it was abandoned. He suggested a similar process also for Gibeon, Bethel, and Shechem

---

21. This seems to have led to the erroneous claims for continuity in this region, too. See throughout this monograph.

(6). Perhaps more influential was Stern, who expressed this view in many places. In his 1975 paper, for example, Stern wrote, "the territory of Benjamin, however, did not suffer destruction at the time and sites such as Bethel, and perhaps even Gibeon and Tell en-Nasbeh, continued to flourish" (1975, 35). In subsequent papers, he repeated this conclusion (e.g., Stern 1983, 120). From Stern's works onwards, this archaeological maxim came to be widespread and widely accepted.

But we should stress that it was based to some extent on an erroneous stratigraphical interpretation of the entire late Iron Age Judahite assemblage. Albright (above) and Stern (e.g., 1975) dated Lachish III and similar assemblages to the early-sixth century, to 597 B.C.E. (instead of the late-eighth century B.C.E.). This helped to push the date of the assemblages that were relatively later in date much lower, deeper into the sixth century.

The widespread view that the sites in Benjamin were not harmed by the Babylonians is exaggerated. While Malamat's evidence is compelling, the archaeological foundations are more shaky. Dating the sites to the mid– or even late–sixth century is archaeologically baseless,[22] and results only from the knowledge that they did not exist in the Persian period on the one hand, and on the assumption that they were not destroyed in 586 on the other.[23]

However, one can accept all of Malamat's (mainly textual) analysis regarding this area, and still date the abandonment and collapse in Benjamin to the 580s or 570s B.C.E. As already noted, it is more than likely that the sites were not destroyed in 586 B.C.E., although a decline probably occurred in the rural sector at this time. Following Gedaliah's assassination, however, much of the population fled, and the region's settlements were gradually abandoned (though it was less devastated than other regions in Judah). Some of the sites were already abandoned in the early-sixth century, while a few others lingered on.[24] This is the only way to understand both the archaeological data and the biblical texts.

---

22. Even at Tell el-Ful, there is not a stratigraphical stratum with pottery that is dated to this period. The entire ceramic discussion is based mainly on finds in a cistern and even these were not sealed and "clean" but rather comprised only part of the finds within the cistern (although they were found within what perhaps can be seen as an inner stratigraphy in the fill, and the assemblage is therefore not artificial).

23. On the basis of the lack of destruction layers, the biblical evidence, and at times some remains like *mwsh* impressions and perhaps some peculiarities in the archaeological record.

24. Stern (2001, 322–23) suggested that some of the sites existed until the beginning of the fifth century, on the basis of the imports unearthed there. This, however, is contradicted by the data, as Stern himself had analyzed in more detail in the past (see, for example, Stern 1982, 31, 32, for Bethel and Tell en-Nasbeh; respectively, with references). Stern also refers to the probable lack of imports at Tell el-Ful (1982, 34), and the situation in Gibeon seems to be similar (32–33).

In most of the sites discussed, the Persian period was hardly or poorly represented. Therefore, even according to the "consensus" these sites were deserted/destroyed/declined before the late-sixth century, and with only limited occupation during the Persian period. The question of their existence during the sixth century is dependent to a large extent on interpretation, and we have seen that this, in turn, is dependent mainly on the Bible.

Indeed, Vanderhooft (2003a, 254, n. 18), after quoting Blenkisopp's protest against the tendency of archaeologists to corroborate their finds with biblical data, wrote: "In fairness, we must be skeptical of the same efforts when linked to arguments that favor continuity between the Babylonian and the Persian periods. The published report of the excavations at Tell el-Ful, for example, cannot have arrived at the dates for phase IIIB (586–538 B.C.E.) by a happy coincidence."

It should be therefore reiterated that the idea of continuity developed—even regarding Benjamin—at least partly as a result of a biblical agenda, not an archaeological one. If not for the biblical story of Gedaliah, there would have been almost nothing in the archaeological finds to suggest that the sites did not end at the same time as Jerusalem (i.e., in 586 B.C.E.). The only hint would have been the absence of a destruction layer in some of the sites. While I find it to be of importance (below), I doubt if this alone would have suggested continuity (it would have probably been attributed to the partial preservation of highland sites; cf. Na'aman 1996, for an earlier period). It is legitimate to harmonize the various types of data, but we should acknowledge that continuity in Benjamin is to a large extent a result of biblical interpretation, and is not based only on archaeological reasoning (more below). This is not to say that those studies were bad scholarship—they were based on good archaeological and historical research. Moreover, the Bible was regarded as reliable source at the time (more so than it is regarded today). But we should acknowledge the biblical influence on the current view of continuity in Benjamin.

SUMMARY

There is a consensus that settlement prospered in the land of Benjamin during the Neo-Babylonian period and that this area was not destroyed by the Babylonians. This view is based on the results of the excavations of the major tells in the region, in which sixth century occupations were discerned.

However, the data from surveys and salvage excavations, pertaining mainly to the rural sector, teach of a crisis in the sixth century. The simplest solution to the discrepancy in data is that the rural sector was harmed by the Babylonians in 586 B.C.E., while the urban sector was less affected. The decline in the urban sector was more gradual.

This is a tempting solution, and is supported by the reality in many other periods. In many instances, security problems led to the abandonment of rural settlements, while urban settlement continued to exist (and might have even prospered due to the relocation of the population from the smaller sites, e.g., Demand 1990). A similar pattern can result from a policy of a central government (Bunimovitz 1998; Faust 2003a; 2007b, and references). The continuation of the central sites in Benjamin, therefore, does not indicate prosperity in all settlements, and it is possible that there was some general decline, as the rural sector disappeared and only the towns survived.[25]

However, even the prosperity of the towns is not archaeologically clear cut. Minimal Persian period remains were observed in most sites, indicating a major decline in the sixth century, prior to the Persian period. The sites did not flourish in the Persian period, and those that existed were small. Even scholars who claim to identify the pottery of the sixth century agree that there is no good way to distinguish the pottery of the early and late Neo-Babylonian period in Judah, or to definitively date when these strata ceased to exist—in 575 or 540.[26] With the absence of significant Persian period settlement in the region, there is no reason to attribute the sixth century settlement, even if we accept this dating, to the entire period. The decline in the central sites started not long after 586, and continued until it reached a nadir later in the sixth century B.C.E.

Additionally, the basis of the sixth century dating is biblical, and the biblical description lies behind many of the attempts to identify sixth-century occupation in Benjamin. It is likely that without the biblical information, archaeologists would have reconstructed settlement abandonment in Benjamin at the same time as in other parts of Judah, that is, to the Babylonian campaigns, as was indeed

---

25. There was most likely some decline even in towns as observed at Tell el-Ful.

26. While it is possible that there are some features in the ceramics of the sites in Benjamin which push us slightly deeper into the sixth century, several points should be remembered: (1) The difference between the dates suggested in this chapter (and in most cases also in the original publications of the excavations results), and those suggested by Lapp and others are only a few dozen years (or less). Proving the later date on the basis of pottery alone is practically impossible, esp. since many Persian period forms appear already in the Iron Age. Such an exercise can be attempted only when we have very good, clear, and large assemblages. (2) We currently do not have even a single "good" and "large" assemblage which can be dated to the sixth century. Even if Lapp is right in suggesting that the discussed assemblage at Tell el-Full should be dated to the sixth century, it is not clear what the significance of the information is, even regarding this particular site. It clearly says nothing about Benjamin as a whole. In most sites, e.g., Gibeon and Tell en-Nasbeh, there is not even one clear locus which can be dated to this period (regardless of its quality). Therefore, it is very difficult to claim that the pottery can date sites to the later part of the sixth century. A broader perspective is needed.

done in the past.[27] Using the Bible is legitimate, but we should acknowledge that the archaeological dating of sites in Benjamin to the sixth century rely upon it to a very large extent. Moreover, the biblical stories, even if accepted, refer only to a few years after the 586 events. Clearly, there is no biblical or other reason to postulate settlement throughout the sixth century.[28] Since we have already seen there is no archaeological reason for this, the decline (if not in 586 B.C.E.) must have occurred during the Babylonian period.

Odds are that settlement declined after the 586 campaigns and mainly after Gedaliah's assassination. The rural sector probably suffered more from the 586 campaign, while the central settlements' decline resulted from Gedaliah's assassination, when people fled to other regions and the administration collapsed. Settlement in the region most likely deteriorated in the first decade or two of the Neo-Babylonian period and it was in great decline before the Persian period. This interpretation is strengthened by the lack of destruction layers in many of the large sites. They were simply abandoned gradually (i.e., not in an abrupt destruction) after the assassination.

This scenario is further strengthened when examining the history of scholarly interpretation of the data from the excavations in Benjamin. The dating to the sixth century is, in most cases, relatively new, and it is questionable whether the dating is based on solid archaeological evidence or assumptions derived from the biblical text (though the discussions in themselves are worthy and are not simply attempts to paraphrase the Bible).

In summary, the lack of destruction layers, the biblical story, and perhaps some peculiarities in the finds make "sixth century dating" tempting. We should stress, however, that it probably relates only to a relatively short period of time after 586, and no more. In other words, even if we accept the new dating (and this is not without problems), there is no reason to attribute prosperity to the

---

27. Apparently, the only archaeological element that supports continuity in the central sites in Benjamin is the lack of destruction. I believe this is significant, but since we are discussing highlands sites, with only limited preservation, it can be doubted whether this would have been sufficient to suggest continuity, with the absence of the biblical evidence. Now that we are "looking" for such continuity, we can identify elements which might support it, but the general lack of destruction would not have been enough on its own.

28. A number of scholars constructed very complex scenarios regarding the authorship of various biblical traditions, relating those to the supposed prosperity in Benjamin in the sixth century B.C.E. (e.g., Blenkinsopp 2003). Whether those reconstructions are possible, however, should be checked independently of the archaeological record. At any event, this monograph did not aim at evaluating those traditions, nor at studying the biblical information. On the nature of the relations between archaeology and biblical studies regarding the study of this period, see more in the summary of this book (ch. 11, endnote 2).

entire sixth century. It appears that the common view of prosperity in Benja-
mion throughout the sixth century is only a scholarly construct, originating in
the Bible's hints that the region was an area of refuge and the new center of the
remaining populations. The rural sites in the region were probably destroyed
or abandoned in 586 B.C.E. The urban sector was not directly destroyed at the
time, but was gradually abandoned after Gedaliah's assassination. In this there
is a marked difference between Benjamin and other regions that were probably
devastated more severely during the Babylonian campaigns.

Finally, it must be stressed that the ideas expressed in this chapter need to
be examined in more detail. Only an in-depth study of all the publications of
the pottery unearthed in the region of Benjamin will allow us to prove, refute,
or refine the conclusions presented here. The main aim of this chapter was to
show that such an examination is in order. As noted, the discussion of Benjamin
can be evaluated separately from the main themes of the present monograph.
Acceptance or rejection of the conclusions here should not influence the overall
arguments of the book.

CHAPTER 10
LIFE IN JUDAH IN THE SIXTH CENTURY B.C.E.

The previous chapters systematically examined the "reality on the ground" in sixth-century Judah. The region suffered greatly from the aftermath of the Babylonian campaigns, there was sharp social and cultural break with the Iron Age traditions, the population decreased dramatically, and most settlements, including rural ones, were deserted. Most of the population either died in the wars or afterwards—from punitive actions or from famine and epidemics. Others were exiled and some fled to safer and more prosperous regions. The polity had collapsed. There is currently not a single piece of evidence to indicate any form of organized political life during most of the Neo-Babylonian period. Nor was it in the explicit interest of any political entity to have organized society in Judah. For all these reasons, Iron Age society collapsed and fragmented, and did not continue as a "functioning society." The present chapter will reconstruct life on the micro-scale in the sixth century and look at questions such as: What was life like? Where did people live? How were they organized? What was the economy? I should state in advance that due to the poor state of knowledge on the period, this is only a preliminary reconstruction.

REMAINING INHABITANTS

The land was not empty; there were probably thousands of people who lived in sixth-century Judah. However, there was nothing that resembled Iron Age settlement or Iron Age society. The cities were destroyed, and only a small number remained and lived amid the ruins. Possible continuity (most likely partial) in the rural sector was observed in only some 15 percent of the Iron Age villages.

Those who remained were few in number, scattered over many areas, and mainly from the lower spectrum of Judahite society. It is likely that there were also survivors from the upper classes who managed to avoid death and exile, but they were not sufficient to organize society. Survivors were probably individuals, and only rarely did entire families (extended families) survive. The Iron Age *bet av* and *mišpāhâ* (e.g., Reviv 1993; Schloen 2001; Faust 2000b; 2005a; 2012) became something of the past.

WHERE DID THEY LIVE?

Can we be more specific on the regions in which people lived in the Neo-Babylonian period?

Cities

A very limited population continued to live amid the ruins in cities, for example, in Jerusalem (e.g., Barkay 1993, 107–8; 2003), where continuity was noted in a few burial caves (although, other mechanisms for the use of the caves were offered, e.g., Lipschits 2003b, 246; 2005, 211, n. 106). It is likely that this was the situation in most cities, as far south as Tel Ira, where people continued to use one of the tombs (Beit Arieh and Baron 1999). The limited number of burials indicates the demographic insignificance of the remaining population (ch. 5). But there were people there.

The situation after the Babylonian destruction at Timnah (Mazar and Panitz Cohen 2001, 282) might illuminate the situation in many urban sites.[1] The last Iron Age town there was quite large, and was destroyed in massive conflagration—the debris were more than one meter deep. At Timnah, however, evidence for reoccupation was found only in one area, in the form of an agricultural installation. Mazar and Panitz-Cohen concluded that "this was a brief phase and may indicate that a few farmers lived in the ruined town for a short while in the early 6th century." The situation in Timnah might represent the situation in other sites, and is indicative of both the demographic collapse and the existence of a few squatters amid the ruins.

Villages

Rural sites are expected to suffer greatly as a consequence of war, and most villages and farmsteads were destroyed or abandoned. Limited continuity was noted in a number of rural sites, though their populations were drastically reduced in comparison to that of the Iron Age.

---

1. It is not clear whether the late Iron Age settlement at Timnah (Tel Batash) was a Judahite city (Mazar and Panitz Cohen 2001, 282), but the situation there can illustrate the reality in other sites.

In other places, the remaining population probably clung to deserted and destroyed forts (e.g., Kh. abu et-Twein), where security from bandits (who probably roamed the region, as some of the remnants probably resorted to this form of life, and gangs from nearby regions joined in) was probably better (or at least people felt more secure; cf. Nowicky 1999, 167).

In some places, perhaps, a few villages or farmsteads were left relatively unharmed. While no solid archeological evidence exists for such a reality, it is possible. We can speculate that this was the situation west of Jerusalem, where continuity is indicated in a few nearby rural sites, for example, Malha and Beit HaKerem (see fig. 6, above), and also in the western part of Gush Etzion, where Kh. Jarish, Horvat Harimon, and Kh. el-Qatt (as well as the fort at Kh. Abu et-Twein) show some continuity with the Persian period (although the finds are very limited, showing significant population decrease in these sites; see fig. 7, above).[2] Why these villages were left as a relative island of continuity is unclear. Maybe they were too remote, or were accidentally overlooked. Or maybe the Babylonians considered them less rebellious. In such specific locales, the Babylonians could have left the "vinedressers and tillers of the land" that are mentioned in the Bible (Jer 52:16) and are referred to frequently in the current debate. Regardless of the reason, we identify such islands of relative continuity. It is possible that production continued on a very small scale during the sixth century there, and perhaps some inter-village trade/exchange took place. Due to the limited number of the sites, however, and with the lack of any indication for organization, this trade could not have been important even on the regional scale.

In light of the above, it is clear that survivors could be found in every region, but there were also relatively larger population concentrations because living together improves social life and security (at least the feeling of security). Benjamin might have been one such area and it is possible that west of Jerusalem (and perhaps the city Jerusalem itself) and parts of northern Judah were also "islands" of settlement. We must note that the area around Jerusalem and in Gush Etzion was excavated more intensively, therefore increasing the amount of data, and the (slightly) larger number of settlements in these areas could be a result of bias in the data. In any event, it is likely that such islands of relative continuity, that is, regions in which limited and partial continuity can be found in a few adjacent sites, will be found in the future in additional regions. A closer examination of those "islands" of settlement show how limited this settlement was, even at its best.

---

2. It is also possible that the relative concentration of sites resulted not from continuity, but from a new settlement peak in the Persian period, and hence more sites were incidentally resettled.

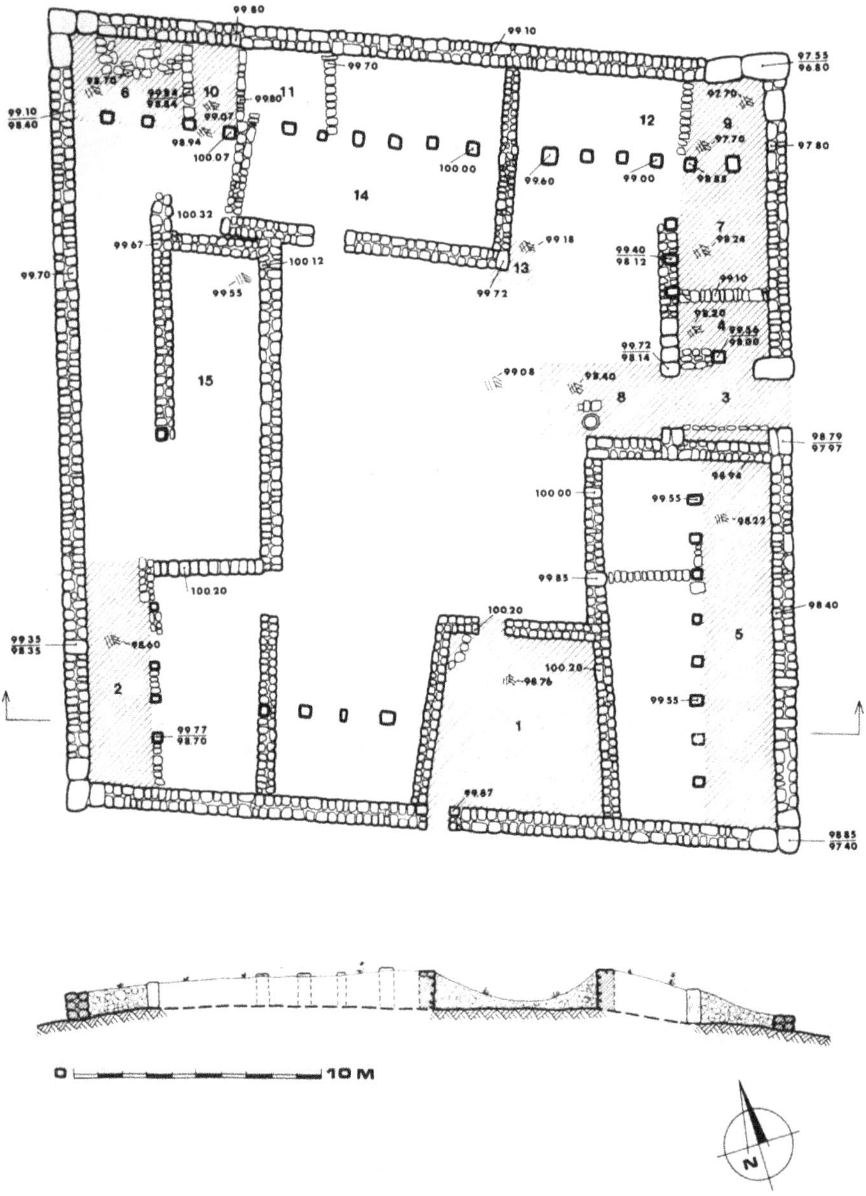

Fig. 17. Plan of the Iron Age estate/fort at Khirbet abu et-Twein (Mazar 1981, 231; courtesy of the Israel Exploration Society and Amihai Mazar).

ECONOMY

In contrast to the seventh century, there was no centralized economy during the Neo-Babylonian period, and we lack evidence for international trade, even along the coast (ch. 3).

The population must have subsided on simple agriculture. The specialization in agriculture that evolved during previous centuries could not have supported the producers, as no network of exchange existed, and was inevitably abandoned even if the knowledge for this production still existed in the first years after the destruction. The population resorted to a "closed" economy, producing what they needed, and exchanging only with neighboring sites. Surpluses were limited, causing the region to be "wiped off" the international trade map. The local communities did not have much to offer; therefore, foreign goods did not reach the region.

Inhabitants probably grew cereals, olives, and vines, although we lack any direct evidence to support this. Herding was probably an important aspect of the economy of the survivors.

Demographic decline, however, has its agricultural advantages for the survivors. There is less need to use poor soil and the better land can be used by the remaining population. It is possible that even with the most basic agriculture, people lived fairly well (from this perspective).

LIFE IN THE SIXTH CENTURY

Life continued in the Neo-Babylonian Period. Khirbet Abu et-Twein and its surroundings present us with a good opportunity to reconstruct life at the time. Khirbet Abut et-Twein (fig. 17) was an Iron Age fort (Mazar 1982), or more likely a royal estate (Faust 2005a, 199–207; 2012) in what is today the western part of Gush Etzion, southeast of Bethlehem. The structure was quite large, measuring some 29.5 × 31 m. Below the fort there was a small Iron Age village (ch. 2).

The pottery found at the site was not stratified (Mazar 1982, 99–101), and can be divided into three categories:

1. "Sherds of vessels typical of Judah in the Iron Age II" (101). ("The bulk of the finds," according to Mazar.)
2. "(S)herds ... of vessels which appear both at the end of the Iron Age as well as during the sixth–fifth centuries B.C." (Some finds.)
3. Forms which do not appear before the Persian period. Mazar stressed that "this group consists of only a few examples."

Mazar (1982, 104–5) therefore concluded that the site was built as a fort in the Iron Age, and was still in use after 586 (although the nearby village was apparently abandoned at the time).[3] Mazar commented on the finds, connecting them to the survivors: "The biblical sources provide clear evidence for the continuation of peasant settlement in Judah by 'vinedresser and husbandmen' as Jeremiah defined them (Jer. 52.16)" (1982, 105).

We can try to understand life at Kh. Abu et-Twein after 586 B.C.E. The entire settlement system in the region had collapsed and most settlements were either destroyed or abandoned, including the Iron Age village that existed below the Kh. Abu et-Twein estate/fort (ch. 2). The majority of the population disappeared; people either died, ran away, or were perhaps exiled. While some inhabit-

---

3. Notably, Hoglund (1992) attempted to date the structure to the Persian period (see also ch. 2), on the basis of the Persian period pottery found at the site, and in light of an architectural typology he developed for the identification of Persian period forts. While this note cannot be used for a very detailed refutation of Hoglund's claims, it should be stressed that his conclusions are flawed in almost every way. First of all, most of the pottery (category 1, above) found at Kh. Abu et-Twein is Iron Age pottery (Mazar 1982), and while some forms (category 2) can be dated to the seventh to fifth century time period, only a few cannot be earlier than the Persian period (category 3). On this basis, Mazar concluded that the site was an Iron Age fort, and that there was some continual usage at the site in the Persian (or Neo-Babylonian) period. Hoglund (1992, 191–95) questioned that, and claimed the site was founded only in the Persian period (in the middle of the fifth century). Since the vast majority of the pottery that was found in the debris is dated to the Iron Age (note that group number 2 is most likely also Iron Age), the site was probably founded then, and the later pottery only shows that there was some usage at the fort at a later stage. This is reinforced by the fact that the village below the fort existed only in the Iron Age (Mazar 1982). The village was a "by product" of the fort (Faust 2005a, 199–207), and the latter must date to the Iron Age. Moreover, architectural dating is a dangerous endeavor even when the data is solid, let alone when it is not. As far as Hoglund's architectural "model" goes, it should be stressed that almost all the examples of Persian period forts he mentioned (and which he used to build the "Judean" typology) are located outside of Judea. His Judean examples are problematic and speculative at best. At some of the sites, not a single Persian period sherd was found (e.g., Deir Baghl; Hoglund 1992, 195–96; cf. Kochavi 1972, 41), while others are multi-period sites, so the dating of the structure that was only surveyed, is doubted (e.g., el Qatt; Hoglund 1992, 196–97; cf. Kochavi 1972, 78). Notably, the most important site in Judah was Kh. Abu et-Twein, discussed here, as it is the only one that was excavated (Mazar 1982). As we have seen, this is an Iron Age site. All this shows that Hoglund's model is built on shaky foundations. And Hoglund uses this "model" to date a certain type of structures to the Persian period, even when no such pottery is found. This procedure is wrong, since pottery is the best dating tool we currently have. Furthermore, I should note that such square structures with courtyards (which Hoglund dates to the Persian period) existed in other periods; moreover, not all the structures fall into the exact category Hoglund discussed. Hoglund's "model" cannot therefore be used to change the dating of Kh. Abu et-Twein. (For additional criticism of Hoglund's model, see also Lipschits 2006, 37, notes 58–59.)

ants probably stayed in nearby villages, a number of people who remained in the region found refuge in the abandoned and destroyed estate/fort, probably because of the security it afforded. Moreover, the fact that it was an estate/fort inevitably allowed them to feel secure, especially if the people now residing in it were former inhabitants of the region, since the building probably symbolized strength and power for them.

The people who dwelled within the walls of the fort probably tilled the land in the area. Due to the relative emptiness, they could use the best soil in the river beds.[4] They probably still used the nearby wine presses that were found near the Iron Age village (David Amit, personal communication), and it is likely that they continued to grow some of the vines of the former village (or of other sites). Cereals were probably grown in the wadies below, and some of the area was used for pasture—perhaps even areas that had been used for vines during the Iron Age.

As noted above, it is possible that people also lived in a few nearby sites (H. HaRimon, Kh. el-Qatt, and Kh. Jarish); and while human activity there was also very limited, it is likely that the population did have some form of economic and social exchange. People most likely exchanged agricultural products or crafts and met on various occasions. There was some kind of loose economic and social system in the region.

One can even speculate (but no more than that) that perhaps those who lived at Kh. Abu et-Twein viewed themselves as the new "rulers" of the region, and living in the estate/fort gave them some prestige. While this is expected under such circumstances when social mobility is great (ch. 7; see even Lipschits 2005, 371; cf. Morris 2006, 66–67; Conlee 2006, 107–8, 113), there is no way to prove it. Regardless of the origin of the population in the place, it is unlikely that entire families survived. In most cases, large kinship groups disintegrated.

Many of the people probably started their life again—marrying, remarrying, having children, etc. While children of the Iron Age were ideally part of a large and extended family (the biblical *bet av*), which in turn formed part of a lineage (*mišpāhâ*), etc., those who grew up in the sixth century were not part of a similar grouping. It is likely that during the first generation the survivors still tried to maintain the world as they knew it (e.g., using Iron Age tombs in some places—not necessarily in the vicinity of Abu et-Twein of course). However, the children of the second generation after the destruction did not have anyone who could even try to transmit to them the "mentality" of this lost world, and who could really tell them "what it was like" (unlike "grand" stories of a lost golden age, ch. 7). They lost any real contact with the mindset of the Iron Age world. In most

---

4. Note that this is not the best ecological niche in Judah, to say the least.

respects, the society those children created could not have been similar to that of their forbearers in the Iron Age, even if they tried (ch. 9). The same holds true for people living in other locations.

Life in the Ruined Cities
As we have seen, it is more than likely that in every city there were squatters who lived amid the ruins, using available materials, scavenging, and practicing poor agriculture nearby (just like at Kh. Abu et-Twein).

Life in Benjamin
We have seen that in this area there were probably more people after 586 B.C.E., and it is possible that the break here was less sharp, and the decline less immediate. Although the situation might have been better in Benjamin, it is not certain whether there was any form of organized life after Gedaliah's assassination and the subsequent disintegration. If so, it still requires evidence—and not just assumptions.

Life in (Possible) Unharmed Villages
In addition to Benjamin, it is possible that some form of life continued in villages which were less harmed. There is no clear evidence of villages that were totally unharmed, but if we can find a concentration of villages with possible continuity (that cannot be attributed to a bias due to a unique concentration of Persian period settlements, ch. 2), then maybe some of the villages (will) represent a higher degree of continuity, and not just reuse by survivors. If such "islands" will be found, life there would not be much different from Kh. Abu et-Twein, with the exception that there were slightly more complex forms of organized life there (perhaps on the village level). However, it appears that in all locales, people led a very simple life.

Discussion
Notably, Ezekiel describes exactly such a reality. After mentioning the fall of Jerusalem (Ezek 33:21), Ezekiel speaks of the survivors in Judah. He refers to (v. 24) "the inhabitants of these waste (ruined) places in the land of Israel," and later (v. 27), "those who are in the waste (ruined) places shall fall by the sword; and those who are in the open field I will give to the wild animals to be devoured; and those who are in the strongholds [*meṣûdôt*; probably rock shelters or hilltops] and in caves shall die by pestilence."

The description of Ezekiel can serve as an illustration (even if it is not historical) to these who remained in the land.

1. Some people lived amid the ruins, in the destroyed cities and villages.
2. Some people lived in the "field." This refers to those who lived in iso- lated structures, and not in settlements. Notably, while (*'îr* in the Bible refers to settlements (any settlement—villages and towns alike), the field refers in many instances to farmsteads which are part of the field (cf. Lev 25:31; see also Deuteronomy 28:3, 16; see extended discussion in Faust 2008a, and many references). The usage of the term *field* was probably meant to differentiate between those who lived in such farmsteads or structures from those who lived in the ruined towns and villages.

    Notably, the first two categories that refer to settlements (*'ārîm*, which equals both cities and villages, referred to in the text as ruins) and to isolated structures (*ḥăṣērîm*, referred to in the texts as the field, which is a common dichotomy in the Bible, see Faust 2008a) cover what can be regarded as regular habitual places.

3. Some people lived in rock shelters and caves. It is likely that *meṣûdôt* refer to mountaintop or hilltop rock shelters that denote places of refuge (e.g., Greenberg 1997, 685; see also Cooke 1936, 368), since they go together with "caves." This category referred to those who hid.

As Greenberg (1997) wrote:

> Inhabitants of the ruins' evidently refers to the survivors who lived in the Ju- dahite towns ravaged by the Babylonians. In the aftermath of the war, people who fled into the open country straggled back to resettle the abandoned sites … The situation in this oracle is that some have returned while others still lived scattered about the countryside (684).

Whatever the historical reality behind Ezekiel's prophecy of destruction, his description can clearly be used to illustrate what life was like for the remaining inhabitants in Judah who lived amid the ruins of towns and/or villages, in the field, and in rock shelters and caves.[5] Whether Ezekiel's description is historical or not, it serves as a good illustration for reality in the sixth century B.C.E.

Summary

The inhabitants of Neo-Babylonian Judah were scattered from Benjamin in the north to the Negev in the south, but were very limited in number. They clung

---

5. It is likely that hiding in caves took place only during the first period after the destruction. After that, people probably returned to live "above ground."

to deserted settlements, mainly cities but in some cases also to villages; used some farmsteads; and found refuge in abandoned and deserted administrative buildings (immediately after the war, many also found refuge in rock shelters and caves, but this could not have lasted long). The economy was simple, not far above subsistence level, and probably only included limited regional exchange.

Some people still clung to Iron Age traditions, but due to the collapse of the social order of the Iron Age, many of the traditions gradually faded away. The usage of *mišpāḥâ* and additional kinship terms, as discussed by Vanderhooft (2009; see ch. 4 above), can show how the people of the Persian period tried to maintain the traditions of the past and used the same terminology, but because of the drastic changes, the same terms denoted different things now, acquiring new meanings. The world of the sixth century still maintained bits of the Iron Age, but was to a large extent very different.

CHAPTER 11
JUDAH IN THE SIXTH CENTURY B.C.E.:
SUMMARY AND CONCLUSIONS

Until not long ago, there was an agreement that the sixth century was a period of low demography, with little trade, and little material remains. This nadir was attributed to the Babylonian destructions of the late-seventh century B.C.E. in Philistia and the early-sixth century B.C.E. in Judah. This view was challenged recently by a group of researchers, predominantly biblical scholars. They revived and elaborated Torrey's claims (although on a more moderate scale) that the exile was of little significance and that most of Judah's inhabitants were not influenced by it. Not only was the land not empty, but most of the population was unaffected by the Babylonian campaign and life continued as usual.[1] These scholars asserted that continuity, rather than break, was typical of the sixth century. They admitted that the urban centers were destroyed by the Babylonians—this is well-known archaeological information that is accepted by all—but suggested that the rural sector (about which we knew very little), was not affected. Since most of the population lived in this sector, then they were unaffected by the Babylonian conquest and destructions.

The dearth of sixth-century finds that was traditionally attributed to the poor conditions and demographic decline of the region was explained by the new school as resulting from the fact that we were discussing a short period of time, with no archaeological characteristics. According to this view, when sixth-

---

1. Scholars who follow this line of thinking, most notably biblical scholars like Barstad, Lipschits, and Blenkinsopp, and also Berquist, McNutt, and others, questioned the biblical "myth of the empty land" that infiltrated modern scholarship. They attacked the claim that the land was totally empty, and that the entire population was exiled. We must note that in so doing, they created straw men, in comparison to whom their view could have been presented as more reasonable. Most previous scholars did not think that the land was totally empty and devoid of population. Nor did they attribute the significant demographic decline only to exile (ch. 8).

century sites were surveyed, finds were attributed to the Iron Age (or the Persian period) and not identified correctly. The claims and counterclaims had brought the discussion to a dead end, and the goal of the present monograph was to decipher the situation in the Neo-Babylonian period, and to enable us to understand the reality of this period.

After presenting the background of the current debate, chapter 1 surveyed the known archaeological data derived from the excavations of large sites, mainly tells. The evidence from these sites comprises the basic information that was addressed by all scholars, and on which all previous views were based. An early-sixth-century destruction layer (or at least abandonment) was found in practically all the excavated central sites, and the destruction was usually attributed to the Babylonians. Regardless of the identity of the agents of these destructions, the country was nevertheless devastated. This is how the traditional view of the desolation of the country was formed.

Supporters of the continuity theory agreed with the fate of the urban sector, but suggested that the rural sector was unharmed by the Babylonians. Some went even further to say that the rural sector prospered in sixth-century Judah. Therefore, chapter 2 examined the reality in rural Judah and the claims that after the 586 events, life in this sector went on just as before. We have developed a method to overcome our inability to identify sixth-century pottery by examining continuity in excavated rural settlements from the Iron Age to the Persian period. Some fifty late Iron Age rural sites were excavated in Judah, and only about seven show possible continuity to the Persian period (usually very limited continuity, with little Persian period remains). Hence, there was a break in rural settlement between the late Iron Age and the early Persian period. The best, and probably only, candidate for causing this break was the Babylonian campaigns and the events which followed, in accordance with the traditional view. Admittedly, we cannot archaeologically date the break in rural settlement to a certain date within the sixth century, but the 586 B.C.E. events and the processes that followed (and even supporters of the continuity school do not deny their historicity) are the only serious candidates for causing the collapse. Anyone who wishes to claim otherwise should suggest another date, and that person carries the burden of proof.

While it is possible that the local pottery of the sixth century is not distinguishable from that of the seventh century as some scholars suggested (and this is the reason for our lack of familiarity with it), chapter 3 examined a class of pottery whose sixth century date is secure—Greek pottery. This easily recognizable pottery is absent from the entire region, even from sites in the coastal plain. While the exact chronology of Greek pottery is not without problems, supporters of the continuity theory follow the accepted dating of Greek pottery. Hence, they must acknowledge a gap in the importation of Greek pottery to the region during the sixth century. Since Greek pottery was circulated in large quantities around the Mediterranean during the sixth century B.C.E., its almost complete absence in the southern Levant is significant and indicates a great decline in the economy of the region at the time. The region was simply wiped off the map of flourishing Mediterranean trade of the sixth century B.C.E. By using Greek pottery, we can date the decline with greater precision. Unlike previous chapters, when we suggested that the 586 B.C.E. events and subsequent processes were the only reasonable candidates to cause the decline (although we could not prove this dating archaeologically), here it is clear that the break occurred precisely in the beginning of the Neo-Babylonian period. The importation of Greek pottery ceased at exactly this time, hence supporting the association of this break with the military campaigns of the early-sixth century.

Interestingly, the long domination of Phoenicia (Tyre) in Mediterranean trade and its hegemony over the Phoenician colonies in the west came to an abrupt end during the first half of the sixth century, and many Phoenician colonies declined or were even abandoned. Concurrently, Carthage took the place of Tyre. Most scholars agree that this change was a result of the long Babylonian siege at Tyre and its subsequent conquest. It appears that as a consequence of the siege, Tyre declined, its colonies collapsed, and Carthage took advantage of the opportunity to become an independent empire. While the almost total lack of Greek pottery in the land of Israel shows how unimportant the region was for the economy of the Mediterranean, the changes in the western Mediterranean also show that the east (Tyre) was in great decline during the Babylonian rule.

Chapter 4 examined social and cultural changes during the transition from the Iron Age to the Persian period. There were several social and cultural institutions which were of the utmost importance in the Iron Age, but which disappeared in the sixth century. The four-room house and the Judahite tomb played a central role in the life of the average Judahite, as they accompanied the individual from cradle to grave. They reflected and shaped Judahite values and society. Both markers of life and death, however, disappeared from the archaeological record during the sixth century. In the early phases after the destruction, there is evidence that some of the few who remained clung to these habits (i.e., using such tombs and houses), but as time progressed these habits became meaningless without the entire social system they were part of, and therefore ceased to be practiced. Other changes in religion and cosmology, and probably also in language, occurred. The cessation of such socio-cultural markers is in accordance with the traditional view of the sixth century.

Chapter 5 examined settlement changes and demographic fluctuations from the seventh to the second centuries B.C.E., that is, from the Iron Age, through the

Persian period, and to the Hellenistic period. This examination clearly revealed that the Persian period was a nadir in both settlement and demography. While this is well-known, a detailed scrutiny of the available data revealed that the nadir was much lower than was usually thought. The demographic trends presented by supporters of the continuity theory are impossible arithmetically, according to their own data. The available evidence showed that settlement and population collapsed in the early-sixth century, and very slowly recovered, only reaching previous levels in the second century B.C.E. The nadir of the sixth century was most likely approximately ten percent of that of the seventh century B.C.E. and, at most approached twenty percent. The data clearly support the traditional view of the sixth century.

The following chapter compared Sennacherib's campaign with Nebuchadnezzar's campaign. While Sennacherib's campaign is usually regarded as disastrous, in actuality there was far more destruction and decline after Nebuchadnezzar, hence putting the results within a proper context.

All the characteristics of life in the sixth century bear the mark of what Tainter (1999; 2000) labeled a post-collapse society. When societies collapse, they exhibit general characteristics. Chapter 7 discussed Judah as an excellent example of a post-collapse society. This explains why the destructions and the demographic decline brought about social changes and disintegration, and the cessation in the use of Iron Age cultural markers. Notably, many facets which Barstad and other continuity theorists claimed were not reasonable in the traditional view of the sixth century find parallels among many other post-collapse societies.[2]

Chapter 8 revisited various aspects of the continuity theory. Among other things, we noted that the "myth of the empty land" was actually a straw man (and even straw men), and that traditional scholars did not consider the land to be "empty" nor did they view "exile" as the only mechanism of demographic decline. The Babylonian campaigns brought death to many people during the war itself, and as a result of the famine and epidemics that affected many of the besieged cities. When the battles ended, many more were executed. The looting of food by the conquering armies increased famine, and the many dead that were lying around brought about epidemics. Some of the population that remained were exiled, while others ran away into regions which were less affected. All these factors brought about the drastic demographic decline (not only the exile). The collapse of the administration made food production in each region insuf-

---

2. There was some continuity of course, but it was relatively limited. These instances are worth studying as part of the regeneration process of Jewish society in the Persian and (mainly) Hellenistic periods (ch. 7).

ficient for the local population, as regions that specialized in one produce could not have exchanged it with the surpluses of other regions. The collapse of the state increased famine even further (at least for some time after the destruction). Those that remained were few and did not form intact social or kinship groups. Society could not continue as usual, and it collapsed.

We also noted that archaeologists observed sparse settlement in various parts of the country, not only in Judah. This runs against the accusation that it is biblical influence that led them to reconstruct such a reality. The biblical "myth" was supposed to influence scholarship on Judah, and not on the coastal plain. The dearth of settlement in the latter, therefore, undermines the significance of the biblical influence on the archaeological consensus of the sixth century B.C.E. as a period of desolation. In addition, we examined the Babylonian interests in the region, and discovered that those should not have led them to spare Judah— far more important regions were devastated by the Babylonians, and there is no reason to suspect the fate of Judah. The chapter also examined evidence for administrative continuity between the Assyrian and Babylonian Empires in the region, and concluded that no such evidence is currently present.

Finally, we noted that it appears that the continuity school is dictated by a biblical agenda, which leads them to force their views on the archaeological data.

Judah in the sixth century was sparsely settled, with possible population concentrations in small areas such as Benjamin. Settlement in the region of Benjamin received a great deal of scholarly discussion. Scholars argued that there was a large degree of stability, and even prosperity, in this area during the sixth century B.C.E. However, the reality in the region of Benjamin is not as straightforward as many think, and chapter 9 showed that the relative continuity in settlement in the sixth century was short lived. While some sites (not all) were not affected by the Babylonian campaigns, the situation probably deteriorated after Gedaliah's assassination. It seems that the region was only slightly better off than other parts of Judah.[3]

Chapter 10 attempted to describe life in Judah in the sixth century B.C.E. Scant architectural remains enabled us to reconstruct the simple life that continued in places like Kh. Abu et–Twein. Here, the remaining inhabitants reused

---

3. The question whether Judah became part of Samaria or became a new province was not dealt with in this book, as the archaeological evidence does not bear any direct evidence in this regard. Still, many scholars (e.g., Vanderhooft 2003b, 227–29; Oded 2003, 68) stressed that there is no indication that the Babylonians established a new province, and in light of archaeological evidence the view that the region became part of Samaria at the time (as maintained by most scholars since Alt [1953, 323], see also Vanderhooft 2003b, 227–29; Oded 2003; and many others) seems more logical (unless the area was too poor, and was simply left outside the province).

an old estate/fort. They probably farmed the land and lived off a simple economy. The situation was similar throughout Judah, where squatters lived amid the
ruins. The reconstruction was in accordance with the traditional view of the sixth
century B.C.E.

We now come full circle to the continuity school's claim that the rural sector
was unaffected by the Babylonian conquests. Even without the positive archeological evidence for the devastation of most of this settlement sector, the mere
logic employed by the continuity school is unfounded. As Tainter (2000, 12)
observed, "when the administrative apparatus collapsed it took the countryside with it," that is, even if the countryside was not harmed directly, it is likely
that it, too, would collapse, as it could not stand on its own (ch. 7). It should
also be noted that many of the claims raised by the supporters of the continuity theory are problematic (ch. 8). In many instances, their reconstructions are
based on assertions rather than on data, or on the insertion of modern concepts;
for example, we have seen how scholars imposed their concepts on the economy
of the Babylonian Empire. Their writing is also based on misunderstanding of
the archaeological literature and, in other instances, an uncritical reading of it.
One does not have to be a "dirt" archaeologist to write about archaeology, but
one must be very familiar with the archaeological data, and understand it and its
limitations in order to do so.

Moreover, it should have been a warning sign for biblical scholars that there
seems to be almost a consensus among archaeologists[4] throughout the generations that the sixth century was relatively "empty" and the region was in ruins.[5]

In sum, there is no doubt that thousands of people lived in sixth-century
Judah. But they were scattered across large areas. The survivors were usually individuals, and did not constitute entire families, and the vast majority came from
the lower classes. They were survivors and did not form an organized society.

---

4. Finkelstein and Silverman's popular book appears to be an exception. However, the book
did not treat the data, and only relied on Lipschits (Finkelstein and Silverman 2001, 307). In
2010, Finkelstein returned to the traditional view that the land was devastated in the sixth century (e.g., Finkelstein 2010, 46), and his population estimates of the Persian period were lower
than those of any other scholars (43–46). Clearly, Finkelstein should be counted as part of the
traditional school. In addition, in a brief article Dever (2009) accepted the view that there was a
large degree of continuity in the countryside (adding that Stern's views need to be modified and
that my figures require "some adjustment"; 33*). However, in this paper Dever did not discuss
even a single site in the countryside.

5. From Watzinger 1935; through Albright 1940; 1960b; 1963; Kenyon 1965; Aharoni 1979;
to "modern" scholars like Shiloh 1989; Stager 1996; Herzog 1997b, 278; Mazar 1990; King and
Stager 2001, 251–58; Dever 2005, 291–94; Master 2007; Finkelstein 2010, 46; Holladay 2009, 88;
and Stern 1983; 2001; 2002.

As Reviv (1993, 196) wrote in his study of Israelite society, "with the elimination of Judah's independence, its society was also eliminated." These survivors joined into small groups, created new communities, and gradually developed new customs and traditions. Continuity with the Iron Age was limited.

It is likely that the demographic nadir was not in 586 B.C.E., but was a few years later when the aforementioned processes "matured." In any event, the process of recovery was slow and lasted several centuries. While many issues are still open and await further study, we can be certain that life did not continue as before in sixth-century Judah.

ENDNOTE 1: HOW THE NEW MYTH WAS BORN

As we have seen above, the rural sector cannot carry the burden assigned to it by some scholars[6] of preserving the majority of Judahites in the territories of what used to be the kingdom of Judah. What was the rationale behind the development of the view that the rural sector preserved the majority of Judahites?[7]

After referring to "recent surveys, undertaken by the Israel Department of Antiquities in the years 1967–1968," Barstad wrote,

> During these surveys *a large number of sites with material remains from the sixth century,* many of them new, were discovered in Judah. There can be little doubt that in these small towns and villages we have direct access to places where large number of Judeans who survived Nebuchadnezzar's invasions were living (1996, 54–55; emphasis added).

Barstad, therefore, defined "Judah after the fall of Jerusalem" as "a society where life went on after 586 B.C. pretty much in the same way as it did before…" (1996, 79; see also Barstad 2001, 7). He claimed that "these towns and villages, especially those at a certain distance from Jerusalem, were allowed to go on in the same unruffled manner as before the upheavals in 586" (1996, 81). Elsewhere, he

6. Most notably Barstad 1996; see also Barstad 2003; Lipschits 1997b, 153–98; 1998b; 2003b, 222; 2004; 2005, 190; Berquist 1995, 15–18; McNutt 1999, 187–88.

7. As mentioned above, this view developed among biblical scholars and theologians without any necessary reference to the archaeological "reality" on the ground (e.g., Carroll 1992; Berquist 1995). Therefore, much of their work is irrelevant for the present discussion, as it does not engage with the archaeological data. Hans Barstad was probably the first scholar that referred to the situation in Judah during the sixth century B.C.E., and his influential work is therefore a good starting point. The following discussion is based on Faust 2003b, 46–47.

referred to "the large majority of the population that actually remained in Judah." Barstad quoted the emergency survey,[8] and referred also to Weinberg (1969).

Weinberg (1969, 84) spoke of "some 2500 sites examined" in the (yet unpublished) emergency survey, 500 of which were "in Judah alone" (from all periods). He claimed that "most of these are villages or small towns, largely nameless. ... Yet, *a number of these* have yielded material from the sixth century, and it now seems clear that it was in such places that *most of the remaining inhabitants* of Judah lived after the more important centers were destroyed by the Babylonians" (emphasis added). Later in his paper, Weinberg (96) mentioned again the emergency survey and the discovery "of the first small settlements" where the population of the sixth century might have inhabited. He assumed that "fine-comb surveying will locate more such settlements, and there should be hundreds of them scattered throughout the land." It should be noted that Weinberg himself did not give much weight to these settlements, and considered the period to be a relatively very poor one.

The emergency survey was unpublished when Weinberg published his paper in 1969. In the final publication of the survey, Kochavi (1972, 23) mentioned only three sites that should be dated to the sixth century.[9] It seems as if Weinberg was orally informed of these few sites before they were published and he referred mainly to them in his publication, when he mentioned "*a number of*" sites that produced sixth century material, out the five hundred sites identified in Judah. These unnumbered sixth century sites, whether correctly identified or not, had been assumed to have been inhabited by the majority of Judah's population when Barstad published his book in 1996 (he did not mention any other survey which supposedly supported his claims; only the 1968 survey and Weinberg's summary). It could be assumed that these few sites were confused with the hundreds of new sites which were discovered during the survey and were mentioned on the same page (84; the vast majority of which, however, had nothing to do with the present discussion) or with the hundreds of sites Weinberg (1969, 96) assumed would be discovered in the future. Whatever was the cause for the confusion, a new "myth" was born—the myth that the "majority" of the population of the (former) kingdom of Judah occupied the smaller sites, and that this "majority" was unaffected by the fall of the kingdom.

---

8. 2001, 7; see also 1996, 78. Note that he did not refer to the new surveys conducted by Ofer (1993b), Finkelstein (1989), Finkelstein and Magen (1993), etc.; although preliminary (and even final) results were available at the time.

9. Even these could have resulted from misidentification that resulted from unfamiliarity with the pottery at the time (Amit and Cohen-Amin in press; Alon De Groot, personal communication).

Later works, even if more updated archaeologically (e.g., Lipschits 2003a; 2003b; 2005) were simply an offshoot of Barstad's thesis, and they all fail to name and locate the many settlements they claim to have existed in the sixth century.

ENDNOTE 2: ON THE IMPLICATIONS FOR BIBLICAL SCHOLARSHIP AND INTERDISCIPLINARY RELATIONS

The period under discussion is extremely important for biblical scholars. It is the period during which, according to many, important parts of the Bible were written. The question of where they were written—in Babylonia or in the land of Israel—is also of great importance.[10] The issue was mentioned in chapter 8, and only the main arguments will be repeated here, in order to develop the theme of the present section.

The interest in the sixth century of scholars like Barstad and Blenkisopp was derived from their understanding that in an "empty" land, or one with little population, texts could not have been written. A desolate land lacked the required apparatus and even surpluses to have scribes. Hence Barstad wrote, "one very important question is whether Neo-Babylonian and Persian Judah had the necessary population or infrastructure to produce the literature that we now find in the Hebrew Bible" (2003, 4). He concluded, "I do believe that it did" (see also Barstad 1996, 18–20, 45, 80–81). Similar quotations can be brought from other scholars as well (e.g., Blenkinsopp 2002a, 37; see also ch. 8). Indeed, our understanding of the archaeology of the "exilic period" in Judah is significant for the possibilities opened (or closed) for biblical scholars' reconstruction of the authorship and editing processes of the texts (for an explicit treatment of this type of the entire Persian period, see now Finkelstein 2010).

Almost all archaeologists who study the material culture and settlement of the sixth century agree that there was very little of it.[11] The land was not literally empty but demography was greatly reduced and society simply collapsed. It was

---

10. For material on the biblical literature of the sixth century, and the importance of the exile, see for example, Jansen 1956; Thomas 1961; Ackroyd 1968; Seitz 1989; Barstad 1996; Sanders 1997; Levitt Kohn 2002; Albertz 2003; Middlemas 2005, and references; see now also Middlemas 2007.

This is the main reason why the "exile" is so important for biblical scholars, from Torrey onward. See also, in addition to the above literature, Grabbe (1998); Carroll (1998); and many others. Various other scholars attempt today to learn about the development within the land of Israel (e.g., Blenkinsopp 2003).

11. From Watzinger 1935; through Albright 1940; 1960b; 1963; Kenyon 1965; Aharoni 1979; and up to scholars like Shiloh 1989; Stager 1996; Mazar 1990; Dever 2005; Master 2007; Stern 1983; 2001; 2002; Holladay 2009; Finkelstein 2010.

biblical scholars and theologians who developed and supported the continuity theory. Their agenda was not derived from an interest in the reality of the period, but rather from the possibilities it opened or closed for biblical interpretations. While this is legitimate, there are dangers to such an approach and in any event it should at least be acknowledged. These biblical scholars and theologians who view the sixth century as settled and prosperous, attempt to force the archaeo-logical record that they realize they desperately need to suit their thesis. Most of them suffer not only from an agenda (not always so hidden), but also from a misunderstanding of the archaeological record. Archaeologists "know" it is impossible—there was no functioning society or polity in sixth-century Judah, and no data on prospering communities came to light. If the reality on the ground during the sixth century bears importance for the possibilities of the cre-ation of the various texts (below), biblical scholars are expected to correct their views on the basis of this reality, and not the reverse, as many are currently doing.

Barstad's agenda, as we have seen in chapter 8, is quite clear. After assuming that there must have been many people in Judah, he wrote

> If, in fact, "most of the population" remained in Judah, as it must have done … this society must have consisted not only of peasants … but also of arti-sans, traders, village and town elders, scribes, priests and prophets. In other words … a functioning society, with many of its political institutions still intact (1996, 18–19).

We have evidence of nothing of the like. But Barstad needs a functioning soci-etyof prophets, scribes, and priests because his dating of various texts and his understanding of their place of authorship is dependent on it (see also Middle-mas 2005, 20).

An even more disturbing approach can be seen in Blenkinsopp's explicit call for archaeologists to confirm his theory; in the last paragraph of his paper, which discusses modern politics and Zionism, he asserted:

> I have tried to show that what has become known as "the myth of the empty land" originated with the dominant Judaeo–Babylonian elite in Judah un-der Persian rule. … During the Hellenistic period, at a time when interest in national and ethnic origins was running high, the myth then instigated one of several accounts of the initial Israelite occupation of the Palestinian hill country supposedly empty of inhabitants … it served in due course as historical legitimation for an exclusive claim to territory, at least in the sense that others could share space only on conditions established by those who claimed to be the original settlers. Our survey, finally, raises the question whether archaeology should allow itself to be co-opted into this process, or

whether its task should not rather be that of contributing to the dissolution of false understandings of the past (2002b, 187; emphasis added).

Paradoxically (and sadly), the plea to "liberate" archaeology from its coopera-tion in the creation of the "myth,"[12] does not involve a call for an independent archaeological agenda that will inform biblical scholars on the material reality in sixth century. Rather, it is an explicit call for a recruited archaeology, in which both the agenda and the conclusions should be biblically (and even politically) driven.[13] While the archaeology of the sixth century B.C.E. should be informed by biblical studies, as the two are closely related, it would be better off with studying the sixth century B.C.E. mainly in archaeological/anthropological terms, that is, to concentrate on concepts such as abandonment of sites and regions (e.g., Cam-eron and Tomka 1993; Nelson and Schachner 2002; Hegmon, Nelson and Ruth 1998), processes of collapse and post-collapse (e.g., Tainter 1988; 1999; Nowicky 1999; Yoffee and Cowgill 1991; Schwartz and Nichols 2006), etc. If the archaeo-logical data are so important for biblical scholars, they will have to come to terms with the results.

Indeed, there can be no doubt that there is an urgent need for a closer coop-eration between biblical scholars and archaeologists and anthropologists—a venture from which all sides will benefit. Both sides should work together, or at least be informed on the developments of the other, to the extent that it might have an impact on what they do. In the present case, biblical scholars need this cooperation much more than archaeologists, as their scenarios are built on archaeological data. However, cooperation is for the benefit of all.

It is clear that Judah suffered a major blow in the sixth century, following the Babylonian campaigns. Life did not continue as usual. This does not require biblical scholars to change their views; however, they must acknowledge the data. The implication of post-collapse Judah for biblical studies should be examined using not only common sense but also information from disciplines like anthro-pology. For example, it would be worthwhile for biblical scholars who assume that if Judah was devastated there could not have been any writing in the region to check this assumption, on the basis of the wide array of anthropological and

---

12. When reading some of the literature on the subject (e.g., Blenkinsopp 2002b; 2002c), it is clear much of it has a hidden agenda, and it is at fault with what it is charging previous genera-tions of scholars.

13. Not all biblical scholars belong to the new school, of course (for example, Meyers and Meyers 1994; Oded 2003; 2010; Schniedewind 2004, and additional references above), but Blen-kinsopp wants an archaeology that will support his views (the reader should perhaps refer to the first part of his 2002b paper, to appreciate why he thinks archaeologists should reach these conclusions).

ethno-historical information available. Is it true that collapsed societies cannot (ever) produce writings (cf. Schwartz 2006, 4)?[14] This should be examined care-fully.[15] And if indeed this is always the case, then scholars who believe that many texts were written in sixth-century Judah would indeed face a serious problem, and might be forced to abandon their scenario. To the best of my knowledge, however, such an examination has never been conducted.

In any event, ignoring the archaeological data, or, even worse, pleading with archaeologists to "create" settlements (e.g., Blenkinsopp 2002b, 187, Barstad 2003, 12) in the sixth century will probably not work, as the great divide between some biblical scholars and archaeologists in the present debate shows.

---

14. Postgate (1991, 244–45), for example, correlated political and material decline with de-cline in writing, but this is irrelevant to the present discussion since he referred to a different literary genre. The issue should be examined through reference to the vast ethno-historical and anthropological literature on writing (cf. Goody 1975).

15. One should also take into consideration the fact that we are discussing alphabetical scrip, which is much simpler to master, and perhaps scribes need not be viewed as full-time spe-cialists. If scribes could work part time in food production, this has significant implications on the likelihood of producing texts in Judah during the sixth century (which, as mentioned above, should be examined in light of the relevant literature from anthropology and related disciplines).

BIBLIOGRAPHY

Ackerman, Susan. 1992. *Under Every Green Tree: Popular Religion in Sixth-Century Judah.* Atlanta: Scholars Press.

Ackroyd, Peter R. 1968. *Exile and Restoration: A Study of Hebrew Thought of the Sixth Century B.C.* London: SCM.

Aharoni, Yohanan. 1978. *The Archaeology of the Land of Israel.* Jerusalem: Shiqmona (Hebrew).

———. 1979. *The Land of the Bible: Historical Geography.* Philadelphia: Westminster.

———. 1982. *The Archaeology of the Land of Israel.* Philadelphia: Westminster.

———. 1993a. Arad, the Israelite Citadles. Pages 82–87 in vol. 1 of *NEAEHL*. Edited by E. Stern. 4 vols. Jerusalem: Israel Exploration Society.

———. 1993b. Ramat Rahel. Pages 1261–67 in vol. 4 of *NEAEHL* Edited by E. Stern. 4 vols. Jerusalem: Israel Exploration Society.

Ahituv, Shmuel. 1992. *Handbook of Ancient Hebrew Inscriptions,* Jerusalem: Bialik (Hebrew).

Ahlstrom, Gosta W. 1982. *Royal Administration and National Religion in Ancient Palestine.* Leiden: Brill.

———. 1986. *Who Were the Israelites.* Winona Lake, Ind.: Eisebrauns.

———. 1993. *The History of Ancient Palestine from Paleolithic Period to Alexander's Conquest.* Sheffield: Sheffield.

Aizner, Anat. 2011. The Finds in Iron Age II Dwellings as a Reflection of Society, MA Dissertation, Ramat-Gan: Bar-Ilan University.

Albretz, Rainer. 2003. *Israel in Exile: the History and Literature of the Sixth Century B.C.E.* Studies in Biblical Literature 3. Atlanta: Society of Biblical Literature.

Albright, William F. 1934. The Kyle Memorial Excavations at Bethel. *BASOR* 56: 1–15.

———. 1940. *From Stone Age to Christianity: Monotheism and the Historical Process.* Baltimore: Johns Hopkins University Press.

———. 1943. *The Excavation of Tell Beit Mirsim: Volume III, The Iron Age.* AASOR 21. New Haven: American Schools of Oriental Research.

———. 1948. Review of Tell en-Nasbeh, Vol. I: Archaeological and Historical Results; Vol. 2: The Pottery. *JNES* 7: 202–5.

———. 1949a. *The Archaeology of Palestine.* Harmondsworth: Penguin.

———. 1949b. The Biblical Period. Pages 3–69 in vol. 1 of *The Jews: Their History, Culture, and Religion.* Edited by L. Finkelstein. New York: Harper and Brothers.

———. 1954. *The Archaeology of Palestine.* Harmondsworth: Penguin.

———. 1957. *From the Stone Age to Christianity.* New York: Doubleday.

———. 1960a. Reports on Excavations in the Near East and the Middle East. *BASOR* 189: 37–39.

———. 1960b. *The Archaeology of Palestine*. Harmondsworth: Penguin.

———. 1963. *The Biblical Period from Abraham to Ezra*. New York: Harper & Row.

———. 1966. Review: Some Recent Reports and Publications. *BASOR* 183: 32–34.

Alpert-Nakhai, Beth. 1997. Beth Zur. Page 314 in vol. 1 of of *OEANE*. 5 vols. Edited by E. M. Meyers. New York: Oxford University Press.

Alt, Albrecht. 1953. Die Rolle Samarias bei der Entstehung des Judentums. Pages 316–37. *Kleine Schriften zur Geschichte des Volkes Israel II*, Munich: C. H. Beck.

Amiran, Ruth. 1970. *Ancient Pottery of the Holy Land: From Its Beginning in the Neolithic to the End of the Iron Age*. New Brunswick: Rutgers University Press.

———. 1975. A Note on the "Gibeon Jar." *PEQ* 107: 129–32.

Amit, David. 1989–90a. Elazar. *ESI* 9: 158–60.

———. 1989–90b. Khirbet Jarish. *ESI* 9: 157–58.

———. 1991. Farmsteads in Northern Judea (Betar area), Survey. *ESI* 10: 147–48.

———. 2009. Water Supply to the Upper City of Jerusalem during the First and Second Temple Periods in Light of the Mamilla Excavations. Pages 94–108. in *Collected Papers. New Studies on the Archaeology of Jerusalem and Its Region, Volume 3*. Edited by D. Amit, G. D. Stiebel and O. Peleg-Barkat. Jerusalem: Israel Antiquities Authority and the Hebrew University (Hebrew).

Amit, David, and Cohen-Amin, R. In press. Iron Age Rural Settlements in the Northern Hebron Hill-Country. *'Atiqot* (Hebrew).

Amit, David, and Jon Seligman. 2010. Archaeology and Conservation in Jerusalem Area – 2009–2010. Pages 10–21 in *New Studies in the Archeology of Jerusalem and its Region: Collected Papers*, vol. 4. Edited by D. Amit, O. Peleg-Barkat and G.D. Stiebel. Jerusalem: Israel Antiquities Authority and the Hebrew University of Jerusalem. (Hebrew)

Amit, David, and Irina Zilberbod. 1998. Mazor, Survey. *ESI* 18: 65.

Armon, Einat. 2002. *Hellenization of the Northern Coastal Plain of Israel during the Persian Period*. M.A. thesis. Bar Ilan University (Hebrew).

———. 2005. The Greek World and the Coastal Plain of Eretz Israel Prior to the Macedonian Conquest. *Cathedra* 116: 5–30 (Hebrew).

Arubas, Benny, and Haim Goldfus. 2007. The Site at Binyanei ha-Uma and Its Role in the Settlement Network Surrounding Jerusalem. *ErIsr* 28: 14–20 (Hebrew).

Aubet, Maria E. 2001. *The Phoenicians and the West: Politics, Colonies and Trade*. Translated by M. Turton. Cambridge: Cambridge University Press.

———. 2007. East Greek and Etruscan Pottery in a Phoenician Context. Pages 447–60 in *Up to the Gates of Ekron: Essays in the Archaeology and History of the Eastern Mediterranean in Honor of Seymour Gitin*. Edited by S. W. Crawford, et al. Jerusalem: Israel Exploration Society.

Aubet Semmler, Maria E. 2002. Phoenician Trade in the West: Balance and Perspectives. Pages 97–112 in *The Phoenicians in Spain: An Archaeological Review of the Eight-Sixth Centuries B.C.E.* Edited by M. R. Bierling and S. Gitin. Winona Lake, Ind.: Eisenbrauns.

Auld, Graeme, and Margreet Steiner. 1995. *Jerusalem I, from the Bronze Age to the Maccabees*. Cambridge: Lutterworth.

Avigad, Nahman. 1972. Two Hebrew Inscriptions on Wine-Jars. *IEJ* 22: 1–9.

———. 1983. *Discovering Jerusalem*. Nashville: Thomas Nelson.

———. 1993. Maresha. Page 951 in vol. 3 of *NEAEHL*. Edited by E. Stern.4 vols. Jerusalem: Israel Exploration Society, 1993.

Avissar, Miriam, and Eliyahu Shabu. 1998. Qula. *ESI* 20: 51*–53*.

Avi-Yonah, Michael. 1966. *The Holy Land, from the Persian to the Arab Conquests (536 B.C. to A.D. 640): A Historical Geography*. Grand Rapids: Baker.

———. 1993. Maresha (Marisa). Pages 948–51 in vol. 3 of *NEAEHL*. Edited by E. Stern. 4 vols. Jerusalem: Israel Exploration Society.

Avner-Levy, Rina, and Hagit Torge. 1999. Rosh Ha-'Ayin. *ESI* 19: 40*, 58–59.

Ayalon, Etan. 1982. Bareqet (Modi'im). *ESI* 1: 6.

Balensi, Jacqueline, M. Dolores Herrera, and Michal Artzi. 1993. Abu Hawam, Tell. Pages 7–14 in vol. 1 of *NEAEHL*. Edited by E. Stern. 4 vols. Jerusalem: Israel Exploration Society.

Bar-Adon, Pessach. 1989. Excavations in the Judean Desert. *'Atiqot* 9. Jerusalem (Hebrew).

Barkay, Gabriel. 1988. Jerusalem as a Primate City. Pages 124–25 in *Settlement, Population and Economy in the Land of Israel*. Edited by S. Bunimovitz, M. Kochavi and A. Kasher. Tel Aviv: Tel Aviv University (Hebrew).

———. 1992. The Iron Age II–III. Pages 302–73 in *The Archaeology of Ancient Israel*. Edited by A. Ben-Tor. New Haven: Yale University Press.

———. 1993. The Redefinition of Archaeological Periods: Does the Date 588/586 B.C.E. Indeed Mark the End of the Iron Age. Pages 106–9 in *Biblical Archaeology Today: Proceedings of the Second International Congress on Biblical Archaeology, Jerusalem, June–July 1990*, Jerusalem: Israel Exploration Society.

———. 1994. Burial Caves and Burial Practices in Judah in the Iron Age. Pages 96–164 in *Graves and Burial Practices in Israel in the Ancient Period*. Edited by I. Singer. Jerusalem: Yad Ben Zvi (Hebrew).

———. 1995. New Excavations at Ketef Hinnom. Pages 8–15 in *Recent Innovations in the Study of Jerusalem, Proceedings of the First Conference*. Edited by Z. Safrai and A. Faust. Jerusalem (Hebrew).

———. 1998a. The Iron Age III: The Babylonian Period. Page 25 in *Is It Possible to Define the Ceramics of the 6th Century B.C.E. in Judah?* Edited by O. Lipschits. Tel-Aviv (Hebrew).

———. 1998b. The Pottery of the Babylonian Period at Keteph Hinnom. Page 5 in *Is It Possible to Define the Ceramics of the 6th Century B.C.E. in Judah?* Edited by O. Lipschits. Tel-Aviv (Hebrew).

———. 1999. Burial Caves and Dwellings in Judah during the Iron Age II: Sociological Aspects. Pages 96–102 in *Material Culture, Society and Ideology: New Directions in the Archaeology of the Land of Israel*. Edited by A. Faust and A. M. Maeir. Ramat Gan: Bar Ilan University. (Hebrew).

———. 2000. The Necropoli of Jerusalem in the First Temple Period. Pages 233–70 in *The History of Jerusalem: The Biblical Period*. Edited by S. Ahituv and A. Mazar. Jerusalem: Yad Ben Zvi (Hebrew).

———. 2003. The King's Palace and "The House of the People" in Jerusalem at the Time of the Babylonian Conquest. Pages 21–28 in *NSJ*, Vol. 9. Edited by E. Baruch, U. Leibner and A. Faust. Ramat Gan: Bar Ilan University (Hebrew).

———. 2006. Royal Palace, Royal Portrait? The Tantalizing Possibilities of Ramat Rahel. *BAR* 32/5: 34–44.

———. 2011. A Fiscal Bulla from the Slopes of the Temple Mount – Evidence for the Taxation System of the Judean Kingdom. Pages 151–78 in *New Studies on Jerusalem*, vol. 17. Edited by E. Baruch, A. Levy-Reifer and A. Faust. Ramat-Gan: The Ingeborg Rennert Center for Jerusalem Studies, Bar-Ilan University. (Hebrew)

Barnet, Richard D. 1958. The Siege of Lachish. *IEJ* 8: 161–64.

Barstad, Hans M. 1996. *The Myth of the Empty Land*. Oslo: Scandinavian University Press.

———. 2001. The Myth of the Empty Land. Pages 7–8 in *Judea and Judeans in the Neo-Babylonian Period, Summaries*. Edited by O. Lipschits. Tel-Aviv.

———. 2003. After the "Myth of the Empty Land": Major Challenges in the Study of Neo-Babylonian Judah. Pages 3–20 in *Judah and Judeans in the Neo-Babylonian Period*. Edited by O. Lipschits and J. Blenkinsopp. Winona Lake, Ind.: Eisenbrauns.

Baruch, Yuval. 1997. Kh. el-Eid: An Iron-Age Fortress in the North of Mt. Hebron. Pages 79–56 in *Judea and Samaria Research Conference: Proceedings of the 6th Conference–1996*. Edited by Y. Eshel. Kedumin-Ariel (Hebrew).

———. 2000. Betar Forest. *ESI* 20: 104*.

———. 2001a. Khirbet Kabbar. *Hadashot Arkheologiyot: Excavations and Surveys in Israel* 113, 97*–98*, 143–44.

———. 2001b. Khirbet Abu Shawan. *Hadashot Arkheologiyot: Excavations and Surveys in Israel* 113, 95*–97*, 141–143.

———. 2006. Buildings of the Persian Hellenistic and Early Roman Periods at Khirbat Kabar, in the Northern Hebron Hills. *'Atiqot* 52: 49*–71*.

———. 2007. A Farmstead from the End of the Iron Age and Installations at the Foot of Khirbat Abū Shawān. *'Atiqot* 56: 25–44 (Hebrew; English Summary: 71*–74).

Batz, Shahar. 2006. The Region of the Southern Hebron Hills from Iron Age II to the Persian Period in Light of Recent Excavations. Pages 55–72 in *JSRS*. Vol. 15. Edited by Y. Eshel. Ariel: Judea and Samaria College (Hebrew).

———. 2007. Continuity and Change in Burial Rites in the Northern Hebron Hills, From Iron Age II Until the Byzantine Period. Pages 43–58 in *JSRS*. Vol. 16. Ariel: Judea and Samaria College (Hebrew).

Bedford, Peter R. 2005. The Economy of the Near East in the First Millennium B.C. Pages 58–83 in *The Ancient Economy: Evidence and Models*. Edited by J. G. Manning and I. Morris. Stanford: Stanford University Press.

Be'eri, Ron and Irina Zilberbod. 2009. Settlements from the Intermediate and Middle Bronze Ages at Ras el-Amud. Pages 81–93 in *New Studies in the Archeology of Jerusalem and Its Region: Collected Papers*, vol. 3. Edited by D. Amit, G. D. Stiebel, and O. Peleg-Barkat. Jerusalem: Israel Antiquities Authority and the Hebrew University of Jerusalem. (Hebrew)

Beit-Arieh, Itzhaq. 1993a. Ira, Tel. Pages 642–46 in vol. 2 of *NEAEHL*. Edited by E. Stern. Jerusalem: Israel Exploration Society.

———. 1993b. Radum, Horvat. Pages 1254–55. in vol. 4 of *NEAEHL*. Edited by E. Stern. 4 vols. Jerusalem: Israel Exploration Society.

———. 1993c. Uza, Horvat. Pages 1495–97 in vol. of *NEAEHL*. Edited by E. Stern. 4 vols. Jerusalem: Israel Exploration Society.

———. 1999. Stratigraphy and Historical Background. Pages 170–78 in *Tel 'Ira: A Stronghold in the Biblical Negev*. Edited by I. Beit Arieh. Tel Aviv: Tel Aviv University.

———. 2003. *Map of Tell Malhata*. Archaeological Survey of Israel. Jerusalem: Israel Antiquities Authority.

Beit Arieh, Itzhak, and Aileen G. Baron. 1999. The Cemetery. Pages 129–69 in *Tel 'Ira, A*

Stronghold in the Biblical Negev. Edited by I. Beit Arieh. Tel Aviv: Tel Aviv University.

Beit Arieh, Itzhaq, and Bruce C. Cresson 1991. Horvat 'Uza, a Fortified Outpost on The Eastern Negev Border. *BA* 54: 126–35.

———. 2007a. Stratigraphy and Architecture (Horvat Radum). Pages 303-317 in Horvat 'Uza and Horvat Radum: Two Fortresses in the Biblical Negev. Edited by I. Beit-Arieh. Tel-Aviv: Tel Aviv University.

———. 2007b, Stratigraphy and Architecture (Horvat 'Uza). Pages 15-76 in Horvat 'Uza and Horvat Radum: Two Fortresses in the Biblical Negev. Edited by I. Beit-Arieh. Tel-Aviv: Tel Aviv University.

Bellamy, Chris. 1990. *The Evolution of Modern Land Warfare: Theory and Practice*. London: Routledge.

Ben-Arieh, Sara. 2000. Salvage Excavations near the Holyland Hotel, Jerusalem. *'Atiqot* 40: 1–24.

Ben-Shlomo, David. 2003. The Iron Age Sequence of Tel Ashdod: A Rejoinder to "Ashdod Revisited" by I. Finkelstein and L. Singer-Avitz. *TA* 30: 83–107.

———. 2005. Introduction. Pages 1–9 in *Ashdod VI: The Excavations of Areas H and K (1968-1969)*. Edited by M. Dothan and D. Ben-Shlomo. Jerusalem: Israel Antiquities Authority.

Ben-Tor, Amnon. 1993. Joqneam. Pages 805–11 in vol. 3 of *NEAEHL*. Edited by E. Stern. 4 vols. Jerusalem: Israel Exploration Society.

Berlin, Andrea M. 1997. Between Large Forces: Palestine in the Hellenistic Periods. *BA* 60: 2–51.

Berquist, Jon L. 1995. *Judaism in Persia's Shadow: A Social and Historical Approach*. Minneapolis: Fortress.

Betlyon, John W. 2003. Neo-Babylonian Military Operations Other than War in Judah and Jerusalem. Pages 263–68 in *Judah and Judeans in the Neo-Babylonian Period*. Edited by O. Lipschits and J. Blenkinsopp. Winona Lake, Ind.: Eisenbrauns.

Bienkowski, Piotr. 1998. Comments on the Papers by Kitchen, Whitelam and Finkelstein. Pages 65–163 in *The Origin of Early Israel—Current Debate: Biblical, Historical and Archaeological Perspectives*. Edited by S. Ahituv and E. D. Oren. Beer-Sheva 12. Beer-Sheva: Ben-Gurion University of the Negev Press.

Biers, William R. 1992. *Art, Artefacts, and Chronology in Classical Archaeology*. London: Routledge.

Biger, Gideon, and David Grossman. 1993. Village and Town Populations in Palestine during the 1930s–1940s and Their Relevance to Ethnoarchaeology. Pages 19–30 in *Biblical Archaeology Today, 1990: Pre-Congress Symposium on Population, Production and Power*. Jerusalem: Israel Exploration Society.

Bikai, Patricia M. 1978. *The Pottery of Tyre*. Warminster: Aris and Phillips.

Billig, Ya'akov. 1995. Horvat Ha-Motza. *Hadashot Arkheologiyot: Excavations and Surveys in Israel* 103: 71–2 (Hebrew).

———. 2007. Beit HaKerem. Page 139 in *New Studies in the Archaeology of Jerusalem and Its Region*. Edited by J. Patrich and D. Amit. Jerusalem: Israel Antiquities Authority and the Hebrew University of Jerusalem (Hebrew).

Biran, Avraham. 1985. On the Identification of Anathoth. *ErIsr* 18: 209–14 (Hebrew).

———. 1993. Aroer (in Judea). Pages 89–92 in vol. 1 of *NEAEHL*. Edited by E. Stern. 4 vols. Jerusalem: Israel Exploration Society, 1993.

Biran, Avraham, and Ram Gophna. 1970. An Iron Age Burial at Tel Halif. *IEJ* 20: 151–69.

Birman, Galit, and Eli Goldin. 1999. Horbat Tittora. *ESI* 19: 54*–55*, 80.

Blakely, Jeffrey A., and James W. Hardin. 2002. Southwestern Judah in the Late Eighth Century B.C.E. *BASOR* 326: 11–64.

Blenkinsopp, Joseph. 2002a. Stern Criticism (queries and comments). *BAR* 28/5: 13–14.

———. 2002b. The Bible, Archaeology and Politics; or The Empty Land Revisited. *JSOT* 27.2: 169–87.

———. 2002c. There Was No Gap. *BAR* 28/3: 37–38, 59.

Bloch-Smith, Elizabeth. 1992. *Judahite Burial Practices and Beliefs About the Dead*. Sheffield: JSOT Press.

———. 2002. Life in Judah from the Perspective of the Dead. *NEA* 65/2: 120–30.

Boardman, John. 1988. Dates and Doubts. *AA* 1988: 423–25.

———. 1999. *The Greek Overseas: Their Early Colonies and Trade*. London: Thames & Hudson.

Bourdieu, Pierre. 1977. *An Outline of A Theory of Practice*. Cambridge: Cambridge University Press.

Brand, E. 1998. *Salvage Excavation at the Periphery of Tel Gadid*. Tel-Aviv: Tel Aviv University. (Hebrew)

Branigan, Keith. 1966. The Four Room Buildings of Tell En-Nasbeh. *IEJ* 16: 206–9.

Bright, John. 1972. *A History of Israel*. Philadelphia: Westminster.

Broshi, Magen. 1975. Nasbeh, Tell en-. Pages 912–18 in vol. 3 of *EAEHL*. Edited by M. Avi-Yonah. 4 vols. London: Oxford University Press.

———. 1979. The Population of Western Palestine in the Roman-Byzantine Period. *BASOR* 236: 1–10.

———. 1993. Judeideh, Tell. Pages 837–38 in vol. 1 of *NEAEHL*. Edited by E. Stern. 4 vols. Jerusalem: Israel Exploration Society.

Broshi, Magen, and Israel Finkelstein. 1992. The Population of Palestine in the Iron Age II. *BASOR* 287: 47–60.

Broshi, Magen, and Ram Gophna. 1984. The Settlements and Population of Palestine During the Early Bronze Age II-III. *BASOR* 253: 41–53.

———. 1986. Middle Bronze Age II Palestine: Its Settlement and Population. *BASOR* 261: 73–90.

Bruins, Hendrik J., Johannes van der Plicht, and Amihai Mazar. 2003. [14]C Dates from Tel Rehov: Iron-Age Chronology, Pharaohs and Hebrew Kings. *Science* 300 (5617): 315–18.

Bunimovitz, Shlomo. 1989. The Land of Israel in the Late Bronze Age: A Case Study of Socio-Cultural Change in a Complex Society. Ph.D. diss. Tel Aviv University(Hebrew).

———. 1998. Sea Peoples in Cyprus and Israel: A Comparative Study of Immigration Process. Pages 103–13 in *Mediterranean Peoples in Transition: Thirteenth to Early Tenth Centuries B.C.E.* Edited by S. Gitin, A. Mazar and E. Stern. Jerusalem: Israel Exploration Society.

———. 2003. Building Identity: The Four-Room House and the Israelite Mind. Pages 411–23 in *Symbiosis, Symbolism and the Power of the Past: Ancient Israel and Its Neighbors from the Late Bronze Age through Roman Palestine*. Edited by W. G. Dever and S. Gitin. Winona Lake, Ind.: Eisenbrauns.

———, and Avraham Faust. 2002. Ideology in Stone: Understanding the Four-Room House. *BAR* 28/4: 32–41, 59–60.

———, and Zvi Lederman. 2003. The Final Destruction of Beth Shemesh and the *Pax*

Assyriaca in the Judean Shephela. *TA* 30: 3–26.

Byrne, Ryan. 2004. Lie Back and Think of Judah: The Reproductive Politics of Pillar Figurines. *NEA* 67: 137–51.

Cameron, Catherine M., and Steve A. Tomka. 1993. *The Abandonment of Settlements and Regions: Ethnoarchaeological and Archaeological Approaches.* Cambridge: Cambridge University Press.

Campbell, Edward F. 2002. *Shechem III: The Stratigraphy and Architecture of Shechem/Tel Balatah.* Boston: American Schools of Oriental Research.

Campbell, Lyle. 1994. Language Death. Pages 1960–68 in vol. 4 of *The Encyclopedia of Language and Linguistics.* Edited by R. E. Asher and J. M. Y. Simpson. Oxford: Pergamon.

Carroll, Robert P. 1992. The Myth of the Empty Land. *Semeia* 59: 79–93.

———. 1998. Exile? What Exile? Deportation and Discourse of Diaspora. Pages 101–18 in *Leading Captivity Captive: The Exile as History and Ideology.* Edited by L. L. Grabbe. Sheffield: Sheffiled.

Carter, Charles E. 1999. *The Emergence of Yehud in the Persian Period: A Social and Demographic Study.* JSOTSup 294. Sheffield: University of Sheffield.

———. 2003. Ideology and Archaeology in the Neo-Babylonian Period: Excavating Text and Tell. Pages 301–22 in *Judah and Judeans in the Neo-Babylonian Period.* Edited by O. Lipschits and J. Blenkinsopp. Winona Lake, Ind.: Eisenbrauns.

Cassutto, Deborah R. 2004. *The Social Context of Weaving in the Land of Israel: Investigating the Context of Iron Age II Loom Weights.* M.A. thesis. Bar-Ilan University.

Cazelles, Henri. 1983. 587 ou 586. Pages 427–36 in *The Word of the Lord Shall Go Forth.* Edited by D. N. Freedman. Winona Lake, Ind.: Eisenbrauns.

Chadwick, Jeffrey R. 2005. Discovering Hebron: The City of the Patriarchs Slowly Yields Its Secrets. *BAR* 31\5: 24–33, 70.

Cogan, Mordechai. 2003. *Historical Texts from Assyria and Babylonia: 9th–6th Centuries B.C.E.* Jerusalem: Bialik Institute (Hebrew).

———, and Hayim Tadmor. 1988. *II Kings.* AB 11. Garden City: Doubleday.

Cohen, Rudolph. 1995. Fortresses and Roads in the Negev during the First Temple Period. Pages 80–126 in *Eilat: Studies in the Archaeology, History and Geography of Eilat and the Aravah.* Jerusalem: Israel Exploration Society (Hebrew).

Cohen-Tavor, Ahia. 2011. "Man Is but the Imprint of His Native Landscape": Survey in the Region of Tel Rehov. Pages 17–18. *The Thirty-Seventh Archaeological Congress in Israel (abstracts),* Ramat-Gan: Bar-Ilan University.

Coldstream, John N. 2003. Some Agean Reactions to the Chronological Debate in the Southern Levant. *TA* 30: 247–58.

———, and Amihai Mazar. 2003. Greek Pottery from Tel Rehov and Iron Age Chronology. *IEJ* 53: 29–48.

Conlee, Christina, A. 2006. Regeneration as Transformation: Postcollapse Society in Nasca, Peru. Pages 99–113. in *After Collapse: The Regeneration of Complex Societies.* Edited by G. M. Schwartz and D. J. Nichols. Tucson: University of Arizona Press.

Cook, Robert M. 1989. The Fracis-Vickers Chronology. *JHS* 109: 164–70.

———. 1997. *Greek Painted Pottery.* London: Routledge.

———, and Pierre Dupont. 1998. *East Greek Pottery.* London: Routledge.

Covello-Paran, Karen. 1998. Horbat Malta. *ESI* 18: 27–28.

Cresson, Bruce C. 1999. Area F. Pages 97–102 in *Tel 'Ira: A Stronghold in the Biblical Negev.* Edited by I. Beit-Arieh. Tel Aviv: Tel Aviv University.

Cross, Frank M. 1962. Epigraphical Notes on Hebrew Documents of the Eighth-Sixth Centuries BC. *BASOR* 168: 18–23.

———, and Józef T. Milik. 1956. Explorations in the Judaean Buqeah. *BASOR* 142: 5–17.

Cunliffe, Barry W. 2001. *Facing the Ocean: The Atlantic and Its Peoples 8000 B.C.–A.D. 1500.* Oxford: Oxford University Press.

———, and Maria C. Fernandez Castro. 1999. *The Guadajoz Project: Andalucia in the First Millennium B.C.: Volume 1, Torreparedones and Its Hinterland.* Oxford: Oxford University Committee for Archaeology.

Dagan, Yehuda. 1998. Settlement Reality in the Shephelah between Sennacherib Destruction and the Restoration Period. Page 8 in *Is It Possible to Define the Ceramics of the 6th Century B.C.E. in Judah?* Edited by O. Lipschits. Tel-Aviv (Hebrew).

———. 2000. The Settlement in the Judean Shephela in the Second and First Millennium B.C.E.: A Test-Case of Settlement Processes in a Geographic Region. Ph.D. diss. Tel Aviv University.

Dahari, Uzi., and 'Ad Uzi. 2000. Shoam Bypass Road. *ESI* 20: 56*–59*.

Dalley, Stephanie. 2003. The Transition of Power from Neo-Assyrians to Neo-Babylonians: Break or Continuity? *ErIsr*27: 25*–28*.

Dandamayev, Muhammad A. 2006. Neo-Babylonian and Achamenid State Administration in Mesopotamia. Pages 373–98 in *Judah and Judeans in the Persian Period.* Edited by O. Lipschitz and M. Oeming. Winona Lake, Ind.: Eisenbrauns.

D'Angelo, I. 2006. Imported Greek Pottery in Archaic Cyrene: The Excavations at Casa del Prpileo. Pages 181–86 in *Naukratis–Greek Diversity in Egypt: Studies on East Greek Pottery and Exchange in the Eastern Mediterranean.* Edited by A. Villing and U. Schlotzhauer. London: The British Museum.

Dar, Shim'on. 1982. Ancient Agricultural Farms Near Wadi Beit-'Arif. *Nofim* 16: 47–60 (Hebrew).

———. 1986. Hirbet Jemein: A First Temple Village in Western Samaria. Pages 13–73 in *Shomron Studies.* Edited by S. Dar and Z. Safrai. Tel Aviv (Hebrew)[Publisher?].

Davidovitz, Uri, et al. 2006. Salvage Excavations at Ramot Forest and Ramat Bet-Hakerem: New Data Regarding Jerusalem's Periphery during the First and Second Temple Periods. Pages 35–111 in *NSJ:* Vol. 11. Edited by E. Baruch, Z. Greenhut and A. Faust. Ramat-Gan.

Davies, Philip R. 2003. Biblical Hebrew and the History of Ancient Judah: Typology, Chronology and Common Sense. Pages 150–63 in *Biblical Hebrew: Studies in Chronology and Typology.* Edited by I. Young. London: T&T Clark.

Defonzo, Ryan J. P. 2005. Iron II Judah: An Intra-Regional Study of Production and Distribution. Ph.D. diss. University of Toronto.

De Groot, Alon. 2001. Jerusalem During the Persian Period. Pages 77–81 in *New Studies on Jerusalem, Proceedings of the 7th Conference.* Edited by A. Faust and E. Baruch. Ramat-Gan (Hebrew).

———, and Zvi Greenhut. 2002. Moza: A Judahite Administrative Center Near Jerusalem. Pages 7–14 in *NSJ* Vol. 8. Edited by E. Baruch and A. Faust. Ramat Gan: Bar Ilan University (Hebrew).

De Odorico, Marco. 1995. *The Use of Numbers and Quantifications in the Assyrian Royal Inscriptions.* Neo-Assyrian Text Corpus Project. Helsinki: University of Helsinki.

De Vaux, Roland. 1965. *Ancient Israel: Its Life and Institutions.* London: Darton, Longman & Todd.

———. 1973. *Archaeology and the Dead Sea Scroll*. London: British Academy.

———. 1993. Qumran, Khirbet and 'Ein Feshkha'. Pages 1235–41 in vol. 4 of *NEAEHL*. Edited by E. Stern. 4 vols. Jerusalem: Israel Exploration Society.

Deetz, James. 1967. *Invitation to Archaeology*. New York: Natural History Press.

Demand, Nancy H. 1990. *Urban Relocation in Archaic and Classical Greece*. Bristol.

Dessel, James P. 1999. Tell 'Ein Zippori and the Lower Galilee in the Late Bronze and Iron Ages: A Village Perspective. Pages 1–32 in *Galilee Through the Centuries*. Edited by E. M. Meyers. Winona Lake, Ind.: Eisenbrauns.

Deutsch, Karl W. 1959. The Limits of Common Sense. *Psychiatry* 22/2: 105–12.

Dever, William G. 1969–1970. Iron Age Epigraphic Material from the Area of Khirbet el-Qom. *HUCA* 40–41: 139–204.

———. 1971. Archaeological Methods and Results: A Review of Two Recent Publications. *Or* 40: 459–71.

———. 1993. Qom, Hkirbet el-. Pages 1233–35 in vol. 4 of *NEAEHL*. Edited by E. Stern. 4 vols. Jerusalem: Israel Exploration Society.

———. 1995. Social Structure in Palestine in the Iron Age II Period on the Eve of Destruction. Pages 416–61 in *The Archaeology of Society in the Holy Land*. Edited by Thomas E. Levy. London: Leicester University Press.

———. 1997a. Bethel. Pages 300–301 in vol. 1 of *OEANA*. 5 vols. Edited by E. M. Meyers. New York: Oxford University Press.

———. 1997b. Qom, Khirbet el-. Pages 391–92 in vol. 4 of *OEANA*. 5 vols. Edited by E. M. Meyers. New York: Oxford University Press.

———. 2001. *What Did the Biblical Writers Know, and When Did They Know It?* Grand Rapids: Eerdmans.

———. 2005. *Did God Have a Wife? Archaeology and Folk Religion in Ancient Israel*. Grand Rapids: Eerdmans.

———. 2007. Archaeology and the Fall of the Northern Kingdom: What Really Happened? Pages 78–92 in *"Up to the Gates of Ekron": Essays on the Archaeology and History of the Eastern Mediterranean in Honor of Seymour Gitin*. Edited by S. W. Crawford. Jerusalem: W. F. Albright Institute of Archaeological Research and the Israel Exploration Society.

———. 2009, Archaeology and the Fall of Judah. *ErIsr* 29: 29*–35*.

Dinnur, Uri, and Nurit Feig. 1993. Eastern Part of the Map of Jerusalem. Pages 58*–70* (English summaries). in *Archaeological Survey of the Hill Country of Benjamin*. Edited by I. Finkelstein and Y. Magen. Jerusalem: Israel Antiquities Authority (Hebrew).

Dobbs-Allsopp, Frederick W., et al. 2005. *Hebrew Inscriptions: Texts from the Biblical Period of the Monarchy with Concordance*. New Haven: Yale University Press.

Docter, Roald F., et al. 2004. Radiocarbon Dates of Animal Bones in the Earliest Levels of Carthage. *Mediterranea* I: 557–77.

Dominguez, Adolfo J., and Carmen Sanchez. 2001. *Greek Pottery from the Iberian Peninsula: Archaic and Classical Periods*. Leiden: Brill.

Dothan, Moshe. 1971. *Ashdod II-III. 'Atiqot* 9–10. Jerusalem: Israel Antiquities Authority.

———. 1985. Ten Seasons of Excavations at Ancient Acco. *Qad* 69–70: 2–14 (Hebrew).

———. 1993. Ashdod. Pages 93–102 in vol. 1 of *NEAEHL*. Edited by E. Stern. 4 vols. Jerusalem: Israel Exploration Society.

Dothan, Trude, and Seymour Gitin. 1993. Miqne, Tel (Ekron). Pages 1051–59 in vol. 3 of *NEAEHL*. Edited by E. Stern. 4 vols. Jerusalem: Israel Exploration Society.

Drinkard, Joel F. 1992a. Direction and Orientation. Page 204 in vol. 2 of *ABD*. Edited by David Noel Freedman. 6 vols. New York: Doubleday.
———. 1992b: East. Page 248 in vol. 2 of *ABD*. Edited by David Noel Freedman. 6 vols. New York: Doubleday.
Edelstein, Gershon. 2000. A Terraced Farm at Er-Ras. *'Atiqot* 40: 39–63.
———, and Mordechai Kislev. 1981. Mevasseret Yerushalayim: The Ancient Settlement and Its Agricultural Terraces. *BA* 44: 53–56.
Efrat, Elisha. 1995. *Elements of Urban Geography*. Tel Aviv: Achiasaf (Hebrew).
Ehrensvard, Martin. 2003. Linguistic Dating of Biblical Text. Pages 164–88 in *Biblical Hebrew: Studies in Chronology and Typology*. Edited by I. Young. London: T&T Clark.
———. 2006. Why Biblical Texts Cannot Be Dated Linguistically. *HS* XLVII: 177–89.
Eilat, Moshe. 1977. *Economic Relations in the Lands of the Bible, c. 1000–539 B.C.* Jerusalem: Bialik Institute (Hebrew).
———. 1978. The Economic Relations of the Neo-Assyrian Empire with Egypt. *JAOS* 98: 20–34.
Eisenberg, Emanuel, and Alla Nagorski. 2002. Tel Hevron (Er-Rumeidi). *Hadashot Arkheologiyot: Excavations and Surveys in Israel* 114: 91*–92*.
Eitam, David. 1979. Olive Presses of the Israelite Period. *TA* 6: 146–55.
———. 1980. The Production of Oil and Wine in Mt. Ephraim in the Iron Age. M.A. thesis. Tel Aviv University (Hebrew).
———. 1987. Olive Oil Production During Biblical Period. Pages 16–43 in *Olive Oil in Antiquity*. Edited by D. Eitam, and M. Heltzer. Haifa: University of Haifa.
———. 1992. Khirbet Khaddash: Royal Industry Village in Ancient Israel. Pages 161–82 in *Judea and Samaria Research Studies: Proceedings of The First Annual Meeting–1991*. Edited by Z. H. Ehrlich and Y. Eshel. Jerusalem: Reuven Mas (Hebrew).
———. 1996. The Olive Oil Industry at Tel Miqne-Ekron in the Late Iron Age. Pages 167–96 in *Olive Oil in Antiquity–Israel and Neighboring Countries from the Neolithic to the Early Arab Period*. Edited by D. Eitam and M. Heltzer. Padova: Sargon srl.
Eitan, Avraham. 1983. Vered Yericho. *Hadashot Arkheologiyot: Excavations and Surveys in Israel* 82: 43–44 (Hebrew).
———. 1986. Antiquities Director Confronts Problem and Controversies (BAR Interviews Avraham Eitan). *BAR* 12\4: 30–38.
Elat, Moshe. 1991. Phoenician Overland Trade within the Mesopotamian Empires. Pages 21–35 in *Ah Assyria... Studies in Assyrian History and Ancient Near Eastern Historiography Presented to Hayim Tadmor*. Edited by M. Cogan and I. Eph'al. Jerusalem: Magness.
Elgavish, Joseph. 1968. *Archaeological Excavations at Shikmona: Field Report No. 1*. Haifa: The City Museum of Ancient Art (Hebrew).
Eph'al, Israel. 1978. The Western Minorities in Babylonia in the 6th–5th Centuries B.C.: Maintenance and Cohesion. *Or* 47: 74–90.
———. 1983. On Warfare and Military Control in the Ancient Eastern Empires: A Research Outline. Pages 88–106 in *History, Historiography and Interpretations: Studies in Biblical and Cuneiform Literatures*. Edited by H. Tadmor and M. Weinfeld. Jerusalem: Magness.
———. 1996. *Siege and Its Ancient Near Eastern Manifestation*. Jerusalem: Magnes (Hebrew).
———. 2000. *Ethnic Changes in the Land of Israel Following the Destruction of the King-*

doms of Israel and Judah. Public Lecture in Memory of the Late Prof. Benjamin Mazar. September 27 (Hebrew).

Erdkamp, Paul. 1998. *Hunger and the Sword: Warfare and Food Supply in Roman Republican Wars (264 - 30 B.C.)*. Amsterdam: J. C. Gieben.

Erlich, Adi. 2006. The Persian Period Terracotta Figurines from Maresha in Idumea: Local and Regional Aspects. *Transeuphratene* 32: 45–59.

Eshel, Hanan, 1987. The Late Iron Age Cemetery of Gibeon. *IEJ* 37: 1–17.

———. 2000. Jerusalem Under Persian Rule: The City's Layout and the Historical Background. Pages 327–43 in *The History of Jerusalem, The Biblical Period*. Edited by S. Ahituv and A. Mazar. Jerusalem, Yad Ben Zvi.

———, and Amos Kloner. 1990. A Late Iron Age Tomb between Bet Hanina and Nebi Samwil and the Identification of Hazor in Nehemia 11:33. *ErIsr* 21: 37–40 (Hebrew).

Eskhult, Mats, 2003. The Importance of Loanwords for Dating Biblical Texts. Pages 8–23 in *Biblical Hebrew: Studies in Chronology and Typology*. Edited by I. Young. London: T&T Clark.

Fabian, Peter, and Itzhak Gilead. 2007. The Iron Age Settlement within the Modern City of Beer-Sheva. Pages 3–4 in *New Studies on Beersheba, the Settlement in the Negev and the Edomites during the Iron Age (abstract booklet)*. Edited by Y. Baumgarten and S. Gal. Omer: Israel Antiquities Authority.

Fagan, Brian. M. 1999. *World Prehistory: A Brief Introduction*. New York: Longman.

Fantalkin, Alexander. 2001a. Low Chronology and Greek Protogeometric and Geometric Pottery in the Southern Levant. *Levant* 33: 117–25.

———. 2001b. Mezad Hashavyahu: Its Material Culture and Historical Background. *TA* 28.1: 3–165.

———. 2004. The Final Destruction of Beth Shemesh and the *Pax Assyriaca* in the Judahite Shephela: An Alternative View. *TA* 31: 246–61.

———. 2006. Identity in the Making: Greeks in the Eastern Mediterranean during the Iron Age. Pages 199–208 in *Naukratis Greek Diversity in Egypt: Studies on East Greek Pottery and Exchange in the Eastern Mediterranean*. Edited by A. Villing and U. Schlotzhauer. London: The British Museum.

———, and Oren Tal. 2009. Re-Discovering the Iron Age Fortress at Tell Qudadi in the Context of Neo-Assyrian Imperialistic Policy. *PEQ* 141: 188–206.

Fargo, Valerie M. 1993. Hesi, Tell el-. Pages 630–34 in vol. 2 of *NEAEHL*. Edited by E. Stern. 4 vols. Jerusalem: Israel Exploration Society.

Faust, Avraham. 1995a. *The Rural Settlement in the Land of Israel during the Period of the Monarchy*. M.A. thesis. Bar-Ilan University (Hebrew).

———. 1995b. Settlement on the Western Slopes of Samaria at the End of the Iron Age. Pages 23–29 in *Judea and Samaria Research Studies, Proceedings of the 4th Annual Meeting–1994*. Edited by Z. H. Erlich and Y. Eshel. Kedumim: Ariel (Hebrew).

———. 1999a. Differences in Family Structure between Cities and Villages in Iron Age II. *TA* 26: 233–52.

———. 1999b. From Hamlets to Monarchy: A View from the Countryside on the Formation of the Israelite Monarchy. *Cathedra* 94: 7–32 (Hebrew).

———. 1999c. Socioeconomic Stratification in an Israelite City: Hazor VI as a Test Case. *Levant* 31: 179–90.

———. 1999d. *The Social Structure of the Israelite Society during the 8th–7th Centuries B.C.E. according to the Archaeological Evidence*. Ph.D. thesis. Bar-Ilan University

(Hebrew).

———. 2000a. Ethnic Complexity in Northern Israel during Iron Age II. *PEQ* 132: 2–27.

———. 2000b. The Rural Community in Ancient Israel during the Iron Age II. *BASOR* 317: 17–39.

———. 2001. Doorway Orientation, Settlement Planning and Cosmology in Ancient Israel During Iron Age II. *OJA* 20.2: 129–55.

———. 2003a. Abandonment, Urbanization, Resettlement and the Formation of the Israelite State. *NEA* 66: 147–61.

———. 2003b. Judah in the Sixth Century B.C.E.: A Rural Perspective. *PEQ* 135: 37–53.

———. 2003c. The Farmstead in the Highlands of Iron II Israel. Pages 91–104 in *The Rural Landscape of Ancient Israel*. Edited by S. Dar, A. M. Maeir and Z. Safrai. Oxford: BAR.

———. 2004a. Mortuary Practices, Society and Ideology: The Lack of Iron Age I Burials in Highlands in Context. *IEJ* 54: 174–90.

———. 2004b. Social and Cultural Changes in Judah during the 6th Century B.C.E. and Their Implications for our Understanding of the Nature of the Neo-Babylonian Period. *UF* 36: 157–76.

———. 2005a. *The Israelite Society in the Period of the Monarchy: An Archaeological Perspective*. Jerusalem: Yad Ben Zvi (Hebrew).

———. 2005b. The Settlement on Jerusalem's Western Hill and the City's Status in the Iron Age II Revisited. *ZDPV* 121: 97–118.

———. 2006a. Farmsteads in Western Samaria's Foothills: A Reexamination. Pages 477–504 in *I Will Speak the Riddles of Ancient Times" (Abiah chidot minei-kedem—Ps. 78: 2b): Archaeological and Historical Studies in Honor of Amihai Mazar on the Occasion of His Sixtieth Birthday*. Edited by A. M Maeir and P. De Miroschedji. Winona Lake, Ind.: Eisenbrauns.

———. 2006b. *Israel's Ethnogenesis: Settlement, Interaction, Expansion and Resistance*. London: Equinox.

———. 2006c. Trade, Ideology and Boundary Maintenance in Iron Age Israelite Society. Pages 17–35 in *A Holy Community*. Edited by M. Purthuis and J. Schwartz. Leiden: Brill.

———. 2007a. Jerusalem's Hinterland and the City's Status in the Bronze and Iron Ages. *ErIsr* 28: 165–72 (Hebrew).

———. 2007b. Rural Settlements, State Formation, and "Bible and Archaeology." *NEA* 70: 4–9, 22–25 (with responses).

———. 2007c. Settlement Dynamics and Demographic Fluctuations in Judah from the Late Iron Age to the Hellenistic Period and the Archaeology of Persian Period Yehud. Pages 23–51 in *A Time of Change: Judah and Its Neighbors during the Persian and Early Hellenistic Periods*. Edited by Y. Levin. London: Continuum.

———. 2008a. Cities, Villages and Farmsteads: The Landscape of Leviticus 25: 29–31. Pages 103–12 in *Exploring the Longue Duree: Essays in Honor of Prof. Lawrence E. Stager*. Edited by D. Schloen. Winona Lake, Ind.: Eisenbrauns.

———. 2008b. Settlement and Demography in 7th Century Judah and the Extent and Intensity of Sennacherib's Campaign. *PEQ* 140: 168–94.

———. 2009. Tel 'Eton 2006–2007 (Notes and News). *IEJ* 59: 112–19.

———. 2011a. The Excavations at Tel 'Eton (2006–2009): A Preliminary Report. *PEQ*.

———. 2011b. The Interests of the Assyrian Empire in the West: Olive Oil Production as a Test-Case. *JESHO*.

———. 2012. *The Archaeology of the Israelite Society in the Iron Age II*. Winona Lake, Ind.: Eisenbrauns.

Faust, Avraham, and Shlomo Bunimovitz. 2003. The Four-Room House: Embodying Israelite Society. *NEA* 66: 22–31.

———. 2008. The Judahite Tomb: Family Response at a Time of Change. *IEJ* 58: 150–70.

———. In press. The House and the World: The Israelite House as a Micro-Cosmos. In *Family and Household Religion toward a Synthesis of Old Testament Studies, Archaeology, Epigraphy, and Cultural Studies*. Edited by Rainer Albertz, et al. Winona Lake, Ind.: Eisenbrauns.

Faust, Avraham, and Adi Erlich. 2008. The Hasmonean Policy toward the Gentile Population in Light of the Excavations at Kh. er-Rasm and Additional Rural Sites. *Jerusalem and Eretz Israel* 6: 5–32 (Hebrew).

———. 2011. *Kh. er-Rasm: The Changing Faces of the Countryside*. Oxford: Archaeopress.

Faust, Avraham, and Zeev Safrai. 2005. Salvage Excavations as a Source for Reconstructing Settlement History in Ancient Israel. *PEQ* 137: 139–58.

———. 2008. Changes in Burial Patterns in the Land of Israel through Time in Light of the Findings from Salvage Excavations. Pages 105–21 in *In the Hill-Country, and in the Shephelah, and in the Arabah (Joshua 12, 8): Studies and Researches Presented to Adam Zertal in the Thirtieth Anniversary of the Mennasseh Hill-Country Survey*. Edited by S. Bar. Jerusalem: Ariel (Hebrew).

———. In press a. *History of Settlement in Ancient Israel: Quantitative Analysis in Light of the Results of Salvage Excavations and Planned Expeditions*. Ramat Gan: The Rennert Center for Jerusalem Studies.

———. In press b. Toward a Quantitative Study of the History of Settlement in Ancient Israel: Burials as a Test-Case. in *Portal Science and Archaeology: Views from the Mediterranean Lands*. Edited by T. E. Levy, S. H. Savage, C. Baru and Ø. LaBianca. London: Equinox.

Faust, Avraham, and Ehud Weiss. 2005. Judah, Philistia and the Mediterranean World: Reconstructing the Economic System of the Seventh Century B.C.E. *BASOR* 338: 71–92.

———. 2011. Between Assyria and the Mediterranean World: The Prosperity of Judah and Philistia in the Seventh Century B.C.E. in Context in *Interweaving Worlds: Systemic Interactions in Eurasia, 7th to 1st Millennia B.C.* Edited by T. Wilkinson, S. Sherratt and J. Bennet. Oxford: Oxbow.

Feig, Nurit. 1996. New discoveries in the Rephaim Valley, Jerusalem. *PEQ* 128: 3–7.

———. 1999. The Environs of Jerusalem in the Iron Age II. Pages 387–409 in *The History of Jerusalem: The Biblical Period*. Edited by S. Ahituv and A. Mazar. Jerusalem (Hebrew).

———, and Omar Abd Rabu. 1995. Jerusalem, Kh. er-Ras. *Hadashot Arkheologiyot: Excavations and Surveys in Israel* 103: 95–99 (Hebrew).

Feldstein, Amir, et al. 1993. Southern Part of the Maps of Ramallah and el-Bireh and Northern Part of the Maps of 'Ein Kerem. Pages 133–264 in *Archaeological Survey of the Hill Country of Benjamin*. Edited by I. Finkelstein and Y. Magen. Jerusalem: Israel Antiquities Authority (Hebrew), 28*–47* (English summaries).

Finkelstein, Israel. 1978. *Rural Settlement in the Foothills and the Yarkon Basin in the Israelite-Hellenistic Periods*. M.A. thesis. Tel-Aviv University (Hebrew).

———. 1981. Israelite and Hellenistic farms in the Foothills and the Yarkon Basin. *ErIsr*

15: 331–48 (Hebrew).

———. 1988. Demographic Data from Recent Generations and Spatial Archaeology. Pages 57–72 in *Settlement, Population and Economy in Eretz Israel in Antiquity*. Edited by S. Bunimovitz. Tel Aviv: Tel Aviv University.

———. 1989. The Land of Ephraim Survey 1987–1989: Preliminary Report. *TA* 15–16: 117–83.

———. 1993a. Environmental Archaeology and Social History: Demographic and Economic Aspects of the Monarchic Period. Pages 56–66 in *Biblical Archaeology Today, 1990: Proceedings of the Second International-Congress on Biblical Archaeology*, Jerusalem: Israel Exploration Society.

———. 1993b. Northern Part of the Maps of Beit Sira, Ramallah and el-Bireh. Pages 15–95 (Hebrew), 13*–23* (English summaries) in *Archaeological Survey of the Hill Country of Benjamin*. Edited by I. Finkelstein and Y. Magen. Jerusalem: Israel Antiquities Authority.

———. 1994. The Archaeology of the Days of Manasseh. Pages 169–87 in *Scripture and Other Artifacts: Essays on the Bible and Archaeology in Honor of Philip J. King*. Edited by M. D. Coogan, J. C. Exum and L. E. Stager. Louisville: Westminster John Knox.

———. 1995a. *Living on the Fringe*. Sheffield: Sheffield Academic.

———. 1995b. The Philistine Countryside. *IEJ* 46: 225–42.

———. 1996. The Archaeology of the United Monarchy: An Alternative View. *Levant* 28: 177–87.

———. 1998. Bible Archaeology or Archaeology of Palestine in the Iron Age? A Rejoinder. *Levant* 30: 167–73.

———. 2000. The Philistine Settlements: When, Where and How Many? Pages 159–80 in *The Sea People and Their World: A Reassessment*. Edited by E. D. Oren. Philadelphia: University of Pennsylvania.

———. 2005. [De]formation of the Israelite State: A Rejoinder on Methodology. *NEA* 68: 202–8.

———. 2007. Jerusalem in the Persian Period and the Wall of Nehemiah. Pages 45–57 in *New Studies on Jerusalem: The 13th Volume*. Edited by E. Baruch, A. Levy and A. Faust. Ramat Gan: Bar-Ilan University (Hebrew).

———. 2008a. Archaeology and the List of Returnees in the Books of Ezra and Nehemiah. *PEQ* 140: 7–16.

———. 2008b. Jerusalem in the Persian (and Early Hellenistic) Period and the Walls of Nehemiah. *JSOT* 32: 501–20.

———. 2010. The Territorial Extent and Demography of Yehud/Judea in the Persian and Early Hellenistic Periods. *RB* 117/1: 39–54.

Finkelstein, Israel, and Yitzhak Magen. 1993. *Archaeological Survey of the Hill Country of Benjamin*. Jerusalem: Israel Antiquities Authority.

Finkelstein, Israel, and Nadav Na'aman. 2004. The Judahite Shephelah in the Late 8th and Early 7th Centuries B.C.E. *TA* 31: 60–79.

———, and Neil A. Silberman. 2001. *The Bible Unearthed: Archaeology's New Vision of Ancient Israel and the Origin of Its Sacred Text*. New York: Free Press.

Finkelstein, Israel, and Lily Singer-Avitz. 2001. Ashdod Revisited. *TA* 28: 231–59.

———. 2004. "Ashdod Revisited"—Maintained. *TA* 31: 122–35.

———. 2009. Reevaluating Bethel. *ZDPV* 125: 33–48.

———. 2011a. Saul, Benjamin, and the Emergence of "Biblical Israel": An Alternative View, *ZAW* 123: 348–67.

———. 2011b. Tell el-Ful: The Assyrian and Hellenistic Periods (with a new identification), *PEQ* 143: 106–18.

Finkelstein, Israel, David Ussishkin, and Baruch Halpern 2006. Archaeological and Historical Conclusions. Pages 843–59 in vol. 2 of *Megiddo IV*. Edited by I. Finkelstein, D. Ussishkin and B. Halpern. Tel Aviv: Tel Aviv University.

Fitzpatrick, Andrew P. 1997. Everyday Life in Iron Age Wessex. Pages 73–86 in *Reconstructing Iron Age Societies*. Edited by A. Gwilt and C. Haselgrove. Oxbow Monographs 71. Oxford: Oxbow.

Foxhall, Lin. 2005. Village to City: Staples and Luxuries? Exchange Networks and Urbanization. Pages 233–48 in *Mediterranean Trade 800–600 B.C.* Edited by R. Osborne and B. W. Cunliffe. Oxford: Oxford University Press.

Francis, David E., and Michael Vickers. 1983. Signa Priscae Artis: Eretria and Siphnos. *JHS* 103: 49–67.

———. 1988. The Agora Revisited: Athenian Chronology c. 500–450 B.C. *Annual of the British School at Athens* 83: 143–67.

Frankenstein, Susan. 1979. The Phoenicians in the Far West: A Function of Neo-Assyrian Imperialism. Pages 263–94 in *Power and Propaganda: A Symposium on Ancient Empires*. Edited by M. T. Larsen. Mesopotamia 7. Copenhagen: Academic Verlag.

Fritz, Volkmar. 1990. *Kinneret: Ergebnisse der Ausgrabunger auf dem Tell el-'Oreme am Seee Gennesaret 1982–1985*. Wiesbaden: Abhandlungen des Deutschen Palastian-Vereins 15.

———. 1993. Kinneret: Excavations at Tell el-'Oreimeh (Tel Kinrot) 1982–1985 Seasons, *TA* 20: 187–215.

———. 1997. Cities: Cities of the Bronze and Iron Ages. Pages 19–25 in vol. 2 of *OEANE*. 5 vols. Edited by E. M. Meyers. New York: Oxford University Press.

———. 2007. On the Reconstruction of the Four-Room House. Pages 114–18 in *Up to the Gates of Ekron: Essays in the Archaeology and History of the Eastern Mediterranean in Honor of Seymour Gitin*. Edited by S. W. Crawford, et al. Jerusalem: Israel Exploration Society.

Funk, Robert B. 1968. The History of Beth-zur with Reference to its Defenses. Pages 4–17 in *The 1957 Excavations at Beth-Zur*. Edited by O. R. Sellers, et al. AASOR 38. Cambridge, Mass.: American Schools of Oriental Research.

———. 1993. Beth Zur. Pages 259–61 in vol. 1 of *NEAEHL*. Edited by E. Stern.4 vols. Jerusalem: Israel Exploration Society.

Gadot, Yuval. 2011. The Rural Settlement along Nahal Rephaim from the Middle Bronze age and until the Hellenistic Period: A Fresh look from Kh. Er.Ras, in *New Studies on Jerusalem*, vol. 17, eds. E. Baruch, A. Levy-Reifer and A. Faust. Ramat-Gan: The Ingeborg Rennert Center for Jerusalem Studies, Bar-Ilan University. (Hebrew)

Gal, Zvi. 1992. *Lower Galilee during the Iron Age*. ASOR Dissertation 8. Winona Lake, Ind.: Eisenbrauns.

———. 2009. The Lower Galilee between Tiglath Pileser III and the Beginning of the Persian Period. *ErIsr* 29: 77–81 (Hebrew).

———, and Yardenna Alexandre. 2000. *Horbat Rosh Zayit: An Iron Age Storage Fort and Village*. Jerusalem: Israel Antiquities Authority.

———, and Rafael Frankel. 1993. An Olive Oil Press Complex at Hurvat Rosh Zayit.

ZDPV 109: 128–40.

Geva, Hillel, and Nahman Avigad. 2000. Area W: Stratigraphy and Architecture. Pages 131–97 in *Jewish Quarter Excavations in the Old City of Jerusalem*. Edited by H. Geva. Jerusalem: Israel Exploration Society.

Gibson, Shimon. 1994. The Tell ej-Judeideh (Tel Goded) Excavations: A Re-appraisal Based on Archival Records in the Palestine Exploration Fund. *TA* 21: 194–234.

———. 1996. Tell el-Ful and the Results of the North-East Jerusalem Survey. Pages 9*–23* in *New Studies on Jerusalem, Proceedings of the Second Conference*, Edited by A. Faust. Ramat Gan: The Ingeborg Rennert Center for Jerusalem Studies.

Gilboa, Ayelet. 1996. Assyrian-Type Pottery at Dor and the Status of the Town During the Assyrian Occupation Period. *ErIsr* 25: 122–35 (Hebrew).

———, and Ilan Sharon. 2003. An Archaeological Contribution to the Early Iron Age Chronological Debate: Alternative Chronologies for Phoenicia and Their Effects on the Levant, Cyprus, and Greece. *BASOR* 332: 7–80.

———. 2008. Between the Carmel and the Sea: Tel Dor's Iron Age Reconsidered. *NEA* 71: 146–70.

Gitin, Seymour. 1989. Tel Miqne-Ekron: A Type-Site for the Inner Coastal Plain in the Iron Age II Period. Pages 23–58 in *Recent Excavations in Israel: Studies in Iron Age Archaeology*. Edited by S. Gitin and W. G. Dever. AASOR 49. Winona Lake, Ind.: Eisenbrauns.

———. 1995. Tel Miqne-Ekron in the 7th Century B.C.E.: The Impact of Economic Innovation and Foreign Cultural Influences on a Neo-Assyrian Vassal City-State. Pages 61–79 in *Recent Excavations in Israel: A View to the West*. Edited by S. Gitin. Dubuque, Iowa: Archaeological Institute of America.

———. 1997. The Neo-Assyrian Empire and Its Western Periphery: The Levant, with a Focus on Philistine Ekron. Pages 77–103 in *Assyria 1995, Proceedings of the 10th Anniversary Symposium of the Neo-Assyrian Text Corpus Project*. Edited by S. Parpola and R. M. Whiting. Helsinki: The Neo-Assyrian Text Corpus Project.

———. 1998. The Philistines in the Prophetic Texts: An Archaeological Perspective. Pages 273–90 in *Hesed Ve-Emet: Studies in Honor of Ernest S. Frerichs*. Edited by J. Magness and S. Gitin. Atlanta: Scholars Press.

Goethert, Rolf, and Ruth Amiran. 1996. A Salvage Excavation on the Eastern Slope of Tel-Arad. *ErIsr* 25: 112–15 (Hebrew).

Golani, Amir. 2005. Horvat Avimor. *Archaeological News: Excavations and Surveys in Israel* 117 (internet Edition).

Goldfus, Haim, and Amir Golani. 1993. Map of the Wadi el-Makukh. Pages 265–338 (Hebrew), 47*–58* (English summaries) in *Archaeological Survey of the Hill Country of Benjamin*. Edited by I. Finkelstein and Y. Magen. Jerusalem: Israel Antiquities Authority.

Gonzales-Ruibal, Alfredo. 2006. Past the Last Outpost: Punic Merchants in the Atlantic Ocean (5th–1st Centuries B.C.). *JMA* 19: 121–50.

Goodblatt, David M. 2006. *Element of Ancient Jewish Nationalism*. Cambridge: Cambridge University Press.

Goody, Jack. 1975. *Literacy in Traditional Societies*. Cambridge: Cambridge University Press.

Gophna (Gofnah), Ram. 1963. "Haserim" Settlements in Northern Negev. *Yediot* 27: 173–80 (Hebrew).

———. 1964. Sites from the Late Iron Age between Beer-Sheba and Tell el Farʻa. *Yediot* 28: 236–46 (Hebrew).

———. 1966. Iron Age *Haserim* in southern Philistia. *ʻAtiqot* 3: 44–51 (Hebrew).

———. 1970. Some Iron Age II Sites in Southern Philistia. *ʻAtiqot* 6: 25–30 (Hebrew).

———. 1992. The Intermediate Bronze Age. Pages 126–58 in *The Archaeology of Ancient Israel*. Edited by A. Ben Tor. New Haven: Yale University Press.

———, and Itzhaq Beit-Arieh. 1997. *Map of Lod*. Archaeological Survey of Israel. Jerusalem: Israel Antiquities Authority.

———, and Yuval Portugali. 1988. Settlement and Demographic in Israel's Coastal Plain from the Chalcolithic to the Middle Bronze Age. *BASOR* 269: 11–28.

Govrin, Yehuda. *Map of Nahal Yatir*. Archaeological Survey of Israel. Jerusalem: Israel Antiquities Authority.

Grabbe, Lester L. 1998. Introduction. Pages 11–19 in *Leading Captivity Captive: The Exile as History and Ideology*. Edited by L. L. Grabbe. Sheffield: Sheffield Academic.

Grayson, A. Kirk. 1991. Assyria 668–635 B.C.: The Reign of Assurbanipal. Pages 144–61 in *The Assyrian and Babylonian Empires and Other States of the Near East, from the Eight to the Sixth Centuries B.C.* Edited by J. A. Boardman.Vol. 3/2 of *CAH*. Cambridge: Cambridge University Press.

Greenberg, Raphael, and Gilad Cinamon. 2000. The Rogem Ganim Excavations: A Community Project for the Rehabilitation of an Ancient Site in West Jerusalem. Pages 44–51 in *New Studies on Jerusalem, Proceedings of the Sixth Conference*. Edited by A. Faust and A. Baruch. Ramat Gan: Bar Ilan University (Hebrew).

———. 2006. Stamped and Incised Jar Handles from Rogem Gannim and Their Implications for the Political Economy of Jerusalem, Late 8th Century–Early 4th Centuries B.C.E. *TA* 33: 229–43.

Greenhut, Zvi. 1994. Recent Archaeological Research in the Periphery of Jerusalem. *Ariel* 100–101: 133–47. (Hebrew)

———. 2006. Production, Storage and Distribution of Grain During the Iron Age and their Linkage to the Socio-Economic Organization of the Settlement in Israel. Ph.D. diss. Tel Aviv University. (Hebrew)

———, and Alon De Groot. 2009. *Salvage Excavations at Moza*. Jerusalem: Israel Antiquities Authority.

Grossman, David. 1994. *Expansion and Desertion: The Arab Village and Its Offshoots in Ottoman Palestine*. Jerusalem: Yad Ben Zvi (Hebrew).

Gudovitz, Shlomo., and Amir Feldstein. 1998. Horbat Tittora. *ESI* 18: 79–81.

Haas, N. 1971. Anthropological Observations on the Skeletal Remains Found in Area D (1962–1963). Pages 212–14 in *Ashdod II-III–Text*. Edited by M. Dothan. *ʻAtiqot* IX-X.

Haiman, Mordechai. 2000. Rosh Ha-ʻAyin Area, survey. *ESI* 20: 45*–46*.

Hallote, Rachel S. 1997. Gibeon. Pages 403–4 in vol. 2 of *OEANE*. Edited by E. M. Meyers. 5 vols. New York: Oxford University Press.

Har-Even, B. 2009. An Iron Age IIB Agricultural Unit at Beitar ʻIlit (West). Pages 65–72 in *Excavations and Discoveries in Benjamin and Judea*. Edited by I. Yezerski. JSP 10. Jerusalem: Staff Officer of Archaeology – Civil Administration of Judea and Samaria, Israel Antiquities Authority. (Hebrew)

Hegmon, Michelle., Margaret C. Nelson, and Susan M. Ruth. 1998. Abandonment and Reorganization in the Mimbres Region of the American Southwest. *American Anthropologist* 100: 148–62.

Herzog, Zeev. 1993. Michal, Tel. Pages 1036–41 in vol. 3 of *NEAEHL*. Edited by E. Stern. 4 vols. Jerusalem: Israel Exploration Society.

———. 1997a. The Arad Fortresses. Pages 113–292 in *Arad*. Edited by R. Amiran, et al. Tel-Aviv: HaKibbutz HaMeuchad and the Israel Exploration Society (Hebrew).

———. 1997b. *The City in Ancient Israel*. Tel Aviv: Tel Aviv University.

Hirschfeld, Yizhar. 1985. *Map of Herodium*. Archaeological Survey of Israel. Jerusalem: Israel Antiquities Authority.

Hizmi, Hananya. 1993. Southern Part of the Map of Beit Sira. Pages 97–131 (Hebrew), 23*–28* (English summaries) in *Archaeological Survey of the Hill Country of Benjamin*. Edited by I. Finkelstein and Y. Magen. Jerusalem: Israel Antiquities Authority.

———. 1998. Horbat 'Eli. *ESI* 18: 51–52.

Hodos, Tamar, 2006. *Local Responses to Colonisation in the Iron Age Mediterranean*. London: Routledge.

Hoglund, Kenneth G. 1992. *Achaemenid Imperial Administration in Syria-Palestine and the Mission of Ezra and Nehemiah*. Atlanta: Scholars Press.

Holladay, John S. 1971. Khirbet el-Qom (notes and news). *IEJ* 21: 175–77.

———. 1992. House, Israelite. Pages 308–18 in vol. 3 of *ABD*. Edited by David Noel Friedman. 6 vols. New York: Doubleday.

———. 1995. The Kingdoms of Israel and Judah: Political and Economic Centralization in the Iron II A-B. Pages 368–98, 586–90 in *The Archaeology of Society in the Holy Land*. Edited by Thomas E. Levy. New York: Fact on File.

———. 1997. Four-Room House. Pages 337–41 in vol. 2 of *OEANE*. Edited by E. M. Meyers. 5 vols. New York: Oxford University Press.

———. 2009. "Home Economics 1407" and the Israelite Family and Their Neighbors: An Anthropological/Archaeological Exploration. Pages 61–88 in *The Family in Life and Death: The Family in Ancient Israel, Sociological and Archaeological Perspectives*. Edited by P. Dutcher-Walls. New York and London: T&T Clark.

Hurvitz., Avi. 1974. The Evidence of Language in Dating the Priestly Code. *RB* 81: 24–56.

———. 1982. *A Linguistic Study of the Relationship between the Priestly Source and the Book of Ezekiel: A New Approach to an Old Problem*. Paris: J. Gabalda.

———. 2003. Hebrew and Aramaic in Biblical Hebrew: The Problem of 'Aramaisms' in Linguistic Research on the Hebrew Bible. Pages 24–37 in *Biblical Hebrew: Studies in Chronology and Typology*. Edited by I. Young. London: T&T Clark.

———. 2006. The Recent Debate on Late Biblical Hebrew: Solid Data, Expert's Opinions and Inconclusive Arguments. *HS* 47: 191–210.

Hutchinson, Richard W. 1962. *Prehistoric Crete*. Harmondsworth: Penguin.

Jackson, Kenneth. 1953. *Language and History in Early Britain*. Edinburgh: Edinburgh University Press.

James, Peter. 2003. Naukratis Revisited. *Hyperbreus: Studia Classica* 9: 235–64.

———. 2004. Review of The Assyrian, Babylonian and Persian Periods in Palestine. *BAIAS* 22: 47–57.

———. 2006. Dating the Late Iron Age Ekron (Tel Miqne). *PEQ* 138: 85–97.

———, et al. 1991. Centuries of Darkness: Context, Methodology, and Implications. *CAJ* 1: 228–235.

———. 1993. *Centuries of Darkness*. New Brunswick: Rutgers University Press.

Jamieson-Drake, David W. 1991. *Scribes and Schools in Monarchic Judah, A Socio-Archaeological Approach*. The Social World of Biblical Antiquity 9. Sheffield: Sheffield

Academic.

Jansen, Enno. 1956. *Juda in der Exilszeit: Ein Beitrag zur Frage der Entstehung des Judentums*. Göttingen : Vandenhoeck & Ruprecht.

Johnson, Barbara. 2001. Attic Pottery. Page 188 in *Timnah (Tel Batash) II: The Finds from the First Millennium B.C.E. Text*. Qedem 42. Edited by A. Mazar and N. Panitz-Cohen. Jerusalem: Hebrew University.

Kaplan, Jacob. 1993. Ashdod Yam. Pages 102–3 in vol. 1 of *NEAEHL*. Edited by E. Stern. 4 vols. Jerusalem: Israel Exploration Society.

Katz, Haya, and Avraham Faust. 2011. The Assyrian Destruction Layer at Tel ʿEton. *ErIsr* 30: 256–74. (Hebrew)

Katzenshtein, H. Jacob. 1973. *The History of Tyre, from the Beginning of the Second Millennium B.C.E. until the Fall of the Neo-Babylonian Empire in 538 B.C.E.* Jerusalem: The Schocken Institute for Jewish Research.

Keegan, John. 1993. *A History of Warfare*. London: Hutchinson.

Keel, Othmar. 1978. *The Symbolism of the Biblical World: Ancient Near-Eastern Iconography and the Book of Psalms*. New York: Seabury.

Kelle, Brad E. 2007. *Ancient Israel at War 853–586 B.C.* Oxford: Osprey.

Kelm, George L., and Amihai Mazar. 1985. Tel Batash (Timnah) Excavations: Second Preliminary Report (1981–1982). Pages 93–120 in *BASOR Supplement*. Preliminary Reports of ASOR-Sponsored Excavations 1981–1983. Edited by W. E. Rast. Winona Lake, Ind.: Eisenbrauns.

Kelso, James L. 1968. *The Excavations of Bethel (1934–1960)*. Cambridge, Mass.: American Schools of Oriental Research.

———. 1993. Bethel. Pages 192–94 in vol. 1 of *NEAEHL* Edited by E. Stern. 4 vols. Jerusalem: Israel Exploration Society.

Kemp, Barry. 1991. Explaining Egyptian Crises. *CAJ* 1: 239–44.

Kempinski, Aharon. 1989. *Megiddo: City-State and Royal Centre in North Israel*. München: C. H. Beck.

———. 1993. Masos, Tel. Pages 986–89 in vol. 3 of *NEAEHL*. Edited by E. Stern. 4 vols. Jerusalem: Israel Exploration Society.

Kenyon, Kathleen. 1965. *Archaeology in the Holy Land*. London: Methuen.

———. 1993, Jericho, Tell es-Sultan. Pages 674–81 in vol. 2 of *NEAEHL*. Edited by E. Stern. 4 vols. Jerusalem: Israel Exploration Society.

Kern, Paul B. 1999. *Ancient Siege Warfare*. Bloomington: Indiana University Press.

Kh. el-Burj 1973. Kh. el-Burj. *Hadashot Arkheologiyot: Excavations and Surveys in Israel* 45: 26 (Hebrew).

King, Philip, and Lawrence E. Stager. 2001. *Life in Biblical Israel*. Louisville: Westminster John Knox.

Kitchen, Kenneth A. 1991. Egyptian Chronology: Problem or Solution? *CAJ* 1: 235–39.

Kletter, Raz. 1991. The Inscribed Weights of the Kingdom of Judah. *TA* 18: 121–163.

———. 1998. *Economic Keystones: The Weight System of the Kingdom of Judah*. Sheffield: Sheffield Academic.

———. 2002. People Without Burials? The Lack of Iron I Burials in the Central Highlands of Palestine. *IEJ* 52: 28–4

———, and Wolfgang Zwickel. 2006. The Assyrian Building of ʿAyyelet ha=Sahar. *ZDPV* 122: 151–86.

Kloner, Amos. 2000. *Survey of Jerusalem, the Southern Sector*. Archaeological Survey of

Israel. Jerusalem: Israel Antiquities Authority.

———. 2001a. Jerusalem Environs in the Persian Period. Pages 83–89 in *New Studies on Jerusalem: Proceedings of the Seventh Conference*. Edited by A. Faust and E. Baruch. Ramat Gan: Bar-Ilan University (Hebrew).

———. 2001b. *Survey of Jerusalem: The Northeastern Sector*. Archaeological Survey of Israel. Jerusalem: Israel Antiquities Authority.

———. 2003. *Survey of Jerusalem: The Nortwestern Sector, Introduction and Indices*. Archaeological Survey of Israel. Jerusalem: Israel Antiquities Authority.

———. 2004. Iron Age Burial Caves in Jerusalem and Its Vicinity. *Bulletin of the Anglo-Israel Archaeological Society 2001–2002* 19–20: 95–118.

———, and Eshel, Esther. 1999. A Seventh-Century B.C.E. List of Names from Maresha. *ErIsr* 26: 147–50 (Hebrew).

———, and Zelinger, Yehiel. 2007. The Evolution of Tombs from the Iron Age through the Second Temple Period. Pages 209–20 in *Up to the Gates of Ekron: Essays in the Archaeology and History of the Eastern Mediterranean in Honor of Seymour Gitin*. Edited by S. W. Crawford, et al. Jerusalem: Israel Exploration Society.

———, and Boaz Zissu. 2003. *The Necropolis of Jerusalem in the Second Temple Period*. Jerusalem: Yad Ben Zvi and the Israel Exploration Society (Hebrew).

Knoppers, Gary N. 2004. In Search of Post-Exilic Israel: Samaria after the Fall of the Northern Kingdom. Pages 150–60 in *In Search of Pre-Exilic Israel*. Edited by J. Day. London: T&T Clark.

Kochavi, Moshe. 1972. The Land of Judah. Pages 19–89 in *Judea, Samaria and the Golan, Archaeological Survey 1967–1968*. Edited by M. Kochavi. Jerusalem (Hebrew).

———. 1974. Kh. Rabud = Debir. *TA* 1: 2–33.

———. 1993a. Malhata, Tel. Pages 934–36 in vol. 3 of *NEAEHL*. Edited by E. Stern. 4 vols. Jerusalem: Israel Exploration Society.

———. 1993b. Rabud, Khirbet. Page 1252 in vol. 4 of *NEAEHL*. Edited by E. Stern. 4 vols. Jerusalem: Israel Exploration Society.

———. 1998. The Excavations at Tel Malhata: An Interim Report. *Qad* 115: 30–39 (Hebrew).

Kochavi, Moshe, and Itzhaq Beit-Arieh. 1994. *Map of Rosh Ha-'Ayin*. Archaeological Survey of Israel. Jerusalem: Israel Antiquities Authority.

Kogan-Zehavi, Elena. 2005. An Assyrian Building South of Tel Ashdod. *Qad* 130: 87–90 (Hebrew).

Kol Ya'akov, Shlomo., and Misgav Har-Peled. 2000. Jerusalem, Ramat Bet Ha-Kerem. *Hadashot Arkheologiyot: Excavations and Surveys in Israel* 112: 86*–87*, 107–108.

Kuhrt, Amelie. 1995. *The Ancient Near East, c. 3000–330 BC*. London: Routledge.

Lapp, Nancy L. 1978a. Other Finds from the 1964 Campaign. Pages 109–16. in *The Third Campaign at Tell el-Ful: The Excavations of 1964*. AASOR 45. Edited by N. L. Lapp. Cambridge, Mass.: American Schools of Oriental Research.

———. 1978b. The 7th–6th-Century Occupation: Period III. Pages 39–46 in *The Third Campaign at Tell el-Ful: The Excavations of 1964*. AASOR 45. Edited by N .L. Lapp. Cambridge, Mass.: American Schools of Oriental Research.

———. 1978c. The Pottery from the 1964 Campaign. Pages 79–107 in *The Third Campaign at Tell el-Ful: The Excavations of 1964*. AASOR 45. Edited by N. L. Lapp. Cambridge, Mass.: American Schools of Oriental Research.

———. 1993. Ful, tell el-. Pages 445–48 in vol. 1 of *NEAEHL*. Edited by E. Stern. 4 vols.

Jerusalem: Israel Exploration Society.

———. 1997. Full, tel el. Pages 346–47 in vol. 2 of *OEANE*. Edited by E. M. Meyers. 5 vols. New York: Oxford University Press.

———. 2007. Some Early Persian Period Pottery from Tell Balatah. Pages 221–27 in *Up to the Gates of Ekron: Essays in the Archaeology and History of the Eastern Mediterranean in Honor of Seymour Gitin*. Edited by S. W. Crawford, et al. Jerusalem: Israel Exploration Society.

———. 2008. *Shechem IV: The Persian-Hellenistic Pottery of Shechem/Tell Balatah*, Boston: American Schools of Oriental Research

Lehmann, Gunnar. 2002. Area E. Pages 73–90 in *Tel Kabr: The 1986–1993 Excavation Seasons*. Edited by A. Kempniski. Tel Aviv: Tel Aviv University.

Lehmann, Gunnar, et al. 2010. Excavations at Qubur al-Walaydah, 2007–2009, *WO* 40: 137–59

Lemche, Niels P. 1988. *Ancient Israel: A New History of Israelite Society*. Sheffield: Sheffield University Press.

Lemos, Irene S. 2002. *The Protogeometric Aegean: The Archaeology of the Late Eleventh and Tenth Centuries B.C.* Oxford: Oxford University Press.

Levin, Christoph. 2006. Review of Richard M. Wright, *Linguistic Evidence for the Pre-exilic Date of the Yahwistic Source. RBL* 1.

Levitt Kohn, Risa. 2002. *A New Heart and a New Soul: Ezekiel, the Exile and the Torah*. Sheffield: Sheffield Academic.

Levy, Thomas E., and Thomas Higham. 2005. *The Bible and Radiocarbon Dating: Archaeology, Text and Science*. London: Equinox.

Levy, Yosef, Martin Peilstocker, and Anat Ginzburg. 2004. An Iron Age Fortress in the Sand Dunes of Rishon Leziyon. *Qad* 128: 92–94 (Hebrew).

Levy, Yosef, and Martin Peilstocker. 2008. Rishon Lezion, the Iron Age II Fortress. Pages 2020–22 in vol. 5 of *NEAEHL*. Edited by E. Stern. 5 vols. Jerusalem: Israel Exploration Society.

Lewis, Theodore J. 1993. Israel, Religion of. Pages 36–332 in *The Oxford Companion to the Bible*. Edited by B. M. Metzger and M. D. Coogan. Oxford: Oxford University Press.

Liphschits, Nili, and Gideon Biger. 1991. Cedar of Lebanon (*Cedrus Libani*) in Israel During Antiquity. *IEJ* 41: 167–75.

Lipschits, Oded. 1990. The Date of the "Assyrian Residence" at Ayyelet Ha-Shahar. *TA* 17: 96–99.

———. 1997a. The Origins of the Jewish Population of Modi'in and Its Vicinity. *Cathedra* 85: 7–32 (Hebrew).

———. 1997b. *The "Yehud" Province under Babylonian Rule (586–39 B.C.E.): Historic Reality and Historiographic Conceptions*. Ph.D. diss. Tel-Aviv University.

———. 1998a. Jerusalem and the Temple Between the Destruction of the First Temple and the Days of the Return to Zion. Pages 27–39 in *New Studies on Jerusalem: Proceedings of the Fourth Confernece*. Edited by E. Baruch. Ramat Gan: Bar-Ilan University (Hebrew).

———. 1998b. The Material Culture of the People that Remained in Judah. Pages 21–23 in *Is It Possible to Define the Ceramics of the 6th Century B.C.E. in Judah?* Edited by O. Lipschits. Tel-Aviv.

———. 1999. The History of the Benjamin Region under Babylonian Rule. *TA* 26: 155–90.

———. 2001. The Policy of the Persian Empire and the Meager Architectonic Finds in the Province of 'Yehud'. Pages 45–76 in *New Studies on Jerusalem, Proceedings of the 7th Conference*. Edited by A. Faust and E. Baruch. Ramat Gan: Bar Ilan University (Hebrew).

———. 2003a. Demographic Changes in Judah between the Seventh and the Fifth Centuries B.C.E. Pages 323–76 in *Judah and Judeans in the Neo-Babylonian Period*. Edited by O. Lipschits and J. Blenkinsopp. Winona Lake, Ind.: Eisenbrauns.

———. 2003b. *Jerusalem between Destruction and Restoration: Judah under Babylonian Rule*. Jerusalem: Yad Ben-Zvi (Hebrew).

———. 2004. The Rural Settlement in Judah in the Sixth Century B.C.E.: A Rejoinder. *PEQ* 136: 99–107

———. 2005. *The Fall and Rise of Jerusalem: Judah under Babylonian Rule*. Winona Lake, Ind.: Eisenbrauns.

———. 2006. Achaemenid Imperial Policy, Settlement Processes in Palestine, and the Status of Jerusalem in the Middle of the Fifth Century B.C.E. Pages 19–52 in *Judah and Judeans in the Persian Period*. Edited by O. Lipschits and M. Oeming. Winona Lake, Ind.: Eisenbrauns.

———. 2007. The Babylonian Period in Judah: In Search of the Half Full Cup. Pages 40–49 in *In Conversation with Oded Lipschits, The Fall and Rise of Jerusalem*. Edited by D. Vanderhooft. JHebS 7.2.

Lipschits, Oded, et al. 2009. Ramat Rahel and Its Secrets. *Qad* 138: 58–77 (Hebrew).

———, et al. 2009. The 2006 and 2007 Excavation Seasons at Ramat Rahel: Preliminary Report. *IEJ* 59: 1–20.

Lipschits, Oded, Omer Sergi, and Ido Koch. 2010. Royal Judahite Jar Handles: Reconsidering the Chronology of the *lmlk* Stamp Impression. *TA* 37: 3–32.

———. 2011. Judahite Jar Stamped and Incised Jar Handles: A Tool for Studying the History of Late Monarchic Judah. Tel Aviv 38: 5–41.

Lipschits, Oded, and Oren Tal. 2007. The Settlement Archaeology of the Province of Judah: A Case Study. Pages 33–52 in *Judah and Judeans in the Fourth Century B.C.E.* Edited by O. Lipschits, G. N. Knoppers and R. Albertz. Winona Lake, Ind.: Eisenbrauns.

Lipschits, Oded, et al. 2011. Palace and Village, Paradise and Obvilion: Unraveling the Secrets of Ramat Rahel. *NEA* 74: 2–49

Liverani, Mario. 1992. *Studies on the Annals of Ashurbanipal II*. Roma: La Sapienza.

———. 2001. The Fall of the Assyrian Empire: Ancient and Modern Interpretation. Pages 374–91 in *Empires: Perspectives from Archaeology and History*. Edited by S. E. Alcock et al. Cambridge: Cambridge University Press.

———. 2005. *Israel's History and the History of Israel*. London: Equinox.

London, Gloria. 1989. A Comparison of Two Contemporaneous Life Styles of the Late Second Millennium B.C. *BASOR* 273: 37–55.

Lubetski, Meir. 1978. New Light on Old Seas. *JQR* 68: 65–77

Luke, Joanna. 2003. *Ports of Trade, Al Mina and Geometric Greek Pottery in the Levant*. Oxford: Archaeopress.

Machinist, Peter. 1992. Palestine, Administration of (Assyro-Babylonian). Pages 69–81 in vol. 5 of *ABD*. Edited by David Noel Freedman. 6 vols. New York: Doubleday.

Magen, Yitzhak. 1995. The Land of Benjamin in the Second Temple Period. Pages 75–102 in *Judea and Samaria Research Studies, Proceedings of the Fourth Annual Meeting 1994*. Edited by Z. H. Erlich and Y. Eshel. Kedumim-Ariel (Hebrew).

————. 2004. The Land of Benjamin in the Second Temple Period. Pages 1–28 in *The Land of Benjamin*. Edited by Y. Magen et al. Jerusalem: Israel Antiquities Authority.

Magness, Jodi. 2001. Early Archaic Greek Pottery. Pages 141–44 in *Timnah (Tel Batash) II: The Finds from the First Millennium B.C.E. Text*. Qedem 42. Edited by A. Mazar and N. Panitz-Cohen. Jerusalem: Hebrew University.

Maitlis, Ytzhak. 1989. *Agricultural Settlements in the Vicinity of Jerusalem in the Late Iron Age*. M.A. Thesis. Hebrew University.

Malamat, Avraham. 1950. The Last Wars of the Kingdom of Judah. *JNES* 9: 218–27.

————. 1983. *Israel in Biblical Times*. Jerusalem: Israel Exploration Society (Hebrew).

————. 1989. *Mari and the Early Israelite Experience*. The Schweich Lecture 1984. Oxford: Oxford University Press.

Manahan, T. Kam. 2004. The Way Things Fall Apart: Social Organization and the Classic Maya Collapse of Copan. *Ancient Mesoamerica* 15: 107–25.

Manor, Dale. 1997. Judeideh, Tell el-. Pages 259–60 in vol. 3 of *OEANE*. Edited by E. M. Meyers. 5 vols. New York: Oxford University Press.

Marchese, Ronald. 1995. Athenian Imports in the Persian Period. Pages 127–81 in *Excavations at Dor: Final Report, Volume Ib*. Qedem Reports 2. Edited by E. Stern. Jerusalem: The Hebrew University.

Marcus, Joyce, and Kent V. Flannery, 1996. *Zapotec Civilization: How Urban Society Evolved in Mexico's Oaxaca Valley*. London: Thames & Hudson.

Markoe, Glenn E. 2000. *Phoenicians*. Berkeley: University of California Press.

Master, Daniel. 2001. The Seaport of Ashkelon in the Seventh Century B.C.E.: A Petrogrpahic Study. Ph.D. diss. Harvard University.

————. 2003. Trade and Politics: Ashkelon's Balancing Act in the Seventh Century B.C.E. *BASOR* 330: 47–64.

————. 2007. Comments on Oded Lipschits, The Fall and Rise of Jerusalem. Pages 28–33 in *In Conversation with Oded Lipschits, The Fall and Rise of Jerusalem*. Edited by D. Vanderhooft. JHebS 7/2.

Mata, Ruiz. 2002. The Ancient Phoenicians of the 8th and 7th Centuries B.C. in the Bay of Cadiz: State of Research. Pages 155–98 in *The Phoenicians in Spain: An Archaeological Review of the Eight-Sixth Centuries B.C.E.* Edited by M. R. Bierling and S. Gitin. Winona Lake, Ind.: Eisenbrauns.

May, Natalie. 1999. Jerusalem, Giv'at Homa. *ESI* 19: 65*–66*.

Mazar, Amihai. 1976. Iron Age Burial Caves North of the Damascus Gate, Jerusalem. *IEJ* 26: 1–8.

————. 1981. The Excavations at Khirbet Abu et-Twein and the System of Iron Age Fortresses in Judah. *ErIsr* 15: 229–49 (Hebrew).

————. 1982. Iron Age Fortresses in the Judean Hills. *PEQ* 114: 87–109.

————. 1990. *The Archaeology of the Land of the Bible, 10,000–586 B.C.E.* New York: Doubleday.

————. 1997. Iron Age Chronology: A Reply to I. Finkelstein. *Levant* 29: 157–1.67.

————. 2011. Tel Rehov in the Assyrian Period: Squatters, Burials and a Hebrew Seal. Pages 265–80 in *The Fire Signals of Lachish: Studies in the History of Israel in the Late Bronze Age, Iron Age, and Persian Period in Honor of David Ussishkin*. Edited by Israel Finkelstein and Nadav Na'aman. Winona Lake, Ind.: Eisenbrauns.

————, David Amit, and Zvi Ilan. 1996. Hurvat Shilhah: An Iron Age Site in Judean Desert. Pages 193–211 in *Retrieving the Past: Essays on Archaeological Research and*

Methodology in Honor of Gus W. Van Beek. Edited by J. D. Seger. Winona Lake, Ind.: Eisenbrauns.

———, and George E. Kelm. 1993. Batash, Tel. Pages 152–57 in vol. 1 of *NEAEHL*. Edited by E. Stern. 4 vols. Jerusalem: Israel Exploration Society.

———, and Nava Panitz-Cohen. 2001. *Timnah (Tel Batash) II: The Finds from the First Millennium B.C.E. Text.* Qedem 42. Jerusalem: Hebrew University.

Mazar, Benjamin. 1993. En-Gedi. Pages 399–405 in vol. 2 of *NEAEHL*. Edited by E. Stern. Jerusalem: Israel Exploration Society.

Mazar, Eilat, and Benjamin Mazar. 1989. *Excavations in the South of the Temple Mount, Jerusalem.* Qedem 29. Jerusalem: Hebrew University.

Mazor, Gabriel. 2006. A Farmhouse from the Late Iron Age and the Second Temple Period in "French Hill," North Jerusalem. *'Atiqot* 54: 1*–12* (Hebrew).

McCown, Chester C. 1947a. *Tell en-Nasbeh, Excavated Under the Direction of the Late William Fredric Bade, Vol. I: Archaeological and Historical Results.* Berkeley:The Palestine Institute of Pacific School of Religion.

———. 1947b. The Cultural History of the Site. Pages 60–63 in *Tell en-Nasbeh, Excavated under the Direction of the Late William Fredric Bade, Vol. I: Archaeological and Historical Results.* Edited by C. C. McCown. Berkeley: The Palestine Institute of Pacific School of Religion.

McNutt, Paula M. 1999. *Reconstructing the Society of Ancient Israel.* Louisville: Westminster John Knox.

Mendels, Doron. 1992. *The Rise and Fall of Jewish Nationalism.* New York: Doubleday.

Meshorer, Yaakov. 1976. Means of Payment Prior to Coinage and the First Coinage. *Qad* 34–35: 51–60 (Hebrew).

Meyers, Carol. 2007. Terracottas Without Texts: Judean Pillar Figurines in Anthropological Perspective. Pages 115–30 in *To Break Every Yoke: Essays in Honor of Marvin L. Chaney.* Edited by R. B. Coote and N. K. Gottwald. Sheffield: Sheffield Phoenix.

———, and Eric M. Meyers. 1994. Demography and Diatribes: Yehud's Population and the Prophecy of Second Zechariah. Pages 268–85 in *Scripture and Other Artifacts.* Edited by M. D. Coogan, J. C. Exum and L. E. Stager. Louisville: Westminster John Knox.

Middlemas, Jill. 2005. *The Troubles of Templeless Judah.* Oxford: Oxford University Press.

———. 2007. *The Templeless Age: An Introduction to the History, Literature and Theology of the "Exile."* Louisville: Westminster John Knox.

Mileveski, Ianir. 1996–97. Settlement Patterns in Northern Judah During the Achaemenid Period, According to the Hill Country of Benjamin and Jerusalem Survey. *BAIAS* 15: 7–29.

Milroy, James, and Lesley Milroy. 1985. Linguistic Change, Social Network and Speaker Innovation. *Journal of Linguistics* 21: 339–84.

Milroy, Lesley. 2002. Social Network. Pages 549–72 in *The Handbook of Language Variation and Change.* Edited by J. K. Chambers, P. Trudgill and N. Schilling-Estes. Malden: Blackwell.

Mitchell, Allen J. 1997. Contested Peripheries: Philistia in the Neo-Assyrian World System. Ph.D. diss. University of California at Los Angeles.

Mook, Margaret S., and William D. E. Coulson. 1995. East Greek and Other Imported Pottery. Pages 93–125 in *Excavations at Dor: Final Report, Volume Ib.* Qedem Reports 2. Edited by E. Stern. Jerusalem: Hebrew University.

Morris, Earl. 2006. "Lo, Nobles Lament, the Poor Rejoice": State Formation in the Wake of Social Flux. Pages 58–71 in *After Collapse: The Regeneration of Complex Societies.* Edited by G. M. Schwartz and D .J. Nichols. Tucson: University of Arizona.

Muilenburg, James. 1947. The History of Mizpah of Benjamin. Pages 45–49 in *Tell en-Nasbeh, Excavated under the Direction of the Late William Fredric Bade, Vol. I: Archaeological and Historical Results.* Edited by C. C. McCown. Berkeley: The Palestine Institute of Pacific School of Religion.

Na'aman, Nadav. 1993. Population Changes in Palestine Following Assyrians Deportations. *TA* 20: 104–24.

———. 1995. Province System and Settlement Patterns in Southern Syria and Palestine in the Neo-Assyrian Period. Pages 103–15 in *Neo-Assyrian Geography.* Edited by M. Liverani. Rome: Stampa a Cura di Sargon.

———. 1996. The Contribution of the Amarna Letters to the Debate on Jerusalem's Political Position in the Tenth Century B.C.E. *BASOR* 304: 17–27.

———. 2000. Royal Vassals or Governors? On the Status of Sheshbazzar and Zerubabel in the Persian Empire. *Henoch* 22: 35–44.

———. 2001. An Assyrian Residence at Ramat Rahel? *TA* 28: 260–80.

———. 2007. When and How Did Jerusalem Become a Great City? The Rise of Jerusalem as Judah's Premier City in the Eighth-Seventh Centuries B.C.E. *BASOR* 347: 21–56.

———, and Ran Zadok. 2000. Assyrian Deportations to the Province of Samerina in Light of Two Cuneiform Tablets from Tel Hadid. *TA* 27: 159–88.

Nadelman, Yonatan. 1993. Jerusalem, Pisgat Ze'ev D (H. Zimri). *ESI* 12: 54–56.

Nahshonim 1961. Burial Cave in Nachshonim. *Hadashot Arkheologiyot: Excavations and Surveys in Israel* 1: 7–8 (Hebrew).

Naso, Alessandro. 2006. Etruscan and Italic Finds in North Africa, 7th–2nd Century B.C. Pages 187–98 in *Naukratis: Greek Diversity in Egypt: Studies on East Greek Pottery and Exchange in the Eastern Mediterranean.* Edited by A. Villing and U. Schlotzhauer. London: The British Museum.

Naveh, Joseph. 1962. The Excavations at Mesad Hashavyahu: Preliminary Report. *IEJ* 12: 89–113.

———. 1963. Old Hebrew Inscriptions in a Burial Cave. *IEJ* 13: 74–92.

———. 1970. *The Development of the Aramaic Script.* Jerusalem: Israel Academy of Sciences and Humanities.

Nelson, Margaret C., and Gregson Schachner. 2002. Understanding Abandonment in the North American Southwest. *JAR* 10/2: 167–206.

Netzer, Ehud. 1992. Domestic Architecture in the Iron Age. Pages 193–201 in *The Architecture of Ancient Israel from the Prehistoric to the Persian Period.* Edited by A. Kempinski and R. Reich. Jerusalem: Israel Exploration Society.

Niehr, Herbert. 2003. The Changed Status of the Dead in Yehud. Pages 136–55 in *Yahwism after the Exile: Perspectives on Israelite Religion in the Persian Era.* Edited by R. Albertz and B. Becking. Assen: Van Gorcum.

Niemeier, Wolf-Dietrich. 2001. Archaic Greeks in the Orient: Textual and Archaeological Evidence. *BASOR* 322: 11–32.

———. 2002. Greek Mercenaries at Tel Kabri and Other Sites in the Levant. *TA* 29: 328–31.

Nijboer, Albert J. 2005. The Iron Age in the Mediterranean: A Chronological Mess or "Flag before the Trade," Part II. *AWE* 4: 255–77.

———, and J. van der Plicht. 2006. An Interpretation of the Radiocarbon Determinations of the Oldest Indigenous-Phoenician Stratum thus Far, Excavated at Huelva, Tartessos (South-West Spain). *BABesch* 81: 31–36.

North, John. 1996. *Stonehenge, Neolithic Man and the Cosmos.* Bristol: HarperCollins.

Noth, Martin. 1960. *The History of Israel.* New York and Evanston: Harper and Row.

Nowicki, Krzysztof. 1999. Economy of Refugees: Life in the Cretan Mountains at the Turn of the Bronze and Iron Ages. Pages 145–71 in *From Minoan Farmers to Roman Traders: Sidelights on the Economy of Ancient Crete.* Edited by L. Shaler, J. Cowey and O. Hoover. Stuttgart: Steiner.

Oded, Bustenay. 1979. *Mass Deportations and Deportees in the Neo-Assyrian Empire.* Wiesbaden: Reichert.

———. 1984. The Kingdoms of Israel and Judah. Pages 99–200 in *The History of Eretz Israel, Volume II: Israel and Judah in the Biblical Period.* Edited by I. Eph'al. Jerusalem: Yad Ben Zvi (Hebrew).

———. 1995. Observations on the Israelite/Judaean Exiles in Mesopotamia during the Eighth-Sixth Centuries B.C.E. Pages 205–12 in *Immigration and Emigration within the Ancient Near East.* Edited by K. van Lerberghe and A. Schoors. Leuven: Peeters.

———. 2000. The Settlements of the Israelite and Judean Exiles in Mesopotamia in the 8th–6th Centuries B.C.E. Pages 91–103 in *Studies in Historical Geography and Biblical Geography, Presented to Zecharia Kallai.* Edited by G. Galil and M. Weinfeld. Leiden: Brill.

———. 2001. Where Is "the Myth of the Empty Land" to Be Found? History versus Myth. Pages 9–10 in *Judah and Judeans in the Neo-Babylonian Period, Summaries.* Edited by O. Lipschits and J. Blenkinsopp. Tel Aviv: Tel Aviv University.

———. 2003. Where Is "the Myth of the Empty Land" to Be Found? History versus Myth. Pages 55–74 in *Judah and Judeans in the Neo-Babylonian Period.* Edited by O. Lipschits and J. Blenkinsopp. Winona Lake, Ind.: Eisenbrauns.

———. 2010. The Early History of the Babylonian Exile (8th–6th Centuries B.C.E.). Haifa: Pardes (Hebrew).

———, and Avraham Faust. 2006. The Land of Judah in the Neo-Babylonian Period—A Review Article. *Cathedra* 121: 171–78 (Hebrew).

Ofer, Avi. 1993a. Hebron. Pages 606–9 in vol. 2 of *NEAEHL.* Edited by E. Stern. 4 vols. Jerusalem: Israel Exploration Society.

———. 1993b. *The Highlands of Judah during the Biblical Period.* Ph.D. diss. Tel-Aviv University (Hebrew).

———. 1998. The Judean Hills in the Biblical Period. *Qad* 115: 40–52 (Hebrew).

———. 1999. The Desert Town of Judah. *Cathedra* 90: 7–32 (Hebrew).

———. 2001. The Monarchic Period in the Judaean Highland: A Spatial View. Pages 14–37 in *Studies in the Archaeology of the Iron Age in Israel and Jordan.* Edited by A. Mazar. Sheffield: Sheffield Academic.

Onn, Alexander, and Yehuda Rapuanu. 1993. Jerusalem, Kh. er-Ras. *ESI* 13: 71.

Oppenheim, Leo A. 1967. Essay on Overland Trade in the First Millennium B.C. *JCS* 21: 236–54.

Oren, Eliezer D. 1993a. Haror, Tel. Pages 580–84 in vol, 2 of *NEAEHL.* Edited by E. Stern. 4 vols. Jerusalem: Israel Exploration Society.

———. 1993b. Sera, Tel. Pages 1329–35 in vol. 4 of *NEAEHL.* Edited by E. Stern. 4 vols Jerusalem: Israel Exploration Society.

Oren, Ronit, and Na'ama Scheftelowitz. 2000. Khirbet el-Bira. *ESI* 20: 50*–51*.

Orton, Clive, Paul Tyres, and Alan Vince. 1993. *Pottery in Archaeology.* Cambridge: Cambridge University.

Osborne, Robin. 1996. Pots, Trade and the Archaic Greek Economy. *Antiquity* 70: 31–44.

Oswald, Alastair. 1997. A Doorway on the Past: Practical and Mystic Concerns in the Orientation of Roundhouse Doorways. Pages 87–95 in *Reconstructing Iron Age Societies*. Edited by A. Gwilt and C. Haselgrove. Oxbow Monographs 71. Oxford: Oxbow.

Pakkala, Juha, Stefan Munger, and Jürgen Zangenberg. 2004. *Kinneret Regional Project: Tel Kinrot Excavations*. Tel Kinrot, Tell el-Orme-Kinnert. Vantaa: Proceedings of the Finnish Institute in the Middle East.

Panitz-Cohen, Nava. 2005. A Salvage Excavation in the New Market in Beer-Sheba: New Light on Iron Age IIB Occupation at Beer-Sheba. *IEJ* 55: 143–55.

Patrich, Joseph. 1994. *Map of Deir Mar Saba*. Archaeological Survey of Israel. Jerusalem: Israel Antiquities Authority.

Pearce, Laurie E. 2006. New Evidence for Judeans in Babylonia. Pages 399–411 in *Judah and Judeans in the Persian Period*. Edited by O. Lipschits and Manfred Oeming. Winona Lake, Ind.: Eisenbrauns.

Peleg, Yuval. 2004. An Iron Age Site at Nokdim in Judaea. Pages 35–42 in *Judea and Samaria Research Studies* 13. Edited by Y. Eshel. Ariel: Eretz (Hebrew; English abstract on pp. VIII-IX)

Peleg, Yuval, and Yaron Feller. 2004a. Betar 'Illit (West). *Hadashot Arkheologiyot: Excavations and Surveys in Israel* 116: 52*–54*, 68–72.

———. 2004b. Har Gillo (West). *Hadashot Arkheologiyot: Excavations and Surveys in Israel* 116: 74*, 100–101.

———. 2004c. Sansanna. *Hadashot Arkheologiyot: Excavations and Surveys in Israel* 116: 65*, 86–87.

———. 2004d. Shim'a, Industrial Zone. *Hadashot Arkheologiyot: Excavations and Surveys in Israel* 116: 63*–64*, 83–85.

Pendlebury, John D. S. 1963. *The Archaeology of Crete: An Introduction*. New York: Biblo & Tannen.

Petrie, Flinders. 1937. *Anthedon, Sinai*. London: British School of Archaeology in Egypt.

Polak, Frank. 2003. Style Is More Than a Person: Sociolinguistics, Literary Culture, and the Distinction between Written and Oral Narrative. Pages 38–103 in *Biblical Hebrew: Studies in Chronology and Typology*. Edited by I. Young. London: T&T Clark.

———. 2006. Sociolinguists: A Key to the Typology and the Social Background of Biblical Hebrew. *HS* 47: 115–62.

Porath, Yosef, Samuel M. Paley, and Robert R. Stieglitz, 1993. Mikhmoret, Tel. Pages 1043–46 in vol. 1 of *NEAEHL*. Edited by E. Stern. 4 vols. Jerusalem: Israel Exploration Society.

Portugali, Yuval. 1988. Population Theories and Their Importance for the Demographic Research in the Land of Israel. Pages 4–38 in *Settlement, Population and Economy in the Land of Israel*. Edited by S. Bunimovitz, M. Kochavi and A. Kasher. Tel Aviv: Tel Aviv University (Hebrew).

Postgate, John N. 1979. The Economic Structure of the Assyrian Empire. Pages 193–221 in *Power and Propaganda: A Symposium on Ancient Empires*. Edited by M. T. Larsen. Copenhagen: Akademisk.

———. 1991. The Chronology of Assyria: An Insurmountable Obstacle. *CAJ* 1: 244–46.

———. 1994. How Many Sumerians per Hectare? Probing the Anatomy of an Early City. *CAJ* 4: 47–65.

Prent, Mieke. 1996-7. The Sixth Century B.C. in Crete: The Best Candidate for Being a Dark Age? Pages 35–46 in *Debating Dark Ages. Caeculus* III. Edited by M. Maaskant-Kleibrink. Groningen: Groningen Archaeological Institute.

Price, Barbara J. 1978. Secondary State Formation: An Explanatory Model. Pages 161–86 in *Origins of the State: The Anthropology of Political Evolution*. Edited by R. Cohen and E. R. Service. Philadelphia: Institute for the Study of Human Issues.

Pritchard, James B. 1959. *Hebrew Inscriptions and Stamps from Gibeon*. Philadelphia: University Museum.

———. 1962. *Gibeon Where the Sun Stood Still: The Discovery of a Biblical City*. Princeton: Princeton University Press.

———. 1964. *Winery, Defences and Soundings at Gibeon*. Philadelphia: University of Pennsylvania.

———. 1969. *Ancient Near Eastern Texts Relating to the Old Testament*. Princeton: Princeton University Press.

———. 1970. Gibeon. Pages 107–9 in vol. 1 of *EAEHL*. Edited by B. Mazar et al. 4 vols. Jerusalem: Israel Exploration Society (Hebrew).

———. 1975. Gibeon. Pages 446–50 in *EAEHL*. Edited by M. Avi-Yonah. London: Oxford University Press.

Rapuiano, Yehuda, and Alexander Onn. 2004. An Iron Age Structure from Shu'afat Ridge, Northern Jerusalem. *'Atiqot* 47: 119–29.

Reich, Ronny. 1975. The Persian Building at Ayyelet Ha-Shahar: The Assyrian Palace of Hazor. *IEJ* 25: 233–37.

———. 1992. Palaces and Residencies in the Iron Age. Pages 202–22 in *The Architecture of Ancient Israel*. Edited by A. Kempinsky and R. Reich. Jerusalem: Israel Exploration Society.

———. 1993. The Cemetery in the Mamilla Area of Jerusalem. *Qad* 103-4: 103–9 (Hebrew).

Rendsburg, Gary. 2003. Hurvitz Redux: On the Continued Scholarly Inattention to the Simple Principle of Hebrew Philology. Pages 104–28 in *Biblical Hebrew: Studies in Chronology and Typology*. Edited by I. Young. London: T&T Clark.

Renfrew, Colin, and Paul Bahn. 2004. *Archaeology: Theories, Method and Practice*. London: Thames & Hudson.

Reuben, Amichai, and Yuval Peleg. 2009. Caves, Winepresses, and a Three-Room Structure to the East of An'ata. Pages 57–64 in *Excavations and Discoveries in Benjamin and Judea*. Edited by I. Yezerski. JSP 10. Jerusalem: Staff Officer of Archaeology – Civil Administration of Judea and Samaria, Israel Antiquities Authority. (Hebrew)

Reviv, Hanoch. 1993. *The Society in the Kingdoms of Israel and Judah*. Jerusalem: Bialik Institute (Hebrew).

Rezetko, Robert. 2003. Dating Biblical Hebrew: Evidence from Samuel-King and Chronicles. Pages 215–50 in *Biblical Hebrew: Studies in Chronology and Typology*. Edited by I. Young. London: T&T Clark.

Ridgeway, David. 1999. The Rehabilitation of Bocchoris: Note and Queries from Italy. *The JEA* 85: 143–52.

Riklin, Shimon. 1993. 'Ofarim. *ESI* 13: 53–54.

———. 1995. A Fortress at Michmas on the Northeastern Border of Judean Desert. Pages 69–73 in *Judea and Samaria Research Studies, Proceedings of the 4th Annual Meeting, 1994*. Edited by Z. H. Ehrlich and Y. Eshel. Kedumim: Ariel (Hebrew).

———. 1997. Bet Arye. *ʿAtiqot* 32: 7–20 (Hebrew).

Risdon, D. L. 1939. A Study of the Cranial and Other Human Remains from Palestine Excavated at Tell Duweir (Lachish) by the Wellcome-Marston Archaeological Research Expedition. *Biometrika* 31: 99–166.

Rom-Shiloni, D. 2009. *God in Times of Destructions and Exiles: Tanakh (Hebrew Bible) Theology*. Jerusalem: Magnes.

Roth, Jonathan P. 1999. *The Logistics of the Roman Army at War (264 B.C.–A.D. 235)*. Leiden: Brill.

Safrai, Zeev. 1998. Ancient Fields Structures: The Villages in Eretz-Israel during the Roman Period. *Cathedra* 89: 7–40 (Hebrew).

Saggs, Henry W. F. 1984. *The Might that Was Assyria*. London: Sidgwick & Jackson.

Sagona, Claudia. 2004. The Phoenicians in Spain from a Central Mediterranean Perspective: A Review Essay. *ANES* 41: 240–66.

Salazar, Christine F. 2000. *The Treatment of War Wounds in Graeco-Roman Antiquity*. Leiden: Brill.

Sanders, James A. 1997. The Exile and Cannon Formation. Pages 37–61 in *Exile: Old Testament, Jewish and Christian Conceptions*. Edited by J. M. Scott. Leiden: Brill.

Sanders, Seth, L. 2009. *The Invention of Hebrew*. Urbana: University of Illinois.

Scheftelowitz, Naama, and Ronit Oren. 1996. *Trial Excavations in Kh. el-Bira Region*. Tel-Aviv: Tel Aviv University. (Hebrew)

———. 1999. Khirbet el-Bira. *ESI* 19: 42*–43*, 62–64.

Schloen, David. 2001. *The House of the Father as Fact and Symbol*. Winona Lake, Ind. : Eisenbrauns.

Schniedewind, William M. 2004. *How the Bible Became a Book?* Cambridge: Cambridge University Press.

Schwartz, Glen M. 2006. From Collapse to Regeneration. Pages 3–17 in *After Collapse: The Regeneration of Complex Societies*. Edited by G. M. Schwartz and D. J. Nichols. Tucson: University of Arizona.

———, and John D Nichols, eds. 2006. *After Collapse: The Regeneration of Complex Societies*. Tucson: University of Arizona.

Schwartz, Seth. 2001. *Imperialism and Jewish Society 200 B.C.E. to 640 C.E.* Princeton: Princeton University Press.

Segal, Orit, Raz Kletter, and Irit Ziffer. 2006. A Persian Period Building from Tel Yaʿoz (Tell Ghaza). *Atiqot* 52: 1*–24*.

Seitz, Christopher R. 1989. *Theology in Conflict: Reactions to the Exile in the Book of Jeremiah*. Berlin: Walter de Gruyter.

Seligman, Jon. 1994. A Late Iron Age Farmhouse at Ras Abu Maʿaruf, Pisgat Zeʾev A. *Atiqot* 25: 63–75.

———. 2007. Archaeological News in the Jerusalem Region, 2006–2007. Pages 7–15 in *New Studies in the Archeology of Jerusalem and Its Region: Collected Papers*, vol. 1. Edited by J. Patrich and D. Amit. Jerusalem: Israel Antiquities Authority and the Hebrew University of Jerusalem. (Hebrew)

———. 2008. Archaeology and Conservation in Jerusalem Region – 2008. Pages 7–16 in *New Studies in the Archeology of Jerusalem and Its Region: Collected Papers*, vol. 2. Edited by D. Amit and G. D. Stiebel. Jerusalem: Israel Antiquities Authority and the Hebrew University of Jerusalem. (Hebrew)

———. 2009. Archaeology and Conservation in Jerusalem Region: 2008–2009. Pages 8–16 in *New Studies in the Archeology of Jerusalem and Its Region: Collected Papers*, vol. 3. Edited by D. Amit, G. D. Stiebel and O. Peleg-Barkat. Jerusalem: Israel Antiquities Authority and the Hebrew University of Jerusalem. (Hebrew)

Shalev, Yiftah. 2009. Tel Dor and the Urbanization of the Coastal Plain of Israel during the Persian Period. *ErIsr* 29: 363–71 (Hebrew).

Shanks, Hershel. 2007. Assyrian Palace Discovered in Ashddo. *BAR* 33/1: 56–60.

Sharon, Ilan, et al. 2007. Report on the First Stage of the Iron Age Dating Project in Israel: Supporting a Low Chronology. *Radiocarbon* 49: 1–46.

Shavit, Alon. 2003. Settlement Patterns in Israel's Southern Coastal Plain during the Iron Age II. Ph.D. diss. Tel Aviv University.

Sherratt, Andrew, and Susan Sherratt. 1991. Urnfield Reflections. *CAJ* 1: 246–247.

———. 1993. The Growth of the Mediterranean Economy in the Early First Millenium B.C. *World Archaeology* 24/3: 361–377.

Shiloh, Yigal. 1970. The Four-Room House: Its Situation and Function in the Israelite City. *IEJ* 20: 180–90.

———. 1973. The Four-Room House: The Israelite Type-House? *ErIsr* 11: 277–85 (Hebrew).

———. 1978. Elements in the Development of Town Planning in the Israelite City. *IEJ* 28: 36–51.

———. 1984. *The City of David I*. Qedem 19. Jerusalem: Hebrew University.

———. 1989. Judah and Jerusalem in the 8th–6th Centuries B.C.E. Pages 97–105 in *Recent Excavations in Israel: Studies in Iron Age Archaeology*. Edited by S. Gitin and W. G. Dever. Winona Lake, Ind.: Eisenbrauns.

Sinclair, Lawrence A. 1968. Bethel Pottery of the Sixth Century B.C. Pages 70–76 in *The Excavations of Bethel (1934–1960)*. Edited by J. L. Kelso. Cambridge, Mass.: American Schools of Oriental Research.

———. 1975. Gibeah. Pages 444–46 in vol. 2 of *EAEHL*. Edited by M. Avi-Yonah. 4 vols. London: Oxford University Press.

Sinopoli, Carla M. 1991. *Approaches to Archaeological Ceramics*. New York: Plenum.

Smith, Daniel. 1989. *The Religion of the Landless: The Social Context of the Babylonian Exile*. Bloomington: Meyer Stone.

Smith-Christopher, Daniel. 1997. Reassessing the Historical and Sociological Impact of the Babylonian Exile (597/587–539 B.C.E). Pages 7–36 in *Exile: Old Testament, Jewish and Christian Conceptions*. Edited by J. M. Scott. Leiden: Brill: Leiden.

Smith, Robert H. 1990. The Southern Levant in the Hellenistic Period. *Levant* 22: 123–30.

Snodgrass, Anthony. 1991. The Aegean Angel. *Cambridge Archaeological Journal* 1: 246–47.

Solimany, Gideon, and Vered Barzel. 2008a. Jerusalem, East Talpiyot. *Hadashot Arkheologiyot: Excavations and Surveys in Israel* 120.

———. 2008b. Ramat Rahel. *Hadashot Arkheologiyot: Excavations and Surveys in Israel* 120. Online: http://hadashot-esi.org.il/report_detail_eng.asp?id=793&mag_id=114.

Sommer, Michael. 2010. Shaping Mediterranean Economy and Trade: Phoenician Cultural Identities in the Iron Age. Pages 114–37 in *Material Culture and Social Identities in the Ancient World*. Edited by S. Hales and T. Hodos. Cambridge: Cambridge Univeristy Press.

Sorensen, Lone W. 1997. Traveling Pottery Connections between Cyprus, the Levant and the Greek World in the Iron Age. Pages 285–99 in *Res Maritimae: Cyprus and the*

Eastern Mediterranean from Prehistory to Late Antiquity. Edited by S. Swiny, R. L.
Hohlfelder and H. Wylde Swiny. Atlanta: Scholars Press.

Sparks, Brian. 1996. *The Red and the Black: Studies in Greek Pottery.* London: Routledge.

Stager, Lawrence E. 1976. Farming in the Judean Desert during the Iron Age. *BASOR* 221:
145–58.

———. 1985. The Archaeology of the Family in Ancient Israel. *BASOR* 260: 1–35.

———. 1993. Ashkelon. Pages 103–12 in vol. 1 of *NEAEHL.* Edited by E. Stern. 4 vols. Jerusalem: Israel Exploration Society.

———. 1996. Ashkelon and the Archaeology of Destruction: Kislev 604 B.C.E. *ErIsr* 25:
61*–74*.

———. 2006. New Discoveries in the Excavations of Ashkelon in the Bronze and Iron
Ages. *Qad* 131: 2–19 (Hebrew).

———. 2008. Ashkelon. Pages 1578–86 in vol. 5 of *NEAEHL* Edited by E. Stern. 4 vols.
Jerusalem: Israel Exploration Society.

Steiner, Margreet L. 2001. *Excavations by Kathleen M. Kenyon in Jerusalem 1961–1967:
The Settlement in the Bronze and Iron Ages.* Oxford: Oxford University Press.

Stern, Ephraim. 1971. A Burial of the Persian Period near Hebron. *IEJ* 21: 25–30.

———. 1975. Israel at the Close of the Period of the Monarchy: An Archaeological Survey.
BA 38: 26–54.

———. 1982. *Material Culture of the Land of the Bible in the Persian Period. 538–332 B.C.*
Wiltshire, England: Warminster.

———. 1983. The Material Culture and Economic Life in the Land of Israel in the Persian
Period. Pages 117–38 in *The Restoration: The Persian Period. World History of the
Jewish People.* Edited by H. Tadmor. Jerusalem: 'Am 'Oved (Hebrew).

———. 1993a. Azeka. Pages 123–24 in vol. 1 of *NEAEHL.* Edited by E. Stern. 4 vols Jerusalem: Israel Exploration Society.

———. 1993b (ed.). *NEAEHL.* Jerusalem: Israel Exploration Society.

———. 1994. The Eastern Border of the Kingdom of Judah. Pages 399–409 in *Scripture
and Other Artifacts: Essays on the Bible and Archaeology in Honor of Philip J. King.*
Edited by M. D. Coogan, J. C. Exum and L. E. Stager. Louisville: Westminster John
Knox.

———. 1997a. Cities: Cities of the Pesian Period. Pages 25–29 in vol. 2 of *OEANE.* 5 vols.
Edited by E. M. Meyers. New York: Oxford University Press.

———. 1997b. The Beginning of the Province of "Yahud" in the Persian Period. Pages
69–72 in *New Studies on Jerusalem: Proceedings of the Third Conference.* Edited by A.
Faust and A. Baruch. Ramat-Gan: Bar Ilan University.

———. 1998. Is There a Babylonian Period in the Archaeology of the Land of Israel? Pages
19–20 in *Is It Possible to Define the Ceramics of the 6th Century B.C.E in Judah?* Edited
by O. Lipschits Tel-Aviv: Tel Aviv University.

———. 2000a. *Dor: Ruler of the Seas.* Jerusalem: Israel Exploration Society.

———. 2000b. The Babylonian Gap. *BAR* 26/6: 45–51, 76.

———. 2001. *Archaeology of the Land of the Bible: The Assyrian, Babylonian and Persian
Periods (732–332 B.C.E).* New York: Doubleday.

———. 2002. Yes There Was. *BAR* 28/3: 39, 55.

———. 2004. The Babylonian Gap: The Archaeological Reality. *JSOT* 28.3: 273–77.

———. 2006. The Religious Revolution in Persian-Period Judah. Pages 199–205 in *Judah
and Judeans in the Persian Period.* Edited by O. Lipschits and M. Oeming. Winona

Lake, Ind.: Eisenbrauns.

———. 2007. *En Gedi Excavations: Final Report 1*. Jerusalem: Israel Exploration Society and the Hebrew University of Jerusalem.

Stern, Ian. 2006. Idumaea in the Persian Period: The Interaction between Ethnic Groups as Reflected in the Material Culture. Ph.D. diss. Bar-Ilan University: .

Stoltz, F. 1995. Sea. Pages 1390–1402 in *DDD*. Edited by K. Van der-Toorn, B. Becking and P. W. Van der Horst. Leiden: Brill.

Tadmor, Hayim. 1975. Assyria and the West: The Ninth Century and Its Aftermath. Pages 36–48 in *Unity and Diversity: Essays in the History, Literature, and Religion of the Ancient Near East*. Edited by H. Goedicke and J. J. M. Roberts. Baltimore: Johns Hopkins University Press.

Tahareani Sussely, Yifat. 2007. The "Archaeology of the Days of Menasseh" Reconsidered in the Light of Evidence from the Beersheba Valley. *PEQ* 139/2: 69–77.

Tainter, Joseph A. 1988. *The Collapse of Complex Societies*. Cambridge: Cambridge University Press.

———. 1999. Post-Collapse Societies. Pages 988–1039 in vol. 2 of *Companion Encyclopedia of Archaeology*. Edited by G. Barker. 2 vols. London: Routledge.

———. 2000. Problem Solving: Complexity, History, Sustainability. *Population and Environment* 22: 3–41.

Talshir, David. 2003. The Habitat and History of Hebrew during the Second Temple Period. Pages 251–75 in *Biblical Hebrew: Studies in Chronology and Typology*. Edited by I. Young. London: T&T Clark.

Thomas, David W. 1961. The Sixth Century B.C.: A Creative Epoch in the History of Israel. *JSS* 6: 33–46.

Thompson, Thomas, T. 1999. *The Mythic Past: Biblical Archaeology and the Myth of Israel*. New York: Basic Books.

Torrey, Charles C. 1930. *Pseudo-Ezekiel and the Original Prophecy*. New Haven: Yale University Press.

———. 1954. *The Chronicler's History of Israel: Chronicles-Ezra-Nehemiah Restored to its Original Form*. New Haven: Yale University Press.

———. 1970. *Ezra Studies*. New York: Ktav. 1910. Repr. Chicago: University of Chicago Press.

Trudgill, Peter. 2002. Linguistic and Social Typology. Pages 707–28 in *The Handbook of Language Variation and Change*. Edited by J. K. Chambers, P. Trudgill and N. Schilling-Estes. Oxford: Blackwell.

Trundle, Matthew. 2005. Ancient Greek Mercenaries. *History Compass* 3: 1–16.

Tufnell, Olga. 1953. *Lachish*, III: *The Iron Age*. London: Oxford University Press.

Ussishkin, David. 1977. The Destruction of Lachish by Sennacherib and the Dating of the Royal Judean Storage Jars. *TA* 4: 28–60

———. 1982. *The Conquest of Lachish by Sennacherib*. Tel-Aviv: Tel Aviv University.

———. 2004. A Synopsis of the Stratigraphical, Chronological and Historical Issues. Pages 50–119 in *The Renewed Archaeological Excavations at Lachish (1973–1994)*. Edited by D. Ussishkin. Tel Aviv: Tel Aviv University.

———. 2011. The Dating of the *lmlk* Storage Jars and its Implications: Rejoinder to Lipschits, Sergi and Koch. *TA* 38: 220–40.

Van Beek, Gus W. 1993. Jemmeh, Tell. Pages 667–74 in vol. 2 of *NEAEHL*. Edited by E. Stern. 4 vols. Jerusalem: Israel Exploration Society.

Van Creveld, Martin. 2004. *Supplying War: Logistics from Wallenstein to Patton.* Cambridge: Cambridge University Press.

Van de Mieroop, Marc. 2007. *A History of the Ancient Near East, ca. 3000–323 B.C.* Oxford: Blackwell.

Vanderhooft, David. 1999. *The Neo-Babylonian Empire and Babylon in the Latter Prophets.* Atlanta: Scholars Press.

———. 2003a. Babylonian Strategies of Imperial Control in the West: Royal Practice and Rhetoric. Pages 235–62 in *Judah and Judeans in the Neo-Babylonian Period.* Edited by O. Lipschits and J. Blenkinsopp. Winona Lake, Ind.: Eisenbrauns.

———. 2003b. New Evidence Pertaining to the Transition from Neo-Babylonian to Achaemenid Administration in Palestine. Pages 219–35 in *Yahwism after the Exile: Perspectives on Israelite Religion in the Persian Era.* Edited by R. Albertz and B. Becking. Assen: Royal van Gorcum.

———. 2007 (ed.). In Conversation with Oded Lipschits, The Fall and Rise of Jerusalem. *JHebS* 7\2.

———. 2009. The Israelite *Mishpaha* in the Priestly Writings, and Changing Valences in Israel's Kinship Terminology. Pages 485–96 in *Exploring the Long Duree: Essays in Honor of Lawrence E. Stager.* Edited by D. Schloen. Winona Lake, Ind.: Eisenbrauns.

Vaughn, Andrew G. 1999. *Theology, History, and Archaeology in the Chronicler's Account of Hezekiah.* Atlanta: Scholars Press.

Venit, Marjorie J. 1988. *Greek Painted Pottery from Naukratis in Egyptian Museums.* American Research Center in Egypt, Volume 7. Winona Lake, Ind.: Eisenbrauns.

Vieweger, Dieter, and Jutta Haser. 2007. Tall Zira'a: Five Thousand Years of Palestinian History on a Single-Settlement Mound. *NEA* 70: 147–67.

Vickers, Michael. 1987. Dates, Methods and Icons. Pages 19–25 in *Images et societe en Grece ancienne: L'iconographie comme methode d'analyse.* Edited by C. Berard, C. Bron and A. Pomari. Lausanne: Institut d'Archeologie et d'Histoire Ancienne.

Von Bothmer, Dietrich. 1947. Greek Pottery. Pages 175–78, 304 in *Tell en-Nasbeh, Excavated under the Direction of the Late William Fredric Bade, Vol. I: Archaeological and Historical Results.* Edited by C. C. McCown. Berkeley: The Palestine Institute of Pacific School of Religion.

Waldbaum, Jane C. 1994. Early Greek Contacts with the Levant, ca. 1000–600 B.C.: The Eastern Perspective. *BASOR* 293: 53–66.

———. 1997. Greeks in the East or Greeks and the East: Problems in the Definition and Recognition of Presence. *BASOR* 305: 1–17.

———. 2003. After the Return: Connections with the Classical World in the Persian Period. Pages 301–18 in *One Hundred Years of American Archaeology in the Middle East.* Edited by D. R. Clark and V. H. Matthews. Boston: American Schools of Oriental Research.

———. 2007. A Wild Goat Oinochoe Sherd from Tel Miqne-Ekron. Pages 61–67 in *Up to the Gates of Ekron: Essays in the Archaeology and History of the Eastern Mediterranean in Honor of Seymour Gitin.* Edited by S. W. Crawford, et al. Jerusalem: Israel Exploration Society.

Waldbaum, Jane C., and Jodi Magness. 1997. The Chronology of East Greek Pottery: New Evidence from Seventh Century B.C. Destruction Levels in Israel. *AJA* 101: 23–40.

Wampler, Joseph C. 1947a. *Tell en-Nasbeh, Excavated under the Direction of the Late William Fredric Bade, Vol. II: The Pottery.* Berkeley: The Palestine Institute of Pacific

School of Religion.

———. 1947b. The Stratification of Tell en-Nasbeh. Pages 179–86 in *Tell en-Nasbeh, Excavated under the Direction of the Late William Fredric Bade, Vol. I: Archaeological and Historical Results*. Edited by C. C. McCown. Berkeley: The Palestine Institute of Pacific School of Religion.

Ward, William A. 1994. Review of I. J. Thorpe, et al. Centuries of Darkness: A Challenge to the Conventional Chronology of Old World Archaeology. *AJA* 98: 362–63.

Waterson, Roxana. 1997. *The Living House: An Anthropology of Architecture in South-East Asia*. Singapore: Thames & Hudson.

Watzinger, Carl. 1935. *Denkmaler Palastinas* II. Leipzig:. Hinrichs'sche.

Weinberg, Joel. 2000. Jerusalem in the Persian Period. Pages 307–26 in *The History of Jerusalem, The Biblical Period*. Edited by S. Ahituv and A. Mazar. Jerusalem: Yad Ben Zvi (Hebrew).

Weinberg, Saul S. 1969. Post-Exilic Palestine: An Archaeological Report. Pages 78–97 in *Proceedings of the Israel Academy of Sciences and Humanities* 5, Jerusalem: Israel Academy of Sciences and Humanities.

Weiss, Danny, Boaz Zissu, and Gideon Sulimany. 2004. *Map of Nes Harim*. Archaeological Survey of Israel. Jerusalem: Israel Antiquities Authority.

Weksler-Bdolah, Shlomit. 1999. 'Alona. *ESI* 19: 68*–70*.

Wesler, Kit W. 1999. Chronological Sequences in Nigerian Ceramics. *African Archaeological Review* 16: 239–58.

Whitley, James. 2001. *The Archaeology of Ancient Greece*. Cambridge: Cambridge University Press.

Williamson, Hugh. 2003. The Family in Persian Period Judah: Some Textual Reflections. Pages 469–85 in *Symbiosis, Symbolism and the Power of the Past: Ancient Israel and Its Neighbors from the Late Bronze Age through Roman Palestine*. Edited by W. G. Dever and S. Gitin. Winona Lake, Ind.: Eisenbrauns.

Wiseman, Donald J. 1989. The Assyrians. Pages 36–53 in *Warfare in the Ancient World*. Edited by J. Hacket. London: Sidgwick & Jackson.

Wolff, Samuel R. 1996. Archaeology in Israel. *AJA* 100: 725–68.

———. 1998. An Iron Age I Site at 'En Hagit (northern Ramat Menashe). Pages 449–54 in *Mediterranean Peoples in Transition*. Edited by S. Gitin, A. Mazar and E. Stern. Jerusalem: Israel Exploration Society.

———. 2002. Mortuary Practices in the Persian Period of the Levant. *NEA* 65: 131–37.

Wolfram, Walt. 2002. Language, Death, and Dying. Pages 764–87 in *The Handbook of Language Variation and Change*. Edited by J. K. Chambers, P. Trudgill and N. Schilling-Estes. Oxford: Blackwell.

Wright, Christopher J. H. 1990. *God's People in God's Land*. Grand Rapids: Eerdmans

Wright, George E. 1963. Review of J. B. Pritchard *The Water System of Gibeon*. *JNES* 22: 210–211.

Wright, Jacob, L. 2008. Warfare and Wanton Destruction: A Reexamination of Deuteronomy 20:19–20 in Relation to Ancient Siegecraft. *JBL* 127: 423–58.

Wright, Richard M. 2003. Further Evidence for North Israelite Contribution to Late Biblical Hebrew. Pages 129–48 in *Biblical Hebrew: Studies in Chronology and Typology*. Edited by I. Young. London: T&T Clark.

———. 2005. *Linguistic Evidence for the Pre-Exilic Date of the Yahwistic Source*. London: T&T Clark.

Yadin, Yigael. 1972. *Hazor: The Head of All Those Kingdoms*. The Sweich Lectures 1970. Oxford: Oxford University Press.

———, et al, eds. 1958. *Hazor I*. Jerusalem: Israel Exploration Society.

Yamada, Shigeo. 2000. *The Construction of the Assyrian Empire: A Historical Study of the Inscriptions of Shalmaneser III (859–824 B.C.) Relating to His Campaigns to the West*. Leiden: Brill.

Yankelevitch, Shalom. 2006. The Pottery. Pages 101–54 in *Tel Tanninim: Excavations at Krokodeilon Polis*. Edited by R. R. Stieglitz. Boston: American Schools of Oriental Research.

Yeivin, Zeev, and Gershon Edelstein. 1970. Excavations at Tirat Yehuda. *'Atiqot* 6: 56–67 (Hebrew).

Yezerski, Irit. 1995. Burial Caves in the Land of Judah in the Iron Age: Archaeological and Architectural Aspects. M.A. thesis. Tel Aviv University (Hebrew).

———. 1997. Burial Caves in the Hebron Hills. *'Atiqot* 32: 21–36.

———. 1999. Burial-Cave Distribution and the Borders of the Kingdom of Judah Toward the End of the Iron Age. *TA* 26: 253–70.

———. 2007. Pottery of Stratum V. Pages 86–132 in *En-Gedi Excavations I*. Edited by E. Stern. Jerusalem: Israel Exploration Society.

———. 2011, Iron Age II Burial Customs in the Samaria Region. *ErIsr* 30: 215–33.

Yezerski, Irit, and Ieshayahu Lander. 2002. An Iron Age II Burial Cave from Lower Kh. 'Anim. *'Atiqot* 43: 57*–73* (Hebrew).

Yoffee, Norman., and George L. Cowgill. 1991. *The Collapse of Ancient States and Civilizations*. Tucson: University of Arizona Press.

Yogev, Ora. 1985. Nahal Zimra. *Hadashot Arkheologiyot: Excavations and Surveys in Israel* 87: 29–30 (Hebrew).

Young, Ian. 2003. Late Biblical Hebrew and Hebrew Inscriptions. Pages 276–311 in *Biblical Hebrew: Studies in Chronology and Typology*. Edited by I. Young. London: T&T Clark.

Zehavi, Alon. 1993. Jerusalem, Manahat. *ESI* 12: 66–67.

Zemer, A., 2009, *Terracotta Figurines in Ancient Times*. Haifa: The National Maritime Museum.

Zertal, Adam. 1992. *The Manasseh Hill Country Survey, The Shechem Syncline*. Tel-Aviv: Israel's Ministry of Defense and Haifa University. (Hebrew)

———. 2001. The Hills of Samaria: Population, Economy and History in the 7th–6th Centuries B.C.E. Page 30 in *Judah and Judeans in the Neo-Babylonian Period, Summaries*. Edited by O. Lipschits. Tel-Aviv: Tel Aviv University.

Zevit, Ziony. 2004. A Review of Ian Young, ed. *Biblical Hebrew: Studies in Chronology and Typology*. *RBL* 8.

Zilberbod, Irina, and David Amit. 1999. Mazor (El'ad), sites 21 and 38. *Hadashot Arkheologiyot: Excavations and Surveys in Israel* 109: 63*–64*.

Zissu, Boaz. 2006. A "Vanished Settlement" from the Iron Age: Excavations Near the "Cave of the Rambam," Upper Kidron Valley, Jerusalem. Pages 33–40 in *NSJ*, vol. 12. Edited by E. Baruch and A. Faust. Ramat Gan: Bar Ilan University (Hebrew).

Zorn, Jeffrey. 1993a. Nasbeh, Tell en-. Pages 1098–1102 in vol. 3 of *NEAEHL*. Edited by E. Stern. 4 vols. Jerusalem: Israel Exploration Society.

———. 1993b. Tell en-Nasbeh: A Re-Evaluation of the Architecture and Stratigraphy of the Early Bronze Age, Iron Age, and Later Periods. Ph.D. diss. University of California at Berkeley.

————. 1994. Estimating the Population Size of Ancient Settlements: Methods, Problems, Solutions, and a Case Study. *BASOR* 295: 31–48.

————. 1997a. An Inner and Outer Gate Complex at Tell en-Nasbeh. *BASOR* 307: 53–66.

————. 1997b. Mizpah: Newly Discovered Stratum Reveals Judah's Other Capital. *BAR* 23/5: 28–38.

————. 1997c. Nasbeh, Tell en-. Pages 101–3 in vol. 4 of *OEANE*. 5 vols. Edited by E. M. Meyers. New York: Oxford University Press.

————. 1999. A Note on the Date of the "Great Wall" of Tell en-Nasbeh: A Rejoinder. *TA* 26: 146–50.

————. 2003. Tell en-Nasbeh and the Problem of the Material Culture of the Sixth Century. Pages 413–47 in *Judah and Judeans in the Neo-Babylonian Period*. Edited by O. Lipschits and J. Blenkinsopp. Winona Lake, Ind.: Eisenbrauns.

Author Index

SITE INDEX

Subject Index

www.ingramcontent.com/pod-product-compliance
Lightning Source LLC
Chambersburg PA
CBHW020405100426

42812CB00001B/204

*9 7 8 1 5 8 9 8 3 7 2 5 6 *